Leo McKinstry is a freelance journalist and author. He has published two books on current affairs in Britain, *Fit to Govern* and *Turning the Tide*, and writes regularly for the *Daily Mail* and the *Spectator*. Born in Belfast in 1962, he is a graduate of Cambridge University. He is married and lives in Essex.

Acclaim for *Boycs*:

'A terrific biography by any sta g. McKinstry has done a ravishing j t. Boycott's broadcasting work, a se n-taught diligence, is fairly evaluated, as ained one-on-one coaching ability. All the old tales are retold for much delight – you sense here for the definitive time – and a number of new ones. Boycott politely refused all McKinstry's requests for an interview. But this book tells it, you fancy, just as it was. And is' Frank Keating, *Wisden Cricket Monthly*

'Admirable . . . remarkably fair, sympathetic and readable . . . McKinstry has a sound knowledge of cricket . . . and has marshalled a mass of original material with impressive skill. The feuds within Yorkshire County Cricket Club are particularly well handled' Hugh Massingberd, *Daily Telegraph*

'Far better and less gung-ho than most sports biographies. Its great merit is its fair-mindedness, not an easy thing to achieve given its heavily criticised subject. Its second virtue is thoroughness. McKinstry has interviewed scores of players, administrators, family members, broadcasters and others who have had dealings with Boycott' Michael Davie, *Spectator*

'Leo McKinstry . . . a felicitous and highly professional journalist . . . He set himself the task of looking beyond "the mythology which surrounds Boycott" and "building a more balanced and realistic portrait" . . . In meeting his own objective, the author has done a magnificent job. We all have our Boycott stories and by dint of many, many interviews, he has hoovered up the best of them . . . It could be the best-selling cricket book of the year. If so, McKinstry will have deserved the accolade for his industry, style and, I believe, judgements' Robin Marlar, *The Cricketer*

'One of the most readable sporting biographies for years. Boycott's life is the stuff of fiction . . . This book is neither hagiography nor hatchet job; it depicts a complex, enigmatic man who could enchant or dismay both on and off the field . . . McKinstry [who] tells his tale well. He avoids cheap and easy judgements and the pap that so often litters sporting biography. His book is a serious attempt to rescue a singular man from the myths that engulf him . . . He will always be a controversial figure, but he is fortunate in his biographer. McKinstry disentangles his tale with insight and clarity. This will not be the last word on Boycott, but it might turn out to be the best' John Major, *Mail on Sunday*

'This perceptive new biography . . . puts a new slant on Boycott's fabled selfishness . . . some of the most enjoyable passages in the book are descriptions of Boycott's spectacular rudeness . . . Throughout, the author has a shrewd eye for the contradictions embodied in his subject . . . by the end of this balanced and not unfavourable book . . . he has made Boycott's numerous contrasting traits . . . seem not only natural but appealing'
Michael Prodger, *Sunday Telegraph*

'Particularly good on Boycott's women . . . Throughout, McKinstry has played an innings of Boycsian craft and meticulousness'
Simon Barnes, *The Times*

'Readable and well-researched' Simon Rae, *The Times Literary Supplement*

'McKinstry comes to his subject without any prejudice or excess baggage and has produced an impartial account of Geoffrey's career. And who could be more fascinating than Boycott?'
Derek Hodgson, *The Independent Sports Book of the Week*

'This new biography, in a league well above the run of cricket books, takes a thorough and balanced view of an intensely complex man. Mr McKinstry has spared no effort to speak to friends, colleagues and opponents going right back to his childhood . . . The result is a warts-and-all biography, but one scrupulously fair to this most difficult of men . . . This is a magnificent, intelligent book' Simon Heffer, *Country Life*

'McKinstry has produced the most thorough study to date on Boycott the man and the cricketer' *Yorkshire Post*

'I have already read the season's best cricket book, having consumed Leo McKinstry's *Boycs* in a handful of late-night sittings. McKinstry has bravely spent the last 18 months immersed in all things Sir Geoffrey. The result is as good a cricket book as you could wish to read: wise, elegantly crafted, impressively well-informed and determined to present a balanced portrait' Marcus Berkmann, *Wisden Cricket Monthly*

'Racy account . . . McKinstry is alert to the contrast in his subject's character: his epic determination and his equally epic greed . . . McKinstry narrates all this with sometimes disbelieving relish, which makes it good fun to read . . . He even goes some way towards exonerating him for his role in the injuries to his former girlfriend, Margaret Moore, in the south of France . . . McKinstry makes a persuasive case for Boycott's innocence'
Robert Winder, *New Statesman*

'This third biography of the English legend is surely the best . . . A meticulously well researched book and well worth the read. Once you've got into the excellent first chapter it is difficult to put down'
The Sunday Times Sports Books of the Year

BOYCS

THE TRUE STORY

LEO McKINSTRY

CORGI BOOKS

BOYCS
A CORGI BOOK: 0 552 14758 3

Originally published in Great Britain by Partridge,
a division of Transworld Publishers

PRINTING HISTORY
Partridge edition published 2000
Corgi edition published 2001

1 3 5 7 9 10 8 6 4 2

Set in Times by
Falcon Oast Graphic Art.

Corgi Books are published by Transworld Publishers,
61–63 Uxbridge Road, London W5 5SA,
a division of The Random House Group Ltd,
in Australia by Random House Australia (Pty) Ltd,
20 Alfred Street, Milsons Point, Sydney, NSW 2061, Australia,
in New Zealand by Random House New Zealand Ltd,
18 Poland Road, Glenfield,Auckland 10, New Zealand
and in South Africa by Random House (Pty) Ltd,
Endulini, 5A Jubilee Road, Parktown 2193, South Africa.

Printed and bound in Great Britain by
Clays Ltd, St Ives plc.

This book is dedicated to David Robertson,
another great Yorkshireman

Contents

Preface and Acknowledgements

Geoffrey Boycott has been a presence in my life since I first fell in love with cricket as a Belfast schoolboy in the early seventies. For me, his appeal lies in the way he embodies a heroic ideal. His struggles to overcome the social disadvantages of his background, the limitations in his natural talent and the contradictions in his own nature are almost epic. He set himself a goal, to become one of the greatest batsmen in the world, and in the face of numerous obstacles – many of his own making – he ultimately achieved it. His story is, rightly, the stuff of legends.

Like most heroic tales, however, accounts of his life have always varied in the telling. It has therefore been my aim to look beyond much of the mythology that surrounds Boycott and build a more balanced and realistic portrait. Using extensive research and inter- views with Boycott's colleagues, friends and family, I tried to provide a deeper understanding of this flawed but compelling sport- ing personality. In particular, I have sought to place Boycott in a wider context than just that of Yorkshire cricket, the subject that dominated the two previous – and partisan – biographies of Boycott, one (the pro-Boycott version) by *Yorkshire Evening Post* journalist John Callaghan, published in 1982, and the other (the anti-Boycott version) written by the late Don Mosey, published in 1985. 'Only a Yorkshireman can properly comprehend the character and characteristics which have given the Boycott story its unique place in the history of English cricket,' Mosey wrote. If that were true, then I, as an Ulsterman living in Essex, have laboured in vain. Yet I believe that this robust view has been part of the problem of interpreting the Boycott phenomenon. By focusing narrowly on

Yorkshire, such an approach ignores the truth that Boycott has always been much more than Yorkshire cricketer. He has also been one of the all-time greats of Test cricket, an England captain, a brilliant coach, a widely read columnist, an iconic broadcaster, and an international celebrity.

Despite my admiration for Boycott, this is not, in any sense, an authorized biography. Boycott politely refused my requests for an interview, though I must record my thanks to him for his assistance in checking facts and in expediting interviews with several of his friends. In the foreword to his 1985 book, Don Mosey wrote of a 'conspiracy of silence' from Boycott's supporters. I am grateful to say that I encountered no such difficulty.

I owe a huge debt of gratitude to all those many first-class and Test cricketers who generously gave me the benefit of their views: Dennis Amiss, Geoff Arnold, Bill Athey, Chris Balderstone, Jack Bannister, Bob Barber, Jack Birkenshaw, 'Dickie' Bird, Chris Broad, David Brown, Alan Butcher, Rodney Cass, Brian Close, Howard Cooper, Colin Cowdrey, Andrew Dalton, Mike Denness, Ted Dexter, Keith Fletcher, Norman Gifford, Graham Gooch, David Gower, Tony Greig, Tom Graveney, Frank Hayes, Simon Hughes, Robin Jackman, Paul Jarvis, Peter Kippax, John Lever, Peter Lever, Tony Lewis, David Lloyd, Brian Luckhurst, Richard Lumb, Mark Nicholas, Jim Parks, Pat Pocock, Graham Roope, Kevin Sharp, Mike Smedley, M.J.K. Smith, Robin Smith, Don Shepperd, Ken Taylor, Bernie Thomas, Derek Underwood, Peter Willey, Don Wilson.

Apart from ex-cricketers, many other figures in the media also contributed, as follows: Peter Baxter, Dave Bowden, Max Clifford, Charles Colvile, John Etheridge, Alan Griffiths, Kelvin MacKenzie, Steve Pierson and Bill Sinrich, plus some who wished to remain nameless.

I would also like to thank the members of Boycott's circle of friends and family who assisted with this project: Philip Ackroyd, Peter Boycott, Peter Briggs, John Callaghan, Alice Harratt, Ted Lester, Lord MacLaurin, Albert Speight, Rachael Swinglehurst, Tony Vann, and Shirley Western. Invaluable memories of Boycott's youth and schooldays were provided by: Des Barrick, Bernard Conway, Bernard Crapper, Eddie Hambleton, Arthur Hollingsworth, Roland Howcroft, Peter Jordan, Terry McCroakham,

Terry Newitt, Ken Sale, and Dudley Taylor. I am particularly appreciative of the help that George Hepworth and Malcolm Tate gave me. My many requests for advice and information were always treated with the greatest courtesy. In addition, Sid Fielden showed me the kindest hospitality during a day's visit to Headingley.

Others who kindly provided assistance and interviews were: Sarah Cook, Alf Evans, Mike Fatkin, Martin Gray, Nigel Grimes, Keith Hayhurst, Councillor Brian Hazell, Brian Holling, Doug Lloyd, Eric Loxton, Keith Rogers, Keith Stevenson and Barrie Wathen. I am grateful to the staff at the *Daily Mail*, the *Yorkshire Post*, and the Westminster Reference Library for helping with newspaper research. Chris Dancy in the BBC archives and Stephen Green at the MCC Library were generous with their time, while Brooke Sinclair and James Perry provided a host of unique insights. This book would not have been possible without the backing of my superb agent, Andrew Lownie, or the staff at my publishers, Partridge, especially Alison Barrow, who commissioned the book, Adam Sisman, who edited it, and Sheila Lee, Katrina Whone and Elizabeth Dobson. Thanks also to Paul Dyson for his excellent and original statistical appendix, and to David Hooper for his legal advice.

Finally I would like to thank my wife Elizabeth for her wise counsel and wonderful support during the long months in which Boycs appeared to dominate my every waking thought.

A NOTE ON THE TITLE: Geoffrey Boycott is universally known throughout the cricket world as 'Boycs', though this is occasionally spelt 'Boyks' or even, in Mike Gatting's autobiography, 'Boyx'. His other main nickname has been 'Fiery', which Boycott says was first used during the South African tour of 1964/65 and is a contraction of 'Geof-fiery'. It was coined, he believes, because he came from the same county as 'Fiery' Fred Trueman, though many have maintained that it referred ironically to his dour batting and public demeanour, just as Chris Tavare was known as 'Rowdy'.

Alternatively, others have said it reflects his quick tongue and temper. The name was generally only used by fellow Test cricketers and never had much currency in Yorkshire. Amongst his followers, GLY (Greatest Living Yorkshireman) or Sir Geoffrey are deemed more suitable.

1

A Contradictory Personality

Wednesday 21 July 1999: Geoffrey Boycott attends an early evening reception at a restaurant in central London where he is one of the guests of honour for the launch of the Federation of International Cricketer Associations' new Hall of Fame. Accompanied by his partner Rachael Swinglehurst, he moves amiably through the gathering, sipping from his glass of champagne and indulging in banter with some of the other guests. Then, in the central ceremony of the evening, he is summoned by the former England batsman Tom Graveney on to a stage to accept his induction into the Hall of Fame. In a polished acceptance speech, mixing modesty, humour and charm in equal measure, he describes Tom Graveney as his boyhood hero and pays fulsome tributes to Ian Botham and Fred Trueman, the two other guests of honour.

Anyone watching this performance who did not know of Boycott's reputation would have thought he was one of the most gracious and popular figures in the cricket world. There was no inkling of the festering animosity that has long characterized his relationships with Botham and Trueman, no sign of his notorious boorishness, no evidence of his supposed inability to socialize with others.

22 January 1998: Geoffrey Boycott attends a press conference in central London, where he gives his response to the decision of a French court to convict him of assaulting his former girlfriend Margaret Moore. With his position as a media sports star under threat as a result of the £5,100 fine and three-month suspended jail sentence, Boycott decides to go on the offensive. Bristling with

indignation, he denounces Ms Moore, accusing her of telling lies about the incident and claiming that she is out to destroy him because he refused to marry her. As journalists begin to question his account, Boycott slips into the belligerent tone so well known by colleagues from broadcasting and cricket. 'Shut up,' he tells one reporter, 'this is my conference, not yours.' Finally, there is a collective admonition for the press: 'I am a public figure and the only people I have to answer to are the public, no one else.'

Alec Bedser, who saw the best and worst of Boycott during his 13 years as chairman of England's Test selectors, once spoke of the Yorkshireman's 'enigmatic and contradictory personality'. And these two events, the champagne reception and the stormy press conference, encapsulate the different sides of Boycott's character. On one hand, there is the brilliantly successful cricketing figure – in his time the greatest run-scorer in the history of Test matches and, after his retirement from the playing arena, a commentator in demand throughout the world – relaxed, affable and generous when basking in the recognition of his achievements. On the other hand, there is the sorry figure with the tangled web of personal relationships and the reputation for selfishness and bad manners, who, in the words of one former England cricketer, 'has left a trail of social wreckage across the cricket world'.

In a rare moment of self-analysis, Boycott once admitted to being baffled by his own contradictions. During an appearance on the BBC radio programme *In the Psychiatrist's Chair*, he told Professor Anthony Clare: 'We are like diamonds. There are so many facets to the diamond and you cannot tell why it glows on one side and why it doesn't on the other. Like me, I don't always understand myself.' We all, of course, have different, often conflicting, aspects to our personalities. Yet for Geoff Boycott the contrasts are much stronger than for others. He is an intensely private man who has lived his entire adult life in the fiercest public gaze. Indeed, almost two decades after he played his final Test, he is still probably the most famous name in English cricket, though many colleagues who have played and commentated with him say that they hardly know him. He has developed an image of self-confidence bordering on arrogance, yet possesses a streak of almost chronic insecurity.

He craves respect yet, through his behaviour, continually alienates those who might provide it. Even his admirers admit that his extreme moodiness and introspection make him something of a Jekyll and Hyde character. Fellow England star and broadcaster David Gower says, 'He has the ability to be extremely charming, and an equal ability to be a complete sod.' Peter Willey, the Test umpire and an England colleague of Boycott's, told me: 'Some days he won't seem interested, then on others he will sit down and talk for hours. He is definitely a split personality – and it's just a shame that the good side has not come out more.' Brutally frank in his opinions of others, Boycott can be overly sensitive of any criticism fired in his direction. His career has been littered with the debris of constant feuds and rows. As Derek Hodgson wrote in *Wisden* on his retirement from cricket: 'He has a facility for making enemies much faster than he made runs.' Always a loner, he revels in the adulation of the crowd, whether as a media star in Calcutta or a century-maker in Leeds. He has displayed great inner strength during his rise to the top but is so emotional that, during much of his career, he burst into tears at professional setbacks. Despite often being the most dour of openers, he built up a personal following that no other English cricketer has ever attained. Even in his batting he could be contradictory: in 1965 he played what is still the greatest innings in a Lord's one-day final and then, less than two years later, he was dropped for slow-scoring against India.

He has accumulated great wealth and adores luxury, always staying in the best hotels and flying first class, yet has a reputation for colossal meanness. 'He is for ever trying to squeeze another few pence out of whoever he is dealing with,' fellow commentator Simon Hughes told me. He professes his undying love for Yorkshire cricket, yet helped to tear the club apart in the seventies and eighties. No one was ever better equipped technically and tactically to lead country and county yet, because of his inability to relate to colleagues, he failed dismally in both jobs when given the chance. Though he left school at 16, and has an accent and mannerisms that are a gift to impressionists, he is more articulate and insightful behind the microphone than a host of far better-educated analysts. A balding bachelor, who lived with his mother until he was almost forty, he has enjoyed a surprisingly exuberant, even chaotic, private life. His cosmopolitan outlook, love of travel and phenomenal popularity in the West Indies, India and Pakistan – Asian children have even taken to copying his accent – are in contrast to the narrow horizons of his upbringing in a tightly knit Yorkshire mining community.

It is, perhaps, because Boycott's own personality is riddled with contradictions that he arouses such violently contrasting opinions in others. For all the antagonism he has incurred during his career, he has a circle of friends and supporters who maintain a passionate loyalty towards him. It is a tribute to his ability to inspire long-term devotion that the key women in his life, Anne Wyatt, Rachael Swinglehurst and Shirley Western, have always stuck by him through his many crises, especially the recent French fiasco. Other close friends, like Tony Vann of the Yorkshire committee, George Hepworth from Ackworth, and Ted Lester, the former Yorkshire scorer, speak of his personal kindness. And while there are numerous ex-players who loathe him, there are also many cricketers who feel just the opposite, such as Paul Jarvis, the Yorkshire fast bowler, who describes him as 'a father figure'. Batsmen like Graham Gooch, Bob Barber and Brian Luckhurst have told me how much they enjoyed playing with him. 'I am convinced that Geoffrey made me a better player, without any doubt,' says Luckhurst. In the same way in the media today there are some who object to Boycott's behaviour, such as Henry Blofeld. In 1999, he gave a newspaper interview headlined WHY I WON'T GO IN TO BAT FOR THAT BULLY BOYCOTT. But again, many commentators, such as Jack Bannister, Charles Colvile, David Gower and Tony Greig, have found no problem in working with him.

All the contrasting flaws and virtues of Boycott have to be seen within the dominant theme of his life: his relentless pursuit of success in cricket. In his seminal book *Rain Men* (often described as cricket's answer to Nick Hornby's *Fever Pitch*), Marcus Berkmann wrote of the hold that the game has over its enthusiasts: 'At some cathartic moment in our stunted childhoods, this ridiculous sport inveigled itself into our consciousness like a virus and never left. In adulthood, you somehow expect to recover from all this. But it doesn't happen. Your obsession remains as vivid as ever.' Boycott, having been drawn in by street games in Fitzwilliam, Yorkshire, and by his uncle Algy's enthusiasm at the local Ackworth club, never attempted to let go of this obsession once he had succumbed. Instead, he made cricket the driving force of his existence.

'Cricket mirrors life, if you think about it. Life, death and change in the middle,' said Boycott philosophically, in May 1999. Many would argue that Boycott's approach to cricket mirrors his personality. The adjectives used to describe his batting could be applied to his character: cautious, tough, single-minded, intelligent. His fear of failure, which compelled him to eliminate all risks, also reflected his insecurity. In an interview on BBC 2 in 1978, Ray Illingworth said: 'In technical terms, Geoff Boycott is the best batsman in the world today. His problem is his own insecurity. He's never trusted people and I think this facet of his personality comes out in his batting style.' Mark Nicholas, the Channel Four presenter, put it to me like this: 'Every time he went to the crease he was batting for self-justification, not only as a cricketer but as a man.' A duck, therefore, was not just a disaster in cricket terms, it was a blow to his self-worth.

Yet it must also be said that cricket helped to mould his character. For Boycott, unique among the great batsmen, was not endowed with phenomenal natural talent. No one who saw him in his early days with Barnsley, Leeds or Yorkshire Colts would have believed that one day he would become a leading international cricketer. Boycott only reached the top through an astonishing effort of will and all-consuming dedication. And in that process, he had to be more ruthless than his contemporaries. Focusing every fibre of his being on his ambition, he eschewed almost everything else in life, marriage, family, friendships, a social life and all the other normal compromises of human existence. He was not interested in being popular or likeable, only in batting himself into the record books.

To many observers, it seemed that nothing and no one could stand in the way of Geoff Boycott, a disastrous attitude in a team sport. His total self-absorption made him careless of the needs and feelings of others. Tales of his rudeness and social ineptitude became legendary in the cricket world. David Brown said to me of his first tour to South Africa in 1964/65: 'He thought of nothing else other than Geoffrey Boycott and the rest of the world could go lose itself.

He treated everybody, public, press, the players, the same. He was intolerably rude.' The outrage he caused was made all the greater by both his gift for ripe language, honed in the back-streets of Fitzwilliam and the dressing rooms of the professional cricket circuit, and the traditional Yorkshireman's love of plain-speaking. But if Boycott had paid more attention to the usual niceties of relationships, I doubt that he would have become such a great player. Social acclaim had to be sacrificed to professional glory.

It would be wrong, though, to argue that Boycott's social difficulties stemmed entirely from his cricket. After all, to this day, long after his retirement as a player, he is still renowned for his isolation and brusqueness. Mark Nicholas has worked all over the world with Boycott and is a great admirer of his talent as a broadcaster, but says that 'he can be so rude to people that sometimes you just want to punch his lights out. It is rudeness born of bad manners.' Even as a child and young man, he could be pig-headed and moody. One of his colleagues at the Ministry of Pensions in Barnsley, where Boycott worked before he signed full-time with Yorkshire, says that he was a loner who did not hesitate to tell other employees to 'get stuffed'. So, parts of his character were already deeply ingrained before he became a professional.

Without going too far down the road of pop psychology, I suggest that Boycott's close relationship with his mother must have been at the heart of the development of these traits. His mother's unconditional support led him to develop a self-absorbed, naïve and childlike outlook on life. This meant that, in some respects, he behaved as he felt. If he was in a bad mood, he did not attempt to cover it up. If he thought someone was 'roobish', he said so to their face. Like a child, he continually wanted his immediate demands fulfilled, and was furious when they weren't. And, like a child, he clung to routine and stability and security – one reason he treasures the loyalty of friends and family.

Given the complex nature of his personality, it is hardly surprising that Geoff Boycott should have been such a controversial figure throughout four decades in our national summer sport. His has been a rollercoaster career, with Kipling's twin imposters of triumph and disaster waiting to greet him at every turn. It is one of the most telling features of his life that each success has invariably been accompanied by some misfortune. Barely a year after his unique achievement of scoring his hundredth first-class century in a Test, he was sacked as Yorkshire captain and was fighting for his career at his beloved county. Only days after becoming the greatest run-scorer in the history of international cricket in 1982, he had to resign from the England tour of India, having appalled his fellow players with his conduct in Calcutta. His reinstatement as a Yorkshire player in 1984 after his sacking the year before only plunged the club deeper into turmoil. At the peak of his career recently as an international commentator, he was brought low by Margaret Moore's case against him.

Yet through all these tribulations, Geoff Boycott has displayed a remarkable fortitude. Lesser men would never have reached the heights he attained, nor would they have been able to cope with the catastrophic lows. Even if he has often been the author of his own misfortune, he has never surrendered, whether it be in taking on the most fearsome West Indies attack of all time at the age of forty or overcoming the sneers of critics to become best Yorkshire batsman of his generation. It was England's finest captain of modern times, Mike Brearley, who wrote this tribute to Boycott during the Australian tour of 1978/79: 'As I stood at the non-striker's end and watched him avoid yet another hostile ball, I felt a wave of admiration for my partner, wiry, slight, dedicated, a lonely man doing a lonely job all these years. What was it that com-pelled him to prove himself again and again among his peers?' He has proved this courage once more since the French trial. Not for him a prolonged sulk or a retreat to some rural villa. Instead, having lost almost all his work, been dropped by the *Sun*, and after his contract with the BBC had come to an end, he was soon back in the commentary box with Talk Radio. This is where he truly belongs, pontificating, hectoring, wisecracking, and exulting about the game he adores. 'You have to remember that he is in love with cricket, more than anything else. He would never knowingly do cricket down,' says Mark Nicholas.

For all his many faults, the game has been richer for his presence.

2

'A Very Quiet Boy'

There can be few more depressing streets in England than Milton Terrace in the village of Fitzwilliam, near Wakefield. Several of the two-storey, red-brick properties are boarded up or derelict, while the shell of a burnt-out car lies along the gutter. Many of the local residents seem without jobs or hope. Truancy among the children is rife, police drugs raids common.

Number forty-five, Milton Terrace, is now as bleak as the rest of the houses in this brick-built warren of despair. Yet this neglected edifice was once home to one of Britain's greatest sporting legends. For almost forty years Geoffrey Boycott lived here, from his early childhood until his mother died in 1978. But when Boycott was growing up in Fitzwilliam in the forties and fifties, the same air of abandonment did not hang over the street. With most of the men working at the local Hemsworth colliery – now long closed – there was a strong sense of community and neighbours knew each other well, a spirit also engendered by the much closer family ties of that era. As Boycott wrote in his own *Autobiography* in 1987: 'As I have got older I've realized that growing up in a community like Fitzwilliam did me a lot of good. In many ways I was lucky to experience a sense of belonging and togetherness which seems to have been lost in so much of life nowadays.'

Geoffrey Boycott – his straightforward Yorkshire parents dispensed with the frivolity of middle names – was born in Fitzwilliam on 21 October 1940. At the time of his birth, his parents did not actually live in the village but in neighbouring Ackworth. In Britain of 1940, because of the lack of antenatal facilities, home births were usually a working-class necessity rather than a fashionable middle-class lifestyle choice. So Geoffrey's mother, Jane Boycott, delivered her first-born in the home of her parents in Earl Street, Fitzwilliam. He was a healthy child, weighing eight pounds, 'a smashing little kid with curly blond hair', in the words of his friend from Ackworth, George Hepworth, who remembers visiting the newborn Boycott.

Both Geoffrey's father Tom and his paternal grandfather Bill were employed in the local pits. As president of the Ackworth Working Men's Club, Bill was a figure of some standing in the local community. The Boycott family originally hailed from Shropshire but had come to West Yorkshire in 1910 in search of work in the coal industry. One Fitzwilliam resident, Arthur Hollingsworth, remembers them both. 'I worked on the coalface with old Bill Boycott, he were a grand chap. Geoff's father Tom were also a gentleman. He were a roadlayer down pit, and he used to look after ponies. He were a quiet chap, very harmless, never liked to cause any friction. Never did much talking either, unlike his son.'

When he was three years old, Boycott's parents moved from Garden Street, Ackworth, to Milton Terrace, Fitzwilliam. Though money was short, his childhood appears to have been happy. He indulged in most of the pursuits followed by boys of his age, cricket and football in the street, trainspotting, going to the pictures, playing with his two younger brothers Tony and Peter. 'He definitely had ball sense from an early age,' says George Hepworth. 'I was five years older than him and I remember once, when he can only have been about two or three, I nipped over the wall, took his ball out of yard and then played with it in the street with his cousin, Gordon Naylor. It was only little plastic football, but he created such a fuss, running to the gate and demanding it back.' His aunt, Alice Harratt, remembers him as 'a quiet boy, pleasant and polite, who kept himself to himself, and always tried to avoid trouble. He was bright as well, and was very neat, always smartly dressed. He became a choirboy and altar server in the Anglican Kingsley parish church.' One of his Milton Terrace neighbours from boyhood, Bernard Crapper, recalls a less angelic side of Boycott: 'Everybody got into fights in those days. We had a gang in our street and a couple of streets down were the enemy. We might throw a stone at them and they'd throw one back. He could look after himself, Geoff. It was the way we were all brought up.'

Much of Geoffrey Boycott's outlook on life was shaped by his upbringing. The long hours and permanent danger endured by his father inspired his famous work ethic and titanic self-discipline. It is also probable that the intensity of Boycott's ambition was fired by his desire to escape the austerity of a Yorkshire mining village. Sensing early on that he had a special talent for cricket, he could not afford to squander it and thereby lose the opportunity to build a new life for himself. 'It's better than working down pit,' Boycott often used to tell fellow professionals, when they complained about their lot. And Boycott's delight in luxury and the accumulation of wealth is understandable in a man who lived in a house with an out-side toilet until he was 25.

But the mining background cannot entirely explain the peculi-arities of Boycott's character, that strange mixture of toughness and sensitivity, boorishness and charm, passion and dourness. After all, many others in the cricket world grew up in exactly the same sort of environment: Fred Trueman, Dickie Bird, Harold Larwood to name but three. When I put it to Doug Lloyd, an Ackworth local with long experience of Boycott, that economic circumstances might provide a clue to Boycott's attitudes, he exploded: 'We all went through those experiences, work down pit, outside toilets, we've all been brought up that way round here, not just Geoffrey Boycott as he likes to make out. Everybody in this area has been in the same position, learning to rough it. When I left school, what did I do? Went down pit. Boycott didn't. He worked in an office. He were really quite fortunate.'

Part of the answer to the riddle of Geoff Boycott lies in the huge influence his mother Jane had over him. Theirs was an intensely close relationship, so close that Boycott never considered leaving the family home while she was alive. Even when he was an international sporting star in the seventies, she still washed and ironed all his laundry. 'I owe it all to Mum,' Boycott has often said, and there is no doubt that Jane doted on her eldest child, doing everything she could for him. Not surprisingly, he says that he resembles his mother much more than his father, believing that he inherited her characteristics of fortitude and resolution. 'She was a very, very determined lady, with a lot of inner strength in a quiet way,' he has said. 'She would never be easily got down.'

Boycott may have also inherited his notoriously sharp tongue from his straight-talking mother. Local Fitzwilliam newsagent Harry Cordon told the *Yorkshire Post* in August 1977, the day after Boycott scored his hundredth century: 'His mother comes in here a lot, a marvellous lady, but like everybody in this part of the world, she's not averse to calling a spade a spade. I suppose Geoffrey himself is very much like that, and that's why some people may not have taken to him.'

The attention that Jane lavished on young Geoffrey may have had a number of paradoxical consequences. One was the feeling that, with such unquestioning parental support, he could achieve anything he wanted – psychiatrists have often referred to the almost messianic sense of purpose that can grip an eldest son who is close to his mother. But on the negative side, the intense love may have also made him suspicious of the outside world, leading him to appear a loner, unable to trust others. Throughout most of his playing career, the only two places he appears to have felt totally safe were either at home or at the batting crease. His neighbour and childhood friend from Fitzwilliam, Bernard Crapper, recalls how Geoffrey's mother appeared over-solicitous towards her son: 'She was all right, but she was over-protective of Geoffrey. She was always coming out to see where he was, checking who he was with. She and Geoffrey were very close. I was in and out of his house, used to play in his yard. But then, after an hour or so, his mother would come out and tell Geoff he had to come in.'

Even worse, Geoffrey may have become somewhat spoilt, at least in emotional terms, a trait that could have lasted to this day. One television producer told me: 'The impression I have long had of him is that of a spoilt child, the brat who always wants his own way.' Despite wartime rationing and low wages, Geoffrey was treated generously by his family. His uncle Albert Speight – Jane Boycott's brother – recalls: 'When he was born during the war, things were very hard to get. My parents used to collect all the sweet coupons so that Geoff would have some chocolate. You see, with him being the first grandson in the family, it was a tremendous boost.' Even his shoes were polished by his parents.

Such a warm atmosphere may have provided Geoffrey with a security that few other children enjoyed. Yet at times, it seems that it was almost smothering, creating a mood of claustrophobia. In fact, Boycott occasionally voices his dislike of the pattern of family and community life in which he grew up. The themes of freedom from commitment, not being tied down to one place, run through his adult life. In an interview on Radio Five in November 1998, when Nicky Campbell asked him about his 'unconventional' lifestyle, he said: 'I grew up in a mining community, saw everybody have kids, have greyhounds, pigeons, an allotment and I wanted to travel.' Again, cricket offered the means of escaping such a narrow existence.

Some observers from Fitzwilliam would argue that the most telling characteristic Boycott took from his mother's side of the family was the Speight gift for causing social friction. 'The Speights could be a bit obnoxious. They had this sort of tough, ruthless attitude,' says Bernard Crapper. Arthur Hollingsworth, the local newsagent, is perhaps most revealing of all on this subject, since he knew and worked with both sides of the family: 'Geoffrey was not a Boycott. The Boycotts were very different from the Speights; they were quiet, whereas the Speights were as awkward as bent nails. I used to drive to his grandfather, old Ned Speight, in my pony and cart to deliver a tub of coal for him. And he wouldn't give you the sweat off his brow.'

Whatever the feelings about the Speights, two of them, Boycott's mother and his uncle Albert (known as Algy), were to play a crucial role in the early development of his cricket, which soon became the driving force of his life: his uncle by introducing him to league cricket and his mother by conducting games in the backyard of 45 Milton Terrace. In the 1850s, it had been W.G. Grace's formidable mother Martha who famously encouraged her children's initial steps in cricket in the family orchard. Ninety years later, in the 1940s, Jane Boycott was to act in a similar fashion, organizing playing sessions at the rear of the house with just a bat, a bin and her two younger sons, Peter and Tony. 'Mum kept on making my brothers and I practise shots and techniques in the backyard until we learned every shot in the book,' Boycott said in 1963.

Because of his special talent for cricket, his parents made

considerable sacrifices to further his career: buying him equipment, paying for cricket lessons and helping him through grammar school. But there was no sense of resentment from his two younger brothers at the support Geoffrey was given. Peter Boycott told me, 'All three of us were treated exactly the same way by our parents. Yes, Geoff got extra help with coaching but as far as Tony and myself are concerned, there was absolutely no favouritism.' Tony, the middle son, is three years younger than Geoff, and worked as a fitter in the coal industry before taking early retirement. Peter, eight years younger than Geoff, followed his father's advice 'not to go down pit' and works as a transport manager. To this day the Boycott brothers remain close. 'There has never been any rift in our family. Geoff puts great store by loyalty. He has always been there for us, a great brother, and, likewise, if he wants help on anything, all he has to do is pick up the phone,' says Peter.

Both Peter and Tony have been useful cricketers without aspiring to the heights achieved by their elder brother. Tony, an opening batsman and left-arm spinner, is still playing, while Peter, a former middle-order batsman, now umpires in the West Riding League. 'Geoff and I are different characters,' says Peter. 'If I had shown the same total dedication as Geoff I might have made it as a professional. But, from his earliest days, Geoff was so self-motivated, determined and single-minded. Anything he puts his mind to, he succeeds at. I'm very proud of him.'

It was, perhaps, inevitable that Boycott, from his earliest years, should have had an enthusiasm for the game, for cricket then was as much part of life in Fitzwilliam as the colliery. Given the great strength of Yorkshire in the 1930s, winning the county championship seven times in nine seasons up to 1939, few local schoolboys could have ignored the game. And cricket then was far more important to our national culture than it is today, especially in the north of England. But what was unique about Geoffrey Boycott was the depth of his passion for it. As his childhood friend from Fitzwilliam Malcolm Tate recalls: 'Going back to his very earliest days, he were always cricket mad, just like me. We used to go for long walks in the fields around the village and we would talk about nothing but cricket for hours on end.'

His ability was also obvious to Bernard Crapper, though it was helped by the fact that Geoff, as a result of his family's support, had better equipment than the other boys in Milton Terrace: 'We used to play games in the cobbled street. The wicket would be a dustbin or a chalk mark on the wall. Only Geoff had a proper bat, the rest of us had to make do with crude bats made from planks or wooden fencing. For bowling we used a well-worn tennis ball with no fur. The ball would bounce off at awkward angles from the cobbles, shooting away in one direction, or keeping low, or going straight up in the air. I have often thought that is where Geoff got his great technique from dealing with the ball coming at all heights and directions. The rest of us would never last very long, with the dustbin often rattling after only three or four balls but Geoffrey, of course, could stay there for quite a time. He did use to sulk if he got out and could be a bit tempestuous.'

Cricket was also played on the tarmac playground of Fitzwilliam Junior School, which Boycott attended from the age of five. The school adhered to the traditional approach of the time, strong on discipline and short on sympathy. Bernard Crapper, who later became chairman of the governors of Fitzwilliam Junior, remembers the headmaster, Mr Perry, as a 'big, ruddy-faced man, who looked like a farmer. He had hands like shovels, with one finger missing from the right one. When you'd get those hands whacked across you, you really knew you'd been hit.' But, in the memory of Crapper, Boycott seems to have been a good pupil. 'Geoff was a little bit better behaved than the rest of us. I think that was his mother's influence. In lessons he would knuckle down. He was certainly a bright lad, good in all subjects, even in music with his recorder. He always seemed to understand everything.'

But some elements of the Boycott temperament were apparent even then. According to Crapper: 'I thought he was a decent lad, and I usually got on well with him. But I knew he could be awkward and was prone to moodiness. I could generally tell what mood he was in and then I would leave him alone. Towards others he could have a standoffish attitude. Some people at school thought he was big-headed, probably because of jealousy at his ability, "He thinks he's somebody just because he's got a bat," they would say.'

Before he had reached the age of 10, Boycott suffered two setbacks of the kind with which his life has been littered. The first occurred when he was just seven years old. Playing with some friends on the railings at the back of his house, he slipped and fell on a mangle lying in the neighbour's garden. There was no obvious external injury but he bled internally through the night and had to be rushed to Pontefract Hospital the next morning. Due to the foresight of the doctor examining him, a ruptured spleen was diagnosed and an emergency operation was performed to remove the damaged organ. As his uncle Algy puts it, 'In those days anyone with a ruptured spleen was very lucky to survive and he was in a critical condition. But he was taken to the hospital just in time and he pulled through.' Situated in the upper left side of the abdomen, the spleen filters bacteria out of the bloodstream. Therefore, anyone who has been through a splenectomy is far more prone to infection. According to some medical experts, the risk of being infected, especially with septicaemia, may be eight times higher. This largely explains why Boycott used to be reluctant to tour south Asia, an attitude that blighted his Test career in the seventies.

The second, even more serious, misfortune occurred in March 1950, when his father was badly injured working down the mine. Tom Boycott's job as a roadlayer meant he was responsible for laying and maintaining the underground tracks on which the coal tubs ran. In an interview with the *Daily Telegraph* in November 1998, Boycott described what went wrong and the sorry aftermath: 'Some idiot sent these empty coal tubs along the line while my dad was still working on it at the coal face. Just mangled him up. Broke his back, broke his pelvis, both knees, ruptured his insides. What a mess. It destroyed his life. From then on he was a broken man. He had a rolling, shambling gait instead of being a six foot one inch upright man.' If any such accident happened today, the employee would, rightly, receive substantial compensation. There were no such rights for miners in 1950 and, despite Tom Boycott's poor health, he eventually had to return to his job underground. 'There were just promises, promises from the union but no compensation. He only got a few tomatoes, eggs and apples when people called,' recalled Boycott. His father never properly recovered from his injuries and died prematurely, seventeen years later. This experience further hardened Boycott. Not only did his family have to go through severe financial hardship as they struggled on his father's meagre sick pay immediately after the accident, but also the treatment by both the union and employer must have made Boycott all the more distrustful of those in authority. Throughout his adult life he has clashed with such figures, whether they be Yorkshire committee men, England selectors, BBC bosses or French judges.

Yet one of the hallmarks of Boycott has always been his willingness to battle through any crisis. Even as a child, he let neither family disaster nor personal health problems disrupt his pursuit of success at cricket. So, at the age of nine, he was selected for the Fitzwilliam Junior School team. The following year, he was its captain. His developing reputation as a talented young cricketer was further enhanced when he won a national newspaper competition, organized to coincide with the 1951 Festival of Britain, for the best all-round performance in a schools match. He had been nominated by Fitzwilliam Junior after taking six wickets for 10 and scoring 45 not out from a total of just 52 in a fixture against Royston. The prize, appropriate for a would-be Yorkshire and England opener, was a Len Hutton bat.

Outside school, Boycott's increasing passion for cricket was deepened by his uncle Algy, who was captain at Ackworth Cricket Club. 'I talked cricket with him from his earliest days,' he says, 'and on Saturdays, for a day out, I would take him on the bus to the ground, maybe give him some tea there, and then he would have some lemonade and fish and chips on the way back. That's really how he first got involved in the game. He was so single-minded as a child. Nothing else mattered to him except cricket.' George Hepworth, who was secretary of Ackworth for more than thirty years, says that Algy was Boycott's first real mentor: 'I can see the pair of them now, Algy with his Brylcreemed hair, and little Geoff alongside, carrying Algy's case and boots. It was Algy who really fed his passion for the game. He was a wise old bird, great at encouraging youngsters.'

George Hepworth has a clear recollection of an early game that Geoff played for the Ackworth Under 15s. 'We were playing against Featherstone and I was captain of the side. Geoff was only about nine years old and he came in as last man, with eighteen still needed. He stayed there and we managed to scrape fifteen runs towards the target before Geoff got out. His mum and dad had been watching and there were tears streaming down his face. He thought he had let everyone down but in fact he had batted well for a little lad. And I thought to myself, This kid, he's got a touch of steel in his make-up, a look of eagle in his eye. I had a gut feeling then that he would go right to the top.'

Recognizing that Geoffrey had genuine ability at the game, Algy suggested that he should receive proper training at the coaching clinic at Rothwell, run by the former Somerset leg-spinner Johnny Lawrence. The combined cost of the cricket lessons and the bus fares to Rothwell came to about 10 shillings, more than Boycott's parents could afford, so Algy and other relatives assisted. Boycott's cricket lessons involved not only a considerable sacrifice by his parents but also real dedication on his part, for he had to make two long bus journeys plus a mile's walk to reach the clinic, often in rain or snow.

Johnny Lawrence's indoor school, the only one of its kind outside London, was little more than a large shed with a wooden floor. It had no proper heating, which meant near-freezing conditions on a winter morning. Each of the two nets had different surfaces: one was a turning wicket, the other fast. What the school lacked in facilities and warmth was more than balanced by Johnny Lawrence's talent as a coach. A deeply religious man who refused to play on Sundays, he had a gift for conveying both enthusiasm and technical advice. Jack Birkenshaw, who attended the school with Boycott, says: 'He was a great coach, one of the best I have ever known. He loved the game, had a passion for it, made you enjoy it, taught you all the subtleties of batting and bowling.' George Hepworth agrees: 'Johnny was an absolute genius as a coach, always able to end a session on a positive note. He should have been put in charge at Yorkshire but the establishment derided him because he hadn't played for England. It was all bunkum. He was something special.'

An impeccably straight technique and confidence against spin were two of the legacies of Boycott's early years at the Rothwell school. The Yorkshire left-arm spinner Don Wilson, another Lawrence pupil, remembers: 'When I bowled at Geoffrey, I could never get him out. He had no strokes but an unbelievable defence.' This is Jack Birkenshaw's verdict: 'He was very defensive and I would not have said he would have ever been a Test cricketer then. There were a lot better than Boycs at that age. But he just kept coming along and improving all the time.' Throughout his playing career, Boycott continued to turn to Lawrence for advice and support. Before an overseas tour, for instance, he would usually have several intensive net sessions at the school.

Boycott was soon able to show his increasing skills in a proper playing arena. When he was twelve, his uncle Algy managed to find him a place in the Ackworth second team. It was not an auspicious start for he made precisely nought but he played well enough in the following game to win his début for the first team at the end of the season, making nine in a match at Goole. At the start of the next summer, 1954, still aged just 13, he played his first game for the Ackworth senior team at home. George Hepworth, on leave from duty in the RAF, was playing in the match. 'We were 87 for 7 when he came in and we took our total to 119, making the scores level. Then I was out to the last ball of the over. The very next ball Geoff put his foot across and cracked a terrific cover drive, which rattled the boundary railings.' Boycott's winning hit brought his first press notice, a mention in the local *Pontefract and Castleford Express*, though thanks to the scorer misspelling his name, he appeared as 'Jeffrey Boycott'.

Boycott's performance made an even bigger impression on George Hepworth. On his return to RAF Bempton, he told the local postmaster, Reg Gardiner: 'Watch out for this kid called Geoffrey Boycott. As sure as God made little apples, this kid will go all the way. One day you may well see him play for England.' For years afterwards, George Hepworth used to tell Boycott of these words to Gardiner. 'I'm not sure he ever believed me. Then, in 1984, I was at the Scarborough Cricket Festival, standing talking to Geoff. By coincidence, a million-to-one shot, Reg Gardiner came by. He turned to Geoff and said, "This gentleman said to me, thirty years ago, to look out for a kid called Boycott. Tha were an age comin' through but, by God, he were right."'

George Hepworth also recalls the time he ran out Boycott in a game against Stanley. Hepworth was trying to win the strike because he fancied taking on Stanley's off-spinner. 'I called him for a quick single and, poor little kid, his pads were almost under his chin while I, serving in the RAF, was pretty fit.' Boycott was run out for 25, but Hepworth went on to reach his 50. 'When I returned to the dressing room, Geoff was still sitting there in his pads, just peering over them. I fell about laughing and said, "Never mind, old cock, it were my fault, I were trying to pinch bowling." He called me a cad.'

As well as playing league cricket for Ackworth, Boycott became involved in local, knock-out competitions. One of the teams he played for was an eleven organized by Bernard Conway, a professional rugby-league player with Hull. Conway has vivid memories of the young teenage Boycott: 'He was not endowed with a brilliant natural talent but he was so single-minded and purposeful. He thought of every game as a battle with the sole aim of staying in.' In the summers of 1954 and 1955, Conway entered his team in the Ackworth knock-out, winning in the second year in the final against the Plough Inn. These matches only lasted 20 overs and batsmen had to retire after scoring 25 runs. Conway recalls that Boycott seemed a little concerned that he would not be able to score quickly enough in the competition. 'At the age of thirteen and fourteen he did not have any power in his strokes. He came to me and said, "What am I to do?" I told him not to worry. "Just get your twenty-five and leave the rest to us." And he usually did, despite some barracking from the crowd. I remember I had a bet with one of the Fitzwilliam locals just before the final. He said to me: "Boycott will lose you this match. He scores so slowly." I replied, "With him in the side, we've already got twenty-five runs on the board. And I'll tell you something else. That lad might play for Yorkshire." "They'll not even let him into the stripping room," was the reply.'

Boycott was to carry on playing for Ackworth until he was sixteen, though he still continued to practise at the ground, even when he was a Test player. As might be expected, the club is proud of its association with the great cricketer and has given him life membership. The Ackworth CC Chairman, Barrie Wathen, told me: 'Geoff is always welcome here. We are honoured to have the connection with him. I know he's a complex character, but personally, I have had a good relationship with him.' George Hepworth says that when he was secretary at Ackworth, 'nothing was too much trouble' for Boycott. 'If we were short of money, he would organize a Yorkshire side to come to the ground for a fund-raising game. He would also help to get us sponsors.'

As always though with Boycott, the picture is complex. Today, other, more critical, voices are raised against him in the club. There are complaints that he has used people for his own ends, and that he has been selfish and rude. In particular, it is argued that he did little to assist when the club embarked on a major fund-raising drive to buy its own ground and thereby remove the threat that the land might be used for building. Fifty thousand pounds was needed to purchase the ground from its then owner, the Moorfield Development Company, and some members believed that Boycott should have stumped up the whole sum from his own pocket. But Boycott told the *Yorkshire Post* in November 1990: 'It would be nice for the club to own their own ground and I have a great emotional attachment to Ackworth. I will certainly do all I can to help the fund-raising, but the club actually belongs to the community and they will have to make the biggest contribution.'

The fund-raising campaign was ultimately successful, the ground was bought, and is now superbly appointed. But the feeling among some senior figures is that Boycott never lived up to his promise. Indeed, it is a symbol of the ill-feeling in certain quarters that when the gates at the entrance to the ground, erected in his honour in 1971, were recently taken down, it was decided not to have his name on their replacements. Keith Stevenson, uncle of former Yorkshire player Graham Stevenson, told me: 'He just used us all the time. He's so selfish, forgets where he came from. People says he's never bought them a drink. Well, I wouldn't want him to.' He told me of two incidents that strengthened his negative opinion of Boycott: 'We used to run testimonial matches here for him in 1984, when money were short because of the miners' strike. At one match, we had a beautiful spread in the clubhouse for tea, all home-made stuff. I was umpiring and as we came off the field at the end of one innings, Boycott says to me, "Is there some tea on, Keith?" I replied, "Ay, we'll have twenty minutes." Then Boycott says, "We're having no break. We're going straight out again." So I told him, "If tha's goin' out, tha's goin' on tha' own, because we're havin' tea with the rest of the teams." And, you know, he stayed in the pavilion, never came down to the clubhouse, though we had laid on all this food for his testimonial. That were Mr Boycott.' The second incident occurred when Keith Stevenson and his father gave Boycott a lift to a match at Middlesbrough: 'Never offered me petrol money, of course, and then he says to my dad when we arrived, "Will thee go down shop and bring me lump of red cheese." Me dad were only a miner but he got him this block of cheese – I know it sounds stupid but Boycott loved red cheese – yet Mr Boycott never paid and never thanked me for the lift. And then, at the end of play, we sat in the car park waiting for him, only to find that he had buggered off with a young lass.'

Another member of the club, Doug Lloyd, who played with Boycott in the Ackworth team as a teenager, is equally scathing: 'You won't get me knocking him as a cricketer but as a man I detest him. He is what you call a self-centred bastard. And he's always had a short temper. I remember when he were a lad, fourteen or fifteen, if he got out he would cry and sulk and sit on his own.' Doug Lloyd has a personal reason for his feelings towards Boycott. His son, Neil, was an outstanding young cricketer, playing for England Schools and the national youth side. Many observers, including Fred Trueman, felt that he was certain to play for England. Yet, within a week of playing a junior test match against the West Indies in September 1982, he died suddenly at the age of just 17. The shock of this tragic blow reverberated throughout Yorkshire cricket. 'All the Yorkshire players and the entire committee came to Neil's funeral, except that bastard Boycott. I've played in his benefit matches, taken time off work for him, and then he never showed up at my son's funeral. That were it for me that day.' Boycott was taken aback by the vehemence of Lloyd's reaction, especially because he had written a letter of sympathy to the family the moment he had heard the tragic news about Neil. He said, 'I don't like funerals. I never go to them. The only funerals I have ever been to are my dad's in 1967 and my mum's in 1978. Doug and his wife were sad – understandably sad – and they took it out on me.'

Even today Doug Lloyd is unrepentant. 'It still touches something in me. When I talk about Boycott, I just upset myself.'

3

'Dedicated Absolutely to Cricket'

From Fitzwilliam Junior School, Boycott, having failed his 11-plus, went to the local Kingsley Secondary Modern School. The teaching there was poor, the cricket facilities almost non-existent. The only positive result of this move was the development of his soccer skills, which he had already revealed playing in defence for Fitzwilliam youth club. As on the cricket field, he always wanted to win on the soccer pitch. He is remembered as a tough, physical player, with enough talent to attract the attention of Leeds United scouts in his mid-teenage years. He even played a few games for the famous club's Under-18 team alongside Billy Bremner.

But cricket remained his first passion. Fortunately for Boycott, after just a year at Kingsley he passed the late-entry examination for grammar school and thereby won a place at nearby Hemsworth, which had both an excellent cricket ground and a cricket-loving headmaster in Russell Hamilton. With this kind of support, Hemsworth Grammar was to be almost as important for Boycott's game as the Lawrence coaching clinic and Ackworth Cricket Club.

Hemsworth was a traditional institution, with a mixed intake of about 800 pupils, high academic and sporting standards, and strong leadership from Hamilton. 'It was a smashing school. If you got there, you had a real sense of achievement,' says one of Boycott's fellow pupils, Terry Newitt. 'Russell Hamilton was both strict and inspiring, the sort of gentleman you looked up to. When he walked down the corridor in his black flowing gown, we'd all jump out of the way.' During his years at the school, Boycott proved himself to be not only an excellent cricketer but also a fine rugby player, a sound academic pupil and a mature, likeable young man. Ken Sale, who taught him biology and rugby, remembers him as 'bright, diligent, anxious to please. In the classroom he was keen and alert. He was as careful in his approach to his studies as he was to his batsmanship. I also remember he was fastidious about his dress, always looking immaculate both on and off the field. As with most school sporting heroes, he was the idol of quite a few of the girls, had a little following of them, though I don't think he was ever involved with any. He was a product of his background, very determined to get on and make the most of his talent at cricket. His personality could be described as intense; he didn't seem to mix much but, underneath, I sensed he was a gentle, vulnerable pupil who tried to hide that vulnerability.'

Boycott was soon established in the Hemsworth First XI and at 15 he was made captain. Sale recalls that he had 'a certain streak of arrogance about his game, which came from being so much better than the other boys'. In one match against the staff, Boycott was dominating as usual. Sale continues: 'So our fast bowler, George Pacey, came on with the threat: "Right, I'm going to bowl as fast as I can straight at his legs." I was fielding down at fine leg and soon Boycott was regularly clipping the ball straight past me. To make such a cool response to an adult fast bowler at only fifteen showed Boycott's talent and character. He had an excellent defence off both front and back foot. He absolutely loathed to give up his wicket and hated any false strokes.'

The cricket coach at Hemsworth, Dudley Taylor, who was also a science teacher, has equally fond memories of Boycott. 'Because he was a late-entry pupil, he was a year older than most in his class, so he seemed more mature. He was well-mannered and hard-working, though he could enjoy a laugh in the classroom.' Taylor says that Boycott was good at all games, even basketball, and remembers him as a 'brave and determined full back in rugby'. As with his soccer, his rugby skills aroused an interest beyond school – Boycott played in one Under 18 trial match for South Yorkshire District against Wakefield. Once more, however, it was his cricket that most impressed Taylor. 'I knew even at thirteen that he would go on to play for Yorkshire. He was a more expansive player then but that is probably because he was in a different class to the other boys. I will never forget the way he played the pull. It was so effortless and the ball sped to the boundary, whereas the rest of us were liable to hit the ball in the air when we attempted that shot. In fact, he was so confident about technique that he actually used to coach the staff team in the nets.'

The tension that characterized many of his relationships in later life appears to have been largely absent during his time at Hemsworth, possibly because Boycott felt relaxed in his pre-eminence. Roland Howcroft, a schoolmate of the time, says: 'He was always quite confident; there was no sense of insecurity about him. He was just a normal lad, liked normal things. On the buses to away games, for instance, he would join in singing with the rest of us. He was always outstanding at cricket, of course. Even in those days he was deadly serious about the game, was never a slogger or tried to hit over the top.'

Another of his Hemsworth contemporaries, Peter Jordan, now a journalist, says: 'He was mature, sensible, never involved in any pranks and because he was serious and dedicated he seemed much older than the rest of us. Yet you could not have described him as a loner. He joined in everything at school and could take part as well as anyone in school debates. But there was never any bullshit with him. He never just talked for the sake of it but if he had something to say, he'd say it.' Jordan was sure that Boycott would play for Yorkshire because of his determination. 'He wanted to practise all the time. It was almost as if he was on a crusade. When he was out, he often didn't come back into the pavilion but would sit on his own, holding an inquest on his dismissal. He was friendly and polite to the girls but nothing was going to stand in the way of his cricket, he was that dedicated. If he'd gone into medicine, he would be a top surgeon by now.'

One of Boycott's closest friends at Hemsworth was the school wicket-keeper, Terry McCroakham, who therefore had some direct experience of Boycott the young bowler. 'At this level, he was fast medium, very accurate, with a good inswinger. Because of his control, he was more reliable than many others.' Against Castleford in 1956, Boycott had the remarkable figures of 7 for 4, though he finished up on the losing side. Like others from Hemsworth in the mid-fifties, McCroakham enjoyed Boycott's company. 'I never found him big-headed at all. There was no side to him, he was just part of the team. Yes, he could hog the strike but then he was a much better batsman than any of the rest of us. I don't think he was a natural; you got the impression that he lived to practise. He was very ambitious, knew where he wanted to go.' McCroakham has stayed in contact with Boycott and remains an admirer. 'Just before the Leeds Test in 1964, he had damaged a hand and was having a net to see if he would be fit to play. I was standing nearby. Though he hadn't seen me for seven years and was now an international player, he came straight over for a chat. To me, he has always been like that, unlike some other of these so-called England stars.'

Sadly, all the school records and scorebooks from this period were destroyed in a fire. However, Terry McCroakham has retained a press cutting from this period, which recorded Boycott's largest innings for the school, when he made 'a fine 105 not out' from a Hemsworth total of 143 for 4 against Normanton Grammar School, 'including two sixes and 14 fours'. Unfortunately rain brought the match to a premature end. Eddie Hambleton, another schoolfriend, remembers that day: 'It started to rain quite heavily and the masters had a consultation. They then said that there were not often centuries in schools cricket so they would play a few more overs to give Geoff a chance to reach his hundred. When we came in about three overs later, Geoff had made 105. Back at school on Monday morning, we consulted the old scorebooks and found that the school record was 106. So Geoff just missed out there.'

The summer of 1958 was Boycott's last at Hemsworth. He passed seven O levels and could have easily stayed on to do A levels, perhaps going on to further education. Ken Sale says that he was certainly competent enough to have gained a good degree at a red-brick university. Dudley Taylor goes even further: 'With his brains and cricketing ability, he might well have got to Cambridge if he had been to public school.'

But two factors made him leave school at 17. First, he felt he had been a burden on his parents for too long. In an interview with the BBC in 1965 his headmaster, the late Russell Hamilton, who had been keen for him to stay on for his A levels, said: 'Always at the back of his mind was the fact that financially he had been a big enough strain on his parents and that he really ought to get himself a job.' The second, perhaps lesser, consideration was Boycott's iron determination to make cricket his career, for which a university degree must have seemed an irrelevance. Everyone who knew him in the mid-fifties was struck by his single-minded ambition to become a Yorkshire cricketer. 'Cricket was always going to be his trade,' says Terry McCroakham. Indeed, the choice of Boycott's occupation appears to have been dictated by his playing ambition, for the post he took up in the Ministry of Pensions in Barnsley, though mundane, offered a great deal of flexibility in his working hours. What Boycott did was to work every shift he could in the winter thereby building up extra leave that could be taken during the summer.

Yet, despite the advantages of this job for his cricket, Boycott's early departure from school left him, in the longer term, with feelings of resentment towards the more privileged. The lack of a university education rankled, and was regularly used as a stick with which to beat his opponents in the supposed 'cricket establishment', with Boycott posing as the champion of the ordinary working public against the public-school, Oxbridge 'gin and tonic brigade'. When Mike Brearley was awarded an OBE, Boycott said, 'If I'd been to Cambridge, I'd have a knighthood by now.' Similarly, this chip on his shoulder has also been reflected in his often boorish antics at official gatherings – 'he could be so disrespectful. You'd be at a reception, chatting to some dignitary, perhaps an Oxford-educated bloke, then Boycs comes barging in, doing the guy down, "all the bloody same, you lot," and so on. You would just feel so embarrassed,' says one ex-England player who toured with Boycott.

Boycott worked as a clerical officer at the Ministry of Pensions from 1958 until 1963. His duties were hardly taxing for a man of his intelligence, but because of his cricket ambitions he never applied for promotion. Even in this job, Boycott demonstrated those patterns of behaviour that became so well known to his cricket colleagues. One fellow employee, who gave Boycott a fortnight's training when he started in his post, told me: 'I liked him and never had any problems with him, perhaps because I had shown him the ropes. But he could be very rude to others, never hesitating to tell someone to get stuffed. There was also a degree of resentment over the time he took off for cricket in the summer. He was something of an eccentric – when he brought in his lunch it often consisted of half a dozen cakes, no meat or bread. The social side of office life, like parties or outings, never interested him. He was very much a loner.'

By the time Boycott entered the civil service, he had already made rapid progress up the ladder of Yorkshire cricket. As well as producing a string of outstanding performances for Hemsworth Grammar, he had also appeared successfully for both the South Elmsall district team – averaging around 70 per game as well as captaining the side – and Yorkshire schoolboys. In the summer of 1958 he was vice-captain for the Yorkshire Federation's Under 18s tour of the Midlands. Boycott had little chance to shine, however, as the tour was ruined by poor weather.

Just as importantly, he was also playing club cricket for Barnsley, in one of the toughest environments in the world, the Yorkshire and Bradford League. Boycott had moved from Ackworth to Barnsley when he was 16, on the advice of his uncle Algy who felt that 'we ought to get him into a higher class of cricket'. Furthermore, Barnsley also had a very good batting track. So Algy had taken Boycott to the winter nets one night at Barnsley's ground at Shaw Lane, where his batting was watched by Clifford Hesketh, chairman of Barnsley and a leading member of the Yorkshire committee. According to Algy, Hesketh took a brief look at Boycott, then said, 'Oh, yes, we'll have him.'

Given the strength of Barnsley, Boycott could not immediately break into the First XI, but he did well for the seconds, enjoying an average of 66. Then, towards the end of the season, he played two games for the senior side, making 43 not out in the second match in a victory against Castleford. In the following two summers, 1958 and 1959, he was a regular member of the Barnsley First XI, performing creditably but with few heroics. One of the leading members of the Barnsley club, Gordon Walker, was later to recall Boycott as a moody loner, with an inclination towards foul language and slow scoring: 'I'd say we had several players who looked better at the time. It's been sheer determination that's made him one of t' best we ever had in county.'

Through a remarkable twist of history, the modest south Yorkshire club at this time included a trio of cricketers who were subsequently to be amongst the biggest stars of modern Britain:

Boycott, Dickie Bird and Michael Parkinson. It is perhaps no co-incidence that all three had the same background, the sons of coal miners who learnt early in their lives the value of hard work and strength of character. But even Dickie and Parky were struck by the intensity of Boycott's ambitions. In a radio interview in the seventies, Parkinson explained: 'He always had this extraordinary, obsessive dedication. I have never met an obsession like it in any athlete. I remember the first game I really clocked his talent was when we were playing Scarborough and they had a bowler called Bill Foord, good enough to play for Yorkshire on a few occasions. And Geoffrey came in at number five. It was a soggy, wet day, and the outfield was damp, with a lot of sawdust on the run-ups. Bill Foord bowled his first ball to Geoff who went on the back foot and hit it like a shell past him. It went right through the pile of sawdust behind the bowler and hit the sightscreen. Foord turned to me and said, "Christ almighty, what's this lad's name?"

'"Boycott."

'"I'll remember that."'

What Dickie Bird remembers most about Boycott at Barnsley was 'his application, concentration and his absolute belief in himself. He had one great gift, mental strength. You can have all the coaching in the world but the most important thing is to be mentally strong.' At Barnsley, Dickie Bird and Michael Parkinson generally opened, and Boycott came down the order, 'though he handled the quick bowlers pretty well. He was a fine player off his back foot, which is always the hallmark of class, whatever the level. His punch through the offside was his bread and butter shot, with a lot of bottom hand in it. Then he would also pick up his ones and twos off his legs. That is all he did. He played to his limitations. His one weakness was that he played with very low hands going forward but that is the way we were coached in Yorkshire to cope with spin and move-ment on difficult pitches. The problem with that technique is that, though it might cover deviation it can also leave your hands vulnerable to the one that suddenly rises.' Dickie Bird is also inter-esting on Boycott's personality: 'He always kept himself to himself, even in those early days. He was very private, didn't mix much with the people. Parky, Boycott and I were all from the same background but we did not go out together in the evenings. All he seemed interested in was playing and practising as much cricket as he could. Yet he was also very confident and I think some of the older players resented that, meeting this young man who had so much belief in himself.'

Achievement with Boycott has usually been accompanied by set-backs, and his teenage years were no exception. Just as he had to cope in childhood with his father's disability and the loss of his spleen, so, when he was about 17, he was faced with a serious threat to his sporting ambitions, that of poor eyesight. When Boycott was told that he would have to wear glasses, he feared it was an end to his hopes of becoming a professional cricketer. In a BBC interview he explained: 'I suddenly found when I was doing my schooling in the classroom that I could not see the blackboard very well. My friends kept pulling my leg about this and said that I needed glasses. It had never struck me at first because I was playing cricket fairly well at school but in the end it got under my skin so much that I had to go and see an optician.' Unfortunately the other boys were right. Boycott was told he would have to wear glasses. He was plunged into the blackest despair.

Uncle Algy takes up the story: 'Geoff would just not accept it. He said that if he had to wear glasses, his future was finished. For three or four days he cried, he were that upset.' At the request of Boycott's mother, Algy went to see his nephew and gave him a stern lecture. 'I told him that other people with glasses had made names for themselves in cricket, like Roy Marshall of Hampshire and M.J.K. Smith of Warwickshire. I said to him, "If you say you're finished, you're finished. But if you fight, you can go on."'

Invigorated by his uncle's talk, Boycott wrote to M.J.K. Smith. The future England captain, who was to be Boycott's first skipper on an MCC tour, still recalls the schoolboy contacting him. 'Fellows used to write to me quite a lot because I was one of those wearing spectacles. I had a standard letter saying that it was not a problem at all. I always used to suggest that they had their eyes tested every year so they knew their eyesight was 100 per cent, which was prob-ably better than some blokes who didn't wear glasses.' Smith further explained that he wore rimless spectacles with shatter-proof plastic lenses, so glass would not go into the eye if they were hit.

Boycott was later to claim that glasses had made him more

introverted, more of a loner. After he exchanged his spectacles for contact lenses in 1969, he told a reporter from the *Sun*: 'I started wearing glasses when I was seventeen and my personality changed dramatically. From a carefree youngster, I turned into a withdrawn character who just couldn't go out and meet people. I cut myself off and everyone began to think I was hostile.' This, to say the least, is something of an exaggeration. Not even the most excitable observer would have ever called the young Boycott 'carefree'. Few teenagers can have been more consumed with such a ruthless sense of purpose. His close friend George Hepworth remembers him as 'very intense, almost an introvert' in his early days at Ackworth, long before he found he needed glasses.

Still, having acquired a pair, Boycott was more optimistic about the future. There was now no reason why he should not return to the playing arena with renewed confidence. But not everyone was so sure. His schoolfriend Eddie Hambleton, who played in the Hemsworth School First XI and also drove Boycott to Barnsley games on the back of his Triumph motorcycle – 'two bags in his hands and no crash helmet' – remembers the first time Boycott wore glasses in a match: 'We were playing at the village of Wath. I was sitting about to watch the cricket as Geoff went out to open. The groundsman, Mr Mansfield, whom I knew well, turned to me and said, "Is Boycott wearing glasses?"

'"Ay, I think he is."

'"Well, that's the end of his career, then, isn't it?"'

Mr Mansfield, like many others before and since, was to be proved hopelessly wrong.

4

A Late Developer

There has long been a fascinating debate as to whether Geoffrey Boycott was a natural cricketer who sacrificed strokeplay for run accumulation, or a self-made professional who exploited every ounce of his limited ability through monumental dedication. Some fine judges of the game, like Ted Dexter, incline to the former view. 'Geoff Boycott and Kenny Barrington would not have been far apart,' Dexter told me. 'People often suggest that they didn't have a lot of talent but they made the best of what they'd got. Well, that's rubbish. I mean, Kenny had more talent in his little finger than most people. And Geoff, in Australia 1970/71, provided some of the best batting I have ever seen.' David Brown, the Warwickshire fast bowler, says: 'You don't get to his position as a purely fabricated player without natural talent.'

Boycott's last opening partner at Yorkshire, Martyn Moxon, agrees: 'People say he was a manufactured player, but that's ridiculous. He was very good indeed, though he was a grafter who was more likely to win you a game on a bad wicket. But he had the ability to take an attack apart when he felt it necessary.'

Support for this argument comes not only from his great one-day performances in the Gillette Cup in 1965 and in Australia in 1979/80 but also from the regularity with which he took centuries off the finest bowling attacks all over the world. Anyone who could score a hundred in the West Indies against Michael Holding, Andy Roberts, Colin Croft and Joel Garner – as Boycott did in Antigua in 1981 at the age of 40 plus – cannot be short of genuine class.

Yet the evidence for the other side is more conclusive. For if Boycott had enjoyed great natural flair, it would have shone through from his earliest days. After all, this is what has happened with most of the top Test batsmen. Colin Cowdrey and Peter May were both talked of as England players while still at school. Len Hutton was said to be good enough for first-class cricket at the age of 14. In truth, Boycott is almost unique in the lateness of his rise to top-level cricket and in the limitations of talent. Yes, he might have had sufficient capability to make a living as a professional cricketer. Yes, he might have been a skilled enough sportsman to have had trials with Leeds and played rugby for his school. But, apart from George Hepworth, no one who saw him as a young man had any inkling that he might become an England cricketer. 'I never thought he would be more than an average county cricketer, certainly not a player who would put his name in the record books,' says Dickie Bird, of their days together at Barnsley. Don Wilson is even more emphatic: 'When he first arrived at Yorkshire, he could hardly hit the ball off the square. I would never have said he'd be a Test cricketer, not at any price.'

What brought Boycott to the Test arena was the depth not of his talent but of his will-power. 'He drove himself to the top with old-fashioned discipline. He was not a natural but he dedicated himself totally to the game,' argues Colin Cowdrey. All the other greats of the game, apart from Boycott, have sent out a signal of their genius almost as soon as they stepped on to a cricket field. Boycott was still languishing in the Yorkshire seconds at 21, an age at which others, like Gary Sobers, Denis Compton, Waqar Younis and Sachin Tendulkar, had already enjoyed great success at Test level. Of his own Test contemporaries, Peter Willey, Dennis Amiss and Keith Fletcher all played for their counties in their teens, while David Gower, Bob Willis, Derek Underwood and Alan Knott were younger when they first played for England than Boycott was when he made his début for Yorkshire.

'He certainly wasn't an outstanding player – he'll admit that him-self. There were lots of players around who were more prolific than Geoff. But he was totally locked into what he wanted to do,' says Rodney Cass, a fellow pupil of the Johnny Lawrence school. The very fact that Boycott had to work so hard to reach Test standard is further proof of his restricted natural ability. It was partly because he had this monumental dedication to cricket that he developed his character traits of self-absorption and unsociability, which later caused such friction in his career. There is one further point. For all his great achievements, Boycott remained chronically insecure about his batting. According to Ray Illingworth, he would always be asking, 'Do you think I'm a good player?' Other England captains have testified to his need for constant reassurance. Such enquiries would hardly have come from someone who had confidence in their innate talent.

Between 1958 and 1962, Boycott did not make the progress he might have hoped. At times he thought he was destined for the scrapheap, another player of youthful promise who was unable to step up to a higher grade. In a BBC interview in 1971 he confessed of his teenage years: 'Every schoolboy who loves cricket envisages that one day he would like to play for Yorkshire and England. I was just the same. But then you find out that there are lots of other boys who are as good as you and many of them much better. It is then that you really begin to despair that you will ever make it.' It was because of this inability to break into first-class cricket during this period that a surprising move for Boycott was mooted. Frustrated by his stagnation in Yorkshire, he was willing to try his luck with Northamptonshire. 'He was fighting for a place in the Yorkshire side but they were such a powerful team and the competition was fierce,' recalls his old Fitzwilliam schoolfriend, Malcolm Tate. 'People like Jack Hampshire and Mike Smedley seemed to be ahead of him. I said to Geoff, "I know everyone wants to play for Yorkshire but there isn't only Yorkshire in cricket."' So, on the advice of Des Barrick, he went down to see if Northants would be interested.'

Des Barrick, a fine county professional, was, like Boycott, a native of Fitzwilliam and a graduate of the Johnny Lawrence school. After failing to win a place in the Yorkshire side, he had joined Northants in 1949. Now it seemed that there was a chance Boycott might do the same. Des Barrick explained to me: 'Geoff wanted to play first-class cricket as soon as possible but he couldn't get into the Yorkshire first team. Now, I thought this young fellow might really be an asset to Northants. I went to the committee, told them about him and said that Yorkshire seemed to be messing him around. So it was arranged that, next time Geoff was playing for

Yorkshire seconds at Northampton, he should see the secretary Ken Turner and have a discussion with him. My memory is that Geoff seemed keen on the idea. And he was certainly good enough to be first class.' The day arrived when the Yorkshire Second XI were playing at Northants, so Barrick went to the office of the Northants secretary, Ken Turner, to tell him of Geoff's arrival. 'As we were half-way down the stairs, Ken saw Geoff standing by the dressing room. He took one look at him, turned to me and said, "It's no use talking to him. He's wearing glasses. He'll be blind in two years. He's no good to us." With that he turned round and went back up to his office. He never even spoke to Geoff. I'll not forget Ken's words as long as I live. Years later I used to tease Ken, telling him "how many bloody runs Boycott would have got you if he hadn't been wearing glasses that day". And whenever Ken wrote to me asking if Yorkshire had any good young players, I would just send him a single line back: "Dear Ken, Boycott, signed Des." Of course, I could not tell Geoff what Ken had said. I let him down as lightly as possible, just saying that I'd had a word with Ken and he might be in touch. If I had given him the truth, it would have broken his heart.'

If Boycott had gone to Northamptonshire, the modern history of English cricket might have been very different. Yorkshire would have been spared the grotesque chaos into which the club was plunged by rows over his character, contract and captaincy. Freed from Yorkshire's hothouse atmosphere, where his every utterance was subjected to frenzied scrutiny by press and public, Boycott might have become a more mellow, less intense figure. The better wicket at Northampton might have turned him into a more aggressive batsman, while, spared the pressures to bring success to Yorkshire as a captain, he might never have gone into Test exile in the mid-seventies. Alternatively, he would not have been so attuned to handling the mental stresses of Test cricket without the competitive spirit instilled in him by Brian Close's Yorkshire. Nor would he have achieved the vast public following in the north that made him a unique figure in British sport. His defensive technique, honed on the damp wickets of Sheffield, Middlesbrough and Bradford Park Avenue, might not have been so polished or his footwork so sure. And would he have lost something of that instantly recognizable accent, which has been such a factor in his broadcasting career?

In the absence of any interest from Northamptonshire, Boycott had to concentrate on Yorkshire. In July 1959, while he was still at Barnsley, Boycott played his first game for the Yorkshire seconds, scoring five and 15. He played one more game that season, making just three runs and thus finishing that summer with an average of only 7.66 in the seconds. The 1960 season, with Boycott now nineteen, went even more badly. After a bright start for Barnsley, he was actually selected as twelfth man for Yorkshire against Sussex at Middlesbrough. But then he pulled his hamstring playing in a match for Barnsley and was out for the rest of the summer.

At the end of the 1960 season, ever more frustrated by his failure to advance, Boycott made another important move, switching from Barnsley to Leeds. With Headingley as its home ground, Leeds was more fashionable, more prestigious and, Boycott felt, more likely to bring him to the attention of the Yorkshire committee. Furthermore, there were two key players at Leeds who already knew him. The first was Johnny Lawrence, Boycott's wily old leg-spinner coach. The second was Billy Sutcliffe, captain of Leeds, the son of the great Yorkshire and England batsman Herbert Sutcliffe and himself a former Yorkshire captain. Boycott later recalled that Sutcliffe offered to give him all the help he could in the development of his cricket, particularly by turning him into an opening batsman. 'Until then, I had never opened the innings and I was somewhat nervous about it. But I thought, If he thinks I am good enough, there must be a chance. So I moved from Barnsley to Leeds and I never regretted it,' Boycott said.

In a 1965 radio interview, Billy Sutcliffe recalled Boycott's arrival at the club: 'When Geoff Boycott joined me at Leeds in 1961 I rated him a good ordinary player of which there are hundreds in Yorkshire. I was soon to realize that this was no ordinary player. A more dedicated man I don't think I have ever met. It used to be said that the great pre-war Yorkshire sides would eat cricket, drink cricket and sleep cricket. I think that sums up Geoff Boycott.' Sutcliffe explained that in the run-up to the season, Boycott attended nets with Yorkshire in the afternoons and Leeds in the evenings, with the result that he regularly practised from one o'clock until nine at night. But Sutcliffe also perceived that there was a darker side to Boycott's approach: 'He hated getting out, in any cricket and at any score. On one occasion I think he hated me. I had been telling him how to hit the ball over the top of the bowler. In one match, he had scored about 80 when he tried this shot, only to be caught brilliantly at mid-on. I never saw that shot again from him.'

Boycott's switch to Leeds soon began to pay dividends. He played well for the club – he topped the season's averages – and also became a regular in the Yorkshire Second XI, finishing with 688 runs at 38.22, including 156 not out against Cumberland. The Second XI captain at the time, Ted Lester – later to become one of Boycott's most loyal supporters in Yorkshire – wrote a far-sighted analysis of Boycott in his official report at the end of the 1961 summer: 'This comparative newcomer to the side has shown considerable promise and his determined batting has been a great asset to the side. He is particularly strong off his back foot but I have the feeling that his very open stance is restricting his off-side play off the front foot. I shall be pleased if the coaches will give this matter careful consideration during the winter practices. When he has the confidence to play more attacking shots, I expect to see further improvement from him. Possesses a very good temperament, and has established himself as the best opening batsman in the side.'

Other problems were apparent, however. Boycott's reputation as a poor runner between the wickets was already well advanced by now, thanks to some poor misjudgements in club cricket. Coupled with his ingrained moodiness, his unwillingness to take risks and his stance as loner, this ensured that he was not universally popular in the Second XI: 'Even in those days,' says Lester, 'I had one of the second teamers come up to me and say, "We don't want Boycott in our side. He just upsets people." I replied, "Look, you needn't worry because if I have any trouble from him, he's out." And I never did have any trouble. He was as good as gold. The one thing I will say, though, is that you had to know when to leave him alone. If he'd just got out, and you tried to talk to him, anything could happen. He was that upset.' On his difficulties with running, Lester has this insight: 'One of the reasons he ran people out was because he knew, if he were going to improve, he had to stay in the middle. So he made sure he didn't allow himself to be run out. The other problem, probably his biggest fault, was that he liked to call at both ends. Some of the other players complained to me about his running and I said to them, "Well, it's up to you. If he runs you out, you run him out next time." But they never did; he was too cute for that.'

One of the Second XI players at the time was the future Nottinghamshire captain Mike Smedley, regarded by many as a better prospect than Boycott. As he explained to me, he experienced his share of difficulties in running with Boycott: 'Often, when we were batting together, Geoff would be taking a short single off the fifth or sixth ball of the over and keeping the bowling. Sometimes they would be close calls, though I don't think Geoff was the one in danger. When Brian Bolus came down from the First XI into the seconds, he was assigned to open with Boycott to try and sort him out, while I was dropped down the order. I don't think Brian had much effect. It started to be a running joke in the Second XI.'

Like everyone else who encountered him, Smedley was struck far more by Boycott's ambition than his ability. 'He was not something particularly special but had to work hard at his technique. Initially, you got the impression he didn't have many shots and would just work the ball around, though once he had gone to Leeds he became more confident. Yet there remained a streak of insecurity. Then, if he was out, he would sulk with a towel on his head. I just put it down to disappointment because he was so keen to do well but I think he should have grown out of it by then.' Smedley recalls that Boycott was quiet, serious and intent on becoming a Yorkshire professional. 'When we were staying in hotels during matches, he and I would wander around the town at night. But all he ever chatted about was cricket. He seemed to have no interest in girls or cars or anything like that.'

Rodney Cass, who first met Boycott at the Johnny Lawrence school, also played with him in the Yorkshire Second XI in the early sixties. 'Technically, he was not a classical batsman then. He played very low, with low hands, mainly because Yorkshire wickets didn't bounce much. We were taught to get our heads right over the ball when we played defensively.' Peter Kippax, the Leeds and Yorkshire leg-spinner, recalls that in his Second XI days, Boycott could be a mixture of bombast at the crease and anguish at failure. In one match against Lancashire seconds, Boycott was due to open against the extreme pace of Colin Hilton. 'I said to him: "Look, Geoff,

Hilton is going to be a hell of a lot quicker than anything you've had before."

' "Won't be any trouble to me, won't be any trouble. I can handle it. Don't worry about me."

'So he's facing Hilton in the first over. Second ball goes just past his nose. Third one tweaks his cap. Fourth ball, the stumps go flying in all directions. Geoff came back into the dressing room, put a towel on his head, sobbed his heart out. He could be very emotional, wore his heart on his sleeve.'

Throughout his time with Barnsley, Leeds and the seconds, Boycott continued to attend the Yorkshire nets, still organized by those stalwarts, Arthur 'Ticker' Mitchell and Maurice Leyland. Leyland and Mitchell had a soft-cop, hard-cop way of dealing with the colts under their command. Leyland, one of England's great batsmen of the thirties, was the genial encourager of youth, while Mitchell was the barking taskmaster. 'Well played, son,' was Leyland's line. 'What sort of bloody shot do you call that?' was the frequent barb to be heard from Mitchell. Little wonder, then, that so many youngsters tried to avoid the nets run by Ticker Mitchell. Yet his growling approach had a purpose: he was looking for character under fire. In fact, he reserved his most fearsome invective for those he most admired, precisely because he wanted to see if they were ready for the tough challenge of playing for Yorkshire. Jack Birkenshaw says of Mitchell: 'He was seriously tough. He would rollick you most weeks. But you learned to respect why he was doing that – if you got through him and kept playing, you'd be a hardened Yorkshire cricketer.'

The promising Boycott, inevitably, received the full Mitchell treatment, his technique and temperament having excited the respect of the old drill sergeant. Fred Trueman later recalled the incident when Mitchell instructed him to give the bespectacled youngster a thorough test against genuine pace. 'He told me: "Let him have it because I want to see what he's really like." Geoff came into the nets when I was warmed up and I started letting it go at him. I could see him getting into line, getting behind it. This went on for about twenty minutes until Arthur Mitchell came along and asked what I thought. I said: "Well, he's a marvellous defence but no shots." Arthur replied: "That's right. If we can teach him to play a few shots, that's all he needs, really. This lad will get runs." And I told Arthur: "I think you may be right."'

As we have seen, Boycott's devotion to practice was almost fetishistic, playing in every game, every net session he could possibly manage. No match was too obscure for him, no distance too long. Philip Ackroyd, a member of the Yorkshire committee and in the fifties a keen club cricketer with a team known as the Ratts, recalls the earnest Boycott playing for his side because 'he wanted a game every day of the week'. Ackroyd recalls 'a brilliant century he made for us, getting his hundred before lunch. He was a fine strokemaker, an excellent hooker and puller. Nobody played the short ball better.'

Ackroyd admits that, even then, he could be a controversial figure. 'He was utterly single-minded. He was a very insular young man and did not mix well. He did not drink and, because of his dedication to cricket, seemed to have no other interests. If he did come to the bar, he would only talk about cricket. He did not pay much heed to women either. In fact there was an umpire who stood in all of our Sunday games and he had an attractive daughter. We tried to push them into each other's company. She thought the world of Geoffrey but he was just not interested, not at all.'

But Boycott was far more interested in women than Philip Ackroyd could have known. While he was still at school, he had privately confessed to a friend his deep attraction to a local girl, even joking about a possible engagement so that he might be able to go beyond just a teenage kiss. In his job at the Ministry of Pensions in Barnsley, his liking for female company was obvious. His first supervisor told me: 'There was a rather pretty girl in the office and on one occasion he took her into the manager's office and tried to kiss her but she broke away. I remember that well because she told us all about it.' The way Boycott deceived so many con-temporaries over his attitude towards the opposite sex was through the simple expedient of remaining highly secretive about this side of his life. Unlike other young men, he was rarely one either to boast of his conquests or to parade his personal feelings. And this was to be the stance he adopted throughout his career, where his urge to seduce was matched by his desire to remain private.

But there was one relationship he could not keep secret. While working at the Ministry of Pensions he met Anne Wyatt, an attractive, raven-haired married colleague with whom he was to share his life, in the most unconventional manner, for the next four decades. Contrary to subsequent press reports, she was not his supervisor but on the same grade as Boycott as a clerical officer. Fourteen years older than him, she was born Ethel Senior in Barnsley in 1926. Her marriage had not been particularly happy before she became involved with Boycott, and she often spoke to colleagues in derogatory terms of her husband, Bob Wyatt. But once Wyatt found out about his wife's affair, he is said to have been so infuriated that he threw all her belongings out into the street, forcing her to move in with her parents. Later, he took even more drastic action to escape his failed marriage, emigrating to Canada.

Ethel Wyatt's romance with Boycott led to a transformation in both her appearance and her name, according to Boycott's supervisor. 'When I first knew her, she was a buxom lady, well-dressed but hardly glamorous. But after she began the relationship with Geoffrey, she went on a crash diet, lost several stone and took to smart suits and high heels. She never wore the same outfit two days running. Before she was with Geoffrey, her hair had grey streaks. But then she had it dyed black and wore it long. She would disappear two or three times a day to do her makeup.' In 1960, she suddenly announced that she wanted to be known as Anne rather than Ethel. Their work colleague says that she and Boycott soon became quite open about their affair: 'They used to meet in a little room at lunchtime, and anyone else who had to go in there felt uncomfortable. I liked her but she was not the most popular person in the office. Her hackles could easily be raised and she was quite prickly. I think some of the ladies were jealous of her because she was so far ahead of them in style and fashion.'

Anne Wyatt was always sensitive about the difference in age between her and Boycott. On England's trips abroad, for instance, she was reluctant to give up her passport to tour management for safe-keeping, though other wives and girlfriends happily complied with this requirement. But pseudo-Freudian claims that she has been a 'mother figure' to him are little more than psychobabble. Why would Boycott need or want such a figure when he was living with his own devoted mother – and would continue to do so for almost two more decades? And how many sons have mothers only fourteen years older than themselves? For Boycott, according to his uncle Algy, the attraction is easily explained: 'Young men are drawn to older women. When you are young there is a sense of mystique about them and Geoff went down that road.' Boycott's childhood friend Malcolm Tate perfectly understood why he should fall for her. 'He was only eighteen and she was a really lovely lady of about thirty. She was intelligent, smart, glamorous, what you would call "a cracker". She was pleasant, easy to talk to. Geoff's mother thought the world of her. Anne was a great influence on Geoff.'

She and Boycott had much in common. Both from mining families, they were always immaculate, intensely private and never afraid to speak their minds. Because her father was a local umpire, she had been brought up to understand cricket, always a necessity with Boycott. 'She mirrored a lot of Geoffrey,' says his friend Tony Vann. 'She's forceful, very straight, knows where she's coming from.' Where they differed in their personalities was that Anne appeared much better mannered than her partner, never going in for his public displays of rudeness. Peter Kippax, who knew both reasonably well, says: 'I found Anne a lovely person. She was genuinely nice, nice with my children when they were very young and that counts for a lot. When we were playing cricket, my wife sat with Anne and they always got on well.' But even Anne could be exasperated by Boycott's moodiness. Kippax recalls an incident when he happened to run into Boycott in Hong Kong – one of Boycott's favourite cities – and he and some other players happened to walk past the pair in the street: 'Geoff just blanked us, didn't say a word. Then Anne turned round to me and said, "It's one of those days, Peter, you know what's it like." I just said, "Yeah, it's OK."'

5

Proving Them All Wrong

An excellent start to the 1962 season in the Second XI led to Boycott's call-up to the first team. In the opening match, he scored another century against Cumberland, 126 not out, which led to the award of his second team cap. Innings of 32 and 87 not out followed against Northumberland, then a century against Lancashire's Second XI, in what was known as the Rosebuds match. Peter Lever, one of the Lancashire bowlers then, recalls that his colleagues, like so many others, thought far more of John Hampshire than Boycott at this time. 'At Old Trafford in the second team, we used to look for Hampshire's name at number four, that's who we were bothered about. Boycott wasn't nearly so talented. You could bowl half volleys at Boycott all day and he would never try and score off them.'

Whatever the junior Lancashire dressing room thought, Boycott's rich vein of early form had made inevitable his promotion to the first team. The greatest English first-class batting career of modern times began on 16 June 1962 against the Pakistani tourists at Bradford, when Boycott went out to open for Yorkshire with Brian Bolus. Astonishingly, he hit the first ball he received for four, a feat he was not to repeat many times in his subsequent 24 seasons as a professional. Soon afterwards, however, he was bowled without adding to his score by the medium pace of D'Souza. In the second innings of the drawn game, he also failed, again dismissed by D'Souza for four.

Despite his poor start against Pakistan, Boycott was selected for the next Yorkshire game, at Northampton, thereby making his first appearance in the County Championship. Dropping down the order to number four, he was dismissed for just six in the first innings, though in the second he battled to 21 not out amidst a dismal Yorkshire collapse, which allowed Northants to win by six wickets. He did even better in the following drawn match against Derbyshire, scoring 47 and 30 as an opener. It was a useful but hardly dazzling beginning, and Boycott now returned to the second team for the rest of the summer, apart from two appearances against Essex and Kent. Against the latter, he hit 18 in the first innings and recorded his first duck for Yorkshire in the second, though he also displayed early signs of that showy confidence, which was a mask for his insecurity. The Kent player Brian Luckhurst, later to be one of Boycott's most successful Test opening partners, recalls that the Kent seam bowler David Halfyard bowled a short ball to Boycott who pulled it straight over square leg for six. 'At the end of the over, Colin Cowdrey, being the lovely man he is, went up to Boycs, whom he had obviously never met before, and said, "Good shot, Geoffrey." To which Boycs replied, in his broadest accent, "Ay, and if he pitches there again next over, I'll bloody hit him there again."'

For all such bravado, by the end of the 1962 season, his average stood at just 21.42 from 150 runs scored in nine innings, while his performances in the colts showed a worrying decline. Many doubted, at this stage, that Boycott was cut out for top-level cricket. With typical candour, he admitted, in a later BBC interview, that most of his first appearances for the county had been inadequate. 'I don't think it took me long to realize all the weaknesses I had. They just rolled my wicket over and said it was like shelling peas.'

A host of young players, of course, go through similar experiences. But Boycott's early problems at Yorkshire might have been exacerbated by the unique pressures of the club, stemming from both its pre-eminent position in English cricket – they won the County Championship yet again in 1962 – and the huge expectations of the Yorkshire public, which has long possessed the most knowledgeable and unforgiving spectators in the world. On the positive side, these twin forces helped to create a ruthless professional outlook. The late Chris Balderstone, who played with Boycott for ten years at Yorkshire, said to me: 'Most of us young lads would have given our right arms to play for Yorkshire. It was every man for himself. You had to be mentally tough to cope, getting your head down and really grafting the whole time.' But, more negatively, this mood also resulted in a profound spirit of caution. With so many players to choose from in the Yorkshire leagues and such high demands from the crowd, youngsters rarely enjoyed any permanence in the team. A couple of failures and they could be out, replaced by yet another bright prospect. So everything was done to eliminate risks rather than exhibit strokes. Brian Bolus was a classic case of what could go wrong. Hovering on the fringes of the Yorkshire team for six years from 1956, Bolus left in 1962, moved to Nottinghamshire and, freed from his Yorkshire shackles, quickly displayed such a spirit of adventure that within a couple of months he was opening for England.

Perhaps even more importantly, many newcomers to the Yorkshire team found the atmosphere intimidating. Yorkshire in the fifties has been described as 'a hard, vicious school', and a legacy of this mood still lingered in the early sixties. Former Yorkshire leg-spinner Peter Kippax recalls: 'I played in Boycott's first game for Yorkshire in 1962. It was a tough side, then; they were real pros. Let's be honest, they were not a welcoming bunch. They were all looking after their places and they did not want any upstarts getting a lead in. I thought the atmosphere was awful. Once, when I was playing one of my first games, I arrived early, put my things on a peg and the next thing I knew, they were right across the table. I had used the spot of someone who had changed there for ten years.'

For some outsiders, Boycott's obstreperous and egocentric nature only reflected this negative Yorkshire mentality. The Warwickshire fast bowler David Brown thinks that Boycott's attitude was typical of the county: 'The Yorkshiremen have always rucked among themselves. When I first played, they were constantly moaning at each other. You could listen to their dressing room and it was a guinea a minute. Boycott might have thought too much about himself but in many respects he was just like the rest of them.'

But for those within the Yorkshire set-up, Boycott's attitude was a particular cause of friction within the club. His fellow colt Peter Kippax says: 'He never got close to anyone; he was definitely not a team man. He made no contribution to the dressing room other than to draw practical jokes towards himself. He was there in the corner and you either left him alone or you took the mickey out of him.' One of the central difficulties was his continued poor running between the wickets. The great Australian all-rounder Keith Miller once said of Boycott: 'He's got every other aspect of his game so organized that I cannot understand why he does not master the elementary rules of running.' Two incidents in the 1962 season added to this sorry reputation. In Boycott's début championship game in Northants, he managed to run out Phil Sharpe by declining a perfectly safe run. Then, in the game against Derbyshire, he and Ken Taylor had put on 67 in their opening partnership when Taylor hit the ball to the leg-side, started to run, then Boycott sent him back and he was out by a considerable distance. As a result of these two disasters, Boycott received a severe lecture from his captain Vic Wilson. Boycott, with characteristic impenitence, refused to give ground or apologize, thereby worsening his standing in the team. As Don Wilson later wrote: 'These incidents were guaranteed to rub colleagues up the wrong way but his conduct afterwards was something less than remorseful. We thought at the time he was just a boy who didn't know any better, but he even makes light of it now. It was never because he was an inveterate bad runner or caller; it was because he was inherently selfish.'

The accusation of selfishness was applied not just to his running but to his whole approach to cricket. There were mutterings that he would not bat in the interest of the side, that his slow rate of scoring reflected his obsession with his average. His sense of isolation was compounded by his anguish at failure, which meant that he retreated further into himself at any early dismissal. As he was later to admit: 'I became very tense and taut and for a long time I used to find it very difficult to discuss getting out with anybody. I used to go very quiet, into my shell. Basically, it was because I felt shame at getting out.'

The strength of Boycott's ambition further reinforced his distance from his team-mates, since he placed professional success above popularity. 'He was determination personified. He practised harder than anyone else, went to bed earlier, did not socialize with the rest of us. He did not have great natural ability, but overcame that problem through sheer grit, for which you have got to admire the man,' says Peter Kippax.

Animosity over Boycott's reluctance to mix socially with his colleagues focused on his dislike of going out drinking. Alcohol has always been an essential part of the cricket scene, with the teetotaller as rare as a long hop from Gus Fraser. The acceptance of that first pint from the gnarled old pro is almost a rite of passage for a young player, and most newcomers feel that they have to prove they can hold their drink as well as their catches. 'I was a very rare bird in cricket when I started,' Boycott said later. 'A young man who didn't smoke and didn't drink, who was shy and introverted and found it difficult to talk to people, who was mad keen on physical fitness.' The problem was worsened by the fact that Yorkshire in the sixties, for all their internal squabbles, were a very social side. Don Wilson explained to me: 'Wherever we went on the county circuit, we entertained; I was the singer and Phil Sharpe played the piano. Now this did not suit Geoffrey in any way whatsoever. But I never said there was anything wrong with him just because he didn't drink. Everyone seems to think because I enjoyed a drink –Trueman, Jimmy Binks, Doug Padgett and Nic, all of us enjoyed pints in the evening – and Geoff didn't, there was a problem. It wasn't that. If he'd have come along out with us and just had a glass of orange, then no one would have minded.'

This claim is open to doubt. In fact there are two recorded incidents of Boycott being humiliated for his early teetotalism. When he had just won his Second XI cap Brian Sellers, the autocratic Yorkshire cricket chairman, having offered to buy a round in a local pub, exploded when Boycott requested an orange juice. 'You can buy your own bloody orange juice,' said Sellers. The other happened at the Balmoral in Scarborough when, amidst a round awash with alcohol, Boycott asked for an orange squash. The landlord brought over a glass ostentatiously decorated with fruit on cocktail sticks. It was a gesture, Boycott felt, purposely designed to make him ashamed. 'The lads thought I wasn't a man because I drank only orange squash,' he said. No wonder he had little time for hanging around bars after that. He believed he had made an effort to socialize, and the response had been crushing.

Given both his modest performances on the field in 1962 and his awkwardness with his team-mates, it is not surprising that his captain Vic Wilson felt that he should not be retained by Yorkshire at the end of the season. Wilson wrote to this effect to the committee, arguing that Boycott was neither a good enough player with whom to persevere nor the sort of person that Yorkshire should have in their squad. The chances of an uncapped Boycott surviving might have looked slim, especially when he was up against his rival John Hampshire. And there was a long-established stream of Yorkshire-born players leaving the club after failing to make the grade as a junior. Of Boycott's own contemporaries, Duncan Fearnley (Worcestershire), Jack Birkenshaw (Leicestershire), Mike Smedley (Nottinghamshire), Dickie Bird (Leicestershire) and Rodney Cass (Essex) were all forced to seek their fortunes elsewhere because of limited opportunities in their native county.

But, as so often with Boycott in a career of interwoven triumphs and disasters, he now had a stroke of good fortune. Vic Wilson announced his retirement in 1962 and Brian Close was appointed his successor. Close had a much more favourable view of Boycott. He told me: 'When they made me captain after Vic left, I said to the committee, "Right, keep him and let me sort him out." You see I realized that he had the ability to concentrate which you do not often find amongst young players. And he was so intent on improving. He spent all day long thinking about his game.'

Thinking about his game was exactly what Boycott did during the winter. Practising at the Johnny Lawrence school, he worked diligently on the deficiencies of his technique which had been so ruthlessly exploited by opposition bowlers, particularly a frailty outside the off-stump. The following summer, 1963, Boycott was a man transformed. After a hesitant start, he cemented his place with a wonderful innings against Lancashire in the Roses match at Bramall Lane, Sheffield. His 145, scored on a difficult pitch against top-class bowling, was not only his first century for Yorkshire but also a performance of such quality that the great cricket writer A. A. Thomson recorded: 'Bramall Lane spectators, a craggy lot not easy to please, were unanimous in asserting that apart from half a dozen artistic masterpieces from Sir Leonard Hutton, this was the finest innings played by a Yorkshire batsman since the war.' What made Boycott's innings all the more admirable was that it took place when Yorkshire were in deep trouble against a Lancashire attack consisting of four future or present England bowlers: pacemen Brian Statham, Ken Higgs and Peter Lever, and the leg-spinner Tommy

Greenhough, with 380 Test wickets between them over their careers. As Boycott walked to the wicket to join Bryan Stott, the scoreboard read 56 for 3. But the 22-year-old was undaunted. He was nursed through his early overs by Stott; then, once he was established, he broke loose and outscored the senior player with a series of flashing drives and cuts. He and Stott eventually put on 249 together and Yorkshire won the game by 10 wickets. As so often, Boycott took some of the gloss off his triumph with a tactless remark. 'I got more than you,' was the first thing he told his senior partner back in the dressing room. Stott was appalled, feeling the comment was stupid and childish. But, then, he was a successful businessman with his own electrical firm and a comfortable living. Cricket was a pleasure for him, whereas for Boycott it was an endless struggle – not just for his livelihood but also for self-justification.

This maiden century was followed by a string of good scores in June: 76 against Somerset, 49 not out against Gloucestershire, 50 against Warwickshire and, against Sussex in the Gillette Cup in front of a crowd of 15,000 at Hove, 71. This brilliant innings – in a losing cause – showed how far Boycott had developed as a stroke-player. Jim Parks, the Sussex and England wicket-keeper, recalls: 'We had a good attack but Boycs was magnificent, played all the shots and had we not run him out I'm sure he would have gone on to win the match for Yorkshire. It was my first sight of him and he looked such a fine player that day.'

Boycott's excellent run of form convinced him, in July 1963, to hand in his notice at the Ministry of Pensions in Barnsley and become a full-time cricketer. As he told his fellow civil servants, he was apprehensive about giving up a secure job in exchange for a precarious living as a sportsman. But it is wrong to exaggerate the risks he took. It was hardly as if the Barnsley branch of the Ministry of Pensions was the only occupation open to him. With his obvious intelligence and drive Boycott could have taken many other jobs if he had failed at Yorkshire. At the end of the 1963 season, for instance, Boycott quickly found a clerical position with the Yorkshire Electricity Board. This was, after all, the era of full employment – in July 1963, the number of registered unemployed stood at 494,000, a figure that any government today can only dream of. Furthermore, as soon as Yorkshire heard that he had left his job, he was offered a guaranteed payment – not a contract, Yorkshire never gave those until 1971 – of £16 a week in summer and £8 in winter, giving him some measure of security.

Yet the very fact that he had now to earn his living from the game reinforced his single-mindedness. Failure became even more unthinkable, dedication to his craft even more vital. Echoing in his head were the words of his former headmaster, Russell Hamilton, who had told him when Boycott sought his advice on becoming a full-time cricketer: 'You should have learnt enough at school to know that if you want to go in for professional cricket, you have jolly well got to work at it, for it is a career.' Never was a school-master's warning more diligently heeded.

But his new status as a professional coincided with a brief dip in his form, as he was shuffled up and down the batting order. Throughout much of his time with Hemsworth Grammar, Ackworth, Barnsley, Leeds and the Yorkshire Second XI, Boycott had been an opening batsman, and in his first match against Pakistan in 1962 he had opened with Brian Bolus. His great recent success, however, had been achieved in the middle order. Now, in July, when he was asked by skipper Brian Close to open once more, he became anxious. Poor scores against Sussex and Surrey only seemed to confirm his doubts about the opening role, but his captain was unsupportive. Close says: 'I asked him to open against Surrey at Bramall Lane and Geoff Arnold bowled him out for a duck. He came in and completely sulked. I gave him a right rollicking about it. I said, "Look, I've taken the decision to make you into an opening batsman because your particular temperament and approach fits it. Now, you go out and do your bloody best and try." He was so sorry for his bloody self that he started to cry. But I made him realize that he had a job to do. I said to him, "Sympathy won't get you anywhere."'

Close was soon vindicated. Boycott, opening the innings against Warwickshire, scored 62 and 28, then scored his second century of the season, 113, in the Roses match at Old Trafford, batting for five hours without giving a chance – a rare double against the old enemy Lancashire. Then, at Sheffield for Yorkshire versus the West Indians he scored a brave 71 against the full might of the West Indian attack, Wes Hall, Charlie Griffith and Gary Sobers. Even better followed in his first match at Lord's, when Yorkshire played Middlesex. Boycott's remarkable innings of 90 was made out of a Yorkshire total of just 144 against a new-ball attack, which included internationals Alan Moss and John Price. Boycott was bitterly disappointed not to have reached a century and, as usual, went into a sulk. But his astonishingly mature innings prompted that most perceptive of sports writers, Ian Wooldridge of the *Daily Mail*, to prophesy that he would soon become 'a permanent opening batsman for England'.

Boycott rounded off this brilliantly successful first full season with the highest score of his career thus far, 165 against Leicestershire at Scarborough. He topped the Yorkshire averages – as he was subsequently to do in every single season until 1978 – with 1446 runs at 46.64, while he also finished second in the overall national batting averages. The conquering hero was wreathed in laurels. Yorkshire awarded him his cap. The Cricket Writers Club named him 'Young Cricketer of the Year', as did the Wombwell Cricket Society. *Wisden* said he was 'easily the most successful batsman in Yorkshire and created a big impression with his reliability'. Former England all-rounder Trevor Bailey, still captain of Essex, was another to be impressed by Boycott. In *Playfair Cricket Monthly* he wrote this judicious analysis: 'Geoff is clearly a dedicated cricketer, prepared to make any sacrifice that will help him succeed in his chosen profession. He has certainly remembered the advice of the old Yorkshire coach who used to say to his pupils, "Get your head over the ball and smell it." I am sure that with his concentration and singleness of purpose, he will make many runs in the years that lie ahead.'

6

An Ideal Temperament

Test cricket could almost have been designed for Boycott. Technically and temperamentally, he was ideally suited to the five-day game. Grinding down the opposition, concentrating for session after session, guarding his wicket with an impeccable defence, this was what Boycott did best. He did not have to struggle with the artificialities of the county set-up, like bonus batting points and sporting declarations, which were to lead to so many rows later in his Yorkshire career. At Test level, he could play his natural game, acting as the bedrock of his side's innings.

In addition, his mental strength made it easier to cope with the overcharged tension of Test cricket. The inner steel in his character, forged in the furnace of the hardest schools in English cricket, the Yorkshire leagues and county club, had been further hardened by all the struggles he had experienced in his early life: the austerity of his family life; his poor health and eyesight; the sneers of those who said he would never make it; and, most recently, the continual refrain that he was not nearly as good as John Hampshire. 'I'll show them' became one of the strongest motivating forces of Boycott's career, ensuring that he would always give his absolute best when playing for his country. For many players, Test cricket has been a means of exposing their inadequacies. For Boycott, it was a vehicle for proving his capabilities.

It was obvious that, by the end of the 1963 season, Boycott could soon be in the reckoning for a Test place, especially because the selectors were having such problems in finding a reliable opening pair. Since the start of the 1962 season, when Boycott made his first-class début, a disturbing number of combinations had been tried, including: Geoff Pullar and Colin Cowdrey; Mickey Stewart (Alec's father) and Cowdrey; Pullar and the Reverend David Sheppard (the future Bishop of Liverpool); Cowdrey and Sheppard; Ray Illingworth and Sheppard; Stewart and John Edrich; Peter Richardson and Stewart; Stewart and Brian Bolus (Boycott's former Second XI colleague at Yorkshire, now at Nottinghamshire); Bolus and Edrich; M.J.K. Smith and Bolus; Bolus and Jimmy Binks (the Yorkshire wicket-keeper, playing in his only Tests on the MCC tour to India, 1963/64) – a display of such feverish selectorial inconsistency that it makes Atherton–Butcher look like the Rock of Ages.

At the beginning of the 1964 season, Boycott made sure that the selectors could not ignore him with two big centuries in May. An innings of 151 against Middlesex at Headingley was followed by his third hundred against Lancashire in consecutive Roses matches. In the *Cricketer* in May A. A. Thomson wrote of his Test prospects: 'It is not a dead cert, but it's the best bet I know in this race.' Boycott himself was far from certain. Though he had been selected for the MCC team against the Australian tourists at Lord's and scored 63, he felt that he had still not yet done enough to win a place for the first Test at Trent Bridge, as he told one of his girlfriends, Shirley Western, a glamorous big-band singer whom he had met in August 1963 at the Empire Ballroom, Leicester Square. Though he was still in a relationship with Anne Wyatt in Yorkshire, Boycott was never one to let such a consideration restrict his freedom to pursue other women. By the summer of 1964, Boycott and Shirley Western were quite intimate, though their opportunities to meet in London were severely restricted by their professional careers: Shirley sang almost every night with the Ken Mackintosh band at the Empire Ballroom, while Boycott had to travel throughout the country during the summer. Nevertheless, as a keen cricket enthusiast, she took any chance she could to see him play at Lord's, the Oval or any other ground in the Home Counties.

During the MCC game against the Australians, Shirley Western struck up a conversation with Ian Wooldridge of the *Daily Mail*. When she told him she was friendly with Boycott, he replied: 'Geoff? Boycott? I didn't think he had any women at all. Fancy him having someone like you. Well, he'll be in the Test side on Sunday.'

'He doesn't think he's done enough.'

'I bet you a fiver he's in.'

'Fiver he's not.'

Wooldridge was right. Immediately he was on the line to claim his money. On Sunday 31 May Boycott's name was included in the twelve for the Trent Bridge Test against Australia. Boycott, understandably, confessed to some anxiety as well as pride. 'Of course I'm on top of the world. A bit worried, too, because there is so much to gain and so much to lose by a place in the first Test against such a team as the Aussies.' The chorus of congratulations was led by *The Times*, which described Boycott's rise to Test cricket as 'remarkable. This time last year he was hidden away at number six or seven, a little-known name. Now he is in everyone's team. He looks, at 23, to have a productive career ahead of him.'

John Edrich had been chosen to open with Boycott, but on the morning of the Test he reported unfit, having trodden on a ball in the nets and twisted his ankle. It was too late to send for a replacement so when England won the toss and batted, Boycott went in to bat with a makeshift opener, Middlesex all-rounder Freddie Titmus. On seeing the bespectacled débutant, Bobby Simpson, the Australian captain, yelled across to his fast bowler Graham MacKenzie, 'Hey, Garth, look at this four-eyed fucker. He can't fucking bat. Knock those fucking glasses off him right away.' Having ignored this greeting, Boycott was immediately involved in a run-out incident with Titmus. In one of the opening overs, Boycott pushed a ball from Neil Hawke on to the leg-side and called for a sharp single. As Titmus responded to the call, he collided heavily with Hawke, a powerfully built Australian rules player, who was charging down the pitch to retrieve the ball. Titmus went sprawling across the turf, far out of his ground, while Hawke lobbed the ball to the wicket-keeper Wally Grout. A run-out was a certainty, yet Grout, to the astonishment of his colleagues, refused to break the stumps. Instead, after a pause, he gave the ball back to Hawke. 'Bloody hell, I thought this was a Test match,' said Norman O'Neill, standing at cover.

Grout's gesture rightly won him universal praise both at the time and afterwards. 'It is doubtful if such exemplary sportsmanship has ever been exceeded in Test cricket,' wrote Chris Clark, in his 1986 book *The Test Match Career of Geoffrey Boycott*. Such a claim ignores the truth that, only eight years later, in another Ashes Test, Boycott himself acted in exactly the same sporting way as Wally Grout. His forgotten act of chivalry took place during the first Test between England and Australia at Old Trafford in 1972. The circumstances were not dissimilar to the Titmus–Hawke incident. Australia were batting and Rodney Marsh, on 10 not out, hit a ball from Tony Greig to mid-on and started to run. But he collided with Greig as Boycott moved in from the leg-side to pick up the ball. Marsh could have easily been run out but Boycott refrained from throwing the ball to wicket-keeper Alan Knott. 'Thanks, Fiery, you're a gentleman,' said Rod Marsh. Yet because of his reputation for selfishness and poor manners, Boycott's action, unlike Wally Grout's, is now barely mentioned in the cricket world.

Despite being reprieved by Grout, Titmus only made 16 before falling with the score on 38. Boycott, however, was still there, 23 not out, at the close of his first rain-truncated day in Test cricket. The next morning he continued for another hour before falling, only two short of his half-century, to a brilliant diving slip catch by Bobby Simpson off Graeme Corling. England then struggled to 216 for 8, when Ted Dexter declared, but, with the third day an even bigger washout than the first, the match drifted to a sodden draw.

Bad luck seemed to be hovering around England's openers at Trent Bridge, for Boycott joined Edrich on the injury list when he broke a finger while fielding. The fracture ruled him out, not only of England's second innings – Dexter opened with Titmus and they put on 90 – but also the Lord's Test as well. He returned at Headingley, making 38 and four in England's defeat. In both innings he was caught at slip off Corling, exposing a weakness against away-swing. In true Boycott fashion, he worked thoroughly in the nets on this deficiency, training himself to assess precisely which balls to leave and which to play.

Australia made the Ashes safe in a gargantuan but tedious run-fest at Old Trafford, what Peter Parfitt called 'the most boring Test match I have ever played in'. Bobby Simpson hit 311 as Australia built up a mammoth total of 656 for 8 declared. England responded with 611, Barrington and Dexter both making big centuries. On a perfect pitch, Boycott might have been disappointed only to make

58, bowled by a MacKenzie leg-cutter, but at least he seemed to have conquered his problems outside the off-stump and had recorded his first Test half-century.

Boycott did even better when playing for Yorkshire against the Australian tourists at Bradford, hitting 54 and 122 against them. The latter innings, however, took place in highly controversial circumstances that reinforced Boycott's growing reputation for single-minded obduracy. On the last day of the match, Bobby Simpson had declared, leaving Yorkshire a target of 323 in 260 minutes. But no attempt was made to go for the runs. Instead, after batting for nearly two hours, Boycott was only 32 not out, with the result that Simpson decided to humiliate him in front of the five thousand spectators by bringing every single fieldsman into a circle just five yards from the bat. Boycott's response was aggressive. He immediately hit spinner Tom Veivers deep into the outfield; then, in the next he hooked Neil Hawke for six and drove him for four. Don Wilson, playing in the game, felt that the Aussies were just laughing at Boycott. 'He'd been in for hours, block, block, block, so, to put it crudely, they decided to take the piss out of him,' he says. But Boycott, through his ability to cope with this showy rebuke, may have enhanced his reputation with them. During the summer, Bobby Simpson expressed his admiration of Boycott, explaining that 'he plays cricket the Aussie way'.

Only a few days later, at the Oval, in another drawn Test shrouded in Stygian gloom, Boycott gave the Australians a further display of his temperament by hitting his maiden Test century, a knock of 113 in England's second innings. Shirley Western, his London girlfriend, well remembers his delight at the achievement. 'We celebrated that night by going to the theatre in the West End to see Harry Secombe and Roy Castle in *Pickwick*. We were walking along Shaftesbury Avenue, and I suddenly said, "Look at the billboard: Boycott Makes Test Hundred."

'"I can't believe, I can't believe it," he kept saying.

'Then in the middle of the show, Harry Secombe stopped and said, "I'd like to say that we have a very special gentleman in the audience who got a hundred today against the Australians." The whole audience clapped. Geoff was so embarrassed and proud. He had never been through anything like that. We went backstage afterwards, where Harry Secombe gave us all champagne. But Geoff wouldn't drink any, saying he had to be at the Test again the next day. He was so shy and endearing.'

With John Edrich dropped after failures at Headingley and Old Trafford, this was also the first Test in which Boycott opened with Bob Barber, the dashing Warwickshire batsman who was to become one of his favourite partners. Both in background and approach to the game, the two could hardly have been more contrasting: Boycott, the miner's son and cautious Yorkshire professional, whose determination to protect his wicket was matched only by his attention to his average; Barber, the Cambridge graduate backed by family money, who was as explosively indifferent to the reputations of bowlers as he was to his own statistics – 'Cricket is far too absorbed in irrelevant numerals,' he told me.

Yet they built up a mutual respect which has lasted to this day. Barber says: 'I never had a problem with him. As far as I was concerned, he was a good fella to have at the other end. And I also felt that if someone wants to lead a quiet life, for God's sake, just let them be themselves. Now, the cricket world, like most other worlds, is a small one with a small number of people. Certain things become received wisdom. So there was this idea that Geoff, because he was determined to get on, was selfish. Well, I can tell you, there was an awful lot of selfishness around then. The real problem with Geoff was that he was more honest than some others. He was quite open that he wanted to score so many runs or get so many hundreds. Many others felt the same but he talked about it and they didn't.'

Nor did Barber have many difficulties in running with Boycott. They developed an understanding during the Oval Test when Barber made it clear that he would not tolerate Boycott hogging the strike by taking a single off the fifth or sixth ball of the over. 'I simply refused to run when he shovelled the ball down to long-leg. Geoff pretty quickly got the message and, from then on, as far as I was concerned, I didn't – until our last match together – have any problem. I would have actually said he was quite a good runner. And though he had a limited repertoire of shots, he was good to bat with because we could play off each other, left hand, right hand, attack, defence.'

Apart from his business interests, one of the reasons that Bob

Barber retired from cricket when he was still at his peak was his disillusion with the shambolic way the English game was organized, even at international level. This was evident at that Oval Test in 1964: 'I thought the whole England set-up was extremely amateur. Virtually no thought was given to tactics. Fifteen minutes before the start of the match, I didn't even know that I was actually opening with Geoff. I was probably picked because I was opening for Warwickshire but no one had confirmed anything. So, just before the start of the game, I said to Willie Watson, one of the selectors, "Look, who's going in first here?"

'"You are."

'"Well, how am I expected to play?"

'"As you feel like."'

For Boycott, his Oval century proved that he had arrived as a Test-match opener. With 291 runs from four matches at an average of 48.50, he was, according to John Woodcock in the *Cricketer*, 'the real find of the series. To say that he has something of Herbert Sutcliffe's phlegmatic temperament is to pay him a high compliment. His batting does not give aesthetic pleasure so much as practical satisfaction.' In the same magazine, the renowned Australian journalist and former Test star Jack Fingleton drew this conclusion: 'Boycott is a good batsman. Whether he becomes more than that depends, I think, on whether he learns to use his feet down the pitch. He is so rigid in his defence that his back foot is anchored and he plays forward defensively with an exaggerated back slant of his bat. I foresee some nasty cracks on the hands against pace bowlers.' It was this style of forward play that Boycott had been taught in Yorkshire, but Fingleton was proved absolutely right. Over the rest of his career, Boycott suffered more than his share of injuries to fingers, hands and wrists.

Boycott's success with England was mirrored by an equally triumphant season with Yorkshire, topping the county's averages with 1427 runs at 59.45. In the overall national averages he finished in fifth place, having completed 2000 runs in a season for the first time. His six centuries included a career best of 177 against Gloucestershire on a big turner at Bristol in September, an astonishing score given that the West Country batsmen could only muster 47 and 84 in both their completed innings. Boycott's achievements in the 1964 season ensured that he was named one of *Wisden*'s Five Cricketers of the Year, that annual certificate of excellence.

His successful first Test series also guaranteed his selection in M.J.K. Smith's MCC party for South Africa that winter – the last official tour England made there before the era of apartheid came to a close. Boycott's inclusion was one of the more straightforward decisions. In making some of the other choices, the pattern of the selectors' thinking – in time-honoured English fashion – ranged from the dubious to the incomprehensible. No room, for instance, was found either for Tom Graveney or Colin Cowdrey, while the uncapped Cambridge student Mike Brearley was picked ahead of Test openers John Edrich, Mickey Stewart and Eric Russell. Much of the blame must be attached to the selectorial chairman, former Middlesex captain Walter Robins, an impulsive, often eccentric figure with a gift for self-publicity and a habit of frequenting the cinema when he was bored with the Test.

By the time of his MCC selection, Boycott had shown himself to be one of the best batsmen in the country. But the same could hardly be said of his fielding. For all his single-minded dedication, he had never given the same attention to this aspect of his cricket as he had to batting. And, surprisingly, Yorkshire gave him no coaching in this area. Jack Birkenshaw says that, in his early days, 'He used to throw a bit like a woman. There was a touch of chucking the handbag about it.' Once he had entered the England team in 1964, his fielding was nowhere near international standard, as was pointed out to him by selector Willie Watson. With characteristic application, Boycott returned to Yorkshire and, guided by batsman Ken Taylor, strove to improve his groundwork. Taylor explained to me how he assisted Boycott: 'I used to drive him a lot to matches then because he didn't have his own car. During the journeys, I would talk to him about fielding, explaining the importance of staying balanced, concentrating the whole time and trying to anticipate what shot the batsman will play. Once we arrived at the ground, we would practise for about forty-five minutes together, throwing the ball to each other. Geoff was always prepared to listen and learn. Though limited in ability, he had tremendous determination. Playing with him every day at Yorkshire

I gradually saw his fielding improve till he became perfectly decent.'

Boycott's two brothers, Peter and Tony, also helped him by giving him practice sessions in the field behind their Fitzwilliam home. Peter would keep wicket behind a single stump while Tony hit the ball in all directions for Boycott to chase. Peter recalls, 'Geoff knew he had this flaw in his game, so he would practise for hours. And soon I could feel the difference in the strength and accuracy of his throws as the ball smacked into my gloves.'

Though he became a reliable fielder with concise movements, an accurate throw and a safe pair of hands, he was still sometimes let down by his lack of pace and power. Bob Barber remembers one incident during the 1966 Oval Test against the West Indies when Brian Close was captaining England for the first time. 'McMorris, opening with Hunte, hit the ball to mid-wicket and Geoff had to go and fetch it. As he picked the ball up, the batsmen got into a terrible dither and both ended up at one end. Then all we got from Geoff was this lolloping, bouncing throw to the same end as the West Indian batsmen, so one of them easily made it back. Closey was absolutely livid and started to advance towards Geoff, uttering a fierce diatribe against him. And there was Geoff, retreating quickly into the outfield.'

Without any real competition, Boycott and Barber were certain to be England's opening pair for the winter tour of South Africa, unless either was totally out of touch. In fact, there were some worrying moments for Boycott in the opening provincial matches, when difficulties over judging the line and length on the quicker overseas wickets led to him hurrying his strokes. From his first seven innings he scored just 151 runs. But then, as he adjusted, he ran into better form, hitting centuries in successive games. His good run continued in the Tests. His opening stand of 120 with Barber – he hit 73 to Barber's 74 – helped to set up an innings England victory, the only result in the five-Test series. In the remaining quartet of draws, he also hit a match-saving 76 not out in the fourth Test at Johannesburg as England struggled on the final day to 153 for 6 and a century in the final Test at Port Elizabeth. His final average was 49.66, while his total tour aggregate was 1135.

This Test series also saw the first international wickets taken by Boycott. With an inexperienced attack stricken by injuries, England captain M.J.K. Smith was forced to turn to Boycott's medium-paced inswingers in the third Test. The results were surprisingly successful. In the second innings Boycott sent down 20 overs and took 3 for 47, including the high-class wickets of Graeme Pollock and Colin Bland, both clean bowled. Altogether he sent down 61 overs in the series.

His bowling might have been a bonus, but it was his batting that really impressed captain M.J.K. Smith. 'It was quite obvious he was a magnificent player,' Smith told me. 'People were already talking, when we went out, about Boycott being a little bit special and they were right. His technique was excellent, with no real weaknesses. He had this marvellous attitude for an opener, get out there, bat all day, and the next. He worked so hard at his game, very hard indeed.' Smith found no difficulties in captaining Boycott. 'Yes, he could be a bit defensive and he was hardly the life and soul of the party. Inevitably, the lads would take the mickey out of him, but that was just part and parcel of team spirit.'

Bob Barber believed that life on tour was more difficult for Boycott, who had never been abroad before this winter. The problem was made worse by the fact that the gauche, introspective young man was surrounded by hardened professionals. 'If you get a group of fellows together – and you will have this as much on tour as anywhere else – you will often see that they find a scapegoat. That's the impression I got with Geoffrey. He did not really fit in. With that lot, it wasn't easy and Geoff did not involve himself in any way socially. I was perhaps the only person who tried to involve him by taking him out. Once, for instance, when we were in Durban, I was conscious of Geoff being on his own so I invited him to come with me up to a game park. He grumbled about not wanting to so I said, "Don't be so bloody daft, get your camera and come on." I think in the end he was quite vulnerable and shy, feeling that the world was against him.'

The camera Boycott took was a 16mm cine machine, which had been lent to him by Harry Secombe. As a first-time traveller, Boycott was keen to have a documentary record of his trip to South Africa. But his use of this equipment at the Test matches also provides an insight into his egocentric nature and his continuing hatred of failure, according to Rodney Cass, his old Yorkshire friend from the Johnny Lawrence school, who was coaching in South Africa that winter. Boycott showed Cass how to use the camera to take some film during the second Test at Johannesburg.

'How much footage do you want of the game?' asked Cass.

'Oh, I only want me, you know, that's all. As soon as I'm out, no more filming,' replied Boycott. So Cass did as instructed and set up the camera in one of the stands to film Boycott. Unfortunately he was out almost immediately, caught behind off Peter Pollock. Cass stopped filming, and after an hour and a half he went to the players' area to return the equipment. Through the dressing-room window he could see Boycott sitting on a bench with a towel on his head. M.J.K. Smith, the captain, told Cass it would be better to come back later. 'So I waited another hour before returning. And when I did, there was Boycs, still in the dressing room covered in his towel.'

Boycott's behaviour was regarded by some of his England colleagues as self-indulgent and self-centred. What Bob Barber felt was shyness and vulnerability, others saw as rudeness and irascibility. David Brown, also on his first tour, says: 'He thought of nothing else other than Geoffrey Boycott and the rest of the world could go lose itself. He could be the rudest, the most ignorant man on God's earth to people like waitresses, attendants or the public. If he'd had a bad day, then the world better look out. I remember at one game coming out of the ground and there were a lot of African kids collecting autographs with bits of tatty paper. He told them to clear off and then got in the car while I signed the lot. He was utterly self-centred and that was just part of his make-up.' David Brown also roomed with Boycott on this tour: 'I was fairly rough and ready in my methods whereas he was always immaculate. So one half of the room looked fine while the other was a mess. He didn't want to socialize, preferring to be his own companion.' Brown had a particular reason to feel aggrieved with Boycott on that tour: 'We had a team Christmas party and both he and I were looking to go our separate ways after that. He came up to me and assured me that the manager, Donald Carr, had said that I could use his motor, as long as I dropped him, Geoffrey, where he wanted to go. So I did this, took the manager's car, gave Geoffrey a lift, and then returned the car later. I never thought another thing about it until the following morning when the manager woke me up on the phone going completely berserk because he'd wanted his car all the previous day. Geoffrey had just stitched me up. He had told me a point-blank lie so that he would be driven somewhere. At first Boycs didn't want to admit it, but once he did, he was quite open about it. You'd need to have a certain mentality just to do it. I had a laugh about it afterwards but Donald Carr took much longer to cool down. He was a very angry manager.'

Like so many others, though Brown was often annoyed with Boycott the man, he admired Boycott the cricketer. 'From the word go, he was the sort of player you wanted in your side. You knew he would never throw his wicket away. As a bowler he gave you wonderful confidence because you knew you could usually stick your kit in the corner of the room and relax all day. He kept himself fit, never carried any weight. He was very careful with his diet, taking honey in his tea. If we were all having steak and chips for dinner, he'd have fish and salad.'

Vice-captain Ted Dexter, who flew out to join the MCC after standing unsuccessfully as the Tory candidate in Cardiff against Jim Callaghan in the 1964 general election, was shocked on his arrival to see how unpopular Boycott was with much of the touring party. He explained to me: 'I arrived three weeks late to find that G. Boycott was totally – and I mean totally – ostracized by the other players. They would not bowl at him in the nets and there was no social contact whatsoever. Not knowing the form I felt it was a bit rough on a young player so I befriended the young Boycott and tried to help him through. In retrospect, I think that it would have been better had I not taken his point of view because he might have learnt a lesson there and then – the lesson that you are playing for a team and not just for yourself.'

Dexter says that he saw the worst of this attitude in the last Test at Port Elizabeth when he became Boycott's first – but certainly not last – run-out victim in a Test match. In Dexter's account, Boycott kept trying to retain the strike by taking a single at the end of each over. 'Of course, the fielders started to get wise and were creeping in. Then Boycott called me for a run and I was flat out, head down, straight through. Yet Boycs hardly moved down the pitch at all. All he did was put his bat down to make sure he wasn't out.' Dexter feels that Boycott was a poor runner because he was unable to trust his partner. 'When he was called for a single, Boycs was always looking out for himself to see if he liked the run first. Once that starts, there is never a relaxed feeling in the partnership.'

David Brown, watching from the pavilion, remembers the Port Elizabeth incident well. 'That run-out was astonishing. Ted stood there in the middle, completely gob-smacked after Geoff dived past him to get in. He came back into the dressing room, sat down and said, "I really don't believe what has just happened to me." How Ted kept his cool I do not know.'

7

'Why the Hell Didn't He Do That Before?'

It is one of the many paradoxes of Boycott's career that his greatest domestic innings should have also become a millstone round his neck. His volcanic 146 at Lord's in the 1965 Gillette Cup final against Surrey, where he displayed every stroke on an awkward pitch and a damp outfield, was cited as an example of the way Boycott could play if the mood took him. From 1965 onwards every act of stonewalling was compared by his detractors to that exhilarating knock.

'He was fantastic that day,' says Don Wilson. 'All of a sudden he was hitting the ball over mid-off and mid-on. We had never seen him lift the ball in the air in our lives. The shots he played were phenomenal. As he came off, the noise was amazing. Every person on the ground stood and applauded him. I couldn't believe this was happening at Lord's, normally a sedate place. The trouble is, people were asking, "Why the hell didn't he do that before?"'

Boycott's innings was all the more extraordinary because it took place at the end of a disappointing season for him, which saw him lose his place in the England side and fail to score a first-class century. After almost two years of rapid advance, Boycott's progress in professional cricket ground to a halt. True, he topped the averages once more for Yorkshire, but this time with a figure of just 34.88 from 942 runs. Overall he fell from fifth to fifteenth in the national averages, with 1447 runs at 35.92.

In the Test matches his final record was equally modest. This was the first summer in which England hosted twin series, with New Zealand and South Africa the visitors. In the opening Test of the season, against New Zealand at Edgbaston, Boycott hit 23 and 44 not out in a nine-wicket victory, though the two main talking points were the icy weather – hot drinks had to be served twice during the second day – and Ken Barrington's painfully slow century. His 137 took 437 minutes, including an excruciating spell when he remained on 85 for 20 overs. As a result of his stagnation, he was dropped for the second Test as a punishment, exactly the same fate Boycott suffered two years later over his perceived tardiness in compiling a double century against India. 'Brighter cricket' was the slogan taken up at this time by the English cricket authorities, worried by dwindling gates and declining popularity. It is telling that Boycott and Barrington should have the same cautious, hard-nosed approach to batting. Both had had a tough upbringing – Barrington was the son of a soldier and first worked in a garage – which compelled them to eschew frivolity and to treat their chosen profession more seriously than most.

Boycott played an important role in England's victory in the second Test at Lord's, scoring 76 as England went after a target of 215 in the final innings. They won by seven wickets with only fifteen minutes to spare, their run-chase made more difficult by the loss of five hours through rain on the last two days. Having missed the third Test at Headingley due to a shoulder injury – his replacement John Edrich hit a record-breaking 310 not out – Boycott returned against South Africa at Lord's. But the Yorkshire opener was unable to re-establish his rhythm, scoring 31 and then a wretched 28 in 105 minutes in the second innings as England struggled to a draw after being set only 191 in four hours. Following the Barrington precedent, there was talk of dropping Boycott as a disciplinary measure, with some outspoken critics even arguing that his innings had cost England victory. In an interview with the *Daily Express*, Boycott explained his philosophy of batting: 'If the selectors want to drop me, that's their business. I am not the world's greatest cricketer. I never will be. But I think I am good enough to open for Yorkshire and England. If I am going on playing for England my attitude to opening the innings will not change. I simply believe the job of the opener is to knock the shine off the new ball by cracking it solidly in the middle and trickling the runs along without taking swipes or risks.'

The selectors reprieved Boycott, but not for long. In the second

Test at Trent Bridge, though he did some useful bowling – in one spell in South Africa's second innings he delivered 19 overs for just 25 runs – he gave another dismal performance with the bat. Out for a duck in the first innings, he was almost strokeless in the second as England wickets fell all around him. After two hours 20 minutes at the crease for just 16 runs, he was finally bowled by left-arm spinner Athol McKinnon. Even the normally measured tones of *Wisden* described this as a 'dreadful effort when courage was needed'.

Boycott's sacking was now inevitable, and for the final Test at the Oval he was replaced by Eric Russell of Middlesex. But the selectors were not so disillusioned as to exclude him from the MCC party for the Ashes tour to Australia that winter, and was picked along with three other openers: Barber, Edrich and Russell. Not all the press were happy about the Yorkshireman's methods. J. J. Warr (who played his only two Tests as a Cambridge undergraduate on the 1950/51 tour) wrote in the *Cricketer*: 'Boycott has transformed the admirable quality of determination into a fetish. Every wicket he plays on is made to look difficult and batsmen later on in the order frequently get themselves out trying to compensate for his slowness. His second innings at Nottingham was exquisitely painful to watch.'

There could hardly have been a more thundering riposte to such comments than Boycott's legendary Gillette innings in September. As with so many matches in the 1965 season, the final was played in damp conditions that were expected to help the bowlers. With his usual vividness, Don Wilson described to me the build-up to the game: 'We set off from Scarborough the day before in torrential rain. By the time we got to Lord's to leave off our bags that evening, the ground was saturated. Lord's used to have the Tavern pub at the bottom of the slope, with some white railings in front of it. And I can tell you, the water had reached the top of those railings. It seemed that there was no way that Yorkshire, or anybody, were going to play in any final the next day.' That night, the entire Yorkshire team – apart from Boycott, of course – set off for a night of revelry in the West End, starting with *The Black and White Minstrel Show* at the Victoria Palace and ending in Snow's Hotel on the Cromwell Road. But the next morning, there was blazing sunshine and the only sign of the heavy rain the night before was the bags of sawdust everywhere. Wilson recalls: 'We had quite a few hangovers round the dressing room. To our horror, we were told that play would soon be under way.'

Fortunately for the groggy players, Surrey won the toss and put Yorkshire in to bat. Unsurprisingly, given the wetness of the outfield and the quality of the new-ball bowling from David Syndenham and Geoff Arnold, openers Boycott and Ken Taylor made a sluggish beginning. Only 20 runs had been scored from 12 overs, when the first wicket, Taylor's, fell. This start was what Surrey supporters had predicted. It was joked at the Oval that all their team had to do to lift the trophy was to keep Boycott batting at one end. But the game was transformed when Yorkshire captain Brian Close strode to the wicket. Suddenly, quick singles were taken, then Boycott began to hit out all around him, despatching Syndenham over square leg and driving Arnold straight for six into the pavilion. By the end of his innings of 146 he had hit three sixes and 19 fours, putting on 192 with Brian Close and ensuring that Yorkshire had made an unassailable total of 317 for 4. With Ray Illingworth taking 5 for 29, Surrey were shot out for just 142. As Yorkshire picked up their first limited-overs trophy, Boycott was the only possible choice for the Man of the Match award.

Boycott has always emphatically denied the claim that it was a lecture from Close, delivered on his arrival at the crease, that galvanized him into action. In his *Autobiography* he wrote: 'So far as I am concerned, at no time did Close tell me to get on with it, or anything remotely similar. The myth about my attitude and motivation that day supports the image of a bold, decisive captain dominating a reluctant subordinate by the force of his personality – but not once did he threaten or cajole me into playing the strokes I played.'

Yet the version Close gave me is very different: 'I'm out there and straight away I get stuck into Boycs: "Come on, you'll run when I tell you to bloody run. Now let's get a move on." I threatened to wrap my bat round his bloody neck. Soon we were getting three or four singles every over and the field started to creep in to close us down. So I said, "Listen, Boycs, if there's anything up, just bloody belt it." Next ball from Geoff Arnold, he cracked it through extra cover for four. No one had ever seen him hit the bloody ball off the square. The spinner came on and I said to him now, "Look, they're all expecting you to push the bloody ball back. Hit it anywhere from long on down to deep square leg." He smashed three in a row. He had never played like that before. The whole point was that it was a cup final. I had to take away from him the worry about getting out. I forced him to do it by relieving him of responsibility. If he got out, he had an excuse. He could say, "It's the captain's fault."'

Apart from this famous knock, 1965 was a pretty miserable season for Boycott. And his problems continued when the MCC tourists set out for Australia under M.J.K. Smith almost two months later. First of all, he developed a severe bout of gastro-enteritis after a stop-over in Ceylon, now Sri Lanka, thereby justifying all his fears – often sneered at by his critics – that the childhood loss of his spleen had left him prone to infection in south Asia. While the rest of the team flew on to Perth, he was detained in a hospital in Singapore. Even when he caught up with the MCC, he was plagued by another medical ailment, sciatica, which had developed as a result of the injections administered by Singapore doctors. This meant he could only play in two of the six first-class matches in the run-up to the opening Test. One of the visitors he received while he was laid up in an Adelaide hospital was that grandest of correspondents E. W. Swanton. As he wrote in *Swanton in Australia*, he was immediately struck by Boycott's passion for his job: 'Visiting the patient, I came to know a zeal for playing and making runs that was more intense than I have ever encountered. The pain at missing this first chance of an innings was clearly far harder to bear than that of sciatica.' As if to echo Swanton's view, when the MCC party were asked by immigration authorities on their arrival in Ceylon to make a written declaration of the purpose of their visit, fourteen players wrote, 'To play cricket'; Bob Barber said 'Holiday'; Boycott just put 'Business'.

His clinical single-mindedness, however, did not always endear him to the other players on this tour. Jim Parks was a room-mate for part of it. 'We used to have to share Boycs out a little bit – he wasn't everyone's cup of tea. I remember Kenny Barrington once said to me, "I don't think I can handle a whole tour with him."' The touring party had a Saturday club, where two barmen would be appointed to make sure that everyone's glass was full. Parks continues: 'Geoff, of course, didn't drink much. All he would have was

Cinzano, so getting him a bottle of that could be a bit awkward if you were the barman. Fine, he didn't want to drink a lot and he was his own man. But the real problem was that all he wanted to do was talk about himself. So when you came back into the room, it was all about how Geoff had played and, really, at eleven o'clock at night, you didn't want to hear this. He wasn't my type of person. I enjoyed a few beers and a good night's sleep. That said, I got on all right with him, didn't mind sharing with him.'

After his horrors against South Africa, Boycott resumed his alliance with Bob Barber, a partnership that was perhaps the brightest feature of England's tour. Bristling with aggression, confident in his strokeplay, Barber was determined to take command from the start. To the delight of his England colleagues at Perth, the very first ball he received on the tour was smacked straight back over the head of the bowler, Graham MacKenzie, and reached the boundary on the first bounce. This was truly the 'brighter cricket' that the English authorities craved. Barber's freedom to attack was enhanced by the knowledge that this was his final tour before giving up cricket for business. He was playing for enjoyment, not for his future.

After a draw at Brisbane – Boycott's 63 not out guiding England to safety on the last afternoon – the second Test at Melbourne saw Boycott and Barber put on 98 for the first wicket in just 16 overs, with Boycott hitting another half-century after being dropped at slip in MacKenzie's first over. In this high-scoring draw he also took his last two wickets in Test cricket, 2 for 32 in Australia's second innings of 426. His second victim was stumped by Jim Parks, who recalls: 'He wasn't the worst bowler, open-chested, fired in his little inswingers. He was very accurate and we could use him to block up one end.' Yet, after this tour, Boycott was only to send down another 25 in the remaining sixteen years of his Test career.

It was in the next Test at Sydney that the Boycott–Barber combination achieved their greatest triumph. In a glorious exhibition of batting, they put on 234 for the first wicket in just four hours, England's highest stand for the first wicket in an Ashes Test since Hobbs and Sutcliffe's 283 at Melbourne in the 1924/25 series. The partnership was almost over before it began. On 12, Boycott was dropped at short-leg off MacKenzie. After that, there was scarcely an error as Barber, backed by his young partner, took a scythe to the Australian attack: 93 were scored up to lunch; 141 in the next two hours. Then Boycott was caught and bowled by the leg-spinner Peter Philpott for 84. Fifty minutes later Barber was out for his breathtaking 185, still the highest score by an England batsman on the first day of a Test against Australia.

The Boycott–Barber stand laid the foundations of a big innings victory. M.J.K. Smith's side, now one up with only two to play, dreamt of regaining the Ashes. But then things started to go wrong for both England and Boycott. In the next Test at Adelaide, Barber and Boycott failed badly in each of their two innings, as England slid to an innings defeat. In the final Test, Boycott's form declined further. Yet instead of giving Barber the strike, he hogged the bowling to such an extent that he took 60 of the first 80 balls, scoring just 15 runs. Then to compound the sin, he called Barber for a ridiculous run after hitting the ball straight into Graham MacKenzie's hands as he followed through. It was the last ball of the over and, as so often before, Boycott was trying to retain the strike. Twice Barber shouted, 'No,' but Boycott ignored him in his charge up the wicket. 'I just walked off the field, didn't bother to run at all. It was unfortunate. Geoffrey must have had some sort of mental block. I did tear into him a bit afterwards but he didn't apologize. Maybe he was just too shy to speak like that. It was the only problem we ever had together.'

Boycott's form continued to desert him as the MCC flew on to New Zealand for a three-match series. In the first two Tests, Boycott failed to reach double figures in any of his three innings and was dropped for the final match, the second time he had been left out of the England side in just eight months. As *The Times* put it, 'The Yorkshire opening bat has looked stale and out of touch since leaving Australia.'

The 1966 season brought only a modest revival in fortunes. As usual, he topped the averages for Yorkshire, scoring 1097 runs at 39.17 and, nationally, he secured ninth place in the averages with 1854 runs at 39.44. He also scored six first-class centuries in the summer, including 164 against Sussex at Hove and, against Nottinghamshire at Sheffield, a century in each innings for the first time in his career.

But none of his hundreds were scored where it really counts, in the Test arena. England's opponents in 1966 were the West Indies, then the unofficial world champions and at the peak of their powers. Led by probably the greatest all-rounder of all time, Gary Sobers, their bowling attack, built around Wes Hall, Charlie Griffith and Lance Gibbs, was just as formidable as a batting line-up of Conrad Hunte, Seymour Nurse, Basil Butcher and Rohan Kanhai. England were hardly in the same league. They lost the series 3–1, tried out three captains, and were plunged into one of those national moods of panic, which have always been a feature of our domestic game since the Victorian era.

Boycott fared little better than the rest of the England team, averaging only 26.57 in the series. His poor form at the start of the summer, combined with his run of failures at the end of the antipodean tour, ensured that he was left out of the side for the first Test at Old Trafford, where England's massive defeat cost M.J.K. Smith the captaincy. Boycott returned at Lord's to open with a new folk hero, the Falstaffian Colin Milburn, whose 94 on his début had been the only highlight of England's performance at Manchester. Yet a far more important and emotional comeback at Lord's was that of thirty-nine-year-old Tom Graveney, out of the side since the Australian tour of 1962/63. Intriguingly, Graveney, despite his attacking style, had always been young Boycott's hero. 'I can't tell you why,' he said, in a BBC radio interview in 1987 with Cliff Morgan. 'The great player of Yorkshire cricket was Len Hutton but as a kid my hero was Tom Graveney, played in Gloucester, two hundred miles away. Elegant, lovely player, aesthetic, front foot, back foot. Sometimes he didn't play for England, they didn't pick him, just like me.'

Boycott soon had the chance to bat with his hero, when they came together at the fall of Milburn's wicket with a score of just eight. They put on 115, with Boycott making 60 and Graveney eventually falling just four short of his hundred. Graveney recalls: 'I had never batted with him before and it was great that day, super. We talked a lot and had no problems at all running between the wickets. It may have been that I was the sort of senior man, an old fella coming back, but he never gave me any anxiety. It may also have been that I did most of the calling. But it was a really enjoyable partnership.' Graveney admires Boycott's cricket but is critical of the Stakhanovite image of toil he has built around himself: 'He tries to paint himself as someone who always had to work very hard but we all worked at our games without making it a chore. I used to have a net every day. I was just giving myself the best chance to get a few runs whenever I went in. I loved batting just as much as he did.'

Apart from a brave 71 at Nottingham, Boycott failed in his other Test innings against the West Indies. This was a worrying period for him. He had failed to average 40 in his last two seasons with Yorkshire. After 24 matches, his Test average now stood at only 36.6, acceptable but hardly high-class. Moreover he had scored only two Test centuries, the last of them 15 matches ago. Of his problems Boycott explained, in a 1971 interview: 'I came on the cricket scene very quickly in 1963. I did rather well and the publicity that surrounded me told everybody that I was going to be a great player. But I think what people forgot is that I came into cricket so quickly that I did not have the maturity and experience. All this caught up with me around 1966 and 1967 and I became very introspective and a little bit nervous.'

By the end of 1966, Boycott was in danger of becoming just another useful but inconsistent performer. But the next 12 months were to take him to a position of far greater public prominence – and not always for the right reasons.

8

'A Great Score, in Anyone's Language'

Today, when eleven England batsmen struggle to make 200 runs between them in any innings, it seems absurd that an England cricketer could be dropped after hitting a double century in a Test match. But that is what happened to Geoffrey Boycott in June 1967, when he scored 246 not out in almost ten hours against India at Headingley, then was excluded from the next Test.

Boycott's Headingley marathon was deemed to have contravened the new ethos of 'brighter cricket' and the selectors decided he had to be punished. What particularly aggrieved them was his batting on the first day. In a full six hours' play, he had made only 106 runs, failing to accelerate even after tea. In the first hour, he hit just 17 runs, followed by eight in the second, 15 in the third, 23 in the fourth, and 21 and 22 in the last two hours. Moreover, he was playing on an excellent pitch against an appallingly weak Indian attack, which was barely of county standard to begin with and plunged below minor counties level in the afternoon, thanks to injuries to medium pacer Rusi Surti (bruised knee) and the left-arm spinner Bishen Bedi (torn muscle). Boycott's inertia drove hundreds of his own Yorkshire spectators to leave the ground after tea although he was near his century, while even a sympathetic journalist like Ian Wooldridge wrote in the *Daily Mail* that his last three hours at the crease 'could not be excused by his nearest and dearest relations'. Far from mitigating his crime, his freer approach the next day, when he added 140 runs in less than four hours, appeared to prove that he could score more quickly if he wanted to. For Boycott's enemies, the Headingley innings revealed the very essence of the man, a selfish player focused entirely on his own performance rather than on the interests of the team or the entertainment of the public.

Yet the absurdity of Boycott's suspension was that his double hundred, far from undermining England's cause, had helped them win by six wickets well before tea on the last day. Test openers are supposed to lay the foundations of a big score – and that was exactly what Boycott had achieved. As the great off-spinner Lance Gibbs told Boycott after his suspension was announced: 'If you had been a West Indian, you would have been a hero. No West Indian would ever get dropped for making a double century.' In truth, the selectors' decision was motivated more by public relations than by cricket. The media were baying for action against Boycott and the selectors felt they had to be seen to do something. But their gesture looked both panic-stricken and patronizing – in effect, the Indian tourists were being told that their Tests should be treated as little more than exhibition matches.

There were other powerful arguments in Boycott's defence. He had been in poor form in the run-up to the Test, making only two scores of over 50 in his previous twelve first-class innings. On the first morning he displayed his lack of touch by continually playing and missing. Instead of throwing away his wicket, however, he battled through the crisis, hitting himself back into form by grinding out the runs. His more vigorous strokeplay on the second day was the result not of a whimsical change of mood but of the renewed confidence that came with a century. England's captain Brian Close recognized the difficulties of Boycott's position, writing later: 'You had to admire the sheer guts of a man so palpably out of form yet so desperately trying to fight his way out of his bad spell.' Close wanted to keep Boycott in the side but was outvoted four to one by the other selectors, Doug Insole, Peter May, Alec Bedser and Don Kenyon. 'I said to them, "Look, I'll give him a right bollocking and tell him not to let it happen again." But the selectors replied that such was his selfishness that it could not be tolerated. So that was it,' Close told me.

One of the central charges against Boycott was that he had 'wilfully disobeyed his captain's orders'. Boycott has always maintained that he never received direct instructions to speed up. His version appears to be backed by Close and, even more explicitly, by one of his batting partners, Basil D'Oliveira. Close's recollection is that he merely said to Boycott at tea that he should see if he could open up, though he should not do anything foolish. Later he went on to the balcony to try to catch Boycott's attention but he admits that Boycott was concentrating so hard that he probably did not see him. In his autobiography *Time to Declare*, D'Oliveira wrote that on the second morning, chairman of selectors Doug Insole came into the dressing room 'to read the Riot Act' and tell the batsmen to give the crowd something to enjoy. 'When it was time to go out to the middle, Boycs led the way and our skipper, Brian Close, said to me just as I was leaving, "Tell Boycs to take no notice, just play his natural game."'

For a sensitive cricketer, who always took immense pride in his professionalism, this rejection was a shattering blow. For the remaining twenty seasons of his first-class career, the selectors' decision rankled with him, a stain on his reputation that could never be blotted out by all his many achievements. Just after his retirement, he told the BBC broadcaster Peter Jones: 'It is a stigma I will always carry. Brian Clough says to me, "Try and forgive them but don't ever forget." Well, I won't forget and I can't forgive because I think it was an unnecessary thing to do.' Some commentators, who refused to be caught up in the hysteria over 'brighter cricket', agreed. John Woodcock wrote in the *Cricketer*: 'The credit he deserved was simply for pursuing the objective he set himself so successfully. In anyone's language it was a great score and I expect that one day, in more taxing circumstances, England will be indebted to him for his obduracy.'

For Boycott, the verdict was as unjust as the one he received in a French court more than three decades later. But resilience in a crisis has always been one of his virtues. Publicly he put a brave face on his humiliation. Brian Close wrote later that he was a 'model of restraint. For the next few days I never ceased to admire the control he displayed in what was obviously a very trying time for him.'

Nevertheless, the decision appeared to affect his batting for the rest of the summer. He only played in two more Tests, one against India and the other against Pakistan, failing to distinguish himself in any of his four innings. It was a throat infection that kept him out of the third Test against Pakistan, while a personal tragedy, the death of his father, required him to stand down from the first.

Boycott heard the news while he was playing for Yorkshire against Surrey at the Oval. 'They asked me to stay and bat, then go home for the funeral. I made 70-odd. It was strength of character,' he later recalled.

Boycott's decision to keep on playing should not be seen as callous. Throughout his life, he was at his most comfortable and secure when he was on the cricket field. In his moment of loss, this man of strong emotions found solace at the crease.

The feeling in Yorkshire that Boycott was a victim of the metropolitan, public-school cricket establishment's prejudice was dramatically reinforced at the end of the summer by the sacking of Brian Close as England captain over allegations – strongly disputed – of unsporting behaviour in a match against Warwickshire at Edgbaston. Amongst those voting in the MCC committee was the skeletal figure of former Prime Minister Sir Alec Douglas-Home who, as Lord Dunglass in the 1930s, had been a passionate supporter of the appeasement of Adolf Hitler. That puts Close's misdemeanours into perspective. At least Close had the consolation of helping Yorkshire to win the championship yet again, with some help from Boycott who, despite his England troubles, headed the Yorkshire averages (1260 runs at 48.46). *Wisden* wrote of his performance, in words that might sum up his whole batting career: 'Only Boycott showed consistent authority throughout the programme. Without his special characteristics of ruthless resolve and concentration, batting consistency would have been hard to achieve.'

That spirit of resolve was to be in even greater evidence in the winter, as Boycott toured the West Indies for the first time and emerged triumphant against Hall, Sobers, Griffith and Gibbs. All his problems of the last two years were put behind him. For perhaps the first time in his career, he looked a genuinely world-class batsman, showing the full range of his strokes and seeking to dominate the bowling. His brilliant form brought him 1154 runs in just 11 first-class games, while in the Tests he scored 463, an average of 66.14. The late Colin Cowdrey, his captain on that trip – appointed in place of Close – said of Boycott's progress: 'By the time of that trip, he had made himself into a very good cricketer. He was much tighter, much less loose than the batsmen of today, and he was brilliant at working out what shots to eliminate in any given circumstance. I also admired his courage against the pace attack. Though he could sometimes go a bit haywire, I actually found him a pretty good judge of a run. I had absolutely no problems captaining him. He might have been reserved, but I found him very astute and shrewd with his advice. He was just a damn good player, great to have in the side.'

Boycott signalled his intentions for the series by hitting four boundaries in Wes Hall's first two overs in the opening Test match at Port of Spain. He went on to score 68, one of the building blocks of a massive total of 568, which should have seen England to victory. At tea on the last afternoon, the West Indies, having followed on, were staring at defeat on 180 for 8. Then immediately after the interval Wes Hall, at number 10, gave a chance to Boycott at short leg. Unaccustomed to fielding in close, he put it down and Hall, partnered by Gary Sobers, saw the West Indies through to safety.

The second and third Tests both ended in draws as well. Then, in the fourth Test, Boycott played one of the most significant innings of his career. On the final day, the match was petering out to a draw when suddenly Gary Sobers made probably the strangest declaration in the history of Test cricket, setting England 215 runs to win in 165 minutes, a seriously achievable target. Apart from sheer frustration at yet another non-result, Sobers' extraordinary action may have been prompted by the belief that England were vulnerable to spin. In the first innings their tail had collapsed to Basil Butcher, an occasional leg-break bowler, in a spell of 5 for 34; indeed, Butcher was so occasional that these were to be the only five wickets he took in a 44-match Test career. But, in England's favour, the pitch was still good and Charlie Griffith was injured.

Boycott and Edrich made a solid start, putting on 55 in 19 overs. At tea, with only 140 needed in 90 minutes and nine wickets still standing, it seemed obvious to almost everyone in the England camp that Sobers had badly miscalculated, everyone that is, except the skipper Colin Cowdrey, who was inclined to caution. Tom Graveney explains: 'In the dressing room, Colin wasn't sure if we should keep going for the runs. Just before tea, Willie Rodriguez had bowled two or three really good overs at Kipper and he hadn't got the runs he thought he should have.' A heated discussion followed. Cowdrey was still not positive but it was the two arch-blockers, Boycott and Barrington, who were amongst the most vociferous in support of a continuing run-chase, Boycott arguing, 'Sobers has given us a real chance. Now let's go and have a bloody crack at it.'

Abandoning his reluctance, Cowdrey played brilliantly, taking the score from 73 to 173 in just 18 overs before he was out. Then Boycott took charge, judging the scoring rate precisely against the clock and hitting off the necessary runs with three minutes – the equivalent of eight balls – to spare. Yet, like his Gillette innings, there was a downside to this triumph, for once again critics were asking why he did not play in this aggressive style more often. Warwickshire fast bowler David Brown says: 'That afternoon we saw a glimpse of what he could do. He played brilliantly and I thought, If you played like that all the time you'd be an absolute revelation.' England just clung on for a draw in the final Test, with Boycott scoring his maiden century against the West Indies in England's first innings, so Cowdrey's team returned home victors by 1–0.

Boycott was now indisputably England's first-choice opener. Despite this success, his awkwardness in company remained a source of exasperation to some of his colleagues. On one occasion he provoked an embarrassing row during a dinner organized in a private room at Trinidad's Hilton Hotel by Vic Lewis, the former band leader, businessman and agent. There were about fourteen people present, including several of the leading England and West Indian players along with their wives and girlfriends. Vic Lewis as the host was at one end and Jill his wife was at the other. Half-way through the meal, there was a loud crash and a commotion. Jill suddenly stood up: 'Vic, I have had to put up with some pretty nasty and preposterous people during your career in showbusiness. But I have never met a ruder person than this man here,' she said, pointing to Boycott. She then stormed off and sat down at the other end of the table.

'Well, she shouldn't be bloody going on about creekit in such a stupid way,' Boycott explained defensively.

One member of that MCC side, Basil D'Oliveira, whose

gregariousness – the hangover appeared to be part of his tour baggage – could hardly have been more different from Boycott's asceticism, later gave this analysis of Boycott the tourist, again highlighting his absolute devotion to cricket: 'He is so wrapped up in his cricket and sometimes this can be misconstrued. You have to know his ways and you find these out over a long period. He never seems to relax. If he does relax, he's sleeping. Cricket is his life and I don't think he has any other interests to help him unwind.'

As a room-mate of Boycott's on that tour, Pat Pocock gained a sharp insight into Boycott's all-consuming passion for his game. Of that experience, he wrote in his wonderful autobiography *Percy: The Perspicacious Memoirs of a Cricketing Man*: 'Rooming with Boycott is a very serious event in a cricketer's life. You are quickly made to realize that you have come to this distant country on business. The thought of enjoyment should not enter your head, since it never entered his. He spoke only of cricket and Yorkshire, since the two things in his mind were synonymous. He spoke, and you listened as that quiet, flat-vowelled voice droned on into the night. It was the voice of a middle-aged man in his mid-twenties, the voice of a man who had never been young.' Yet Pocock saw another, more generous side to Boycott's character, as he explained to me: 'In Barbados, where it was bloody hot, he would bat in the nets for more than fifty minutes. He would go on and on, often against the local bowlers. When he had finished, he came out, took his pads off and then individually thanked each bowler in turn, no matter where they were on the ground. He was brilliant at that. I remember one guy had gone right over to the other side of the field and Boycott followed him just to thank him. He was able to do that because it related to his batting.'

After his Caribbean triumph, there were high expectations of Boycott for the 1968 season. But Boycott's summer turned into a damp squib. Plagued by a serious back injury, which caused him to miss half the season, Boycott performed disappointingly on his three Test appearances against Australia, averaging only 32 and failing to pass 50 in any innings in yet another drawn Ashes series. For Yorkshire, he was only able to play 10 matches in 1968, though he performed superbly in May and June before his back froze, scoring no less than five centuries in the county championship. Returning to competitive cricket at the end of the season, he confirmed his class once more by hitting 93 and 115 in a Scarborough Festival match for an England XI versus the Rest of the World.

It was during this Scarborough Festival that Boycott over-indulged in alcohol for one of the few times in his career. With Yorkshire having won the title yet again, champagne celebrations were soon under way during the Yorkshire–MCC fixture. To the surprise of his colleagues, Boycott was as keen to imbibe as the rest of them. Don Wilson says: 'I can tell you the champagne was flow-ing. And Geoff had a few, very nearly fell into the rubbish tip at the rear of the bar.' Fred Trueman's memory was just as graphic: 'It was the only time I have ever seen him drink. We were batting and we had just come off for bad light. And Geoff was sitting on the floor, with his pads on, his back against the wall, drinking champagne. There were a few MCC players in the dressing room laughing at him. He just said, "Yeah, you can laugh. But you'll be out there all day tomorrow because I'm going to get a hundred." And he did' – 102 not out, in fact, despite the hangover.

1968 was to be a crucial turning-point for Yorkshire. Two of the great stalwarts of the glory years, Fred Trueman and Ray Illingworth – later to be key figures in the club's battle with Boycott in the eighties – retired, the former because of advancing age, the latter because of the committee's refusal to give him the security of a contract. Illingworth then joined Leicestershire in 1969. Yorkshire's years of effortless superiority were drawing to a close. This was to be the last year in which the championship trophy went to Headingley and, in retrospect, those Scarborough celebrations held to mark yet another triumph should perhaps have been a wake.

9

'So That's What You've Been Up To'

Boycott once famously said: 'Given the choice between Raquel Welch and a hundred at Lord's, I'd take the hundred every time.' He also told Professor Anthony Clare during his interview for *In the Psychiatrist's Chair*: 'My mother used to warn me: "Stay away from the girls, Geoffrey, they get you in the woods, they get you into trouble." Always follow your mum's advice.' This was little more than a rhetorical smokescreen to disguise his fondness for women but, outside the cricket world, such comments have indeed led to occasional speculation that Geoffrey Boycott might be gay. After all, to pseudo Freudians his lifestyle has many of the features of the homosexual stereotype: resolutely unmarried; an intense relationship with his mother; a streak of vanity about his appearance; a penchant for creating drama around him; fastidiousness about his diet, clothes and personal hygiene; a degree of sensitivity combined with emotional insecurity; a preference for Cinzano over beer; and a love of performing for the crowd.

In the wake of revelations about Boycott's personal life arising from the French court case, such an idea has proved absurdly wide of the mark. In fact, an alternative image has been created, that of Boycott as the voracious womanizer who accumulates his sexual conquests just as eagerly as he used to pile up the runs. His friend Ted Lester, the scorer for Yorkshire throughout Boycott's career, told me: 'He has had a good run as far as women go. I've seen him with a lot of crumpet you'd be delighted to go with. There have been a lot of women in his life, but I will say this, he's always got rid of them by eleven o'clock so he could get his eight hours' sleep.'

Many others have testified that, throughout his playing days, he was not the Puritan that the public once thought. David Gower, fellow commentator and Test cricketer, says: 'On tour he was never gregarious with the team but every now and then you might catch him in the hotel corridor furtively ushering some brunette into his room and you think, Ah, so that's what you've been up to.' Peter Willey, an England tourist of the Gower era, backs this up: 'I knew all about his women. That's why he often stayed on a separate floor in the team hotel, so he could get people in and out when he wanted to. Everywhere he went he was with different women. He could be very charming with them but he was always secretive about that side of his life, never brazen.'

Sometimes his liking for female company would impinge on other players. One of the England tourists on the 1970/71 tour to Australia told me of this comical incident. 'In Melbourne, I was sharing a room with another player, and Boycs, who was sharing with John Hampshire, overheard that we would be away for the weekend on separate trips. But my visit fell through at the last minute, so I returned to the Windsor hotel in the mid-afternoon. I went up to the porter to ask for my key but was told it had gone so I had to go up to the room to check what was happening. When I got there the door was locked but I could hear whispering inside. I knocked a few times and there was no answer, though the whispering became louder. Eventually I said to whoever was in there, "Listen, if you won't let me in, I've got two choices. Either I kick the door down or I call the manager to get a spare key." At this moment the sheepish figure of Boycs opened the door, wearing only a towel, while I could see a woman scurrying around in the background.

'"I thought thee were away for t' weekend," he said.

'"What's that got to do with you? Why couldn't you stay in your own room?"

'"Cos Hamps is there. Listen, thee won't say owt about this, will thee?"'

At first glance, it might seem strange that Boycott should be so successful with women. When it comes to looks, he is hardly Brad Pitt. Pale, balding, of average height (5 foot 10) and bespectacled for much of his career, he could never have competed with the glamour boys of British sport, like George Best or James Hunt. As fellow players have testified, his single-mindedness about cricket could make his conversation somewhat limited. Nor could he have ever been described as the most romantic of souls. In an interview with the *London Evening Standard* in June 1999, when asked what Anne Wyatt and Rachael Swinglehurst (the mother of his child, Emma) had given him in their long relationships, he replied, 'I don't know.' Then asked if he knew what they loved about him, he continued, 'It's no use guessing what other people bloody think. I just give them what I am. There are no hidden agendas. I'm open and frank. If they misunderstand my intentions, they can't be listening.' And finally, in response to the question as to whether he had ever been in love, he said, 'I don't know.'

One accusation sometimes made against Boycott is that he can behave like a male chauvinist. Simon Hughes, the Channel Four analyst who worked for several years with Boycott at the BBC, told me: 'In the commentary box if there are women around he'll definitely make a comment about their appearance, like "Nice tits." To use the word lech is perhaps unfair, but he certainly has an eye for the ladies, of any age.' One television producer who, given the vituperative nature of his comments, understandably wished to remain anonymous, says: 'His attitude towards the production staff can be terrible and his treatment of some of the women is appalling, with offensive and sexist comments about their physique. You often hear him with a woman, talking about her appearance to her face. There is a serious cringe factor with him.'

It is interesting to note that it is often men, particularly in the politically aware media, who appear shocked by Boycott's attitudes. And while many of today's women might also be outraged by his robust expressions of his masculinity, others take far less offence or are even flattered. Rachael Swinglehurst, whom he first met in 1974, said in an interview with the *Daily Mail* in December 1998: 'In a relationship he wants to be the man and he likes his women to be feminine. He's a boobs and bottom chap and he makes you feel terrific. He's got a lovely body, which has made me look after mine.'

While some of Boycott's utterances might be deeply inappropriate for the modern workplace, there can also be something patronizing about certain men jumping to condemn Boycott on behalf of supposedly aggrieved women. A classic example of this was an incident that took place on the 1992 England tour to New Zealand, where Boycott worked as both a commentator and batting coach. During one match, when he was giving a voice test to the TVNZ production staff, he told attractive TV sound operator Mary Graham, 'I'd rather spend a week than a day with you,' and also how much he liked her legs. Meant as a compliment, the remarks were noted by a male colleague in the TVNZ daily log, with some criticisms attached. Immediately, the station's equal-opportunities procedures swung into action. Boycott found himself at the centre of an inquiry into allegations of sexual harassment and had to defend himself in the press against charges of being a 'sex pest'. But as the station's inquiry soon found, Boycott had no case to answer. Crucially, Mary Graham had taken no offence at anything he had said and was surprised at the fuss. Boycott was immediately cleared. TVNZ's director of sport John Knowles reported that the allegations of harassment were 'totally and absolutely groundless. The vital party – the woman herself – has absolutely no complaint about Geoff's conduct.'

The reality is that Boycott, while he might be bombastic, rude and self-centred with men, can be charming in the company of women. And charm is perhaps the secret of his appeal to the opposite sex. Many of those I have interviewed have spoken of this quality, a mixture of empathy and charisma. The Surrey and England cricketer Graham Roope, who toured several times with Boycott and was at the other end of the pitch when Boycott scored his hundredth hundred in 1977, recalls two examples that highlight this trait. The first occurred during the 1977/78 tour of Pakistan. 'We went to a function at the British High Commission and there was only one eligible lady there. Well, most of the lads were quite keen, women you could talk to being so rare in Pakistan. But the moment he saw her, Boycs was in there, swept her absolutely off her feet. Usually he was quite secretive about his women but here he did it quite openly. He won her over immediately, and I remember she even got time off from the High Commission and went all over the place with him.' The second happened during 1996, when Boycott was working for the BBC during the Trent Bridge Test against India. 'It was my wife's birthday. We were round the back of the pavilion and we bumped into Boycs, who was rushing from one commentary job to another. The conversation went:

'"Roopie, how are you?"

'"Great, how are you?"

'"Great. And who's this gorgeous lady?"

'"She's my, er, third wife."

'"You've got it right at last." He shook hands with her, gave her a great big hug and said, "You look after him, lass, he needs a good Yorkshire lass to look after him." We carried on talking like this. He was just marvellous, charming. Eventually he said, "I've got to dash, please excuse me. All the very best." And after he left, Ruth said to me, "I can see why you don't ever have a bad word to say about him. He's great."'

As always with Boycott, though, the position is complex and it would be foolish to claim either that his behaviour towards women is never disagreeable or that all the reports of his bad manners have been solely the result of misinterpreted flattery. The driver who took him round the country in 1987 on the tour to promote his auto-biography, published by Macmillan, says his conduct towards the young female publicity staff could be appalling: 'It was a six-week tour and I found him incredibly rude. During the course of the tour, he virtually dismembered the publicity girls who accompanied him, leaving them in floods of tears by telling them they were complete wallies, knew nothing, talked rubbish. He would say to them, "You aren't professional, why don't you just bugger off home?" He used foul language all the time he was in the car, and there was a stream of continuous sexual innuendos. The poor little girls were really just cannon fodder for him. One girl, who was meant to accompany him for about three days on the south-coast part of the tour, came down to Bournemouth in the morning with Boycott and got the train straight home that night. Of course he would be just as rude to his marketing director, Martin Neild, now managing director of Hodder and Stoughton. If Martin was in the car, he'd carry on with the lines like, "Don't talk to me, I don't want to talk to you. If I've got to have you in the car, you just sit there and shut up." Once, he even turned on Martin Neild's girlfriend, who was nothing to do with the book and did not work for Macmillan. He phoned Martin at home, upset after his appearance on the radio programme *In the Psychiatrist's Chair*, and when she took the call, he ranted and raved down the line for about five minutes. She was not intimidated, however, and when he finished she simply asked, "Is there a message, Mr Boycott?" '

On another occasion, during a dinner at a Macmillan sales conference, where he was the guest speaker, he caused some embarrassment with his boorish attitude towards a young female representative. Calling her 'Blondie' throughout the evening, he insinuated that the two of them would soon be on their way to an upstairs bedroom. Like several others, she was left in tears by the Geoffrey Boycott experience.

Boycott has been called, even by friends, a Jekyll and Hyde character, and such accounts, compared with this warmth of Graham Roope's testimony, certainly bear out this truth. Nevertheless, it does appear that women, especially mature, accomplished ones, have been more likely to be greeted by Dr Jekyll than Mr Hyde. Boycott seems more at ease amongst women. 'I find I get on better with women than men. In general. They are more decent. Men can let you down,' he once said. This may be because he does not feel the need to be so competitive all the time. With women, he can relax and be himself. With men, especially those in the cricket world, he constantly feels he has to prove something.

As we have seen, Boycott is often dismissed as a old-fashioned chauvinist – a product of his 1940s macho northern upbringing – yet he is surprisingly modern in many of his views on women. For him, a woman's role has never been to stay at home and look after the children. A strong supporter of Mrs Thatcher, he welcomes the idea of women running top companies. Unlike a large section of the cricket establishment, he was an advocate of women's membership of the MCC. As Rachael Swinglehurst puts it: 'He's not a man's man, going down the pub and saying, "You stay at home, woman, in your place." He's all for equality. The most important people in his life have been women and he has tremendous respect for us.'

All women with whom he has had serious relationships have been strong, independent, professional women. There may not be a typical 'Boycott type' of woman physically – unlike, say, Robert de Niro's devotion to black women or Rod Stewart's to blondes – but what all his longer-term partners have in common is their success in business and their careers. His first serious girlfriend, Anne Wyatt, rose up the public-sector ladder to be a senior Social Security official. Shirley Western, with whom he had a ten-year affair, was a top West End singer who put her career before marriage. Rachael Swinglehurst did so well in running pubs in Yorkshire that she has long enjoyed financial independence. Sylvia Reid, whose affair with Boycott hit the headlines in the early nineties, was an ambitious, Porsche-driving sales manager for a housing-development company. And Margaret Moore, though she ultimately turned out to be a bankrupt and a fraud, gave Boycott at least the illusion that she was head of a high-flying computer business.

As in other branches of the entertainment industry, like politics and pop music, a host of women are drawn to sport because of the sexual allure of its associations with glamour, fame, wealth, power and physical performance, as well as the endless opportunities thrown up by evenings in bars and nights in hotel rooms. It was the great wicket-keeper Godfrey Evans who boasted that he had bedded over a hundred women just on his England trips overseas. To avoid such temptations, a top cricketer would either have to be in a remarkably strong marriage or hold devout religious and moral beliefs.

Boycott falls into neither category and has exploited his sporting life as much as anyone. In fact, he probably had more offers than most because of his position as one of the biggest names in English cricket. He also had other attributes, such as his immaculate appearance, the trappings of his wealth (first-class travel, top hotels, BMW and Mercedes cars) and his mixture of self-confidence and vulnerability, which is always appealing to women. There is also his physical fitness. 'He's not a selfish lover. Quite the opposite. He still has a super-muscular body,' Rachael Swinglehurst once said. It is untrue, however, that he is as spectacularly well endowed as cricket legend has claimed ('I've been in every county dressing room in England and only Viv Richards is bigger,' one Yorkshireman wickedly told me). Tony Greig gave this idea greater currency when he repeated it on the ITV programme *The Life and Loves of Geoff Boycott*. However, Greig admitted to me that his comments had been a joke: 'On that programme, I was trying to lighten up the whole thing, give them something they would use, without all the usual old stuff about his selfishness. So I was thinking to myself, what do I do here? Now you hear all these stories about Boycs being marked out of ten by women and it just seemed logical to throw in something which said, "Hey, listen, I've seen him in the showers, he's a fit boy. It may well be that we've got him all wrong. Maybe he's just a great lover." As for the truth about his endowment, well, I think he's just about average. He's just a normal bloke.'

Boycott would be the first to accept that his personal life has been unconventional, to say the least, even if his sexual exploits have not reached the epic levels sometimes claimed. But there are two other powerful points to note in his favour. First, he has never been a hypocrite. He has broken no marriage vows, never claimed to be something he was not. There has been no posing as the family man, no false claims about fidelity and love. While some might find his attitudes distasteful, at least he has always been honest. Second, despite his unorthodox approach to relationships, he has still managed to inspire remarkable loyalty in the three women who have mattered most to him, Anne, Shirley and Rachael, something that few adult men could claim about their partners.

By far the longest of those relationships has been with Anne Wyatt, his colleague from the Ministry of Pensions. She had hardly fallen for a successful sportsman when she took up with him but perhaps she was attracted by the hunger for success that burned within him. Throughout their years together, she did everything she could to further his career, acting as a source of endless advice and support. He always called her 'my lady friend', and today he says she is a 'very special person'. To her must go much of the credit for the change in Boycott from introspective Yorkshire opener of the early sixties to major international sporting celebrity of the seventies. She encouraged him to improve his speaking style in public, to wear more fashionable clothing, to ditch his spectacles in favour of contact lenses, even to have a hair transplant when his baldness was spreading right across his pate. Peter Briggs, another of Boycott's loyal friends, told me: 'She was a tremendous asset to Geoff. She helped to make him what he is today, taking care of his business affairs and organizing so much of his life.' Forthright and uncompromising, she was his protector and mentor during his cricket career, forever compiling press cuttings, relaying to him anything that was said about him, even giving him advice about his cricket and business. 'That's just what Anne says,' he would say to friends, when some suggestion was made. More threateningly, he would warn journalists and colleagues that 'Anne's coming over with the cuttings' when she was flying out to join him on tour. So confident was she of Geoff that she was probably the only cricket follower in England who remained calm during his astonishing hundredth hundred at Headingley in 1977. She explained, 'No, my heart's not thumping. I feel perfectly all right. You see, I always knew he was going to do it.'

That was one of the rare comments she made to journalists. Anne Wyatt has always zealously guarded her privacy and has never given any interviews. She and Boycott once caused an amazing scene at a Foyles literary luncheon in November 1982 when a photographer tried to take a picture of them together. While Boycott chased the cameraman, she threw a glass of water at him. Unfortunately, as well as hitting the photographer, she also showered the elderly widow of the author A. G. Macdonnell. Explaining the cause of her outburst, Anne Wyatt said, 'I'm very private. I just want to get back to my garden and I wish I had never come.' In 1998, during the height of the Margaret Moore business, she explained her refreshingly old-fashioned principles in never talking about her life with Boycott: 'I've always deliberately kept out of the way. Geoff was the star, not me. I've never run to the press about anything. It might be the modern way of doing things but it's not mine.'

Though the insecure Boycott probably needed this rock to cling to during the storms of his career, her undiscriminating loyalty could also be a problem, encouraging him to see enemies at every turn and to pursue a course that might be ultimately self-destructive. His mood of disillusionment and isolation during his last tour to India in 1981/82 was exacerbated by Anne, who went around saying, 'Geoff can't live in conditions like this and eat this terrible food,' when that was exactly what the rest of the team had to do. Instead of being merely his partner, like other wives and girlfriends, she came to be regarded by some as a kind of Svengali or mother-figure, the older woman exerting a sinister control over his life. Her nickname in cricket circles, 'The Black Widow' – which also referred to her raven hair – partly reflected this outlook. Of course this was nonsense: no cricketer as independent and intelligent as Boycott would have ever allowed himself to be dominated in this fashion.

Though their relationship was as complicated as Boycott's personality, there is little doubt that, in the seventies and early eighties, she was hurt by some of his wanderings. According to one of his friends at the time, she would be suspicious and anxious about any evidence that might point to an affair, such as a letter with a stranger's handwriting. Boycott's brother Peter told the *News of the World* in November 1987, when reports of his relationship with Rachael Swinglehurst first emerged, 'Geoff's still living with Anne – and she'll be bloody furious about this other woman. It'll put her nose out of joint. She'll kick and scream but he'll probably just tell her, "Stop your moaning, woman!"' However, by the late nineties she was more philosophical. When told of Margaret Moore, she said, 'When someone goes out the door, how on earth are you supposed to know what they are doing? Once they're out of sight, then the matter is out of your hands. Geoff is over twenty-one and in charge of his own destiny. I don't want other people's sympathy.'

The most frequently asked question about Boycott and Anne is why they never got married. After all, Anne divorced her husband in 1974 and, once Geoff's mother died in 1978, they lived together as a couple in a converted farmhouse in the picturesque village of Woolley, near Wakefield. The house was decorated to her taste: elegant, feminine, patterned soft furnishings and upholstery, 'a bit twee', as one visitor put it. This was to be their home for almost 20 years, until they bought a house in Bournemouth into which Anne moved on her own. Physical passion had disappeared long before that – 'My relationship with Anne has for many years been only business,' Boycott said in 1998. Anne moved to the new south-coast home in 1998, partly to be near her brother and partly because, now in her seventies, she wanted to be in warmer climes than West Yorkshire. Boycott remains in Woolley.

Though Boycott is rightly seen as the resolute bachelor, the decision not to wed may have been mutual. His sister-in-law, Sylvia Boycott, explained to the *Sunday Mirror* in March 1982, 'It has been said that Geoffrey does not want to marry but in fact it's Anne who is not keen. She once told me that her attitude towards marriage was "Once bitten, twice shy."' Even so, Boycott has always hated the idea of marriage. 'I'd rather drop dead first,' he said in 1998, adding that he had a terror of not being a success as a husband. 'I don't want to fail at it. I cannot bear failure. I was just the same with cricket.'

Boycott's feelings about marriage, which go much deeper than just fear of failure, reflect the two contradictory strands of his mother's influence. On one hand, she provided him with a level of unconditional, uncritical backing that any wife would have struggled to match. On the other hand, he must have felt suffocated sometimes by this relationship, given the vehemence with which, as an adult, he has spoken of the need for freedom. 'I knew from an early age I didn't want to stay in the mining village where I was born, and get trapped in a terraced house with an allotment and a pigeon loft. Marriage meant settling down in one place. I never wanted that. I always wanted to travel. Always. I hate it when football wives can't stand life in a northern town when their husbands are earning huge money. I say get a divorce,' he said, in an interview in 1998.

This desire for independence further exposes the fatuity of claims that Boycott was always seeking a mother figure. If he had been, he would have wanted to settle down and be looked after. Instead, he was the very opposite, cherishing his freedom. Few men have ever been more at ease in solitude or less anxious about loneliness.

Marriage might have restricted his ability not just to travel but also to see other women. Even in the first years of his relationship with Anne, he did not want to be constrained. In the summer of 1963 he met the blonde, diminutive, self-confident big-band singer Shirley Western, and began a ten-year affair, which lasted until she moved down to the south coast. She still lives there today, in a flat in Littlehampton, which she shares with her second husband, the ex-professional footballer Roy Dew.

Born Shirley Dodds in Stockwell in January 1936 – on the same day as King George V's funeral – she was brought up in a theatrical family, who performed in music halls over Ireland and England. It was a precarious existence, especially because the advent of the cinema had badly hit variety acts. Soon after Shirley was born, the family moved to Glasgow – to this day she has a noticeable Scottish accent. First on stage at Queen's Park in Glasgow at the age of just three singing 'Burlington Bertie', she began to appear regularly in her teens as a chorus girl touring round Scotland. Like Boycott, she always had a single-mindedness about her singing career. 'This is why when we met we had great respect for each other, because both of us were so ambitious,' she told me.

Her ambition was to sing with a big band so, at eighteen, she came down to London to try to fulfil that dream. With her singing talent obvious, she was taken up by a Canadian agent who told her she had a great voice for country-and-western music. It was at his suggestion that she changed her name to Western and began to sing at the US bases in southern England with her own band. At the time she was the youngest band leader in the country. Intriguingly, one of her saxophone players was Benny Green, the cricket enthusiast and writer, who encouraged her interest in the game. Following a successful TV appearance on *What's My Line?*, she started a job with Ken MacKintosh in 1958. She also made the briefest of appearances as an extra in *Carry On Girls*. It might have been a larger part but for her resemblance to a certain famous British comedienne. 'There was a gang of us chasing Barbara Windsor and Sid James. Suddenly they stopped the filming, and the director said: "You, with the blonde hair, come out of there."

'"What have I done wrong?"

'"You haven't done anything wrong, but you're too like Barbara Windsor. It looks as though you're chasing yourself."

'It annoys me the way the media goes on about that film, calling me a one-time actress in *Carry On* films rather than a successful professional singer. It is the least important thing I have ever done.'

It was through her job with the Ken MacKintosh band that she came into contact with Geoff. 'I had always loved cricket since moving to England. Benny Green, of course, taught me a lot about it and some of the other members of my band used to play regularly. When we were touring around we used to meet up with the Yorkshire players, especially Don Wilson, who really liked the big bands. He liked me as well. He always says, "I could never understand why she preferred Geoff to me."' One Sunday night, Don Wilson took Boycott to the Empire, Leicester Square, then brought him backstage to meet Shirley: 'In those days, I was quite shapely and glamorous. When he met me Geoff exclaimed that he had never seen "anything like that in Fitzwilliam". Immediately there was a spark between Geoff and me. He obviously felt it and so did I. It was very strange, because he was quite a lot younger than me, still an unknown player, and I'd been around with the bands. I suppose I was charmed by his naïvety.'

The next day, Shirley went along to see his superb innings of 90 against Middlesex. She told him it was a 'great knock, to which he replied: "It were bloody awful, I should have got a hundred."' Shirley says, 'It was then that I realized how single-minded he was about being a great cricketer. But that made him all the more appealing because I like professional, motivated people.' That day signalled the start of their relationship, though it was another 18 months before their romance became more intimate. Shirley told me: 'In those days, you didn't just jump into bed with the first person that came round. It had to be a serious, thought-through step.' Shirley says that she was much more gregarious than Boycott but denies that he was ever mean. 'He was just careful. He did not think he should be throwing away his money on drink when he had a family at home who had been struggling all their lives. But when he was with me, he never worried about buying me a bottle of wine or a meal or a few drinks.'

Neither of them gave any thought to marriage because they were both so heavily focused on their careers. 'It would have been impossible. No way did I want to give up my big band, and he was away so much. I never went up to Fitzwilliam, never knew about Anne Wyatt, and I never knew what his relationship was like with her. But in our relationship, though it was not casual, there was no engagement. It was just loving, respectful. To me, he was always very easy company. Yes, he could be moody, especially if he had not scored many runs. But he was never nasty or rude with me. A lot of people found him difficult, self-centred but it wasn't that. It was because he did not have a lot of conversation other than cricket, though he did like to talk to me about showbusiness. In fact, he found my work as interesting as I found his. I think he enjoyed the lifestyle of my world, especially because showbusiness people respected him as a star, whereas his fellow cricketers were awfully critical of him.'

Boycott and Shirley drifted apart from about 1973 when she left the Ken MacKintosh band and moved to Sussex. There was no animosity at all and they remained friends. When she started up her own band again in Worthing, she asked Boycott to preside at the official launch. He agreed enthusiastically, even cutting short a holiday to do so. He was his usual mixture of charm and bluntness, making a brilliant speech, signing numerous autographs and ticking off a local photographer who wanted him to pose at a certain angle with a cricket bat.

'Could you hold the bat properly?' said the photographer.

'You take bloody photo and I'll hold bloody bat,' was the reply.

Just before this Worthing event, Boycott had phoned up Shirley to ask if he could 'bring a lady friend'. Shirley – in another indicator of the lack of any bitterness at the end of their romance – made no objection. The 'lady friend' turned out to be Rachael Swinglehurst, the third of the Boycott trio of serious partners.

10

Disciple of Hobbs

During the winter of 1968/69, England embarked on a hastily arranged tour of Pakistan, following the cancellation of the tour to South Africa because of the notorious D'Oliveira affair. As a Cape Coloured, D'Oliveira had been refused entry to the land of his birth by the apartheid Vorster government.

Boycott turned down the invitation to tour Pakistan. His spleen problems were cited as the cause but there was an additional reason: his decision, made at the end of the 1968 season, to switch from glasses to contact lenses. It took him several months to adjust and he was concerned that his batting might be affected by the change. One of his particular anxieties, which shows the extraordinary thought he always gave to every detail of batting, was that the new lenses might make him blink too much, as he explained in April 1969: 'Whereas my specs have acted as a shield against dust, now they have to act normally. If I blink at the wrong time, then I am either out or I have stopped something almost as lethal as a bullet with my head. And contact lenses are just like any other foreign body in the eye – they make you blink like mad.' Alternatively, the lenses might improve his vision and thereby increase his output. 'If I succeed, it could be worth a thousand more runs a season.'

Perhaps the most obvious change in Boycott over the coming months was felt in his character rather than his cricket. Suddenly, with his spectacles gone, Boycott blossomed into a more open, expansive personality. He was more co-operative with the press, less diffident with the public. He was quite frank in attributing this difference to his contact lenses, explaining two years later, 'They have completely changed my life. They have made me happy, confident and relaxed where once I was shy and edgy. I have no problems in communicating now.' This was hardly the full picture, since Boycott was to have just as many problems with press, public and players in the remainder of his career. But it is true that, without this surge of new social confidence, it would have been more difficult for him to become a major sporting and media star.

On the field, however, he was to experience some difficulties during 1969. It was a disastrous summer for Yorkshire, without Illingworth or Trueman for the first time in almost 20 years and they slumped to thirteenth place in the table, the lowest position they had occupied in their history. Boycott hit Yorkshire's only century, but, as *Wisden* commented, 'he did not touch the heights expected of him,' scoring only 785 runs at 43.61 and falling to seventeenth in the national averages at 38.87 from 1283 runs. The tone for an awkward season was set in the traditional opening fixture at Lord's in April between the MCC and Yorkshire, the champion county. Boycott, whose changeover to contact lenses had been well publicized in the run-up to the start of the season, was twice dismissed cheaply, in the first innings by Ken Higgs for just six and in the second by Alan Ward for a duck. At the interval after Boycott's duck, all the players were sitting down to lunch when Higgs, a straight-talking, undemonstrative Lancastrian, spied Boycott at the other end of the table. ''Ey up, Boycs,' he called. 'Has thee thrown tha bloody contacts off t' balcony?'

In the Tests of 1969 his fortunes were equally mixed. He started superbly against the West Indies, scoring a match-winning 128 on a difficult pitch at Old Trafford. Another century followed in the draw at Lord's. This was also the match in which his great rival John Hampshire scored a century on his England début, five years after Boycott's first Test. That time-gap would have astonished those who watched them together as Yorkshire colts, when Hampshire, the dashing stroke-maker, was seen as a far better prospect. But he never had the same inner steel as Boycott, while in May 1963 his confidence had been undermined by a sickening blow he received on the head from a Charlie Griffith bouncer. The after-effects of that injury plagued him for the rest of his career, ruining his ability to concentrate and condemning him to endless nights of insomnia.

After his own success at Lord's, Boycott saw his international form desert him for the remainder of the season. At Headingley in the third Test, he fell to Sobers for 12 and 0, though England won an exciting match by 30 runs and hence beat the West Indies in a series for the last time in the twentieth century. Against New Zealand, Boycott had a disastrous sequence, making just 101 runs at 20.20 in the three Tests. Twice he was out for a duck to the lively but hardly world-beating Dick Motz. It is one of the quirks of Boycott's Test career that his record against New Zealand, the weakest of the Test nations, should be so poor. When he left international cricket in 1982, his average in 15 Tests against them stood at only 38.17, compared to 45.94 against the much more powerful West Indies and 47.50 against Australia.

Even worse was to follow for Boycott in 1969 against Sussex at Hove where he was involved in a puerile incident with England fast bowler John Snow, with whom he had a fractious relationship. Despite his sometimes cantankerous attitude, Boycott is not by nature physically aggressive – one reason why Margaret Moore's claims about the assault seem so astonishing. But his exchanges with Snow, whom he often called 'Prima', could occasionally degenerate from teasing into something more threatening. Once they squared up to each other in the dressing room on the Caribbean tour of 1967/68, only to be separated by Tom Graveney. Before the start of this match at Hove, Boycott was, as usual, winding Snow up, telling him, 'I'll take another century off you today, Snowy, just you wait until I get going.' But it was different when they were out on the field as Jim Parks, keeping wicket that day, recalls: 'Snowy bowled a bouncer to Geoff, who went to hook it but instead gloved it straight to me. I was sure it was out. But Geoff didn't walk – in those days most players did – and the umpire, Charlie Elliott, gave him not out.'

The next ball, Boycott played Snow down to third man, and as he completed his first run, he smacked his bat against Snow's legs. Boycott says he 'tapped him lightly, playfully', though Snow recalled it as 'quite a rap'. Coming on top of the umpiring decision, it was hardly a clever move by Boycott. In his fury, Snow kicked away Boycott's bat as he turned for the second run, making him stumble. Amazed at what he had seen, the umpire intervened to try to calm the situation, but to no avail. Snow then announced that he would be going round the wicket once Boycott was facing again. He raced and bowled what Jim Parks describes as 'the best bouncer I have ever seen in my life. It was perfect, chest high, straight into Geoff who had to protect himself with his left hand.' Boycott's hand was badly broken. He had to miss the Gillette Cup final at Lord's and was out for the rest of the season.

Having recovered from this injury and fully adjusted to his contacts, in 1970 Boycott started to display the kind of form that, over the next few years, was to raise him on to a pedestal as one of the leading batsmen in world cricket. The stroke-inhibiting terror of failure that had characterized many of his early England appearances had now vanished, along with the Yorkshire-educated technique of low hands and slightly open stance. The long years in the nets, spent perfecting and polishing every aspect of his game, had turned him into the most aesthetic and classical of players, with a cast-iron defence and a full range of shots.

Boycott demonstrated his growing authority in the 1970 series against the Rest of the World XI held as replacement for the cancelled tour of England by the South Africans. While these fixtures lacked the full Test status, there was no doubting the quality of England's opposition, with a side including Gary Sobers, Graeme Pollock, Rohan Kanhai, Clive Lloyd, Mike Proctor, Graham MacKenzie and Intikhab Alam. Not surprisingly, England, led by Boycott's old Yorkshire colleague Ray Illingworth, lost the series 4–1, but the actual margin of victory was closer.

Ironically, in view of his later excellent form, Boycott felt so out of touch early in the summer that he asked the selectors not to pick him for the first three Tests. Returning for the fourth match at Headingley, he made 15 and 64, the latter innings helping to set the Rest of the World a target of 223. At 62 for 5, England looked certain of victory, but then Sobers and Intikhab put on 115 and the Rest of the World, in a gripping finish, scraped home by two wickets.

This was the first match in which Brian Luckhurst opened with Boycott. He says: 'There is no doubt that he was the premier batsman in the country by then. He was such a fine player, looked so strong and secure, his attitude began to rub off on me. I'm convinced that Geoffrey made me a better player because he looked so solid. I feel very privileged to have batted with him.' There was, though, the perennial difficulty of his running between the wickets. Luckhurst says: 'Before I left for Leeds, the Kent boys said to me, "Good luck. And watch the running with Geoff." That's the sort of reputation he had. Sure enough, we had a mix-up right at the start of the match when Boycs hit the ball to Clive Lloyd, then changed his mind twice before sending me back. Fortunately Clive fumbled the ball on an old wicket otherwise I probably would not have made it. We sat down in the dressing room that evening to discuss the running, sorted it out and we never had another problem. It was fine after that.'

Another man playing with Boycott for the first time at international level in that Leeds game was Tony Greig. Even on his début his natural ebullience shone through as he exploited the many-layered ironies of the Rest of the World series. Here was a white South African playing alongside a Cape Coloured South African, D'Oliveira, whose inclusion in the England team had led to its exclusion from apartheid South Africa, while their opponents, the multi-racial Rest of the World team, had a group of white South Africans playing under the leadership of a West Indian, Gary Sobers. Greig could not resist an elaborate joke in this situation, once he had been given the cue by Boycott's rather elephantine attempt at humour. Boycott had come into the dressing room and, seeing Greig and Basil D'Oliveira sitting beside each other, said: 'Mr Vorster wouldn't like this very much. Here I am playing alongside you two.'

Greig takes up the story: 'I was brought up in an environment that encouraged leg-pulling and mickey-taking, so I decided to take him to one side and confront him. "Listen Geoff," I told him, "I'd really appreciate it if you didn't raise that business again because it's very difficult for me to be in the same side as Basil. I'm not sure how much you know about South Africa, but basically, well, he's black, so please don't bring up anything like that again." Boycs was quite shocked. It was totally and utterly untrue, of course, but the other players knew what I was up to. Dolly encouraged me to keep it going. Illy was in on the joke but kept a straight face when Boycs went off to him to explain that "Greigy's a bit touchy about playing with Basil." Eventually Boycs came to me and said, "Look, I'm really sorry, I didn't mean to touch a nerve." I burst out laughing, as did Basil.'

Greig says that Boycott took the joke well: 'The point is that Boycs often engages mouth before brain. Once you accept that, it is actually very easy to get on with him. I consider him a good friend and we have always had an interesting relationship. He has the capacity to dish it out and to cop it. I'm the same.'

The final international of the summer at the Oval saw the Rest of the World win more easily but not before Boycott had hit one of the most masterly innings of his career. On a pitch taking sharp spin, he made 157 in six and a quarter hours, 'batting almost impeccably, using his feet to drive, getting on his back leg to cut and hook,' according to the *Daily Telegraph*. Apart from Boycott, the other England hero of the Oval game was débutant Peter Lever, who took 7 for 83 in the first innings, a performance that guaranteed him a place on the winter trip to Australia. Born in 1940, the Lancashire paceman was an exact contemporary of Boycott and over the sixties had enjoyed the challenge of bowling to him. Lever recalls: 'I got him out a fair number of times but he also got runs. He wasn't a butcher but a collector. He would never take you apart. If you bowled six straight balls, he would just push forward at you, he was that orthodox. But even if he lacked something in talent and was a self-made batsman, he'll still always go down as a great player, one who did the business at the top for nearly twenty years.'

Peter Lever also tells a story about an encounter with Boycott after his great bowling performance, a story that has all the Boycott ingredients of defensiveness, eagerness to learn, bombast, insecurity and, beneath his crustiness, an anxiety to please. 'In the dressing room after I'd got my seven wickets, Boycs looked across and said, "Does thee fancy a meal, then?" And I looked round behind to see if he was talking to somebody else. "Aright, you daft bugger, I'm talking to you."

'"Oh, who's paying, then, Geoff?"

'"I am, I'm bloody paying."

'"Well, this I can't miss."'

The two went to the restaurant at the Clarendon Court hotel. Lever continues: '"Order what you want," Boycs said. We chatted away about cricket, just the pair of us. And I kept thinking to myself, I wonder why Geoffrey, who has never been known to be over-generous in buying meals, has brought me here? I couldn't resist it any longer and when we get to the coffee and sweet course, I say, "Geoff, if you don't mind me asking, why have you brought me here?"

'"Well, can't I just bring one of my mates?" he replies, looking a bit aggrieved.

'"Come on, Geoff."

'"Well, there were a question I wanted to ask you."

'"Yes?"

'"Does thee think I've got chink in my armour?"

'I struggled to keep my face straight. Probably over the last decade I had bowled against him as much as anyone in the country. And he's waited nearly ten years just to say this. But I replied, "Yes, you have one. No one denies you're a good player, you've proved it. But you can't hook."

'"Course I can bloody hook."

'"If that's the reply I rest my case."'

Lever and Boycott then talked more about the art of hooking, with Lever arguing that the shot was too much of a gamble. 'It was funny how the meal ended up. I had a missing front tooth – one was knocked out playing football – and the false one was on a post. I had lost it occasionally when turning round to appeal. So as a replacement I had this piece of chewing-gum, moulded into the right shape, on a matchstick. You could hardly tell the difference. Of course, when I had a meal I had to take it out. During the day, I had been using the chewing-gum when my false tooth had come out. So that night, when I was with Boycs, I put it on my side plate. Later on, we were talking and I must have laughed at something – and you don't laugh too often with Boycs – when he suddenly said, "Hang on, tha's got a tooth missing."

'"Yes," and I look down and it's gone. "Oh, shit, I put it on side plate, and the waiter's taken it."

'"I'll get it." And he's off. He's burst through door into kitchen. And I follow him in there and everybody's standing to attention and Boycs is up to his elbows in a bucket of swill. And then I tell him, "It's all right, Geoff, I'll make another. It was just a piece of chewing-gum." You should have seen his face.'

Boycott's excellence for England in the second half of the season matched his success with Yorkshire, for whom he scored 1425 runs at 50.89. Included in that aggregate was the then highest score of his career, 260 hit in just seven hours against Essex at Colchester. In all first-class matches in 1970, he made 2051 runs at 55.43, bringing him to fifth place in the national averages.

Yet this record was far surpassed by the brilliance of his achievements in Australia in the winter, where his astonishing consistency was instrumental in ensuring the return of the Ashes after twelve years in Australian hands. Interestingly, the MCC captain, Ray Illingworth, wanted Boycott to be his vice-captain. But once Illingworth was named skipper, the selectors offered this position to Colin Cowdrey. Bitter at being passed over for the England captaincy yet again, Cowdrey took several weeks to ponder his decision, then eventually accepted with such reluctance that his form and mood suffered disastrously. Illingworth has written that if Boycott had been appointed his deputy the history of English cricket in the seventies might have been different. Boycott would have been Illingworth's automatic successor in 1973, the sulk over Denness would not have occurred, nor the farcical three-year exile from 1974.

Illingworth proved a superb, if attritional, captain on an awkward trip. There were continual rows over umpiring decisions – two of the worst involving Boycott – while the final Test in Sydney was marred by crowd trouble. More seriously, Illingworth had a poor relationship with his manager, David Clark from Kent, an archetypal establishment figure who had no understanding of the growing intensity of Test competition. Frostiness between the manager and team descended into outright contempt when, half-way through the series, Clark tactlessly told the press he would rather see Australia win than have the remaining Tests drawn. Clark's ill-conceived efforts may have actually united the England side under Illingworth, but ultimately it was the quality of his side that helped him regain the Ashes: Alan Knott, John Snow, Basil D'Oliveira, Derek Underwood, Brian Luckhurst, John Edrich, Peter Lever, Bob Willis (on his first tour) and Illingworth himself produced high-class performances, especially when the pressure was at its greatest.

Above all, there was Geoffrey Boycott, now at the physical and technical peak of his career. His record on this tour was phenomenal, in both Test and state matches. In all first-class games, he scored 1535 runs at 95.93 with six centuries and seven half-centuries, while in the Tests he hit 657 runs in 10 innings at 93.85. His first Test captain Ted Dexter, covering the tour for the *Sunday Mirror*, told me that Boycott provided 'some of the finest batting I have ever seen on that Australian trip. He was absolutely superb. I would say he was the last of the great sideways-on English players; left shoulder and forearm were in the right position.' Of one of his performances, Richie Benaud wrote: 'His driving off the front foot was as close to perfection as you can get.'

Boycott opened his account with a powerful 173 against South Australia on the first day of tour. He was infuriated, however, when Illingworth suggested the next morning that once he had reached his double hundred he should make way for other batsmen. The idea of deliberately getting out was abhorrent to Boycott – even in benefit and league games he would rather retire hurt than throw away his wicket – and, still seething at the captain's instruction, he was dismissed off the third ball the next morning. The quarrel continued in the dressing room afterwards, and several days passed before Boycott would speak to Illingworth again. Eventually the problem was sorted out. In the subsequent match against Queensland, Boycott willingly retired hurt on 124.

In a state game against New South Wales, fellow opener Brian Luckhurst gained an insight into Boycott's supreme powers of concentration, though the incident he refers to shows how Boycott's actions could so often be interpreted as selfish. A short ball from the pace bowler Dave Renneburg jagged back and went straight into Luckhurst's chest. 'I went down on one knee and later discovered that I had two cracked ribs. As I knelt there, I looked down the other end where Geoffrey was prodding the wicket. "You OK, Geoff?" I asked.

'"Yes, I'm fine."

'It wasn't that he had no concern. It was that he didn't want to break his concentration by coming down the wicket so he just stayed out of the way. I suppose it was a little funny that here I was, in a bit of pain, and there he was repairing the pitch. But it didn't matter to me because I understood what he was doing.'

Luckhurst and Boycott enjoyed a good start to the series, putting on 92 for the first wicket at Brisbane in a high-scoring draw. A second draw followed at Perth in what was the first ever Test staged on Western Australia's ground. Once again Boycott and Luckhurst played well, with opening partnerships of 171 and 60. With the third Test abandoned because of rain, the stalemate was finally broken at Sydney, where Boycott gave the crowd a majestic display of batting. In the first innings, he scored 77 in an opening stand of 116 from just 31 overs, only falling when, ignoring the dinner-table advice of Peter Lever, he hooked straight to square leg. Then in the second innings, his 142 not out on an increasingly awkward pitch set up a massive England victory, secured by John Snow's blistering 7 for 40. In his book about the 1970/71 battle for the Ashes, *Captains Outrageous*, the Australian writer R. S. Whitington lavished praise on Boycott's 77: 'Boycott demonstrated that he is clearly the outstanding batsman on either side, technically and temperamentally. More than ever, he reminded me of the Surrey master, Sir Jack Hobbs.'

Inevitably for Boycott, there had to be a negative side to this Sydney glory. It came in the form of perhaps the most notorious of all cricket stories about him. During the second innings at Sydney, he and Basil D'Oliveira enjoyed a fourth wicket partnership of 133. For much of it they had to face the unorthodox spin of Johnny Gleeson, who propelled the ball off a bent middle finger in the manner of Jack Iverson, the tormentor of England in the 1950/51 series. All the tourists, trying to read this eccentric action, found it impossible to work out whether Gleeson had sent down an off-break or leg-break. But during his long stand with Boycott, D'Oliveira is said to have strolled down the wicket to tell Boycott that he had finally worked Gleeson out. Boycott is alleged to have replied, 'Oh, I sorted that out a fortnight ago, but don't tell the buggers up there,' pointing to the England dressing room.

For almost thirty years, this incident has been paraded as an example of Boycott's extreme self-centredness. The very fact that it has been given such widespread credence might seem to reinforce its veracity. Yet Boycott himself has always strongly denied using such words, arguing that he never learnt to read Gleeson. Basil D'Oliveira refused to confirm them when approached by Boycott for his own *Autobiography* or by me for this book. Then there is the intriguing claim in Pat Pocock's memoirs that the incident actually occurred in the Old Trafford Test of 1968. He wrote, 'In later years I would listen to Boycott's supporters deny that the great man's game was tainted by selfishness. And I would remember Old Trafford.' When I interviewed Pat Pocock, he confirmed this recollection, saying that he had been told it directly by Basil. Given all these inconsistencies, it seems likely that what actually happened was that, at some stage, in either 1968 or 1970/71, Boycott, in one of his leaden attempts at humour, may have made some private joke about playing Gleeson and D'Oliveira, always an exuberant raconteur and humorist, relayed it to some of the players and press. Gradually, through years of repetition and embellishment, the line may have been transmuted into an iron statement of policy by Boycott. Nevertheless, the very fact that it has been regarded as such reveals the suspicion with which Boycott has long been held by the cricket world. No one would dream of attributing such a remark to John Edrich or Alan Knott.

After another draw in the fifth Test, in which Boycott made 12 and 76 not out, England were in a tremendously strong position in the sixth Test at Adelaide, having bowled Australia out for 235 in response to 470. Illingworth refused to enforce the follow-on, citing the burden on his pace bowlers as the reason, and Australia escaped with a draw. In a series full of umpiring controversies – England's bowlers did not win a single lbw verdict throughout the Tests – Boycott was caught up in yet another at Adelaide, when he was given run-out by Max O'Connell in the first innings for 58. So aggrieved was he by this decision that he dropped his bat to the ground and stood with his hands on his hips in disbelief. His display of petulance led to an eerie silence across the ground, followed by a roar of anger. Greg Chappell then picked up Boycott's bat, handed it back to him and, along with several other Australians, told him to 'fuck off back to the pavilion', gesturing the direction with their thumbs. Boycott eventually made his solitary way from the crease amidst a crescendo of boos. The criticism in the press the next day was almost as noisy. The *Daily Express* called his outburst 'a disgrace', while *The Times* described it as 'a lamentable exhibition'.

After further argument, Illingworth issued a statement saying that Boycott was sorry that 'he showed a degree of displeasure at a decision he thought was a poor one', hardly the fulsome apology the press were demanding. Boycott's behaviour may have also caused him long-term damage. The moment he saw Boycott's bat fall to the ground, the great Australian Keith Miller said to a colleague, 'That will cost him the England captaincy.' And there was always a suspicion that, throughout the seventies, this incident was treated by Lord's as proof that Boycott did not have the right temperament to lead his country.

Adelaide was to be Boycott's last Test on his brilliant but controversial trip. Just after this, in a meaningless one-day game on an under-prepared track at Sydney, a ball from Graham MacKenzie broke his forearm, putting him out of the rest of the tour. For Boycott the fracture was a double blow: not only did he miss the final Test, which England narrowly won and thereby clinched the Ashes, but he also lost the chance to overtake Wally Hammond's record of most runs on a tour of Australia, made in 1928/29. At the time of the break, Boycott was only 18 short of the record. Yet, after some of his earlier rows, Boycott took it well. Bernie Thomas, the England physiotherapist, recalls: 'He was very good about it, really. I took him off to St Vincent's, the local Catholic hospital run by the Sisters of Mercy. He was excellent with the nuns, charmed them all. Fortunately the sister on duty knew her cricket, so that made a nice little match with Boycs.'

Boycott always maintained that the MacKenzie break caused him permanent damage in his left wrist, restricting its movement. A full two years after the injury, he had a manipulative operation to lessen the problem, while in his left pocket he often carried a squash ball in a sock, continually squeezing it to loosen his wrist joints. 'People probably think I'm an ill-mannered Yorkshire bugger who can't take his hands out of his pockets, but that's why,' he once said. Bernie Thomas is less sure: 'But you only have to look at his record afterwards to realize that it never caused him a great deal of trouble when batting.'

Indeed. Eleven years later, Boycott was still playing Test cricket.

11

Master of His Own Destiny

Any list of top British post-war sportsmen would be certain to include the names of Nick Faldo and Geoffrey Boycott. Each was the supreme practitioner in his chosen field: Faldo, winner of more majors than any other Briton; and Boycott, the greatest English opening batsman and highest Test run-scorer of his time. What is also remarkable about this pair is how much they had in common. Both were fascinated with money, played at the highest level well into their forties, and had unconventional, even chaotic, private lives. They each had supreme mental strength and total dedication to their craft, which more than compensated for their limited natural talent. But the achievement of technical perfection came at a high price, for they were unpopular within their respective sports, seen by many colleagues as self-centred, obsessive, graceless and difficult.

The great humanist psychiatrist R. D. Laing liked to ask, 'Who's doing the diagnosing?' when he was confronted with claims about an individual's supposed mental disorder or schizophrenia. What he found was that such assertions often revealed more about the proponent of the claims than the subject of them. The same, to a lesser extent, is undoubtedly true of some of the criticism of Faldo and Boycott, which frequently came from players looking for an excuse for their professional inadequacies. John Callaghan, who covered almost every Yorkshire game for the *Yorkshire Evening Post* from 1973 to the end of Boycott's career, used to listen to a barrage of woe against Boycott, usually delivered in the bar after a few pints. Then he would say to the cricketers involved, 'Well, who are you going to blame when he's gone? Because you still won't be better players.' Even some within the Yorkshire side felt this. Paul Jarvis, one of the few genuinely talented players to emerge from Yorkshire over the last two decades, told me: 'Boycott, in my mind, was what everyone wanted to be. But some people were jealous of what he had achieved. So their way of trying to get out of their lack of ability and dedication was to pull Boycott down, saying that he just played for his average while they played for the team.'

While professional jealousy exists in every sport, it is probably at its worst in cricket. This is because cricket, uniquely among team games, is based on a series of individual confrontations. At the start of every delivery, the batsman and bowler are on their own, like knights in a jousting contest. Since cricket is so individualistic, the scope for accusations of selfishness is so much greater. But in truth, if a player does well for himself, he generally does well for his side. The ex-Australia coach Geoff Marsh used to encourage his batsmen to be selfish: 'Bat for yourselves and you'll bat well for Australia,' he tells them. The former England fast bowler Geoff Arnold told me, 'Boycott was a very selfish person when it came to cricket but I didn't mind that at all. I wish we had a bit more selfishness these days. Today we're crying out for people to play like him.' There are only very rare occasions in the first-class game, and almost never in Test cricket, when a cricketer can damage his own side's prospects by playing in his own interests. Thus, when Boycott played one of the slowest ever Test innings, 77 in seven hours at Perth on the 1978/79 tour, his captain Mike Brearley said that the innings was 'invaluable' in securing an England victory.

There is another reason why cricket is prone to internal bitterness: the sheer amount of time cricketers spend together. Because of batting, rain and intervals, they are more likely to be in the dressing room than on the field during a match. Indeed, apart from prisoners, submarine crews and public schoolboys, it is hard to think of any group of males who spend more time banged up with each other. All this gives endless scope for bickering and faction-fighting, with the loners, like Boycott, becoming the focus of discontent.

Boycott's problems with his colleagues were hardly unique. In fact, it is rare to find a great cricketer who is universally liked and respected amongst his peers. Sir Donald Bradman, for instance, was loathed by many in his Australian side in the 1930s, especially Jack Fingleton and Bill O'Reilly. A clash of backgrounds was partly to blame: Bradman hailed from the Protestant Anglo-Australian rural conservative tradition, whereas O'Reilly and Fingleton were staunch republican Irish Catholics. But Bradman's astonishing supremacy also invoked animosity, leading to accusations that he was a loner, that he would not buy his mates a drink, that he hogged the limelight, that he was a poor captain – exactly the same litany of complaint that was made in Yorkshire against Boycott in the seventies.

Bradman's rival, Wally Hammond, probably the greatest of all England middle-order batsmen, was even more widely disliked. His Gloucestershire county captain, Basil Allen, was once talking to Plum Warner at Lord's. 'That Wally Hammond of yours really is a wonderful chap,' said Warner. Allen replied, 'If you want my honest opinion, Plum, I think he's an absolute shit.' Morose, introspective, racked by jealousy of Bradman and failures in business, Hammond was an awkward, often brusque companion.

The same pattern can be seen throughout cricket history. Boycott's predecessor as Yorkshire and England opener, Sir Len Hutton, might have been adored by the public, but several colleagues complained about his sarcasm, his unwillingness to help youngsters, and his inclination to watch pace-bowling from the non-striker's end. Colin Cowdrey has generally been regarded as the most affable of players, yet, according to Ray Illingworth's autobiography, 'he was not generally liked by cricketers'. Illingworth himself does not escape criticism. Pat Pocock writes in his memoirs, 'The entire county circuit knew of his shrewdness, his tendency to self-protection, his reluctance to submit himself to long spells of work and his habit of putting himself on to bowl at certain, favourable times of the day.'

Perhaps the most interesting example is that of Sir Richard Hadlee, the record-breaking New Zealand all-rounder. Massively dedicated, like Boycott, constantly in search of technical perfection, he admits that his own professional ambitions brought him into frequent conflict with less talented members of the New Zealand side. In his candid autobiography *Rhythm and Swing*, Hadlee records the time his captain Jeremy Coney accused him of disloyalty: 'You've never had the team's interests at heart,' said Coney. 'You are only one, but there are ten others in the team. They accept you for what you are because they need you but they don't respect you. I don't respect you as an individual.' Exactly this type of language was to be used against Boycott throughout his career.

At the other end of the scale, Mike Gatting was a much-loved cricketer amongst professionals, his genial rotundity a continual source of amused affection from his colleagues. Gatting had far more natural talent than Boycott, yet he ended up with a Test average of just 35.5 compared to Boycott's 47.7. The difference between the two was summed up by an incident on the 1977/78 tour of New Zealand, when Boycott was captain and Gatting was on his first overseas trip. As usual Boycott was seeking some net practice and needed a couple of bowlers. Gatting later wrote that Boycott 'turned his gaze on myself and Paul Downton. We had teamed up to play golf and were looking forward to it. Instead, we had to bowl at a grim Boycott in the nets. He had us running in, knackered, for nearly two hours.' Did Gatting not feel that, rather than whining about his missed golf, he should have tried to learn something from bowling to the finest technician in the world?

Popularity has never sat easily with cricketing excellence. The drive to reach the top will usually clash with the urge to be one of the lads. But in Boycott's case the problem was made worse by his restricted ability, which meant that he had to be even more single-minded than most. If Boycott was to succeed at the highest level, he had to be more tough, ruthless, devoted, self-critical, prepared and focused than any of his contemporaries. And that attitude was bound to clash with the expectations of less-demanding colleagues. In fact, Boycott is quite open about his difficulties in playing a team sport. 'I cannot help feeling that I would have achieved more had I taken up golf as a profession instead of cricket. Golf is unique among ball games in that it allows the individual to be master of his own destiny. Success or failure depends entirely on how he alone shapes up to the challenge presented by the occasion and the course,' he wrote in his 1990 book *Boycott on Cricket*.

Yorkshire committee man Sid Fielden, who was close to Boycott in the early eighties, gives a graphic example of Boycott's rigorous standards. 'We were watching a video of him batting, and the screen showed him hitting the ball through the covers for four. "Magnificent shot," I said. He replied, "That just shows how much you know about batting. My left foot was in the wrong place. I could have been out. I allow myself two mistakes a season."' His single-mindedness was allied to a burning passion, which set him even further apart from his team-mates. Though he may have appeared dour in his approach to run-scoring, he was actually a highly charged, turbulent character. In a revealing interview with the cricket enthusiast and film critic Barry Norman in the *Observer* in May 1973, he admitted, 'I'm supposed to be cold and calculating – sphinxlike, they call me – but I'm not like that at all. I don't show emotion much but inside, if the crowd is with me, I'm on fire. I play emotionally.'

Though some of the animosity that Boycott aroused in the cricket world can be attributed to envy and jealousy, that is hardly the complete explanation: even those who had no axe to grind at all were frustrated and angered by his behaviour. Too often, Boycott's single-mindedness came across as selfishness, plain speaking as gratuitous rudeness, and insecurity as tiresome moodiness. 'Maybe his mother liked him but I don't think the man has ever really had a friend. On the whole cricket circuit, I don't believe there is a player who would put his hand on his heart and say, "Yes, I enjoyed Geoff's company." The man simply cannot relate to fellow human beings,' the former England fast bowler Fred Rumsey said in 1982.

At times Boycott seemed almost wilfully to court unpopularity with his colleagues, playing up to his image as the hard-bitten, blunt Yorkshireman dedicated solely to his game. Pat Pocock tells this indicative story: 'I was playing in South Africa in the winter of 1971/72 for the Northern Transvaal and Boycott had been brought out to play for the same team by a wealthy sponsor. When he arrived later than expected, there was some argument as to whether he would play against Rhodesia or not. Eventually he agreed to. Typically, he went out and scored a hundred, taking on Mike Procter who was bowling very fast. When he was out, he was sitting in the dressing room, wrapped in a towel with a cold drink in his hand. Our captain, Jackie Botten, one of the nicest guys you could ever meet in your life, went over to him and said, "Well played, Geoffrey, great knock." Boycs looked at his hand, then turned away and ignored him. A few moments later I said, "What the hell was all that about, then, Boycs?" And he just said, "Listen, Pat, I haven't come over here to be popular. I've come over to bat."'

On another tour two years earlier, Tony Lewis saw the same refusal to compromise or be part of the team when he was in charge of the 1969/70 MCC goodwill trip to Sri Lanka and the Far East. He told me, 'There were certain corners of his life which I thought were extremely selfish, like the fact that he would allow nothing to get in the way of his own game. We gathered at Lord's before we left for the Far East and were told by the management that, because of baggage restrictions, we would have to cut down on our kit. A lot of people said, "Fine, we'll share." But not Geoffrey Boycott. He was going on tour as Geoffrey Boycott and there was no way he would go without every part of his equipment.' Later on the tour, when the MCC were playing Hong Kong, Boycott opened with the Glamorgan batsman Alan Jones on a misty, damp morning. Soon Jones was scoring regularly, yet Boycott hardly hit a run at all, continually padding up to balls outside the off-stump. The crowd were puzzled, having heard so much about this great English batsman. Lewis says, 'Then, to my amazement, when the batsmen were offered the light, Boycott came off. I immediately went round to the dressing room to ask him what on earth he thought he was doing. "We've come eight thousand miles to show them first-class cricket and then you bring us off."

'"You'll never understand what it's like to be a great player."

'I'm afraid what I said in reply to that is pretty unprintable. But that summed up Geoffrey. He was dedicated to the exclusion of everybody else. It was a pursuit of professionalism that was to leave him increasingly isolated.'

His loud mouth and a short fuse could also cause deep offence. Ted Lester, the Yorkshire scorer, recalls one match between Yorkshire and Kent, when during the lunch interval he was sitting down with John Shepherd, the Barbadian fast bowler. 'Shepherd wasn't eating anything so I said, "What's the matter with you, John?" He replied, "Ted, I have been a supporter of Geoffrey Boycott all my life but today, when he was out, I said, 'Bad luck.' And all I got in reply was a mouthful of abuse. I'll tell you what, I will never support him again." You see, that's Geoff, saying things without thinking.'

Channel Four presenter Mark Nicholas has always enjoyed working with Boycott, and rates him at the highest level as both analyst and batsman. But he says that he has seen him behave 'bloody badly. In a 1980 Gillette Cup game at Southampton the two teams were sitting down to lunch on the top floor of the old pavilion at Southampton. We were all sitting there and the old duck, very nice lady, who served the food came along and said to Boycott, "Do you want some potatoes, dear?" then just spooned them on to his plate before he had answered. She had, of course, twenty-five men to serve during a very short lunch break. He said, loudly and rudely, "No, I don't bloody want your bastard potatoes." Then, with his hand, he swept the potatoes off his plate, right across the table and down on to the floor. He stood up, pushed the table away and then stormed out of the room. The poor lady was left standing there, about to burst into tears, while the table was in mayhem. You can imagine what the room thought of Boycs then.'

Jealousy would never be a motivating force with either the wicket-keeper Bob Taylor or left-arm seamer John Lever, both supreme professionals with excellent records who were universally regarded as great tourists. Yet both occasionally found cause to be offended by Boycott's conduct. Taylor writes in his autobiography *Standing Up, Standing Back* that he found Boycott 'difficult and uncommunicative'. On the 1977/78 tour of New Zealand, Taylor was shocked when Boycott, having just been dismissed in the first Test, pushed aside an eight-year-old schoolboy who had had the temerity to ask for his autograph, giving him a sample of his ripe Pontefract vernacular. The little boy almost tumbled to the ground and started to cry. To be fair, Boycott later apologized and signed the boy's book. John Lever, a regular tourist between 1976 and 1982, says, 'He could be pretty rude and he would hide behind his Yorkshire bluntness as an excuse. Certainly you sometimes wondered if he gave it a lot of thought before he opened his mouth. I will always remember, towards the end of my career, talking in company with him and some others. In front of everyone he said, "Well, here you have Jake, a swing bowler, a good bowler, but no, not a great one. At the top level, he lacked a yard of pace, just wasn't quick enough." It was 100 per cent true but hardly what I wanted to hear.' Sometimes this kind of criticism had a purpose, continues Lever:

'He was an expert at winding up bowlers so he could have some serious practice. He'd say anything to stir you up a bit so he would have a better net. "Ah, you're not really bowling, Jake. You're not coming in very well. Are you injured, Jake?" Then, in your annoyance, you'd come rushing in and he'd suddenly feel he was having a good net.'

The complaint that Boycott would rarely socialize is also cited as more evidence that he wasn't a team man. John Lever recalls this incident on the tour to Pakistan in 1977/78: 'Boycs came into the team area and picked up a bottle of wine to take back to his room. And Ian Botham immediately had him in a headlock and was threatening to pull out some of his hair. "This is the team room, and if you want a drink, you come and drink with the boys, not in your own room. Now do as you're told, Fiery, or I'll pull this lot out," joked Both, grabbing a handful of hair. We all thought Boycs' behaviour was a bit strange because in the hotel, there is nothing else to do. But that was a sign of Fiery's attitude, he just preferred his own company.' Throughout Boycott's career there were persistent complaints that he never bought anyone drink, a sign, it was said, of his unfriendly attitude. Boycott could justifiably point out that he never drank much, so why should he waste time and money in bars just to please others. But players like Alan Knott (a teetotal, devoutly Christian family man) had solitary habits without being stuck with labels like 'mean' or 'self-centred'.

It was Boycott's approach to batting in the middle that probably aroused the strongest grievances. Some, particularly in Yorkshire, felt he was engaged in his own personal war against the opposition without regard to the context of the match or the needs of the team. In a scathing article in the *Cricketer* in 1978, Richard Hutton called Boycott a 'one-pace player' who 'tended to play a different game from everyone else'. Hutton wrote that 'on the slow and wet pitches which abounded in Yorkshire, he displayed a technique which none of us possessed, in that at times he made batting look horribly difficult. He could get bogged down to such an extent that his only way out was to call for and run desperate singles without reasonable regard for his partner's safety. Furthermore, the temptation to concentrate the strike on himself in favourable conditions was not always resisted. All this created pressure on the other batsmen.'

Boycott could legitimately argue that he was the only great player in a weak Yorkshire batting side in the seventies and eighties so he had to make sure that he stayed at the crease. If he failed, collapse was almost inevitable. The same defence could be made of his admittedly poor running. If there was a mix-up, it was more important that he stayed than a less able colleague. Legitimate maybe, but it was hardly an opinion likely to endear him to others.

Even his supporters could be left disappointed. Paul Jarvis, who has the greatest respect and affection for Boycott, said to me, 'He could be so wrapped up in his own game. Looking back, I now think there were times he could have done more to protect the lower order. I remember one instance at Middlesbrough when Malcolm Marshall was steaming in and they had the off-spinner Nigel Cowley on at the other end. I had gone in after Marshall had got a wicket with the last ball of the over. So Boycott had six balls of Cowley to face and he blocked every single one back to the bowler. Three balls later Marshall bowled me. A lot of other top batsmen in that situation would at least have tried to look for one.'

David Gower told me an extraordinary tale about the 1979 Edgbaston Test against India that sounds more like an incident from a kindergarten sandpit than a Test match. To put the story in context, it should be noted that Gower, just 22, was in only his second summer of Test cricket, while Boycott, 38, had played 80 times for England. 'At the end of one over, he pushed it wide of cover and called me for a run. I said, "No." Innocently, I had not realized that he wanted the strike. The following over, I pushed one into space, an easy single, and called him for a run. He just stood there and said, "No." At the end of the over, rather surprised, I went up to him and asked what was going on. He replied, "Well, if you're not running for mine I'm not running for yours."'

According to Gower's autobiography, Boycott proved equally uncooperative during the Jubilee Test against India in Bombay in 1980. Gower, who was going through a dismal run of form, went along to Boycott's hotel room to get him to sign some autograph sheets. When Gower arrived, Boycott looked up and said, 'I can tell thee what tha's doing wrong, tha knows.' There followed a pause. 'But I'm not going to.'

The tendency to play his own game was even more stark in club matches, which Boycott, to the fury of other players, would often treat as nothing more than a glorified net. If he was not playing for Yorkshire or England, he would often try to get a game with Leeds, the club that had first brought him to Headingley. The Leeds people were happy to have such a big name in their midst but the home players did not always feel the same way. Peter Kippax, one of Boycott's contemporaries as a Yorkshire colt in the early sixties, was captain of Leeds by the seventies and recalls: 'Geoff used to play for us occasionally when he wanted some practice. But in the end the rest of the lads ganged up, came to me and said, "If you pick him again, we don't want to play." So I had to say no to Geoff. To be honest, I don't blame them either. Geoff didn't speak to them in a particularly nice way; he didn't offer them anything in the dressing room; he always wanted to hog the strike. He was an individual in a team sport and he did not make any contribution to team spirit.' Martin Gray, who occasionally appeared for Leeds, reinforces this point: 'Boycott was my hero but that all changed the day I played with him for Leeds. He just treated the match like batting practice. His attitude was just unbelievable. He couldn't care less if we won or lost. I batted with him and we had a partnership of over a hundred. He got ninety-six and I got six. In every over, off the fifth or sixth ball he would take a single and keep the strike. To all the other balls he hit either four or nothing. He was such an arrogant, selfish man that I changed my opinion of him completely. He sickened me totally.'

Boycott's reluctance to accelerate – what Richard Hutton described as his 'one-pace' approach – meant that many top bowlers, though greatly respecting him, did not fear Boycott as they did the likes of Viv Richards or Clive Lloyd. Because he was so utterly orthodox, he would resist launching an all-out assault. 'The downside of bowling to him was that he was so hard to remove. The upside was that he was never likely to destroy you, make a mess of your figures,' says Robin Jackman, of Surrey and England. Other England Test bowlers agree. Norman Gifford, the Worcestershire slow-left armer, told me: 'When Barry Richards was in he would really move, whereas Boycott would stay in one gear. He was an accumulator. You could almost see him studying the percentages as the ball came down. He didn't mind blocking at all and had this tremendous patience. Even if you tied him down, he would still not make a mistake by trying to hit out.'

In the final analysis, whatever their reservations about his character and his style, few of his contemporaries could deny that he was a remarkable batsman. He might have been mean and moody, but he was also magnificent. For more than twenty years, against all kinds of bowling attacks, on all kinds of pitches across the world, he piled up the runs with a consistency that few other cricketers in the history of the game have matched. Every Test nation would adore to have him in their side today, but none more so than England whose batsmen are so utterly lacking in his virtues of diligence, application, technique, concentration and patience. England's last world-class spin bowler, Derek Underwood, has particular memories of his skill: 'On a wicket where the ball was really gripping, I'd bowl to him and somehow it didn't seem to turn at all. That's how good he was. I'd only realize that the ball was really turning when Boycs took a single. Then I was bowling at someone else and suddenly I'd be beating the bat twice an over.'

It was the greatest of modern swing bowlers, Sir Richard Hadlee, who gave this tribute to the Yorkshireman: 'The names of other batsmen may flow freely as outstanding players of my time but Boycott's the one I rank above them all, at least from a fast bowler's perspective. He was anything but flamboyant; there wasn't a batsman who was more dreadfully dour than him. But he was prolific, phenomenally so, and he was a true practitioner of the batting art in its purest, technical form. A man despised by so many for his single-mindedness and selfishness, he was the batsman I found the hardest to dismiss. He wasn't the best aesthetically, but he was certainly the best at preserving his wicket.'

Or, as John Lever puts it, 'With Boycs, you really had to get the bugger out.'

12

A Question of Captaincy

Tactically, few cricketers have been better equipped than Geoff Boycott for the role of captain. Temperamentally, few can have been less suited to the job. Because Boycott had relied on dedication rather than flair to reach the top, he had thought more analytically about the game than any of his Yorkshire or England contemporaries. From his earliest childhood days watching Ackworth, he had been fascinated by the study of techniques, bowling changes, field placings. Throughout his career, he kept a dossier on other professionals, with notes on their weaknesses and strengths. It is precisely because Boycott gave such thought to the mechanics and tactics of cricket that he was such a brilliant coach and became one of the game's finest commentators.

Where Boycott fell down was on the equally important man-management side. Wrapped up in his own game, he was unable to inspire and motivate his players. A captain has to put the needs of others before himself, but Boycott's own batting always came first. One of the reasons Brearley was so respected by the England team was that he never let his regular crises of personal form interfere with his leadership. The same was certainly not true of Boycott. Moreover, his sharp tongue, inability to trust, sense of insecurity and constant moodiness made it difficult for him to win the support of the players under his command. Like that other great batsman but unsuccessful captain, Wally Hammond, he tended to bark his orders, never recognizing that loyalty has to be earned rather than demanded.

Boycott was captain of Yorkshire for eight seasons, from 1971 to 1978, and the club did not win a single major trophy during that period. This was a sorry record for the greatest county cricket club in England, a club that had virtually monopolized the championship over the previous decade. Yet it would be wrong to heap all the blame for this decline on Boycott's shoulders. For the reality is that, compared to all his predecessors, Boycott had a dismally weak side under his command. The departure of players of the calibre of Brian Close, Ray Illingworth, Fred Trueman, Doug Padgett, Ken Taylor and Jimmy Binks (all capped by England) between 1968 and the end of 1971 had left the cupboard of talent pitifully bare. And this exodus had occurred while other counties were filling their ranks with overseas stars like Barry Richards (Hampshire), Asif Iqbal (Kent), Clive Lloyd (Lancashire), Graham MacKenzie (Leicestershire), Gary Sobers (Nottinghamshire), Majid Khan (Glamorgan) and Rohan Kanhai (Warwickshire). Such a cosmopolitan policy for Yorkshire was ruled out by the club's romantic but self-destructive insistence on sticking with home-grown talent. In these circumstances, even a combination of the vision of Winston Churchill, the wisdom of King Solomon and the cunning of Sherlock Holmes would have struggled to conjure a winning side. By the time Boycott took over, Yorkshire were already living on the faded glories of their past.

What made the task all the more difficult for Boycott in 1971 was that the atmosphere in the club had been poisoned by the sacking of Brian Close at the end of 1970. At the time of this decision, Yorkshire was run as an autocracy by its formidable chairman Brian Sellers, whose rule over the club stretched back to his captaincy in the 1930s. A tough disciplinarian who brooked no internal dissent, he was one of those frightening individuals whose bite was just as bad as his bark. When Illingworth had left in 1968 after the refusal of his request for a contract, Sellers, instead of looking rationally at the need for greater player security, said, 'He can fucking go and so can anyone else who wants to.' Two years later Sellers decided that Close, despite his excellent record, had to go because of his age and fitness – a piece of nonsense given that he was to play for England against the West Indies six years later – and his dislike of one-day cricket.

All hell broke loose once the news of the dismissal became public. An action group was formed by Yorkshire members to protest at the decision, a forerunner of the two campaigns on Boycott's behalf in 1978 and 1984 when his position was under threat. Within a year Sellers, worn down by the continuing divisions over his move, had resigned as chairman. Yet even with the author of this disaster gone, the reverberations of the Close affair continued to be felt throughout Boycott's career, manifested in growing distrust between the committee and the team, and between the committee and the members.

Before his sacking, Close had been of the opinion that he should be succeeded by Boycott, having been impressed by his willingness to study tactics. He felt, however, that Boycott would need several more years of grooming before he was ready for the role. Now, because of Close's premature departure, Boycott was thrust into captaincy. Not all of the committee had shared Close's opinion of Boycott's suitability. Several members preferred the more affable, less intense figure of Don Wilson. In fact the voting was six all, and was only decided by the casting vote of chairman Brian Sellers. The very fact that Boycott was so narrowly elected against Wilson only reinforced the sense of division within the club. Several of the members who had voted against him simply could not accept him in the role. Ted Lester, who as well as being Yorkshire's scorer during the seventies was also Boycott's confidant, told me, 'He never got the support he deserved from the committee. After the captaincy was decided on a casting vote, the half that didn't want him never wanted him. They were always angling to get rid of him. After one match-winning innings by Boycott I was speaking on the phone to one committee man to give him the result. "Who got the runs?" he asked. "Boycott," I replied. "I wish we'd lost," he replied. That was the kind of attitude Geoff had to put up with all the time.'

Because his career in the seventies was ultimately to be so blighted by rows over the captaincy, Boycott now says, in retrospect, that he wishes he had never taken the job. 'It would have been much easier for me to let others shoulder the responsibility of decision-making while I got on with the job of accumulating runs for Yorkshire and England. I wish I had had the foresight of Herbert Sutcliffe, who declined his invitation to captain the county in 1927,' he wrote in his 1990 book, *Boycott on Cricket*. But he was speaking there with hindsight, and in truth he had badly wanted the position since he was first involved in serious cricket. As early as 1963 he had told the Yorkshire secretary, John Nash, that his twin desires were to play for England and to captain Yorkshire. Boycott was in Australia in 1970 with the MCC side when he received the news of his promotion. His passion for the job shone through his comments to the *Yorkshire Post*, telling the paper that the Yorkshire captaincy was 'the greatest thing ever to happen to me. It has left me just speechless, shivering like a leaf.' But he also expressed confidence about the forthcoming season. 'Yorkshire is such a fine side that I think we should be up at the top in all competitions, one day and all.'

As events turned out, he could have hardly been further from the truth. Yorkshire, in *Wisden*'s bald statement, 'had the worst season in their history'. Finishing thirteenth in the county championship, they went seventeen matches without a win at one stage, the longest sequence without a victory the club had ever seen. Moreover, they were knocked out in the first round of the Gillette Cup and finished second from bottom in the John Player League.

In one respect, Boycott had an outstanding first season as captain. With the bat, he was in astonishingly prolific form, becoming the first Englishman to average over 100 in a season. In all matches that summer he scored 2503 runs at 100.12, with 13 hundreds, a record of consistency in post-war English cricket never achieved by any other player. As he had shown in Australia the previous winter, he was now the complete opening batsman, almost impossible to dismiss once set. Ted Lester, who as a player and then scorer had been involved in first-class cricket since 1945, says: 'Of all the players I've watched, I don't think anyone ever got themselves out less. He was outstanding on poorer pitches, the best I have seen at picking up the length and leaving the ball alone outside the off stump.' Amongst his many notable innings were a vast 233 against Essex at Colchester in six hours and 25 minutes, his second double hundred in a row against this county, and 182 not out on a turning pitch at Lord's. In the three Tests he played that summer, he continued where he had left off against Australia, scoring two more excellent hundreds. Of his 112 made at Lord's against a strong Pakistan attack – his third century in consecutive Tests – Ken Barrington wrote prophetically in the *Daily Mail*: 'Geoff Boycott is fast developing into England's greatest post-war batting star. Peter May, Colin Cowdrey, Tom Graveney and Ted Dexter have all scored more runs in Tests [Barrington modestly omitted himself] but if he keeps his form he will have outstripped them all by the end of his career.'

One of the members of that Pakistan side, Mushtaq Mohammad, is full of praise for Boycott's approach, as he told Richard Sydenham, author of a study of the great Test openers. 'He had such a tremendous temperament. The way he batted used to frustrate sides, and I can remember we gave him a lot of stick just because we couldn't get him out. We'd say, "Come on, you boring bastard, it's not a ten-day match." But he would absorb all the stick and just get on with his batting.'

Yet Boycott's triumphs, far from being lauded by colleagues, became another source of discontent. The fact that he had scored so heavily but his side had performed so badly was said to be proof that his run-glut had not been in the interests of Yorkshire. Once again, he was accused of batting too slowly, of putting the pressure on his colleagues through his prolonged occupation of the crease, of giving more priority to his average than to his team. One particular example of this selfishness was alleged to have occurred in the final game of the season against Northamptonshire at Harrogate, when he declared Yorkshire's innings closed with his own score on 124 not out, thereby ensuring that his average was above three figures. His critics on this occasion chose to ignore that Yorkshire actually won the match in two days by an innings, so the timing of Boycott's declaration could have only helped the result. The absence of championship bonus points for Yorkshire was said to provide further evidence of the damage caused by his flood of runs. Despite scoring over 300 runs in the first innings on nine occasions, only two other counties won fewer bonus points (awarded for every 25 runs over a total of 150 in the first 85 overs) than Yorkshire. At the annual dinner of Harrogate Cricket Club that winter, Fred Trueman launched a scathing attack on Boycott: 'It will never cease to amaze me that a man can average for the first time in history 100 in every innings he played, yet what did we get? Somewhere near the bottom in the batting points league. I think it is disgusting.' Again, though, the charge contained more invective than substance. As the *Yorkshire Evening Post*'s John Callaghan wrote, bonus points – one of those innovations brought in by the drive for 'brighter cricket' – had never been taken seriously by Yorkshire. So the club's 47 points in 1971 was actually only two behind the 1970 total of 49, and higher than in 1969 (30) and 1968 (46). Moreover, Boycott was absent with injuries or on Test duties for parts of the 1971 season and the side performed even worse without him around. When Don Wilson and Doug Padgett were acting as skippers, the side collected just three points from seven matches. In all but one of those fixtures, Yorkshire were bowled out for under 200 in their first innings, again emphasizing how much they relied on his batting.

But the very fact that such claims could be made about Boycott, even if they did not stand up to serious statistical analysis, shows how badly he was distrusted by his players. 'It didn't matter what the rest of us did; Geoff was only concerned with his own performance. It was no way to captain a side,' the late Tony Nicholson, the Yorkshire fast-medium bowler, once said. Andrew Dalton was another unimpressed with Boycott's captaincy. Hailing from Leeds grammar school and Newcastle University, Dalton had first played for Yorkshire in 1968 and was seen as an outstanding prospect, nicknamed by some 'the boy born to be king'. With two centuries in 1971, he had begun to fulfil his great promise, yet within a year he had left the club, disillusioned by its sour atmosphere. Highly intelligent and a successful businessman, he has never spoken publicly before now about his brief career under Boycott's leadership. 'Boycott had a thoughtful approach to captaincy,' Dalton told me, 'and managed his resources to reasonable effect when things were going well for him personally – that is, when he had scored a lot of runs. But I remember against Surrey in a John Player Sunday League match at the Oval, Boycott was out cheaply, came into the dressing room, put a towel on his head and sulked in a far corner, neither near the team nor near the cricket. I thought this was quite extraordinary for a captain, never mind a team member.' Dalton continues: 'My own feeling on the captaincy was that the job should have gone to Doug Padgett as a holding operation, allowing time for Richard Hutton or John Hampshire to come through. There were certainly other options than Boycott. He was not a natural leader and was never inspirational. Nor was he a team player. Everyone had problems with him because of what appeared to be his self-obsession. The team would have been much better off without him.'

Boycott's relationships with colleagues cannot have been helped by some of his more forthright comments to the press. As usual there was the problem of interpretation: what Boycott saw as honest plain-speaking, others regarded as insufferable arrogance. 'Jack Nicklaus and Tony Jacklin are great in their sphere. Men like Gary Sobers and myself have just as much class in ours,' he told the *Sunday Express* in July 1971, adding, 'I don't need people to tell me I'm a good player. I know I am.' Boycott had no time for those who said he was conceited: 'Why not be realistic? I don't agree with the public-school attitude of pretending that success is just a bit of good luck,' he explained to *Reveille*.

By far Boycott's greatest media controversy of the 1971 summer came in the aftermath of the Roses game at Old Trafford in May, just before the first Test against Pakistan. In an unfortunate sequence of events, Boycott, with characteristic maladroitness, managed to offend the Lancashire chairman and team, his own side, and the England chairman of selectors. His problems started on the Saturday evening of the game, when he complained to the press that Lancashire had deliberately bowled wide of the stumps to stop him scoring. Cedric Rhoades, the Lancashire chairman, angrily dismissed Boycott's allegations of unfair play and forced an apology from him.

The furore, splashed all over the Sunday papers, appeared to have a damaging physical effect on Boycott. On the final afternoon on Tuesday, when Yorkshire had been set 165 to win in three hours, Boycott declined to bat on the grounds of illness, reportedly suffering from 'nervous exhaustion'. After the match was drawn, Boycott retreated to his Fitzwilliam bed with some sleeping tablets.

Regrettably, he and Yorkshire had failed to keep England chairman Alec Bedser informed of his condition. Only when Bedser phoned Boycott's mother from a Droitwich hotel was he told that Boycott would be unable to play in the Test at Edgbaston. Understandably aggrieved at being kept in the dark, he became even more annoyed when, during the Test, Boycott rose Lazarus-like from his sick bed to hit 169 for Yorkshire against Nottinghamshire at Leeds.

Boycott's strongest internal critics were the triumvirate of Don Wilson, Phil Sharpe and Richard Hutton. Now, all three might be said to have been motivated by jealousy for each had a reasonable claim on the captaincy, but Wilson argues that the real cause of the difficulties was Boycott's attitude. 'Tactically, Geoff knows about the game, my goodness he knows it – as proved by his commentary, which is very good. And even though I don't like him, I would never deny that he was a great player, a truly great player. The trouble was that if he hadn't scored a hundred, he really couldn't give a damn. There were times when we were like a yacht without a rudder because he was thinking about his own game. There was a terrible atmosphere in the dressing room. He never thought of anybody but himself.'

Wilson's role as vice-captain was made all the more difficult by his own catastrophic loss of form following the MCC tour to Australia where he had done little but net bowling. 'Basically, I'd got the yips. I could barely even mark out my run. I can tell you that the 1971 season was probably the most miserable I ever had in cricket, absolutely dreadful. But because Geoff was such an incredible perfectionist, he had no time for anybody who lost their form. There was one situation against Warwickshire at Birmingham where I bowled a full-toss to Alvin Kallicharran who hit it for six. Boycott was furious and made his anger obvious – really, that broke my heart.'

On the surface, the 1972 season saw some improvement in Yorkshire's fortunes. In the county championship they moved up from thirteenth to tenth place. The newly established Benson and Hedges Cup welcomed them to Lord's as finalists, while they also reached fourth place in the John Player League. Boycott's own domestic form for Yorkshire was as good as ever: he topped the national averages with 1230 at 72.35. But he missed a good part of the season after breaking his finger in the first round of the Gillette Cup against Warwickshire. As a result of this injury, his appearances in the Ashes series were limited to just the first two Tests, where he failed to reach 50 in any of his four innings. In fact, Boycott looked extremely uncomfortable against the raw pace of Australia's new bowling hero, Dennis Lillee, enjoying his first full Anglo-Australian series. In the second innings of England's defeat at Lord's, Boycott was dismissed by Lillee in a bizarre fashion, as he allowed a short ball to fly straight into his ribcage rather than swaying out of the way of it. The ball then bounced off his padding, lobbed over his shoulder and dropped behind him on to the off-bail.

Despite slightly better results, Yorkshire remained a place of strife. Andrew Dalton, confirming his talent with a match-winning performance against Middlesex, was by now so frustrated that he decided to quit the game despite the pleas of committee men. 'I resigned from Yorkshire primarily because there was such an unpleasant atmosphere in the dressing room. In my letter of resignation I said that the relationships between the captain and the senior professionals were too poor to induce me to keep playing. Boycott then asked me to retract what I had written. I replied: "No, because that is my judgement about the team. Look, I have nothing personal against you and I will not be going to the press about this." I also told him that he was a half decent captain and could go on to be a better one but I would not withdraw my judgement.'

During the season Boycott even fell out briefly with his most loyal supporter, Ted Lester, after a row at Chelmsford in the match against Essex. 'He had just been invited to go to India as vice-captain on the MCC tour. He didn't know what to do, whether to go or not. The game progressed, but he just wasn't interested. Eventually, Tony Nicholson and John Hampshire forced him to make a declaration because it was getting so silly.' The total looked impossible for Essex, but, according to Lester, Boycott completely lost control in the field because he was so distracted, enabling Essex to savage the Yorkshire attack with impunity in their successful run-chase. 'We got back into the dressing room and Boycs said, "I am never going to declare again." He was absolutely livid. And then I said to him, "Well, you lost the game by the way you captained the side." That did it. He really went off the rails then, swearing and shouting. For a few days after that, we were not on speaking terms. It was one of the few occasions that he lost control.'

Boycott's dilemma over the 1972/73 tour to India and Pakistan, led by Glamorgan captain Tony Lewis, was understandable. On one hand, the offer of the vice-captaincy could put him in line for the England leadership, the role he now wanted almost as much as the Yorkshire job. On the other, he had his usual concerns over health arising from his lack of a spleen – as we have seen, he had been extremely ill in Ceylon on the way out to Australia in 1965/66. In a subsequent discussion with Lord's, Boycott sought a guarantee that he would be flown back to England in the event of his needing any medical treatment. When the MCC felt unable to give this blanket commitment, he turned down a touring place.

Now, there was nothing unusual in a Test star rejecting a tour of the sub-continent. Along with Boycott, Ray Illingworth, John Snow and John Edrich did so in 1972/73, as did Ian Botham twelve years later. In the past, Test greats like Jack Hobbs, Peter May, Jim Laker, Fred Trueman, Trevor Bailey and Alec Bedser had all avoided going on England duty in India. But Boycott always had a unique gift for attracting controversy and soon his decision was whipping up another media storm. Boycott's central mistake was not to be frank about his health worries. Instead, he issued a bland public statement explaining that he had declined the tour invitation for 'personal and domestic reasons'. This fed speculation that his decision had been motivated by resentment against Tony Lewis's appointment. He then gave more ammunition to his detractors by going on a coaching holiday to South Africa. So fierce did the criticism become that Boycott was compelled to provide a public explanation of his spleen problem. From reticence on the subject, he now went to the other extreme, giving a bulletin filled with gruesome details about anthrax, typhoid and cholera.

This plunge into medical analysis did him little good with the England team, who felt he had let them down. There were mutterings about his 'picking and choosing' his England tours, while on the team coach the players came up with new lyrics to the old song, 'She'll be coming round the mountain when she comes . . .' The opening line went 'You can stick your Geoffrey Boycott up your . . .' Yet, beyond the abuse, the desire to have Boycott in the ranks was a reflection of his importance to England. Tony Lewis says: 'There is no doubt that, with him, we would have won the series. We were bowled out for 163 in the second Test on a real shirt-front when set only 191 to win. Boycs would have got us through that.'

Boycott remained equally unpopular with many of his Yorkshire team-mates. At the end of the 1972 season, he had an explosive row with Don Wilson in a Southampton hotel. 'I just blew my top at him, really tore into him. I was drunk, admittedly, and there were quite a few heated words. Our relationship couldn't sink much lower,' says Wilson.

All might have been forgiven in Yorkshire if Boycott had commanded a winning side. Just the opposite was true. It might have seemed that, after the 1971 season, it would have been impossible for Yorkshire to sink any further, but they managed it in 1973. In what *Wisden* called 'a disturbingly unsuccessful season', the club finished in fourteenth place in the county championship, the lowest position in their history, and went nowhere in the Benson and Hedges Cup. Most shamefully of all, they were knocked out in the first round of the Gillette Cup by Durham, the first ever defeat of a major county by a minor in the competition. With the bat, Boycott was his usual masterful self, finishing second in the national averages with 1527 at 63.62. Yet his detractors pointed out that Yorkshire did not win a single championship game under his leadership, while three victories were secured by acting captain Phil Sharpe when Boycott was away on Test duty.

In any troubled institution, the man in charge has to take the flak. By mid-1973, the chorus of disapproval was growing louder. Fred Trueman, who had quickly become one of Boycott's most bitter critics, told the *Sunday People*: 'To be honest, I think he has had long enough in charge to prove whether he can do the job or not – and for me it is his only failure in a brilliant career. The time has now come to find another man capable of doing the job.' Other Yorkshire greats, like Len Hutton and Herbert Sutcliffe, took to the press to express their doubts. It seemed that, unless there was some radical change, Boycott's days as captain might be numbered. Meanwhile, over his Test career, even darker clouds were now gathering.

13

'The Worst Win for English Cricket'

By the start of the 1973 season, Boycott was acknowledged to be England's finest batsman. He had played in 51 Tests, scored 3620 runs and 10 centuries at an average of 47.63 per innings. Interestingly, this figure is almost exactly the same as his final Test career average, 47.73, which shows how consistent Boycott was throughout his 18 years in international cricket.

Boycott was as solid as ever in the Test matches of 1973, averaging 64 against New Zealand and 50 against the West Indies. But, as usual, controversy was drawn to him like a moth to a flame. The summer was barely under way when he landed in trouble during the Test trial match at Hove in May (MCC Tourists v. The Rest). Already in bad odour because of his withdrawal from the Indian tour, he caused more anger by running out David Lloyd for nought in the Rest's second innings. In one of those mental aberrations that plagued his career, he hit the ball straight to mid-off, said, 'No,' then ran past Lloyd and dived in. What made it all the worse was that he 'retired hurt' just 15 minutes later with a supposed leg strain, walked briskly from the field, then travelled up to Hull where he was fit enough to play for Yorkshire against Nottinghamshire the next morning in the Benson and Hedges Cup.

The young Lancashire batsman Frank Hayes, who was playing with Boycott for the first time, recalls, 'Poor Lloydie was on a pair, and for Boycott to run him out like that after saying no was just dreadful. But there was something even more personal that happened to me. When we were in the field I dropped Graham Roope – Boycs knew that I usually had a good pair of hands – and Roopie went on to get a hundred. The next day, Boycs had pinned a press cutting against my place in the dressing room, a cutting which mentioned my dropped catch. I was so upset I said to Boycs, "What have you done that for?" And he replied, "You've just got him in the Test side and he's not a fookin' player's arse." I'll always remember those words. No other professional would dream of doing something like that. That was Boycs. He messed so many players up. Most people who played with him thought the guy was a pillock, never gave a damn about anyone else; that's the view of him from his fellow professionals.' Another young uncapped player, Bob Woolmer, was on the receiving end of Boycott's pepperiness. When he was lying in the bath with Boycott after the game, he had the temerity to say that Kent felt Boycott had a weakness playing down the leg-side. 'It was either a very brave or very naïve statement. For the next few minutes I was gasping for breath under water,' Woolmer wrote later.

Despite being described privately as 'not a player's arse', Graham Roope was to experience a different side of Boycott when they played together for the first time in the Trent Bridge Test against New Zealand a fortnight later. Once again, we see Boycott's contradictory nature, boorish one day, charming the next. In the nets on the eve of the Test, Boycott asked Roope to bowl his inswingers at him, in order to be fully prepared for the type of attack favoured by New Zealand's Bruce Taylor. Then Boycott offered to return the favour by bowling at Roope. 'I remember Illy saying, "He won't be bowling to you. He'll be off, back to the dressing room." Anyway, I got my pads on, returned, and Boycs was still there. He looked up, "Are you ready?" "Yep." He turned his cap on back to front and he bowled at me for twenty minutes. Illy and the rest were absolutely speechless. When I came out of the net, Ray said to me, "I've played with bugger for years and he's never bowled a single ball to me in the nets, not one."'

England won the first Test narrowly by just 38 runs, after New Zealand made a heroic effort to reach their target of 479. Opening with Dennis Amiss for the first time, Boycott scored only his second half-century against New Zealand as they put on a stand of 92 on the first day. In England's second innings, Boycott, the specialist at running out his partners, was appalled to find himself on the receiving end of a mix-up and was dismissed for one. When Dennis Amiss later reached his century, Boycott stood up and told the England dressing room, 'The bastard's taken all my runs.' Amiss recalls: 'He was obviously upset about it. He threatened to run me out in the next Test match. So I had to go to Ray Illingworth our captain and say, "You've got to sort this out. Boycs seems to think I'd done it on purpose but it was just one of those things." Ray called us together after the dinner at the next Test, took us outside. Ray handled it superbly. After Boycs had been going on a bit, Ray turned to him and said, "Hang on, it's just bad luck. Dennis has apologized. Now, you stay here and sort this out, otherwise you'll never play for England again while I'm captain." I liked Ray for that. Here he was, telling a Yorkshireman that there were other people just as important in the team. Though the row was settled, we weren't likely to be the best of friends immediately after that. I rang him up a few weeks later and his mother answered the phone. "Can I speak to Geoff?" I asked.

'"I'll just get him. Who's calling?"

'"Dennis Amiss."

'"He's not in," she replied, and put the phone down.'

Boycott and Amiss operated well enough to put on 112 in the second innings against New Zealand at Lord's, with Boycott eventually hitting an excellent 92, following a first innings knock of 61 made in awkward, seaming conditions. The match ended in a tense draw, thanks to Keith Fletcher's 178. In the final Test of the series at Leeds, Boycott's 115 on a rain-affected pitch showed great skill and ensured an England win by an innings.

The other visitors that summer were the West Indies. Under Rohan Kanhai, they were showing the first signs of that extraordinary depth in talent which would, by the end of the decade, turn them into perhaps the strongest Test side cricket has ever seen. Facing an attack of Bernard Julien, Keith Boyce, Gary Sobers, Vanburn Holder and Lance Gibbs, England were utterly outclassed and beaten 2–0, though Boycott performed creditably, scoring 97 in the first Test – amazingly, for a man who regarded a century as more valuable than a De Beer diamond, he walked after snicking Julien to the keeper – and 56 not out in the second Test.

The defeat at the final Test at Lord's by an innings and 226 runs, the second heaviest loss in England's history, was both a forewarning of things to come and the death knell of Illingworth's four-year reign as England captain. This last Test was filled with controversy, an IRA bomb scare, crowd trouble and Boycott's truculence serving as the combustible ingredients. On the Saturday afternoon, the packed stands of Lord's had to be cleared after an IRA telephone warning that a bomb had been planted on the ground. No device was found and the 90-minute interruption did nothing to impede the West Indies' rapid progress to a mammoth victory. After making 652 for 8 declared, they bowled out England for just 233, forcing the home side to follow on. Boycott was out in a worrying fashion in the first innings, when on just four he tried to hook a short ball outside the off-stump from Vanburn Holder and was caught at slip. It was the beginning of a difficult period for Boycott against the short ball, as his normally rigorous mind was assailed with confusion as to whether he should hook, duck or sway.

The bouncer problem soon cropped up again in the second innings. There were 85 minutes remaining on the third day when openers Boycott and Amiss had to go out a second time, with England still 419 runs behind. Amiss fell quickly to the pace of Keith Boyce, as did nightwatchman Alan Knott. Brian Luckhurst then joined Boycott for the remaining few overs. All appeared to go steadily until the last over of the day, bowled by Keith Boyce. The first ball was a bouncer, which Boycott hooked down to fine leg but the batsmen did not take a single. Then, off the very last ball of the day, Boycott hooked again, but this time in the air and straight into Kallicharran's hands at square leg. For a batsman who had become a byword for caution, it was, in the words of Crawford White of the *Daily Express*, 'an astonishingly irresponsible shot'. Neither the spectators nor the England dressing room could quite believe it. Caribbean supporters went wild with delight and Boycott was badly manhandled by the invading crowd as he walked from the field. One man even briefly had him in a stranglehold before he struggled free.

The ugly scenes only deepened Boycott's already foul temper, which he blamed for his reckless dismissal. In his *Autobiography*, he explains that he had batted so horribly out of character in the last over because of his fury at the actions of his partner, Brian Luckhurst. He says that Luckhurst, on his arrival at the crease, asked Boycott to take as much of the bowling as possible. Then, in

A proud fourteen-year-old with the first of many trophies.
The lopsided grin and the immaculate dress sense are already evident.

Already surrounded by Yorkshire admirers, the young Geoffrey Boycott demonstrates how to play the game. Courtesy George Hepworth

'I owe it all to Mum.' Boycott tries on his MCC blazer before his first overseas tour, to South Africa in 1964/65. Express Newspapers

Boycott's home, 45 Milton Terrace, Fitzwilliam, where he lived with his mother until her death in 1978. Yorkshire Post

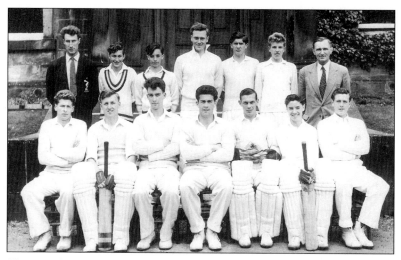

Hemsworth Grammar School XI. Boycott is on the front row, extreme right of the picture; his friend Terry McCroakham is sitting two places away from him, wearing wicketkeeper's gloves. Boycott's headmaster Russell Hamilton is directly behind him – the other teacher is Les Tate. Courtesy George Hepworth

Ackworth Cricket Club, 1956. Sitting at front, fifteen-year-old Boycott adopts an unusually informal pose. Also in the picture are George Hepworth (*middle row, second from right*) and Geoffrey's uncle, Algy Speight (*in white cap at back*). Courtesy George Hepworth

Bowling in the nets, 1967.

One of the finest one-day innings ever played: Boycott's 146 in the Gillette Cup Final, Yorkshire v. Surrey, 1965.

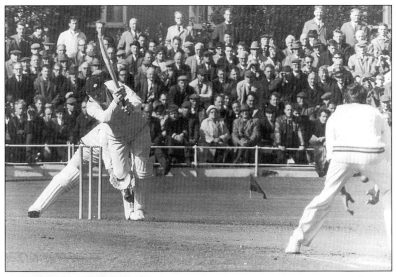

Boycott punches through the leg-side, Yorkshire v. Gloucestershire, Harrogate, 1967. PA News

The Buddy Holly look, 1968. Hawke to Hutton

Boycott plays a straight bat to Australia's Graham McKenzie on his Test début, England v. Australia, Trent Bridge, 1964. © Hulton Getty

The captain: of Yorkshire in 1971 (*above*) and England in 1978 (*below*).

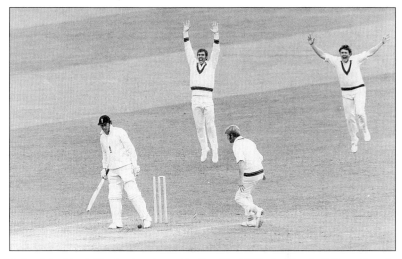

A freak incident, England v. Australia, Lord's, 1972. A rising ball from Dennis Lillee hit Boycott, dropped behind him, and then rolled on to the off-stump, just hard enough to dislodge the bail. PA News

Boycott acknowledges the applause for his hundredth Test as he walks out to open the innings with Graham Gooch, England v. Australia, Lord's, 1981. Patrick Eagar

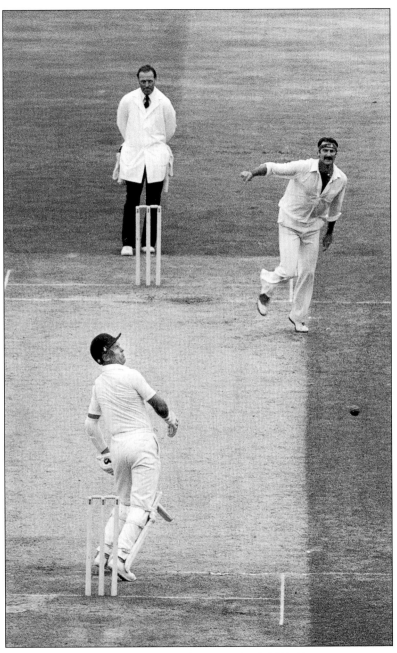

Still foes in middle age. Boycott v. Lillee, The Oval, 1981. Boycott went on to score a century. Patrick Eagar

the last over of the day, Luckhurst allegedly refused an 'obvious and easy single' when Boycott hooked safely down to square leg. That would have given Luckhurst the strike for the remainder of the over. Boycott says he was so enraged that when Boyce delivered the next bouncer he lashed out at it. 'It was the only time I have ever surrendered my wicket through pure hot-headedness and I was sure Luckhurst had done as much to get me out as the West Indies had.'

That is Boycott's record of events of this notorious episode. Brian Luckhurst remembers it differently, and his version shows how badly cricketers can misunderstand each other out in the middle. Speaking for the first time about that Saturday evening, he told me: 'There was only one over left, and it was to be bowled by Keith Boyce. I walked down the wicket and said to Geoffrey, "You've been batting all evening. Do you fancy taking the last over?" And Geoffrey said, no, he didn't. So I said, "Fine." Very first ball of the over, he hooked magnificently down to fine leg. I started to run but then Geoffrey gave me the command to stay. He had obviously changed his mind. He played the next four. The last ball Boycott hooked and Kallicharran had him. I waited to go off with him and as he passed me he said, "Are you happy now?" And he never spoke to me from that day until I went to Leeds in 1974 to captain Kent against Yorkshire.'

What Luckhurst understandably resents is the accusation that he was a coward and deliberately refused a single to avoid the strike. 'He definitely gave me the signal not to run after he hooked that ball. Unfortunately this gesture was never captured on film by BBC TV because the camera obviously followed the ball down to square leg. I might have had a number of weaknesses as a player but being a coward was not one of them.' So it seems that this incident arose from two misunderstandings. First, Luckhurst's question, 'Do you fancy taking the last over?' which was meant as a genuine, sympathetic inquiry, may have been interpreted by Boycott as a display of his partner's reluctance to face the bowling. Second, there was the mix-up over the signals and running, always an occupational hazard with Boycott at the crease.

That was not the end of the matter. At three o'clock on Sunday morning, Boycott was taken to hospital with a nosebleed so severe that it needed cauterization by casualty doctors. The cause of the haemorrhage was almost certainly stress. But the hospital visit inevitably started rumours that punches had been thrown by Illingworth at Boycott in the dressing-room quarrel. 'Shut your mouth or I'll shut it for you,' Illingworth is supposed to have said. There is no truth in this story. Not only is it denied by Boycott, and Illingworth, but also every England player I have interviewed who played in that game (Luckhurst, Amiss, Hayes, Fletcher, Greig, Arnold and Underwood) has dismissed it as a myth. 'It's garbage. It just didn't happen. And I would have known about it if it had,' says Tony Greig with his usual frankness.

Boycott's indignation at the end of this disastrous series was worsened by the news that the Kent captain Mike Denness was to replace Illingworth as England skipper on the MCC tour to the West Indies in 1973/74. Given that he was England's most experienced cricketer and a seasoned county leader, Boycott had good reason for thinking that he should have been appointed instead of Denness, who had not even been considered good enough for a place in the side against the West Indies. Moreover, though Denness had a successful record at Kent, he had a far stronger team under his command than Boycott had in Yorkshire. And other cricketers had doubts about Denness. His county colleague Bob Woolmer said that 'When he put you on to bowl, he seemed to have no clear idea what he wanted from you.' Boycott's rejection only strengthened the view that he was the victim of a privileged Home Counties cricket establishment, 'the purblind mandarins of Lord's', in the words of his old Barnsley team-mate Michael Parkinson. Once, in a rage, Boycott told his friend the journalist Ian Wooldridge that 'a bunch of southern public-school smoothies are determined that no miner's son from Yorkshire will captain England,' though this is just a tiresome piece of inverted snobbery of the kind in which Yorkshiremen love to indulge. After all, Denness's predecessor Illingworth was hardly a public-school type, while Denness himself was a Scot.

Tony Lewis had been the first choice as Illingworth's successor, having been deemed to have done a good job on the India tour. But persistent injuries during 1973 led to his retirement from the game at the end of the season. As chairman of selectors Alec Bedser later admitted, if Boycott had gone to India as vice-captain under Tony Lewis, he would have then probably become captain of the

1973/74 tour to the Caribbean. There were other, wider doubts about Boycott, including his poor record over three seasons with Yorkshire, his awkward relationships with his colleagues, and his volatility, demonstrated not just in the recent Luckhurst row but in a large number of incidents, like the run-out dispute in Australia in 1970/71.

It was only with some reluctance that Boycott went to the West Indies under Denness. Even before the party had left, he had made clear his unwillingness to co-operate with the new skipper, as Mike Denness explained to me: 'I knew that Boycs loved his nets so I wrote to him asking if he would be willing to organize the net practices on tour. He wrote back a totally negative response, saying he wouldn't do it, it wasn't his responsibility as he wasn't captain or vice-captain. So that hardly got things off to a good start. I thought to myself, This is going to be a hard man to deal with because already he has said in black and white that he doesn't want to be any assistance at all.'

Mike Denness speaks frankly about his opinion of Boycott on this trip, saying he was 'difficult' throughout. 'I had almost every player at some stage of the tour come and make the suggestion to me that we send Boycott home. There was a feeling that he generally didn't want to have anything to do with the rest of us. On a number of occasions I went knocking on his door to sit down and have a chat with him in the evening but he was always "far too busy". As the senior man, he never contributed anything. At meetings, when asked a question, he would say, "I just want to hear what the captain has to say." I had a feeling that he was constantly undermining me.'

Given this glaring lack of support, Denness was surprised that Boycott agreed to serve on the tour selection panel along with Tony Greig and Donald Carr, the manager. It was at one of their meetings, when they were discussing team selection, that Denness had a disturbing insight into the turmoil of Boycott's mind. Denness had asked Greig for his opinion, then turned to Boycott: 'He just laid into Greigy, saying, "They always ask you first. I've read all the articles you've written about me. Anne's coming out to Barbados and she's bringing the scrapbook with all the comments you've made. Nobody ever thinks about me." Tears were pouring down his eyes. He seemed so depressed. And I said, "Come on, all we're doing is picking teams here. Now cut all of that out and let's concentrate." Donald Carr didn't say anything. He was taken aback by this exhibition. But I kept thinking, Why is Boycs behaving like this? Is it because he isn't getting the attention, he isn't having the success? What's the reason for it? He was certainly a very complex man. There was a lot of insecurity about him. Yes, he would keep telling you what he had done, how he was "good enough for a hundred any day", but all that could be a front for his lack of confidence.'

Tony Greig also recalls the temperamental side of Boycott: 'On that tour, he really had his nose put out of joint. All he wanted to do at that stage was to captain England. He didn't like Denness at all and he was being on the whole, I thought, a very negative influence on the team. I confronted him and said, "Look, can I help? You're obviously unhappy and you're upsetting other people." He just grunted and then I gave it to him. The guy broke down. He was obviously at the end of his tether. The exchange caused a rift between us and we didn't say much for a week.' Fortunately Anne Wyatt and Greig's wife arranged for the four of them to get together over dinner and amicability was restored. 'Actually I felt sorry for him and I tried to go in to bat for him with the rest of the management team. I told them that he was England's best batsman and they had to try to accommodate him by, say, organizing for him to have better net practice so he felt more comfortable.'

For all his personal troubles, Boycott remained the epitome of dedication, thinking about his cricket all the time. Frank Hayes roomed with him for three weeks in Jamaica on tour. 'He was a loner, suited himself in what he did. He didn't come to the functions where we were meant to fly the flag. One night I came back to the hotel from an event at the British High Commission, planning to change from my corporate uniform into a T-shirt, then have a few beers and a meal at the bar. I went into the room and there was Boycs, practising in front of the mirror, back and across, or playing the forward defensive.

'"I have found the secret for you and I," he said.

'"How do you mean?" I said, changing into my T-shirt.

'"The wickets here, lad, they skid, skid and bounce. Back in Lancashire and Yorkshire, the short one has a bounce like a tennis ball so it gets up here, and both of us can hook." He had actually been working it all out while I was at the function. And I said, "Boycs, I'm putting my T-shirt on, I'm going downstairs, having a beer and a meal. You suit yourself but I've had enough of all that, seriously, and I don't need it." Off I went. It is a very true story and it shows that Boycs and I were like chalk and cheese. I wanted to see the world while he was focused only on his game. I must admit, though, if I'd had his dedication and application, I would have been a better player. But I didn't. I had other things to do.'

Boycott made a flying start in the MCC's first game, hitting the largest score of his career, 261 not out against the President's XI. But once the first Test began, he was again quickly in trouble against the West Indian pace attack of Boyce and Julien. For the third time in successive Test innings, he was dismissed cheaply, trying to hook the bouncer. His downfall heralded an England collapse to 131 all out, to which the West Indians replied with 392. England, facing a deficit of 261, made a tremendous start to their second innings, thanks to a 209 opening stand between Amiss and Boycott. After his initial difficulties with Boycott in the previous summer, Amiss was now feeling more at ease with him. 'We began to work well on that tour. Once he had accepted me, seen me scoring runs, it was good to bat with him. Communication was much better than it had been. We were always telling each other, "Keep going, see off the new ball, get them tired, just don't get out." Though he had his problems on that tour, it still gave you real confidence to have him at the other end because he was such a great player.'

The efforts of Boycott (93) and Amiss (174) were to no avail as England's middle order fell apart and the West Indies won the first Test by seven wickets. It seemed that England were again heading for certain defeat in the second Test at Jamaica as well, when at 271 for 7 in their second innings on the last day, they were only 41 ahead. But then came one of the great Test escapes. The tail rallied around Dennis Amiss as he piled up a monumental 262 not out to see England through to an improbable draw.

Though Boycott had scored 68 in the first innings at Jamaica, in the third Test it was agreed to drop him down the order to number four. The aim was both to strengthen the middle order and to protect him from the new ball, against which he had looked vulnerable at times during the previous five West Indian Tests. Boycott disliked the move. He found the anxiety of waiting his turn almost unbearable and was dismissed for just 10 and 13. Tony Greig has this description of Boycott down the order: 'Out of sheer habit, he padded up from the start and wandered around the dressing room fully prepared to bat, though that did not eventuate until the mid-afternoon. He was like a caged lion, muttering and chatting to himself just to relieve the tension.'

England scraped another draw in the third Test, thanks to a fighting century by Greig, and then saw the fourth Test almost washed out by rain, though not before Boycott had failed for the fourth innings in a row. His disillusion is reflected in a letter he wrote to Ted Lester back in Yorkshire: 'This tour has been one hell of an event. I will be glad to get back to my own team. I am disappointed about my Test scores but I feel I have not really played badly – just somehow the scores have eluded me. Two injuries at the wrong time in Jamaica upset my rhythm, confidence and practice. Since then I have not really found my touch and the disorganization has not helped.'

Despite being completely outclassed and without their best batsman on good form, the tourists had managed to reach the final Test at Trinidad just 1–0 down. Now there was to be a dramatic change in fortunes for England and Boycott. Batting first, England made 267, thanks largely to a superb defensive knock of 99 by Boycott. He should have been out when he was just nine due to a mix-up in the running but he was desperately unlucky to fall just one short of his century when a diving Murray caught him down the leg-side. The West Indies looked to be cruising to a decisive first innings lead at 208 for 2 but then Tony Greig, bowling his off-spinners, took five wickets in 20 balls. His final figures were 8 for 86 as the West Indies gained a lead of just 38. England were soon in trouble again at 44 for 2, Denness the victim of a dreadful run-out by Boycott. Denness had almost completed a straightforward single when Boycott, at the striker's end, sent him back. 'I covered a hell of a distance to be out by about a yard, almost twice the length of the pitch. I don't know whether it was deliberate or not but, to tell you the truth, it just didn't make sense. He showed no emotion whatsoever.'

Fortunately for England, Boycott held the innings together with another fine defensive century before being bowled by Gibbs for 112 with an extravagantly turning off-break. England had set the West Indies a respectable target of 226. At 63 for no wicket, victory looked assured for the home side but then Tony Greig ripped through the middle-order again with 5 for 70. England came away winners by just 26 runs and, against all the odds, had drawn the series. With 13 wickets Greig received most of the plaudits, though he was quick to stress that without Boycott's runs he would have had nothing to bowl at.

Boycott had mixed emotions at this result. He might have played two of his greatest match-winning innings for England, but in doing so he had almost certainly enabled Denness to retain the captaincy. Before the last Test, the press had predicted that Denness was a certainty for the sack. Now he could go home with an unbeaten record. As he stood at the presentation ceremony, Boycott turned to Bernard Thomas, the physiotherapist, standing beside him: 'Bernard, that's buggered my chances of the England job.'

And Boycott was never afraid to say to someone's face what he was thinking. As Mike Denness went round the dressing room congratulating his team on its remarkable triumph, he reached the unsmiling figure of Boycott. 'Unfortunately, that is the worst win we could have had for English cricket,' were Boycott's words.

It was to be four years before he would tour for England again. Ironically, he would end up as captain on that next trip.

14

'I Just Want to Play for Yorkshire'

Throughout the years of 1974 to 1977, when Boycott went into voluntary exile from Test cricket, he received continual requests to come back to the international stage where he belonged. Like some talented but capricious Hollywood actor who suddenly refuses to make another movie, he had a stream of supplicants at his door, begging him to parade his skills before the public. Yet all such clandestine manoeuvres came to nothing.

It is a tribute both to Boycott's own stature as a batsman and Alec Bedser's patience as chairman of selectors that he was able to return in 1977 without any blemish on his record. Throughout Boycott's exile, it was regularly said that he had 'played his last game for England', yet Bedser had never viewed it that way. In his book *Twin Ambitions* Bedser wrote that he always tried to 'make allowances for what I believe at bedrock to be a sensitive nature longing to be liked. Without exception every selection committee I served on appreciated the strains and pressures his application and style imposed upon him to maintain his performances.' Bedser may have had this understanding with Boycott because he, too, was from a working-class background, had left school early to earn his living in a mundane office job and had risen to the top through sheer dedication. It would be hard to find someone further removed from the northern imagery of a gin-soaked, public-school clique running the England team.

There was a variety of reasons for the start of Boycott's exile: concerns about the Yorkshire captaincy; resentment at Denness being promoted above him; a worrying decline in form; the work-load of his benefit year; and sheer exhaustion after playing Test cricket for a decade. But the roots of all these causes lay in Boycott's temperamental character. While his excessive pride fuelled his resentment at not gaining the England post, his insecurity heightened his fear of failure when his touch briefly deserted him. At the very moment when he most needed the support of colleagues, his aloofness and inability to stop worrying only furthered his distance from the team. As John Hampshire later wrote of the 1974 season: 'If Geoff had just been able to join in our off-duty relaxations or even in the dressing-room leg-pulling as one of us, then it would have gone a long, long way towards easing the tensions which crept into our lives. But he couldn't. He was completely absorbed in cricket during every waking moment.'

Boycott returned from the Caribbean in a mood of disillusionment with the England set-up, a mood that worsened with confirmation that Denness was to remain as England captain for the three-Test series against India. In addition, there was more trouble brewing at Yorkshire. The sniping about his captaincy continued from the old guard of Sharpe, Wilson and Hutton and several of the committee men. The organization of his benefit was soon in difficulties, when the expert fund-raiser Roy Parsons – a local businessman who had raised over £120,000 for Yorkshire players over the previous fourteen years – walked out, citing 'differences of opinion with Boycott'. Angered at what he saw as the interference of Boycott's friends, Parsons told the press: 'I don't want to be caught between two or three stools and made to look a fool.' Fortunately for Boycott, the disagreement was soon settled and Parsons returned, but the brief row was another burden on Boycott's already anxious mind.

His own form for the county had dipped alarmingly at the beginning of the season. Apart from a century against Cambridge University, he scored only 75 runs in his first seven first-class innings. Then in the Roses match at Headingley at the end of May, he was the cause of more discontent at the club, with even the chairman John Temple expressing public concern. Set a target by Lancashire of 244 runs in 210 minutes, Yorkshire, following Boycott's lead, refused to chase the runs and instead settled for a tame draw. According to the *Daily Mail* he drove the Leeds crowd to 'distraction and desertion with his morbid innings of 79'.

In the next first-class game, the Test trial at Worcester, he seemed to have battled himself back into the runs with a century in each innings. The veneer of cockiness returned, and he told local reporters, 'If I played at Worcester every week, number four would have to go to t' pictures on Saturday afternoons.' But hopes of a more permanent revival were quickly snuffed out by a totally unexpected force, the medium-pace bowling of Indian tourist Eknath Solkar. Over his long career, Boycott played heroically against some of the greatest bowlers cricket has seen, among them Dennis Lillee, Peter Pollock, Michael Holding and Kapil Dev. Solkar, with his modest left-arm seamers, was nowhere near that standard. More of a batsman than a bowler, in his entire Test career he took just 18 wickets at 59.44. Yet in the summer of 1974 he was to be Boycott's nemesis, dismissing him cheaply four times in six successive innings. Their first meeting, Yorkshire versus the Indians, saw Solkar trap Boycott lbw for 14. Then at Lord's in the MCC game, he had Boycott twice caught at slip for 12 and 1.

The final humiliation for Boycott came in the first Test at Old Trafford. He was dismissed on the first morning for 10 by Abid Ali, almost as innocuous a medium-pacer as Solkar. Soon after he and Amiss had arrived at the wicket for England's second innings on Saturday evening, he was out to Solkar yet again, this time caught behind by Engineer for six. It would be another thirty matches before he would wear an England cap again.

Boycott has always dismissed the suggestion that Solkar had any sort of hypnotic influence on him, arguing that his batting troubles against India were entirely the result of his own poor form and concerns about Yorkshire. Indeed, he regards as a myth the widely held belief that he had a weakness against left-arm seam bowling, pointing out that, during his long Test career, he performed well against the likes of Liaqat Ali, Geoff Dymock, Bernard Julien and Trevor Goddard. And it is true, as the statistical appendix to this book shows, that no single bowler, not even Gary Sobers, had a special hold over Boycott. Nevertheless, many who played with Boycott feel that left-armers exposed the only real flaw in his technique. The cause, they believe, was his classical side-on orthodoxy, which meant that he did not always open his stance enough for the change in line. Alan Butcher, who used to bowl occasionally left-arm seam-up for Surrey, told me, 'I always fancied my chances against him because I knew of his problems against my type. Because he did not fully adjust his stance or pick-up, he could end up playing across the line.' John Lever, probably the best exponent of this type of bowling England has produced since the Second World War, thinks the explanation is simpler. 'His whole approach was based on practice, on working out his game in the nets. But there are not a lot of left-armers around, you just don't see them. So he probably never got the practice that he wanted against my type.'

Whatever Boycott's record against left-armers, his dismissal by Solkar at Old Trafford – Solkar's only wicket of the entire series – plunged Boycott into a new pit of despondency. Weighed down by all his recent anxieties at Yorkshire and filled with contempt for Denness's England leadership, he sought out Alec Bedser to tell him that he was 'in no mental or emotional condition to play well for England'. Mike Denness vividly recalls speaking to Bedser shortly after this conversation: 'Alec came to see me and said, "He's just told me that he doesn't want to play Test cricket any more."

'"Well, Alec, that's his decision. What are his reasons?"

'"He hasn't really given us any."

'"Are you disappointed about that?"

'"Mike, it wouldn't worry me if he never played Test cricket again."

'"Those are strong words, Alec, I'll hold you to them."'

It is understandable that Bedser was temporarily exasperated by Boycott's self-imposed martyrdom. After all, Denness was Bedser's choice as skipper and he cannot have taken kindly to Boycott's ostentatious dislike of this decision. But Bedser was never a man to bear grudges. Shortly before the second Test he rang Boycott again to check on the position, only for Boycott to confirm that he wished to concentrate on leading Yorkshire.

Freed from the stresses of international cricket, Boycott saw a big improvement in his form as his confidence returned. He finished up in fourth place in the national averages, with 1783 runs at 59.43. As usual, he topped the Yorkshire averages. However, Yorkshire saw little change in their fortunes. The team finished tenth in the table, and had no success in any of the four one-day competitions. The divisions over Boycott's captaincy remained as wide as ever. Towards the end of the season, three of the old guard, Tony Nicholson, Don Wilson and Richard Hutton, circulated a petition amongst the capped players, demanding that the committee sack Boycott as captain. But Phil Sharpe refused to sign, then John Hampshire informed the rest of the team that he had recently talked to Boycott, who had told him he was considering retirement at the end of the season. The problem appeared to have resolved itself. 'We were overjoyed,' said Richard Hutton later.

There is no doubt that during 1974 Boycott was so unhappy that he did talk, in somewhat melodramatic terms, about quitting. A letter to Alec Bedser, written in September, mentioned that he had been contemplating retirement. He was now thirty-four, the same age at which Peter May and Ted Dexter had left the game. His benefit looked like being a record-breaking success, which would give him the financial security he had always wanted since his first days as a professional. But retirement was never a serious prospect. Cricket was all that mattered to him. What would he have done instead? He was still at his peak as a player. His hunger for runs remained as strong as ever. Even today, Boycott says that he would give everything away, his wealth, home, celebrity status, just to have another five years' playing for Yorkshire.

Though the old guard's petition went nowhere except the bin, there was growing dissatisfaction in the Yorkshire committee with Boycott the captain. At a meeting on 12 September, he faced a grilling from committee members about the club's poor record under his command and was asked if he would be willing to play under another captain. Boycott later wrote that he was 'surprised by the weight and vehemence of the opinion against me at the meeting'. By a single vote he was re-elected captain for 1975. He knew now that there would have to be a radical transformation in Yorkshire's performance next season, otherwise his dismissal was certain. Sid Fielden, who had come to know him well through work on his benefit, recalls: 'He was worried to death about Yorkshire and his own position. He said to me, "They're going to make John Hampshire captain and if I don't play for them next year instead of England, then they could finish bottom. I just have to concentrate on Yorkshire."'

So, far from contemplating retirement, Boycott wanted to put even greater energy into his native county. But he felt he could only do so without the distractions of Test cricket. And it was this desire to remain out of the international arena that was to create by far the most controversial decision of his career: his refusal to tour Australia in 1974/75. Boycott received his invitation to tour Australia, under Mike Denness, at the end of August and by 19 September he had still not confirmed his acceptance, prompting the MCC to send urgent telegrams to his home demanding an answer. Yet it had initially appeared that he was keen to go. When the touring party was announced, he told the *Daily Mail*: 'During the past three months it seems that I have been the only one to make no comment about whether I would go to Australia. Now it is finally settled, perhaps we can now return to some sanity about my career.'

In reality, however, Boycott probably never intended touring. Brian Luckhurst (who was later picked as Boycott's replacement) told me of an intriguing conversation he had with Boycott just after the touring party was announced: 'We travelled to Yorkshire to play a Sunday league match and I was captain because Mike Denness was injured. As we walked out to toss up Geoffrey said to me: "Send me a postcard from Sydney."

'"What the hell are you talking about? I'm not going, you're going."

'"You send me a postcard from Sydney," he said again, with a smile.'

Boycott travelled to London on 23 September to set out his reasons to Alec Bedser and TCCB secretary Donald Carr for declining a tour place. Essentially, they were much the same as those that had led to his withdrawal from the Test side during the summer. He still had no respect for Mike Denness as a leader. He felt he needed to continue to rest from international cricket, especially because his benefit had taken up more time and energy than expected. Though his form had improved for Yorkshire, he had still been through a difficult time in recent Tests. The pressure of media intrusion had been relentless, and he feared it would be stronger than ever during another Ashes tour. The question of the Yorkshire captaincy still hung over his career, unresolved and a source of increasingly bitter dispute. And there was one very personal reason, which he understandably did not want to make public. His mother was in poor health, crippled by arthritis, and as the eldest son who lived with her, he felt he had some responsibility to look after her. As Boycott was later to explain in his interview with Professor Anthony Clare on *In the Psychiatrist's Chair*, 'She got rheumatoid arthritis six or eight months after my father died. She was in terrible pain, taking thirty-two aspirins at one stage, which was giving her hallucinations. She was singing and murmuring, virtually going crazy.'

With hindsight the legend grew up that the real reason Boycott missed the tour was his fear of Dennis Lillee and Jeff Thomson, who tore England apart that winter with unplayable fast bowling. Mike Denness, in his autobiography *I Declare*, gave this eloquent description of the effect of the Lillee–Thomson barrage on the human body as he watched David Lloyd come back into the dressing room: 'Within seconds, the whole of his body was quivering. His neck and the top half of his body, in particular, were shaking. He was shell-shocked, suffering from the effects of never having to move around so quickly in all his life.'

This was the experience Boycott was accused of trying to avoid. But the claim that he was scared of Lillee and Thomson is absurd. For a start, no one even knew that the Englishmen would be facing this pair. Thomson was a complete unknown at the beginning of the series, having played only one highly unsuccessful Test against Pakistan (0 for 110 in 19 overs), while Lillee was still recovering from a serious back injury, which had almost finished his career. More importantly, one of Boycott's greatest qualities was his bravery against pace. This was the man who, in 1981, flew out to the West Indies at the age of almost forty-one when the quartet of Holding, Roberts, Garner and Croft were in their pomp. 'He had a fantastic defence. He never showed any nerves, even against the best bowling. He was a tough competitor, never shirked anything,' is the verdict of Jack Birkenshaw, an exact contemporary of Boycott and one of England's finest judges of a cricketer. Paul Jarvis, Boycott's former Yorkshire team-mate, feels the same: 'The one area of his play that I really respected was his gutsiness. He was such a tough character. If he got hit he would carry on. At Sheffield in 1983 against Kent, Graham Dilley got one to bounce with the new ball and come back at him, hitting right on the jaw. He scored a hundred but at the end of the day his face was wrecked, all twisted and swollen up. He looked like the Elephant Man. A lot of other people would have gone off to hospital.'

What ultimately lay behind Boycott's withdrawal was fear not of pace but of failure. If the last tour of the West Indies had been difficult, the summer's single Test had been even worse. For a perfectionist cricketer whose entire sense of worth was built around batting achievements, he found the thought of several months of Test struggle, under a captain he despised, too grisly to contemplate. Only a year before he had told Barry Norman, in the *Observer*, 'The only thing I'm bloody frightened of is getting out. I don't like getting out. I bloody don't. I like getting hundreds.'

During the winter, Boycott received the news that his benefit had raised the vast sum of £20,639, easily beating the Yorkshire record of £7000 set by Tony Nicholson in 1973. Boycott was delighted for it was proof that, even if he was unpopular with colleagues and the cricket establishment, he was adored by the public. He told the *Yorkshire Post*, in January 1975, 'I'm as emotional as the next man and I can't tell you how much this demonstration of people's affection means to me. I have always thought of myself as a people's player. Most of my support has come from the grass roots, from people who really enjoy their cricket. Until last year, I never realized just how many well-wishers I really had.'

It has to be said that, for all the outrage Boycott had provoked over the previous 12 months, his decision to opt out of international cricket was amply justified by Yorkshire's great revival in the 1975 season, what he later called 'my happiest hours in cricket'. Available for every game that summer, he led them to second place in the championship, the highest position they have ever achieved in the thirty years since the end of the Close era. Boycott's batting played a key role, for he scored more runs than anyone else in the country, almost 2000 at 73.65. But his captaincy also seemed to improve as he made a greater effort to understand his players. This process was helped by the departure of Don Wilson, Phil Sharpe and Richard Hutton, all of whom he regarded as a negative influence in the dressing room. His most senior player, John Hampshire, immediately saw the difference in his style: 'He made a conscious and obvious effort to get closer to the other members of the team. He let his hair grow a bit longer and took to wearing discreetly flared flannels. He became a good companion to go out with and he genuinely made an effort to change his personality.'

As had occurred at Hemsworth Grammar twenty years earlier, Boycott was able to relax when surrounded by a group he felt respected him. Apart from Hampshire, most of the team were much younger and therefore he held more authority over them than he had over Wilson, Sharpe and Hutton. Richard Lumb was one of those newer players, capped only the year before. Lumb recalls: 'In the earlier years of his reign as captain he certainly enjoyed the respect and support of most of the young players. Tactically he was very good, I thought, but always somewhat negative, safety first. He certainly knew the game inside out. Watching him from the other end helped me mould my technique. I will always remember in 1971 at the pre-season nets, Geoff had come back from Australia with a broken arm, could not bat and was squeezing a squash ball continuously. Suddenly he turned to me: "How tall are you, Richard?"

'"Six foot three."

'"Ay, if I had your height and John Hampshire's strength I would be t' greatest player the world has ever seen."'

Medium-pace bowler Howard Cooper was another young player who saw a positive side of Boycott. 'He was a very thoughtful captain. He had a good philosophy, which I have taken and used throughout my life. He used to say that in captaincy, 20 per cent of the decisions are definitely wrong – those are easy to discard. But the rest, if you really work at them, may succeed. If a side is behind a decision that is made, you are likely to force something to happen. I found him quite encouraging. The fact that he had sufficient confidence in me to put me on for the last over in one-day games made me feel a mature member of the team. In another respect he was a good captain. Though he did not socialize much, he would always spend his captain's expenses. He would also come into the bar, buy everyone a drink and be with us for about half an hour.' But Cooper, though he has great affection for Boycott, feels that he could be unsympathetic. 'He did give you advice but he used to think that we were machines. He could not understand why bowlers could not send down six balls in exactly the same spot.'

Apart from Boycott's leadership and batting, another reason for Yorkshire's success in 1975 was the cricket World Cup, which meant that for much of the summer the other 16 counties were without their overseas stars. For the first time since the sixties, Yorkshire were playing on a level field and reaped the benefit. But in 1976 normal service was resumed. Yorkshire were lumbered once more with the disadvantage of their home-born policy and slipped back to eighth place in the championship. Nor did they achieve anything in the limited-overs competitions. Boycott was injured for much of the season – disc trouble and, inevitably, a broken finger – which deprived the county of their best batsman for no fewer than 18 fixtures in all competitions. Critics of Boycott's captaincy should note that the side performed no better when he was absent. Indeed, one of their most humiliating defeats occurred in the Benson and Hedges Cup when, with John Hampshire in charge and Boycott watching from the sidelines, they were badly beaten by a combined Oxford and Cambridge team at Barnsley.

But Howard Cooper believes that Boycott failed to build on the good work of the previous season. 'What he had then was a team that had matured over a period of five years but it all went wrong in 1976. If he had stood back and instead of pulling us all the time – which is what he had done up to this point – just guided and pushed us, then we might have been even more successful.' But, again, even if Boycott had displayed the most delicate man-management, it is doubtful if allowing the likes of Arthur Robinson, Barrie Leadbeater, Colin Johnson and Mike Bore to express themselves would have achieved a higher ranking. The old problem remained: Yorkshire simply did not have in-depth quality.

While Boycott was struggling with the captaincy once more, he was the recipient of yet more entreaties to return to the Test side. At times the talks must have resembled the worst sort of seventies trade-union negotiations, with meetings held and offers made but, after much rhetorical wandering around the subject, no apparent progress. Alec Bedser, despite what he had said to Denness, phoned Boycott twice in 1975 and 1976, and both times received the same answer, that Boycott wanted to concentrate on Yorkshire. Former England captain Ted Dexter, now working as a journalist, also had a go: 'I took the trouble and drove down to Kent where Yorkshire were playing and I managed to sit with him for an hour. It was an extraordinary conversation. I should think there were about four passages to it. Each time he would get to a point where he would seem to be on the verge of agreeing about a Test return, then suddenly the gates would come down again and he would say, "No, I'm not doing it. Fook 'em. I just want to play for Yorkshire. I'm only interested in Yorkshire." He had this real chip on his shoulder that he hadn't been treated properly, that he had been rejected.'

When Tony Greig was made England captain after Denness's run of failure, he was desperate to get Boycott back in the side. He explains, 'He was one of the top five batsmen of my time and I always wanted him to play. One of my very first questions to Alec Bedser when I took over was "Boycott?" and I kept wanting him all the time I was in charge. We were desperate for a decent opener; we even had to resort to bringing back old-timers like Brian Close to inject a bit of bulldog into the side. Sure the bloke was slow on occasions, but our problem was scoring runs, not the speed at which they were scored. Besides, who cares when you're playing Test cricket? Our problem was how to survive. Our worry wasn't scoring four hundred too slowly, it was getting a decent first innings total.'

Greig went so far as to offer Boycott the vice-captaincy for the winter tour of India when they met at Hove early in the 1976 season. Boycott admits he was tempted by the offer, especially because Greig promised to arrange for food to be flown in from Australia to India so he would not have to worry about his health. But then Boycott broke his finger and was out of action until the end of July. Later in the summer, the issue of the vice-captaincy arose again when Boycott was visited by England selector Charlie Elliott. Greig says Elliott was sent on a 'mission to offer him the vice-captaincy and reported back that Boycott had refused'. Boycott's slant is different. He says that Elliott told him he was a fool not to play for England, but implied that the Indian tour might not be the best time to return because it would raise further suspicions that he only favoured playing Test nations without the ferocious attacks of the West Indies and Australia.

Given that Boycott was sending so many conflicting messages and failing to respond to so many appeals, it is hardly surprising that the question of his vice-captaincy to India drowned in a mud of confusion. The fact is that, yet again, he had deprived himself of a golden opportunity to step up to the England captaincy. As Greig puts it, 'If he had come with me to India as vice-captain, we would have won the series even more easily, we would have won the Centenary Test, and he would have been ready to go when I lost the England job because of Packer.'

15

Achieving the Impossible Dream

While England were touring India under Greig, Boycott spent the winter of 1976/77 in Australia, playing with outstanding success for the Sydney grade side Waverley, as well as carrying out commentary and coaching work across New South Wales. His record-breaking achievements at Waverley and the warm hospitality he received in Australia helped to bring about a more positive attitude towards resuming his Test career. In an interview in January 1977 with the *Sun*'s John Sadler, he explained: 'I'm fit and relaxed and completely at ease. As far as England are concerned, I feel different compared with three years ago when I stopped playing for them. I've stood back from the international scene and realized that to get out for nought is not the end of the world. If I failed, I used to think my world had caved in. That's changed. And my time out here has helped to change it.'

But as he contemplated a return to the Test arena, he was also considering another, far more lucrative offer, from Kerry Packer, who was eagerly recruiting stars for his World Series Cricket venture. When they met just before the Centenary Test in March 1977 at Packer's office, the Australian tycoon explained that he wanted Boycott for his Rest of the World team. They also discussed other players who might be approached, as well as the possible captain of the Rest of the World, with the names of Tony Greig, Clive Lloyd, Eddie Barlow, Ray Illingworth and Boycott himself mentioned. At first Boycott was enthusiastic. 'I'm in,' he told Packer after their initial meeting. The money on the table, estimated to be around £60,000 over three years, was certainly tempting.

Then, during the Centenary Test, Boycott was seen by Packer

executive Austin Robertson, who brought him the contract to sign. Boycott immediately became suspicious because he was told that the lengthy document was secret so he could not take it away to have it checked by his solicitor. Moreover, during this discussion, it became clear that the Packer contract might interfere with Boycott's commitments to Yorkshire, especially because World Series Cricket were considering an operation in England. Boycott would never have dreamt of giving any cause a higher priority than his own beloved county. Having shown his reluctance to sign up immediately, Boycott never heard from the Packer organization again. 'He wasn't happy and he wanted to discuss it further. He wasn't given another chance,' wrote Dennis Lillee, one of Packer's key playing lieutenants, in his book *My Life in Cricket*.

According to Lillee, Boycott's other objection, apart from the Yorkshire problem, was that he had not been promised the job of captaining the Rest of the World team. 'He said he wanted to be captain of the World XI or to be able to name the captain of the team. The man he named as the only captain he'd play under was Ray Illingworth, a rather ironic choice in the light of future relationships with Yorkshire,' said Lillee. It is true that Boycott was interested in this job and, as he had demonstrated with England and Yorkshire, he could be prickly on the question of leadership. But, given that Packer was then in the early stages of recruitment, the captaincy was hardly likely to be a major issue. One allegation that can definitely be scotched is that Boycott refused to sign because he objected to playing under Tony Greig. That is nonsense, as a glance at the chronology would demonstrate. Boycott held his discussions with Packer and Robertson before and during the Centenary Test. Greig did not have his first meeting with Packer until after the Test was concluded.

The saga has another intriguing element. One reason why Kerry Packer might not have been keen to pursue Boycott after the initial hesitation over his contract was because he was not enamoured of Boycott's attitude. Packer had asked Boycott to have a look at his son playing cricket, as Boycott later revealed: 'I went up to the net in the garden some time after Christmas and he wasn't a bad little player. His father was there and he had strong views about his son's cricket – with which I disagreed. Dad thought he knew more about cricket than me. I told him that making money was his job and playing cricket was mine.' It would not have been the first time someone took offence at Boycott's plain speaking.

For a man with a reputation for being mean and self-centred, Boycott emerges with great credit from the Packer business. He was the first player to turn Packer down and, even if there were other factors, his loyalty to Yorkshire was his primary motivation. In view of some of the justifiable criticisms of his long career with the club, it should always be remembered that when he was given what he believed to be a stark choice between money and Yorkshire, he chose the latter.

Once the story broke at the start of the 1977 season and the details became clear, Boycott was suddenly in the unlikely position of being the hero of the cricket establishment. The departure of Greig from the captaincy, to be replaced by Brearley, brought him renewed hope for his chances of the England job he so coveted, particularly because Brearley was untested and without international batting pedigree. There was growing talk of a return to Test cricket, even from those who, only a year earlier, had argued that he had played his last game for England. On 14 May, just five days after newspapers first exposed the Packer circus, Alec Bedser publicly announced that 'The selectors will consider all players who are available. If Boycott tells us he has changed his mind, then there is no possibility of his being ignored because of anything in the past.'

In response, Bedser received a phone call from John Callaghan, the *Yorkshire Evening Post* journalist and a good friend of Boycott's, asking if he would be willing to meet Boycott. Bedser replied that he had always been willing to talk to him at any time. Soon afterwards he received another call, from Boycott himself, and the two agreed to meet at the Watford Gap service station on the M1, half-way between their Surrey and Yorkshire homes. The two men duly arrived at the car park and Bedser suggested they go inside the building for a coffee. Ever suspicious about the press, Boycott said he preferred the privacy of Bedser's car. So the two climbed into his white Austin Princess, just the kind of solid, mundane and very British vehicle that the chairman was bound to own.

The conversation had a somewhat circular feel, ranging over many cricket matters yet continually returning to Boycott's sense of injustice over his treatment as a Test player, especially on the question of the captaincy. Nothing was firmly resolved but Bedser tried to reassure Boycott that there was absolutely no prejudice against him among the selectors, stressing that all of them (John Murray, Ken Barrington, Charlie Elliott and himself) were ex-professionals without the slightest interest in social class or background. Bedser further said that he knew of no policy directive from Lord's to the Test and County Cricket Board (TCCB) that had banned Boycott from the captaincy. The reason he had not succeeded Illingworth in 1973, Bedser explained, was because it was felt he was too absorbed in his own game. But he promised that, if the England captaincy were to fall vacant again in the future, the appointment would be made, as it always had been, entirely on merit. Later Bedser wrote that he 'reminded Geoffrey that the selectors never wanted him out of the side, had always regretted his absence, and if he made himself available again the slate would be wiped clean'. Bedser's concluding words to Boycott were: 'The ball is now in your court.'

Boycott, as we have seen, was on the verge of agreeing to play again. He now hesitated, thrown into turmoil by his conflicting feelings of pride and fear. He desperately wanted to prove himself in cricket's greatest arena against the finest players. Yet the same sense of pride meant that he was terrified of letting himself down. If he failed an army of critics would be waiting to gloat. The memories of all the pressures that had driven him into exile were still at the front of his mind. He was like a driver who has been in a crash, knows he must get back on the road but is fearful of another accident.

After several weeks of agonizing and more discussions with friends, Boycott finally took a deep breath and rang Bedser on the evening of Saturday 11 June with an unconditional offer to play for England again. The team had already been picked for the first Test against Australia at Lord's when Boycott made his call, with new captain Mike Brearley down to open with Boycott's old partner Dennis Amiss, who had been through a torrid time against the Australian attack over the last three years. This match was a rain-interrupted draw, and the Brearley–Amiss partnership remained for the second Test at Old Trafford. Brearley had been keen to include

Boycott in the England team for Manchester but, as he wrote in his book *The Return of the Ashes*, 'I could appreciate the reluctance of some selectors; they felt they didn't want to come just when Boycott whistled or change a team that had been doing very well for one individual.' Amiss was again disappointing, and by the conclusion of England's nine-wicket victory at Old Trafford he had scored just 43 runs in four innings that series.

The failure of Amiss made the return of Boycott inevitable. The stage was now set at Trent Bridge for one of the most romantic of all cricketing comebacks. On the morning of Thursday 28 July, Boycott walked out to field in a Test match for the first time in more than three years, receiving a far friendlier welcome from the crowd than he had expected. Fortunately for his jangling nerves, Australia won the toss and batted. Alongside Boycott was a young, confident débutant by the name of Ian Botham, who soon proved his liking for Test cricket by running through Australia's middle order to take 5 for 74.

Australia were all out for 243 before the close of the first day, having passed 100 with just one wicket down. Brearley and Boycott then had an awkward three overs to face that night, bowled by Len Pascoe and Jeff Thomson. Understandably, Boycott was a riot of nerves but still managed to get off the mark. The next morning, the pressure grew even greater as Boycott battled to cope with both the high expectations of the 20,000-strong crowd and the fierce hostility of the Australian attack. Indeed, the bowling was so aggressive that Dickie Bird had to warn Pascoe after he bowled four bouncers in an over at Boycott. England were soon in serious trouble at 34 for 2, Brearley and Woolmer having fallen cheaply. In spite of the atmosphere of crisis, Randall started breezily on his home ground.

But then, when he had made 13 and the score had reached 53, Randall lost his wicket in probably the most renowned of all Boycott's many run-out disasters. At this stage, Boycott, though defending staunchly, had become almost strokeless. In a desperate attempt to get his score moving again, he played Thomson back down the pitch towards mid-on and called Randall through for an impossible single. The bowler took a few strides, picked up the ball and threw it to wicket-keeper Rod Marsh, who eagerly demolished

Randall's stumps. As a shaken Randall left the field after this act of self-sacrifice, Boycott stood at the other end of the pitch, dropping his bat on the ground and covering his face with his hands in shame. Boycott's distress at running out the favourite local son did not impress the cynical Ray Illingworth. In his bitter book *The Tempestuous Years*, Illingworth highlighted Boycott's conduct as emblematic of his selfish attitude. 'Geoffrey gave it all the drama he could muster,' wrote Illingworth. 'I've looked at the video of that moment many times to make sure I wasn't imagining anything – and I wasn't. There it is every time. Geoffrey gives a quick glance to make sure the throw has gone to Randall's end, he makes double sure of his own safety with a quick grounding of the bat, and then come the histrionics.'

This sneering is too harsh on Boycott. He might have acted out of self-preservation – as he always did when he was running – but his despair at the consequences was certainly genuine. He gave Randall that rarest of Boycott gestures, the direct, personal apology. John Lever, who was twelfth man in that England side, recalls: 'He was genuinely upset at what he had done, for Derek was such a decent, sincere bloke. Fiery felt the same way about him as the rest of us.' With the Nottinghamshire crowd against him and his batting now reduced to near paralysis, Boycott was in the depths of a personal crisis. 'No cricketer can have ever been through a more daunting, at times, harrowing test of character,' wrote Pat Gibson in the *Daily Express*. Boycott's torment was not helped by England's continuing collapse at the other end. From 53 for 3 England staggered to 64 for 4 as Greig was bowled by Thomson and then 82 for 5 as Geoff Miller was caught off Pascoe. It was at this moment that wicket-keeper Alan Knott strode to the wicket to play the innings of his life. And, in doing so, he helped Boycott break free from his miserable immobility.

The partnership was almost over before it had begun. When just five runs had been added, Boycott, with only 20 to his name after three hours at the crease, edged Pascoe to second slip, where Rick McCosker spilled a straightforward, knee-high chance. The history of the Ashes has produced many famous dropped catches: Fred Tate letting off Joe Darling in 1902 at Old Trafford, Arthur Carr putting down Charlie Macartney in 1926 at Trent Bridge and

Graham Thorpe missing Matthew Elliott at Headingley in 1997. But none of these had the same influence over a series and a career as McCosker's dropping of Boycott. If he had held that catch, England would have been 87 for 6, and would have probably slid towards defeat. All Boycott's worst fears of failure would have been confirmed by this painfully awkward innings compounded by the Randall run-out. He would have become the focus for the kind of torrent of press criticism that he so dreaded.

Once he had seen Alan Knott take the initiative from the bowlers with his impish, unorthodox strokes, Boycott started to regain his confidence. A cover drive off Walker for his first boundary showed that the old authority was returning. Soon, as the Australian attack wearied in the late afternoon, he was matching Knott stroke for stroke. At the end of the second day, he was 88 not out and Knott was on 87. The next morning they both quickly reached their centuries. Their partnership of 215 had equalled the England record for the sixth wicket against Australia when Boycott fell to Jeff Thomson for 107, caught at slip, ironically, by McCosker.

As he returned to the pavilion, he savoured the cheers of another 20,000-strong crowd. Basking in their adulation, he had proved all his doubters wrong. In future, Boycott would always say that this was the greatest innings of his life because of the burden of expectation and the danger of failure he had to overcome. In a BBC interview in 1987, Boycott revealed: 'That was the most pressure I could think about, there were people there willing me to get out, the hatred ran very deep. Then to run the local hero out. It would have been the easiest thing in the world to give a slip catch and get away from the stage, the pressure, the tension, the hurt. I just wanted a hole to appear and swallow me up. But something inside would not let go and I held out through sheer character and will-power, not really skill, until Alan Knott came in and got me going, talked to me, got me relaxed. That was by far my best innings.'

Thanks to Boycott and Knott, who made the highest of his five Test centuries, England had a lead of 121. Australia were bowled out again for 309 and, with Boycott (80 not out) sharing an opening stand of 154 with Brearley (81), England easily reached their target of 189 to go 2–0 up in the series. In his victorious return to

Test cricket, Boycott had spent no less than 12 hours at the crease as well as batting on every single day of the match, a feat only previously achieved by M. L. Jaisimha of India when playing against Australia in Calcutta in 1959/60.

Boycott's century at Trent Bridge was the ninety-eighth of his career. In the following game, for Yorkshire against Warwickshire at Edgbaston, he scored his ninety-ninth. By a delicious twist of fate, Boycott's next first-class innings was to be in the fourth Test. So he now had the chance to become the first man in history to hit his hundredth hundred in a Test match. As if that was not rich enough in its dramatic possibilities, the match was also to take place on his home ground of Headingley in front of his own Yorkshire public.

The media, of course, adored the story. So much attention was now focused on Boycott the potential centurion that it was easy to forget that England were actually playing Australia in a Test that might decide the fate of the Ashes. Moreover, some of the more excitable journalists and members of the public, talking blithely of Boycott's excellent chance of pulling off the triumph, seemed to ignore the fact that a Test century against Australia was a rare commodity. It could not just be produced at will. Many of Boycott's Test contemporaries, including Dennis Amiss, M.J.K. Smith, Peter Parfitt, Jim Parks and Peter Willey, never scored a century against the Australians despite good Test records, while Boycott's own hero, Tom Graveney, managed only one Ashes ton in a career lasting 79 matches.

With the expectations of public and press reaching fever pitch, Boycott was now faced with another Olympian test of his ability to withstand pressure. The night before the Test he retired early from the team dinner but was barely able to sleep. Boycott was a player who always treasured his eight hours' sleep, but he was still awake at three o'clock in the morning, trying to calm himself by watching television and ordering tea from the night porter. Unsurprisingly he felt tired and nervous when he arrived at Headingley on Thursday. His anxiety must have increased when he saw the huge crowd that had already filled the ground long before the start. Even though his heart was pumping hard, Boycott still managed to present that front of confidence, which was so much part of his character. 'If I get to lunch I'll make it,' he told Bob Willis, when he came back to the dressing room after his net.

England won the toss and at eleven thirty he and Mike Brearley walked out to open. The calm unruffled start Boycott was hoping for did not materialize. 'It's about time we had a wicket in the first over,' whispered Rod Marsh to Greg Chappell next to him. That is exactly what happened as Mike Brearley edged Thomson's third delivery into Marsh's gloves. Woolmer now joined Boycott and for the next two hours batting was never easy.

Walker, Thomson and Pascoe all extracted swing and movement from the hazy atmosphere and a pitch that was moist enough to have prompted thoughts from Chappell about bowling first if he had won the toss. When he was 22, Boycott edged Walker in front of first slip but a diving Marsh just failed to reach the ball. Four runs later a vicious delivery from Pascoe glanced his wristband and shot through to Marsh. The Australians appealed loudly; Boycott rubbed his forearm calmly. 'Not out,' said umpire Lloyd Budd. Boycott went into lunch on 34, with England 76 for 1. In the next session, Boycott was rock-solid, calmly defending, clipping the ball to leg or punching through the off-side with his trademark back-foot drive. Boycott lost two more partners in the afternoon, Woolmer on 82 and Randall at 105. But then Greig stayed with him until tea, when Boycott's score had reached 69. He was now just 31 runs away.

Throughout the day there was an air of expectancy from the crowd, as if they believed that Boycott had been destined by fate to march inexorably towards his century. Yet few of the spectators realized how close he came to being dismissed in the final session. The Australians were sure that, on 75, Boycott had been caught behind off left-arm spinner Ray Bright as he went to turn him on the leg-side. Certain that Boycott had nicked the ball, Bright was so furious at the rejection of the appeal that he had to be calmed down by his captain and reprimanded by the umpire. But it was not just the Australians who thought Boycott was out. The English players felt the same way. At this crucial moment Tony Greig was batting at the other end. 'Boycott was out, without any shadow of a doubt. It couldn't have been anything but his bat. But why should he walk? None of the Aussies did.' Graham Roope (nicknamed Cyril by the

England team) was due in at the fall of the next wicket and watched the incident closely from the pavilion. 'It was such a big nick. He had a clip at it down the leg-side and it was a fine catch by Marsh who had gone a long way. At that moment, Mike Brearley said to me, "Cyril, you're in." I was so convinced it was out that I actually got up off the bench, put my gloves on and then Bill Alley turned it down. When we came off at the end of the day, several players said to him in the dressing room, "Bloody hell, Boycs, you got away with that one." He never said anything about that but was quite happy to talk about the earlier appeal off his forearm.'

When the England score reached 201, Tony Greig was bowled by Thomson. Roope went out to join Boycott. Slowly the Yorkshire-man inched into the nineties – he scored just 10 runs in the first hour after tea. A single off Pascoe took him to 96 and he retained the strike for the next over to be bowled by Greg Chappell. Policemen moved into their positions on the boundary. Roope says, 'The atmosphere was electric, with the ground jam-packed. Boycs was, of course, completely wrapped up in himself. I was usually a great one for talking to my partner but I thought I better steer clear at this moment. He was obviously a bit nervous but I was more nervous for him.'

At 5.49 the special moment arrived. Boycott leant into a full-length ball from Greg Chappell and stroked it to the boundary for four. As he completed the shot, he held both his arms aloft in triumph. Immediately he was engulfed by a flood of ecstatic supporters washing across the ground. Play was held up for no less than 10 minutes as the spectators celebrated, Boycott briefly losing his cap in the mêlée. The Australians watched half bemused as the normally restrained Yorkshire public gave an exhibition of un-bridled joy such as had rarely been seen east of the Pennines. On his return to the dressing room, the champagne was flowing. But in Roope's recollection, Boycott remained astonishingly calm. 'He never really let go. Having done it, it didn't seem anything more than a day's work to Boycs – that's the impression I got. He had a glass of champagne, took his gear off, had a shower and then left. Next morning he was back in the ground early, having a net. It was almost like just another day to him.'

But even if he could not show it in front of his team-mates, it was much more than just another day. It was, without doubt, the happiest of his life. Through all the twists and turns of his career, this was to be the one occasion he could look back upon with unadulterated pleasure. In a BBC interview soon after the triumph, he recorded his true feelings. 'I really didn't want to bat that morning. In fact, when the cheers went up that England were batting – I know all the crowd wanted England to bat and see if I could do it – I was really dreading it because I had not had any sleep and I was pretty up-tight about it. I thought I would not be able to keep my concentration and stamina going. I think I must have been so up-tight and on a high about the occasion that the adrenaline was flowing and once I had been into the nets and had a bit of practice I came back and sat down for about ten minutes before I went out to bat. I was all right then.'

Of the stroke from Greg Chappell's bowling he said, 'It was like a magic moment. I knew just as I hit it that it had gone for four. My arm was up for the hundred long before it went past the bowler. It was not as an exhibitionist but as a sigh of relief after all the strain and pressure and excitement of achieving an impossible dream. I suppose it is like that for many women who have their first baby, what a tremendous experience it must be for them. I will remember it for the rest of my life. No matter how many more noughts I make I will remember that moment.'

16

'Go and Run the Bugger Out'

Boycott had not just delighted the public with his unique achievement; he had also helped to ensure the return of the Ashes. His massive score of 191 was the cornerstone of an innings triumph at Headingley that saw England take an unassailable 3–0 lead in the series. As Ian Botham put it, 'The Aussies, shell-shocked at having to bowl at Boycott for twenty-two and a half hours since his return to the England side, capitulated without much of a fight.' Perhaps the most fulsome tribute came from his old friend Brian Clough, who had delayed his attendance at a Nottingham Forest board meeting because, he said, he was transfixed by Boycott's innings at Headingley. 'I apologized for my late arrival. I hadn't been watching cricket. I had been watching Boycott.' Clough then launched into the kind of anti-establishment language so beloved by northerners. 'Boycott, over the years, has been misguided, mishandled, misunderstood, criticized and crucified. And only because he was different. He asked for one thing from the public and the cricketing lords – he asked for recognition of his talent. Nothing more. He wanted to captain his country and he should have done.'

Boycott finished the series with an average of 147.33 from 442 runs and, for the first time in his Test career, saw his overall average rise above 50. And by the end of the summer the establishment seemed as favourable as the rest of the country towards Boycott. In a symbol of his new standing with the cricket authorities he was rewarded with the vice-captaincy of the England side for the twin tour of Pakistan and New Zealand that winter. It was the first time he had agreed to travel to the sub-continent, having always pleaded health problems as grounds for refusal in the past. Cynics muttered that his elevated status must be behind the move, though this trip to Pakistan was far shorter than Greig's 1976/77 tour (four months) or Tony Lewis's in 1972/73 (almost five months).

Before the touring party left, Boycott performed another important role for the TCCB and the International Cricket Council (ICC), going into the witness box on their behalf in the legal battle against Kerry Packer. The Packer players, led by Tony Greig, John Snow and Mike Procter, were contesting the ban that the TCCB had imposed on players who had signed up with the Packer organization. Boycott's appearance in the High Court immediately sparked a controversy. A few days earlier, on learning that Boycott was to go into the stand as a witness for the TCCB, Tony Greig had phoned him to ask, 'How the hell did you get involved in this?' Then, in typical Greig fashion, he warned Boycott that he and his solicitors were going to work through the weekend so 'we'll have some mud to throw at you'. This conversation was reported to the judge, Mr Justice Slade, who took the eminently sensible line that Greig had been speaking in jest. Greig now has mixed views about his judicial clash with Boycott. 'That conversation was a big mistake on my part. I should never have done it. But I was really upset about Geoff, wondering how he had got caught up with the TCCB. If there's one person who had an axe to grind at the establishment, it was him.'

Boycott was given a tough time in the witness box by the barrister for the Packer organization, Robert Alexander, QC, but as he was to prove in his commentaries, verbal fluency has always been one of Boycott's gifts. Unintimidated by either Alexander or the High Court surroundings, Boycott was, according to journalist Henry Blofeld, 'impressive and entertaining' in the witness box. His essential argument was that a cricketer could not have two masters, Packer and the TCCB, since they were in conflict. Packer wanted players 'body and soul' and this would inevitably undermine their commitment to the counties. Therefore the ban on Packer-contracted players was reasonable. He also vigorously denied suggestions that he had been motivated by hopes of becoming England captain, while he brought laughter to the courtroom when answering a question about the attractions of local star players. The example of Derek Randall at Trent Bridge in the summer was cited, to which Boycott replied, 'Randall at Trent Bridge? I thought they were all Yorkshiremen come to see me.'

Boycott's efforts were to no avail. Mr Justice Slade came down unequivocally in favour of Packer's World Series Cricket, arguing that the ban amounted to an illegal restraint of trade. Boycott had done himself a great deal of good with Lord's by his sterling defence of their actions although, given his long self-exile from Test cricket, his new pose as a champion of national allegiance looked hypocritical to many. And within five years his words about loyalty were to return to haunt him in an even more stark fashion. After the tour to South Africa in 1982, Boycott and his fellow rebels stood accused of exactly the same crimes as the World Series pirates: disrupting Test cricket for the sake of their own bank balances; plotting in secret because of their venture's dubious nature; and breaching their commitments to the England Test side. In fact, it is one of the ironies of this mercenary business that the lawyer to whom Boycott and his rebels turned for advice was none other than Robert Alexander, QC, the man who had questioned him so closely during the Packer trial.

The Packer affair rumbled on through the winter, creating flashpoints in Test cricket across the globe. But Boycott's first business, as always, was cricket, and he soon found the dry, slow wickets of Pakistan to his liking. With the dead bat dominant, the drawn series was played at a funereal pace – Bob Willis called it 'the most boring tour I have ever experienced'. The tone was set by Mudassar Nazar in the first Test at Lahore where he took 557 minutes to score his century, still the slowest hundred in first-class cricket. Boycott's solid 63 in England's reply helped to save the follow-on and ensured a draw.

Boycott was carrying on his excellent form of the summer, but his mania for occupying the crease was now to be a cause of serious annoyance to his colleagues. At Christmas time, between the first and second Tests, England played two up-country games in Sahiwali. Omitted from the side because of the management's anxieties about potential health problems, Boycott stayed behind in Lahore, where he was meant to fix up some nets. On the England team's return he was asked about the arrangements for the net practice, to which he said, 'Oh, I've done better than that. I've organized for us to have a match at the Lahore Gymkhana ground, with half of us in each side. Every player can bowl as much as he likes or bat as much as he likes.' Bernie Thomas recalls: 'Of course, he opened the batting, and he stayed and stayed. We kept sending messages out to him, but he just carried on. Roopie was having a particularly bad time waiting to go in and when Boycs was consulted he said, "Well, he can have a net tomorrow." Which happened to be Christmas Day. So that didn't go down too well. There was nothing malicious about it. It was just Boycs.' Nor did Boycott improve his popularity when he was asked by the media about this strange session. 'I know they want to get some practice but it's most important of all that I am in form. I am the number-one batsman,' he said, one of those characteristic Boycott remarks whose tactlessness is not diminished by its truth.

At least Boycott could point to his personal results as some justification for his approach. In the second Test at Hyderabad, he top-scored in both England innings, 79 in the first and 100 not out in the second. These two innings brought his Test aggregate since his Trent Bridge comeback to 684 runs at 136.80. The last day might have been an awkward one for England, batting on a turning pitch against Abdul Qadir, the first of the modern generation of great international leg-spinners. But Boycott and Brearley, in the best opening stand they had together, put on 185 to ensure another draw.

Just before the third Test, on 15 January, England played a one-day game against Sind at the Gymkhana ground in Lahore. The match was due to be nothing more than a friendly workout but, for Boycott, it had immense consequences. In England's innings, a ball from Sikander Bakht reared unexpectedly and broke Mike Brearley's left forearm. Out for the rest of the tour with this serious injury, Brearley returned to England that night. Suddenly and by default, Boycott had the job he had craved throughout his career. There was now the chance to prove his doubters wrong, to contradict all the claims that he was temperamentally unsuited to Test captaincy.

In the first days of his captaincy, Boycott was involved in yet another Packer crisis, caused by speculation that Pakistan were planning to include three World Series-contracted players, Zaheer

Abbas, Imran Khan and Mushtaq Mohammad, in their side for the final Test at Karachi. The England players were furious at this possibility and threatened a strike. Lord's was thrown into panic. In a flurry of phone calls between Karachi and London, Doug Insole, chairman of the TCCB, begged Boycott not to allow his team to take such unprecedented action. Boycott stood firm and backed his players to the hilt, with the result that Lord's felt compelled to send a telegram warning the Pakistan board that the England team might refuse to play if the Packer trio were selected. Boycott also made his team's views known directly to the Pakistani officials, and publicly branded Test cricketers who had signed with Packer as 'disloyal traitors' with a mercenary attitude of 'have bat, will travel'.

This remark provoked a furious retort from Tony Greig, now out in Sydney with World Series Cricket. He made a statement to the press, which claimed that the 'threatened strike is the work of Geoff Boycott and his cronies'. It was in this article that Greig wrote his famous phrase that 'Boycott has the uncanny knack of being where fast bowlers aren't'. Therefore, argued Greig, he had no right to criticize other players who had taken the brunt of the Australian and West Indian attacks during his three years of exile. Within a week of this outburst, Greig had been stripped of the Sussex captaincy and was soon to be finished with English cricket.

Greig was wrong to suggest that Boycott was a sort of militant leader like Red Robbo, the British Leyland union activist of the time, whipping up the mood in the England camp for a strike. In fact, in his phone calls with Lord's, he was only a conduit for the views of others, like John Lever, Bob Taylor, Ian Botham and Chris Old, who felt just as strongly about Packer. Even if he had tried to do the bidding of Insole and agreed to a climbdown, it is doubtful that many players would have followed. In fact, Boycott came out well from this crisis. Although diplomacy was not one of his strengths – he always belonged to the Prince Philip rather than the Talleyrand school of international relations – his firm stance and plain talking helped to convince the Pakistan board of the risks they were taking by flirting with Packer. It should also be said that the Pakistan players, some of whose places were under threat, felt just as adamant as England in their opposition to the Packer trio. So, crucially, did the country's military leader, General Zia, who exercised a strong influence over the Pakistan board. During the Karachi Test, Boycott had tea with the General, leaving him in no doubt about the strength of feeling against Packer. And perhaps Boycott picked up from the all-powerful Zia a few ideas for the future management of Yorkshire CCC.

Boycott was filled with pride to lead England out for the first time when the Karachi Test finally got under way without strikes or stoppages. Unfortunately the match ended in another soporific draw, the eleventh successive time England had failed to achieve a result in Pakistan. The explanation, said new vice-captain Bob Willis, lay in the flat pitches which 'should be blown up'. Boycott felt the Pakistanis' attitude towards losing also bred excessive caution. He said, 'Where I come from a national disaster is when a pit roof collapses and twenty men die. Here it's a defeat at cricket.'

Boycott's style of leadership attracted mixed reviews from the players. John Lever told me, 'He wanted the job so badly and you could sense that it meant a lot to him when he was in charge, the old bulldog spirit of pride in his country. Tactically he was good, but he was too wound up in his own game to be a great captain. Because of his complex way of thinking and his blinkered approach to batting he could find it hard in that role. The morning of a Test match, he was going to get his own net, get his own game sorted out. It was then down to someone else to deal with the rest of the side.'

Graham Roope recalls, 'As a captain, he could think too much of himself, but you couldn't fault him for his cricketing ability or knowledge. He was also very helpful to me at times. In the Test at Karachi, I batted about ten hours in the game and got about eighty runs. He talked to me all through my innings, telling me to concentrate all the time. He also worked with me on my technique, teaching me to play more effectively off the back foot.' Another equally balanced view comes from Derek Randall, who had some difficulties with his batting on that tour. In his 1992 autobiography *Rags* he said this: 'Boycott seemed to believe that every young bats-man had the same mentality as himself. He tried to sort out my problems but his style of play was totally alien to mine. His efforts had the opposite effect to that he intended. He should never have been made captain of England, since he didn't mix easily with other players.' But Randall also recalled a time in Pakistan when he was feeling particularly low and Boycott took him to a restaurant that served roast beef and Yorkshire pudding. 'It was a great night out and really cheered me up. So he wasn't as self-centred as is made out.'

Phil Edmonds was the one player in the England team who was more enthusiastic about Boycott's captaincy than Brearley's. Edmonds, whose relationship at Middlesex with Brearley was at best difficult and at worst hostile, always got on well with Boycott. Though they were from very different backgrounds – Edmonds was the son of a colonial businessman, had been born in Zambia (then Northern Rhodesia) and educated at Kent public schools and Cambridge – they had much in common, both being loud, individualistic, sensitive, unpredictable and opinionated. Frances Edmonds' words about her husband, 'he has a reputation for being awkward and arrogant because he is awkward and arrogant', could easily be applied to Boycott. Both had careers riddled with controversy and conflict. Reflecting their difficulties with a team context, both have said that they should have been golfers rather than cricketers.

In an interview for Simon Barnes's superb study *Phil Edmonds: A Singular Man*, Edmonds explained, 'I found it easy to play cricket with Boycs. He would stand at mid-off and take the piss out of me when I was bowling. I knew he thought I was a good player and that always helps. He might have been a terrible captain, but I found it easy to play under him. I could call him all kinds of names, ask him how he could play like that, patting back half volleys? He never took offence with me. But Brears – I could never talk to him.' It is perhaps no coincidence that Edmonds achieved his best Test figures, 7 for 66, in that Karachi Test, far better than any of his Test performances under Brearley.

After the satisfactory, if hardly spectacular, start in Pakistan, Boycott's captaincy problems began to pile up on the second leg of the trip in New Zealand. The opening Test at Wellington was bad enough, when England were defeated by the Kiwis for the first time in forty-eight years. On winning the toss, Boycott had put New Zealand in, and a total of just 228 appeared to justify the decision. But then England responded with 215, of which Boycott made a painfully slow 77 in seven hours 22 minutes, though, in mitigation, he was badly cut above the eye attempting to hook Richard Hadlee. England seemed to have regained the initiative when they bowled out New Zealand for 123, Bob Willis taking 5 for 32. With a target of just 137, the tourists were confident of victory. But then Boycott was dismissed for one by an inswinging yorker from Dick Collinge, and the rest of the batting order folded like a deck of cards, all out for 64. Boycott, whose ripe tongue caused palpitations to manager Kenny Barrington throughout the tour, was gracious in defeat in public, but seething with his team in private. 'It was not pleasant. He was having a bad trot himself and when other batsmen failed he accused everybody of playing like schoolkids. He did not shout but he was brutally blunt,' wrote Mike Gatting.

It was in the second Test at Christchurch that Boycott's reputation as a captain plumbed new depths. This time England batted first after winning the toss and reached 418, thanks to a brilliant first Test century from Ian Botham. Then in the field they had New Zealand deep in trouble but, due to several dropped catches, just failed to enforce the follow-on. Morale was sinking but Boycott was incapable of raising it. 'Come on, keep going, just one more wicket to get and we've still got a good lead,' Bob Taylor said to Boycott, only to be met with the reply, 'You fuck off back behind the wicket and leave it to me.' When England batted again, it was obvious that they needed quick runs if they were to force a victory. Yet Boycott again failed to provide a lead. Just as he went out to open the batting, his partner Brian Rose asked him, 'I suppose we're going to go out and slog it?' Boycott said, 'You play it your way, I'll play it mine.'

But Boycott's way was hardly what England needed. The rest of the team became increasingly frustrated at his stonewalling until, at the fall of Derek Randall's wicket – he was disgracefully run-out by New Zealand's Ewan Chatfield backing up at the non-striker's end – Ian Botham marched out to join his captain. 'Don't worry, lads, Boycs will be back in here before the end of the over,' he told the dressing room as he left.

Botham has always been quite open about his deliberate running out of Boycott. He says that he set off for the middle with the 'clearest, if most extraordinary' of instructions from vice-captain

Bob Willis to 'go and run the bugger out'. If those were his orders, he was certainly diligent in carrying them out. Botham hit the ball to short extra cover, set off for an impossible single and Boycott was run out by about ten yards. 'What have you done? What have you done?' Boycott mumbled on his way back to the pavilion. 'I've just run you out,' replied Botham.

Appalled at this dismissal contrived by his own side, Boycott returned to the dressing room and sat on a bench with a towel on his head, muttering to himself, 'What am I doing? Playing with children?' The captain should have been sorting out the batting order and the pace of the innings, but Boycott sank deeper into his black hole of introspection. Eventually Phil Edmonds approached him: 'OK, Boycs, what are we doing now?' Still covered in his towel, Boycott replied, 'You and Willis are in charge of this tour – you work it out.'

The next morning the England team, presuming that Boycott would declare, were practising their fielding and bowling. Graham Roope recalls: 'Next thing Boycs comes marching over the ground, stops the practice and walks up to Both and I and asks: "Have you done any batting this morning? You haven't, have you?" So I said, "No. I thought we were going to declare." And Boycs replied, "I'm the fucking captain of this side. I'll decide when we will declare." Ian is about to explode when I grabbed him by the arm and said, "Come on, we'll do batting."'

With only 20 minutes left before the start of play, England had still not declared and Bob Willis was becoming increasingly angry because he needed to do his loosening-up exercises. Roope continues, 'In the end Bob, Kenny Barrington and Boycs were in the passageway, shouting and hollering. Then Kenny comes in and says, "We've declared." We went out and the roller was still going up and down the pitch – that's how close it was. And Willis absolutely flew in. The first ball hit Taylor straight in the chest, it whistled through so fast. It was the quickest I've ever seen a white person bowl.'

Willis took 4 for 14 as New Zealand were blown away for 105. England won by 174 runs, but none of the victorious side thought that had anything to do with the captain. Boycott had more trouble in the final Test, when he scratched the cornea of his right eye and had to miss the last two days of the drawn match.

Boycott might have gained the England captaincy by default, but if he had shown real qualities of leadership, it is possible that he would have retained the job beyond this tour. Making Boycott captain in the longer term would have resolved the perpetual difficulty of an England line-up weakened by Brearley's inadequate batting. And while this might have been harsh on Brearley, winner of the Ashes in 1977, the selectors had the recent precedent of another Yorkshireman taking over from an injured southern Oxbridge incumbent. In 1969, Ray Illingworth had been appointed to the England job when Colin Cowdrey had damaged his Achilles tendon. Despite Cowdrey's good record in his two previous series (victory in the West Indies and a draw against Australia), Illingworth kept the job even when Cowdrey recovered.

There was no chance of this happening with Boycott. Christchurch and Wellington had realized all the worst fears about his volatile approach and his inability to work with his players. His vice-captain Bob Willis felt he was just too cautious, writing that the 'lasting impression Boycott gave to all the players with him during that trip was of a terror of being beaten and having to face the consequences'. It was not just on the field that there were problems. The tourists were also irked by his obsession with net practice, which might be suitable for him but could be detrimental to others. On one occasion, before a match in Dunedin, he had the entire team taken at eight thirty in the morning for a net session on sub-standard pitches, which only succeeded in undermining the confidence of the batsmen. His lack of a sense of proportion was also shown in his reports on the umpiring, which often ran to several pages of foolscap covering every minor incident. Both hosts and members of the touring party were embarrassed by his forthright tone and lack of social grace. He was said to have behaved particularly badly in one fixture against the Young New Zealand XI in the remote township of Temuka on South Island, where his complaints about the wicket, the facilities, the journey and the meals prompted this view from John Delaney, the local policeman who doubled up as groundsman: 'He is a self-centred arrogant man who wants everything to go his own way or out comes a vicious tongue.' Again, Boycott could defend himself strongly against all these charges, arguing that they only reflected his hatred of losing, his dedication, his attention to detail and his frankness.

But the England authorities could never see it that way. Kenny Barrington, the manager, whose relationship with Boycott had been difficult throughout the tour, did not recommend that he retain the captaincy. By the start of the 1978 season, Mike Brearley was at the helm again. He later wrote of Boycott, in an article in the *Sunday Times* in October 1983: 'When he took over after I broke my arm, he won little except the recognition that he was not the man to captain England.'

17
'The Worst Months of My Life'

Ever since Boycott had taken over the Yorkshire captaincy there had been sniping against him. At the Headingley Test in 1972 this conversation took place between Richard Hutton and several members of the Yorkshire committee.

'Richard, would you be prepared to captain the county?'

'Yes, on one condition: Boycott is as far away from Yorkshire as possible.'

'The removal of Boycott will have to be handled as delicately as a military operation.'

As the journalist John Callaghan recalls, only a year later, when he began his career with the *Yorkshire Evening Post* in 1973, 'it was suggested to me by the secretary, Joe Lister, that if I wanted to ingratiate myself with the inner sanctum, then I should write stuff to help them get rid of Boycott'.

Though 1977 was another poor summer for Yorkshire – they won just six of their 21 championship games – Boycott's glorious return to Test cricket and his unique triumph at Leeds meant that most of his critics were temporarily silenced. 'If we had tried to sack him then, we would have been torn to pieces,' one later admitted. But once the season was over, Don Brennan, a member of Yorkshire's cricket selection committee, called for Boycott's dismissal. In the post-Headingley climate of adulation, where most of the Yorkshire public thought that Boycott deserved a knighthood rather than the sack, this was a courageous if incendiary move. 'Geoff Boycott is a great player,' Brennan told BBC Radio Leeds, 'but to my way of thinking he is not a leader. A captain should, in my opinion, be able to sacrifice himself, his own game, for the benefit of the side.'

Brennan's explosive words immediately provoked outrage. To give an outlet to this strength of feeling, a Reform Group was established in October by several Yorkshire members with the aim of supporting Boycott. One of the group's leading figures, Peter Briggs, a Manchester-based accountant, explained to me his motivation for backing Boycott. 'Brennan's comments were completely ill-judged. You have to remember in the seventies Yorkshire were really an apology for a side, with Chris Old, John Hampshire and Geoff the only players of quality, yet Geoff had managed to bring them to second place in the table in 1975. Tactically he was excellent. If he had a fault it was that he was so much better than any of the rest of the side and so could not easily relate to them. He was criticized for slow scoring but he was mindful of his responsibilities. If he was out, that was it.' This last point is backed up by the Middlesex spinner Phil Edmonds: 'I remember once talking to Boycs after a county match when he'd been batting really slowly, asking him, "How can you play like that?" And he said, "Ay, but if you'd got me out, you'd have run through the lesser players." There was some truth in that.'

Initially, the Reformers were dismissed as unruly troublemakers but that kind of arrogance was only too typical of Yorkshire's higher echelons, which had long been contemptuous of both members and players. 'The Yorkshire committee in the seventies was a cliquey bloc filled with people who were more interested in social status than in the mechanics of cricket,' says John Callaghan.

Sid Fielden tells this story of an exchange he had soon after he had been elected to the committee in 1982: 'I remember coming back to our seating area at Headingley and another committee man asked me: "Where have you been?"

'"Walking round the ground."

'"What for?"

'"To talk to members."

'"You don't talk to members. Don't you realize that you have joined the most exclusive club in the world?"

'"Yes I know, Yorkshire County Cricket Club."

'"No, the bloody committee."'

It is not surprising that in such a culture, a large section of the membership should have little respect for the committee, a mood reinforced by the botched handling of the Close and Illingworth departures. There was a groundswell of support behind the new Reform Group and a petition expressing no confidence in Brennan quickly gathered 828 signatures. Sensing the popular mood, the committee reappointed Boycott as captain at the end of October.

Another committee meeting on 10 November brought a decision of perhaps greater significance. This was the agreement to appoint Ray Illingworth as Yorkshire's new manager with effect from 1 April 1979. The committee put a positive gloss on this move, stressing that the manager would assist the captain in much of the technical and administrative side of running the team. Illingworth himself joined in this chorus of rhetorical harmony: 'I have no fears about not getting on with Geoff. I can't see our duties overlapping and obviously neither of us will be looking for confrontation. We have played together and got on well,' said Illingworth. Rarely since Chamberlain's 'Peace in our time' broadcast has a public utterance been more horribly damned by events.

While Illingworth was playing out his final season at Grace Road in 1978, Yorkshire was to be gripped by its deepest crisis yet over the captaincy. The summer started badly for Boycott. He suffered yet another finger injury, this time in a one-day international against Pakistan, and John Hampshire took over the captaincy while he recovered. In previous seasons, the side's performance had usually been worse in Boycott's absence, weakening the argument that his captaincy was somehow detrimental to it. This time it was different. Under Hampshire Yorkshire enjoyed a string of good results, including wins over Worcestershire, Leicestershire and, tellingly, Lancashire in just two days. There was now widespread talk that Yorkshire would be better off without Boycott, so much so that Boycott felt compelled to write to *The Times* confirming that he wanted to stay in his job as Yorkshire captain.

One of the biggest complaints about Boycott, in comparison to Hampshire, was that he failed to establish a good team spirit in the dressing room, especially through his attitude towards the younger players. Bill Athey was one of Yorkshire's rising stars in the late seventies but was often appalled by his leadership. He told me: 'There was a lot to admire about him. He was always fit for the job, he practised hard and he had absolute dedication. In other ways, though, he was a shocking professional. In the way he batted, the team was very much second place. That always put us under pressure. He thought about his own game to the exclusion of everyone and everything else. I remember once in the Benson and Hedges Cup at Middlesbrough when he got out. The order had been mucked around a bit and I just said to him when he came off the field, "Where am I batting?" His reply was "Please yourself." I was pretty shocked because I was only a youngster and you don't expect that from senior players, let alone the captain.' Athey also says that Boycott never gave him any help with coaching, perhaps because he feared Athey could develop into a rival. 'He would never impart any of his great knowledge. He had so much to offer but just wouldn't give it.'

The Yorkshire batsman Richard Lumb, who had looked up to Boycott when he started his career in 1970, grew more critical over the years. 'He was certainly not very forthcoming with advice. As a captain, he could never be described as a motivator of players. He was too tied up in his own game and was bad at getting the best out of others. Hamps was a more popular choice as leader. He could be more attacking and the atmosphere changed when he led in Boycs's absence.' Lumb is also interesting on batting with Boycott, with whom he shared 27 century opening partnerships, second only to Holmes and Sutcliffe for Yorkshire. 'We did have some good times but it wasn't always easy. He would often keep the strike when he fancied it. I can remember sometimes going six or seven overs and only facing a mere sprinkling of the ball. But he could also avoid the strike when he wanted to. In one Benson and Hedges game at Bradford against Hampshire, Andy Roberts bowled five overs in succession and I faced all but three of his deliveries. Boycs did not seem too keen to get down to his end. But then he has hardly been on his own as far as pinching or avoiding the strike goes – not by a long way.'

Frank Hayes told me an amusing fact, which shows how Boycott was regarded by Yorkshire's traditional enemy, Lancashire: 'In the seventies, if you got Boycott out in a Sunday League match, you were fined by the Lancashire dressing room. We wanted him in. We used to have fines in the team for many errors, like a misfield, and the money would go to an end-of-season party. One of these fines was for getting Boycott out in a Sunday League game – he could bat diabolically in that competition. Looking back, his record in charge with Yorkshire was terrible.'

The simmering discontent within the dressing room finally boiled over at the county ground in Northampton in July, when the Boycott–Hampshire rift became public. Like most of the rest of the Yorkshire side, John Hampshire had never been close to Boycott. But neither had he been part of the anti-Boycott faction led by Wilson, Sharpe and Hutton in the early seventies. Straightforward, honest and affable, he had little time for plotting and scheming against the appointed captain. But shortly before the Northampton game, he had had dinner with Ray Illingworth when Yorkshire were playing Leicestershire. As they discussed the future of Yorkshire the following season, Illingworth told Hampshire that Boycott did not trust him. Now, according to Boycott, Illingworth was referring to a chance comment that Boycott had made four years earlier, during the height of the Wilson–Sharpe–Hutton row but, whatever the truth about its origins, Hampshire was furious.

Hampshire gave vent to his mood in an extraordinary performance during Yorkshire's first innings against Northamptonshire. The home side, batting first, had made 280 for 7 in their allocated 100 overs. Boycott then replied in his most majestically turgid fashion. In his first three hours at the crease, he scored just 53 runs, compiled from 11 twos and 31 singles. At the other end, Bill Athey hit a brilliant 114, completely dominating his second-wicket stand of 202 with Boycott. Eventually Boycott was out in the ninetieth over for 113, which brought Hampshire together with Colin Johnson. It was now that Hampshire took his unprecedented action. Instead of hitting out to gain the final bonus point, he simply blocked his way through the remainder of the innings, he and Johnson putting on just another 11 runs from the final 10 overs. Hampshire was later to explain that his protest was not premeditated but rather a response to what had happened earlier in the Yorkshire innings. 'Call it a brainstorm if you like, but towards the end of that innings I just decided I was going to play the way we had seen Boycott play so many times,' he wrote.

There was an immediate uproar after the game. The Yorkshire president, Sir Kenneth Parkinson, who had been a spectator at

Northampton, described it as 'one of the worst days of my life'. But Yorkshire, terrified of more bad publicity and increasingly disillusioned with Boycott's leadership, refused to take any firm action at all beyond a mild private rebuke for both batsmen over slow scoring. Boycott's days as captain were now numbered. His authority had been fatally damaged by both Hampshire's 'go-slow' and by the committee's refusal to back him. His dwindling standing was emphasized by a private poll carried out by off-spinner Geoff Cope, which asked the Yorkshire squad whether they still wanted Boycott as skipper. According to his findings, 95 per cent of the capped players wanted a change. What made it all the worse for Boycott was that there now seemed a credible alternative in his old rival from his days in the colts, John Hampshire, who had impressed in the field and with the bat. While Boycott's form fluctuated, Hampshire was enjoying his best ever season. No longer could Boycott claim to be head and shoulders above the rest of his side. For the first time in 16 years, he failed to top the Yorkshire averages. In games for Yorkshire, he scored a creditable 968 at 50.94 but was eclipsed by Hampshire's 1463 at 54.18.

Boycott's fortunes with England during the summer of 1978 were equally varied. He was initially kept out of the Test series against Pakistan because of his hand injury but even when he had recovered the selectors refused to pick him until the last two Tests. Unhappiness with his captaincy and scoring rate in the winter against New Zealand, combined with worries about his lack of match practice, were the reasons. Boycott's return to the England side at Trent Bridge against New Zealand was almost a replica of his previous summer's effort against Australia, though it lacked the same emotional charge. Just as he was dropped early on at slip by McCosker in 1977, so in 1978 Geoff Howarth missed him in exactly the same position off Richard Hadlee when he had scored just two. Boycott went on to score 131 in England's innings victory. In his book about the 1978 summer, *Diary of a Season*, Bob Willis records how Boycott at Trent Bridge set up camp in a small anteroom off the main dressing room where he could be alone with his thoughts. Every time Boycott came off at an interval, 'He would retire to his private room and meditate for a while before emerging to tell us what a difficult wicket it was to bat on.' But Boycott fared less well in the final Test, falling for 24 and four, the latter dismissal achieved with a snorting delivery from Richard Hadlee that shattered his stumps.

Boycott might have enjoyed his Test century, but he was exhausted by his other trials of the last few months. On 15 September, at the end of the season, he left for a much-needed holiday in Bermuda. While he was out there, he was given the tragic news that his mother had died. Though she had first been diagnosed as suffering from terminal cancer in August 1977 and had become progressively more ill throughout the year, Boycott had not realized that she was so close to the end. Even in her final weeks, her first thoughts were for her beloved son and his professional troubles. 'Don't let the buggers get you down,' she said, just before he left for Bermuda. Her death came as a crushing blow. In his book *Put to the Test*, Boycott wrote of her last few months: 'We were very close, my mother and I, and I relied on her a lot. It is always a hard thing to lose a very special parent. If you are married and live away from home it is bad enough, but it is a dreadful experience to live with someone you love and see them deteriorate from week to week.'

Boycott's aunt Alice Harratt says, 'When the doctor told Geoff that she had cancer, he said he would do anything in the world, spend any sum, to help her get better. "Geoff, all the money in the world couldn't cure her," the doctor said.'

As if his life had not been thrown into enough chaos after he returned to his bleak, empty Fitzwilliam home, he was instructed to attend a meeting of the cricket committee on 29 September, the meeting at which the county decided to recommend his dismissal as captain. The timing of this move could hardly have been more inept. Afterwards, as a storm of protest began to swirl around Headingley, the committee pleaded in mitigation that it had offered to postpone the meeting in view of Boycott's bereavement but Boycott had said that he was willing to attend. Though technically correct, this was hardly relevant. Boycott knew that the committee were going to discuss the captaincy but he had no idea that he was about to be sacked. Conversely, the Leeds establishment were all too aware of the action they were going to take. Only the hardest of hearts would have failed to recognize the terrible new burden they were about to impose on a proud, emotional man, who had just lost the most important person in his life.

With bovine insensitivity, the committee pressed ahead. Soon after the meeting had finished, Joe Lister issued a statement which read: 'The Yorkshire County Cricket Club, after long and careful consideration, have decided that the interests of the club would be best served by offering the captaincy to J. H. Hampshire. The committee very much hope that Boycott will continue to extend his invaluable services as a player and have offered him a two-year contract to continue as such.'

Ultimately the committee might have been right in their decision. Boycott, because of his complex personality, was probably not suited to the role of captaincy. But, as usual, the leading committee men handled the matter so badly for so long that they created gaping wounds in Yorkshire cricket, which did not heal for the next decade. They failed to explain their position, treated the members with contempt, sent out contradictory messages, showed no understanding of their key players as individuals and acted without any consistency. It is, in essence, the story of English cricket administration.

Boycott was almost too distraught to react at first and said nothing in public until a sensational appearance on the BBC's *Parkinson* show on Saturday 7 October, which highlighted both his best and worst sides. In a lacerating attack on the Yorkshire committee, he was eloquent, boorish, coherent, aggrieved, egotistical, brilliant at marshalling his facts but unfortunate in his presentation of them. For instance, he referred to how he had given compassionate leave to Chris Old when he had lost his father, surely a personal and private matter that should not have been aired on prime-time Saturday night TV. But his criticism of the mismanagement of the club certainly hit home, and two sentences were especially memorable: first, 'In their haste to sack me, they could not even wait for my mum to be buried,' and second, 'They are small-minded people, people who feel that they always know best, who always feel that they are right.' Boycott concluded that it was 'difficult to think rationally or categorically. The only thing I want is to captain Yorkshire.'

Boycott already had vociferous public support, made all the stronger by the committee's heavy-handed reaction to his *Parkinson* appearance. His words about 'small-minded people' seemed to be confirmed by yet another letter he received from Joe Lister, Yorkshire secretary, full of blather about TCCB rules relating to 'public pronouncements by registered cricketers'. The committee were increasingly on the defensive, and at their meeting on 23 October they were subjected to another fusillade when Boycott's solicitor Duncan Mutch made an emotive two-hour speech, demanding that the committee 'change this unjust decision'. Then Arthur Connell, the chairman, gave the official reply, which after all the manoeuvres over the previous eight years at least had the virtue of honesty: 'It is nothing to do with what Mr Boycott has done or has not done. It is to do with what he is. Captaincy is above all a matter of leadership and the ability to persuade the other members of the team to play right up to and on occasions beyond their potential. This is the quality which in the sincere opinion of the majority of this committee Mr Boycott lacks.'

Outside these committee meetings, the pro-Boycott forces, led by the Reform Group, were growing in strength. Emboldened by their victory over Don Brennan in the previous year, they now accumulated finance, publicity and legal arguments in their battle to force the reinstatement of Boycott. Boycott's critics have been in the habit of sneering at the Reformers for their blinkered, hysterical stance. Yet there is no doubt that this group tapped into a deep reservoir of popular support for Geoff Boycott. And it is interesting to examine why Boycott should have had such a phenomenal appeal for the Yorkshire public. Even Botham in Somerset, Compton in Middlesex or Hammond in Gloucestershire never quite achieved the intense personal following that Boycott attracted in Yorkshire in the seventies and eighties. To the casual observer, this might seem odd, for few batsmen have had a greater reputation for dourness and caution. The PR supremo Max Clifford summed up the views of many when he told Boycott: 'Geoffrey, you were the reason I lost interest in cricket. Three or four hours of watching you score ten runs was quite enough for me.'

The explanation for the popularity of Boycott lies in both the state of Yorkshire cricket and his own character. The Yorkshire public are arguably the most passionate cricket followers in England and, in the words of Boycott's contemporary, Mike Smedley, 'They tend to put their heroes on a pedestal.' When Boycott was at the peak of his career, he was in the unique position in Yorkshire's history of being the only great player in his side. In previous eras, there were usually two or three outstanding players at the club, which meant that no one cricketer became the focus of popular adulation. So the careers of George Hirst and Wilfred Rhodes ran together, as did those of Maurice Leyland and Herbert Sutcliffe, Bill Bowes and Hedley Verity. In the post-war era, the regular successes of Hutton, Illingworth, Watson, Close, Wardle and Trueman all prevented any one player gaining pre-eminence. But after 1970 Boycott was on a different plane from his colleagues and therefore he was the only candidate for the pedestal. Moreover, the very failures of Yorkshire as a side meant that he became the main source of cricketing pride in the county. They might not win the championship but, by God, they had the best opening batsman in the world, an attitude reinforced by his remarkable Test match summer of 1977. Indeed, the sheer scale of achievements was certain to appeal to a well-informed cricketing public renowned for its interest in statistics. By the late seventies, the accumulation of records had developed a compelling momentum of its own. Again, as Mike Smedley puts it, 'People used to go and watch just to see him score runs rather than to see Yorkshire win games.' And the continual attacks on Boycott, inexplicable to ordinary cricket followers who knew nothing of committee politics or dressing-room spirit, cast him all the more vividly in the role of heroic martyr. He was the only successful feature of the club, went the thinking, so why on earth were the insiders so keen to denigrate him?

Boycott's personality and attitude also helped win him popular support. His bloody-minded obstinacy, which caused such offence within the cricket world, appealed to a Yorkshire public that cherished independence and plain speaking. His loyalty to his native county was obvious, and had been graphically demonstrated in 1977 by his refusal to sign up to Packer. His total dedication to his batting, his pride in his appearance, and his Spartan lifestyle all reinforced the popular image of a man who lived only for Yorkshire. In a tough, northern environment, Boycott was also very much a man of the people, not just in the sense that he came from a mining background – though that was important in establishing the distance between himself and the so-called 'gin and tonic brigade' on the committee – but also because he was keen to be in touch with the ordinary members and spectators, what he called on the balcony at Headingley in 1977 'me own Yorkshire folk'. Sid Fielden sums up Boycott's appeal in this way: 'He would speak to people all the time and they looked upon him as "Our Geoff". He was never aloof and would often allow kids to bowl at him when he was practising. Because he came from a mining community, people felt he was one of them.'

In another, more subtle way, his batting could be seen as representative of the ordinary public. Because he did not possess exceptional natural ability, he had fought his way to the top through sheer graft. In the eyes of many cricket lovers, therefore, he was the heroic embodiment of Yorkshire grit triumphing over flair. He showed that greatness could be achieved not just by the genius but also by the little man willing to battle heart and soul for his dream. His friend Tony Vann, later the organizer of the Members 84 Group, explains why he so admired Boycott at the crease: 'As a cricketer, I was a slow opening batsman. I wasn't talented. I had to make the most of my ability, so perhaps I saw part of me in the way he played. I understood, at a much lower level, what his game was about. I admired him as a cricketer, a craftsman, a technician.'

In contrast to his difficult reputation within the cricket world, Boycott's image with much of the wider public was of a courteous and reliable figure. Some ex-professionals might laugh at such a description, but it was not based entirely on myth. Boycott was always punctilious in dealing with his correspondence, despite the huge volume of mail he received, and, thanks partly to Anne Wyatt's excellent organization, he handled the administrative side of work more efficiently than most. Personally he might be awkward but professionally he rarely let anyone down. He was very good about responding to requests for autographs or assistance. In September 1985, for example, an Elsie Smith, aged 89, was in hospital recovering from a fall when she received a phone call from Geoff Boycott after a neighbour had written to him asking him if he would send a get-well message. One of Elsie's friends told the *Yorkshire Post*: 'She was really down when suddenly a porter came along saying, "Geoff Boycott to speak to Elsie Smith." She was thrilled. When I went to see her, her eyes were sparkling and it really made her day.' Ted Lester gives this example of Boycott's warmth towards young people: 'I was at Scarborough, standing beside Geoff. A young girl, aged about fourteen, came up to him and said, "I just wanted to thank you so much for writing to me when I was in hospital. It did me the world of good." I thought to myself that this was the kind of little thing Geoff does but people never know about.'

Sid Fielden says: 'I have seen this man do the most fantastic things. We have a scheme where we invite people from disabled organizations to be at the cricket. I remember him having a long chat here at Headingley with a group of blind cricket enthusiasts. They loved every minute of it and Geoff was genuinely moved by the experience. Another time at Abbeydale, Sheffield, we were running a schoolboys' competition and I got Michael Holding to do the presentation of prizes in one interval and Geoff in the other. These lads were thrilled. I had a letter from one of the fathers saying that his son will never forget that day and wanted to say thank you for arranging for him to meet two great stars.'

Against this background, it is little wonder that the Reformers should find such strong public backing for their cause during their long years of battling with the committee. But in the autumn of 1978 they were not yet strong enough to win the war. At a special meeting in Harrogate on 9 December, their resolutions expressing no confidence in the cricket committee and demanding the reinstatement of Boycott as captain were both defeated.

Boycott learnt of the confirmation of his sacking while he was out in Australia with the MCC touring party. It was a highly emotional time for him. On the plane to Australia, he wrote to his Yorkshire friend Ted Lester saying, 'These last few months have been the worst of my life, watching my mother get gradually worse and finally seeing her deteriorate so rapidly that she was unrecognizable as the strong, determined lady I knew. Living with her, being aware of the problem, and constantly knowing there was not a damn thing I could do to help, I have never experienced anything like it.' After further expressions of regret about losing the captaincy, he concluded, 'I don't know what I shall do now. Take time to think is the most important thing. Just get over my mum, settle down a bit here, try and play cricket and see what evolves.'

As it turned out, Boycott found it impossible to settle down to cricket in Australia. Clearly still in distress, he struggled to focus on the task of opening for England. At one stage he even considered returning to England to put his case at the Harrogate special meeting but instead sent six pages of foolscap outlining his grievances. With his mind so preoccupied, he had his worst ever series, averaging just 21.92 in six Tests and scoring only one half-century. During his appearance on *Parkinson* just before the tour party left, Boycott had joked privately with the audience off-air that he could not guarantee scoring 1000 in Australia – as on his great 1970/71 trip – but he could guarantee that he would score more runs than Mike Brearley. He was wrong. Boycott's tour aggregate was only 533 compared to Brearley's 538.

Throughout the trip there was continual evidence of the pressure he was under. Deficiencies crept into his technique as his confidence waned. His footwork lacked rhythm, his stance became more open and too often he played across the line. More of a loner than ever, he was also given to occasional displays of bad temper. During the state match against Western Australia, he was reported to the authorities after loudly calling umpire Don Weser 'a fucking cheat' for turning down an lbw appeal from Ian Botham. No action was taken once he had made an apology. Another awkward incident occurred when he encountered the new Yorkshire captain John Hampshire, who was playing for Tasmania that winter.

As winners of the Australian Gillette Cup Tasmania were to play the tourists in a game at Melbourne. The day before the match, Hampshire and Boycott found themselves at the same net practice. Hampshire broke the ice, asking Boycott, 'Are you all right, then?' 'Yes, are you?' was Boycott's reply. This cordiality was apparently further strengthened by Hampshire then sending down a few deliveries to Boycott. During the session, Hampshire suggested that they might have a chat later. The next day Hampshire received a message via Chris Old that Boycott would be willing to meet him, provided his friend, journalist and ghost-writer Terry Brindle, was also present. Hampshire thought this idea was nonsense. His answer came in one word: 'Bollocks.'

During the early part of the tour, Boycott was still in a quandary as to whether to accept Yorkshire's offer of a two-year contract.

Throughout the county's long history, there was not a single precedent for a deposed captain to remain as a member of the side. Moreover, other counties and clubs were expressing an interest in acquiring his services. 'If he and Yorkshire were to part company, we would certainly want our hat in the ring,' said Worcestershire's secretary Mike Vockins. 'He is a world-class player and it is difficult to imagine how any county could overlook the possibility of getting a player of that ability.' Another inquiry came from Lancashire League club Accrington who said that 'Boycott is the kind of big name on which our league thrives. People will flock to see a player of his calibre score a century or a duck.'

As he was to prove time and again, however, Boycott could not bear to part from his native county, no matter how great his frustration or bitterness. On 31 January 1979, the final deadline he had been given for acceptance of his two-year contract, he announced that he would be staying with Yorkshire. 'I have accepted Yorkshire's offer chiefly because I am a Yorkshireman. I have given my life to Yorkshire cricket and I want to see the team which I helped to build go on and win something for the greatest county in the game. If that is an emotional view, I am not ashamed of it.'

Though he failed disastrously with the bat for most of the series, his one major innings of 77 at Perth helped to secure an England victory. It was one of his slowest ever innings, lasting some 454 minutes, and at the end of the first day he was just 63 not out, having failed to reach the boundary once. 'What annoyed us was that the man simply refused to play shots, even to half-volleys. Actually I was bored watching him bat,' said Australian captain Graham Yallop. During his innings, Australian Liberal MP Jack Birney sent a telegram to Boycott and the press box that read, 'You have done more harm to Australian cricket than the Boston Strangler did to the reputation of door-to-door salesmen.' Even Boycott, happy to be in the runs again, was able to laugh about that. But what Birney and Yallop ignored was the crucial role that Boycott played in weathering the storm of the attack, holding up one end while David Gower scored his first century against Australia. Unfortunately Boycott was unable to repeat this effort in the remaining four Tests, in which he did not score another 50.

Boycott's loss of form could have been a hammer blow, but the Australians, without the Packer stars, were a desperately weak side and England ran out winners by a record 5–1 margin.

Boycott was now 37 and a shadow hung over his county and Test careers. 'I think he has almost reached the end of the road,' wrote Australian captain Graham Yallop. In an article in the *Observer*, under the heading 'Autumn of an Ageing Lion', Scyld Berry asked if Boycott was now beginning to show the signs of his advancing years. 'Could it be that his reflexes are beginning to slow? The ageing lion will have to sharpen them to reassert his supremacy.'

18
Return of the Master

Because his talent for attracting controversy matched his gift for making runs, Geoffrey Boycott has never really received the credit he deserved for his magnificent, 18-year Test career. Whatever the complaints about his behaviour at Yorkshire, there can be little dispute that his Test performances put him among the all-time greats. Peter May is often referred to as the finest English batsman produced since the war, yet Boycott averaged more per innings over a much longer career against tougher bowling attacks around the world. Similarly, of the four Englishmen who have scored more than 7500 Test runs, Boycott, Cowdrey, Gooch and Gower, Boycott at 47.72 has the highest batting average. At the twin peaks of his Test career, in 1970/71 and 1977, Boycott was probably the best opening batsman in the world. The supreme Indian Sunil Gavaskar could justifiably lay claim to that title at other times in the seventies and early eighties, but Boycott still enjoys a better Test record than all of his other great contemporary openers, Bobby Simpson, Bill Lawry, Glenn Turner, Keith Stackpole, Roy Fredericks, Desmond Haynes, Conrad Hunte, Gordon Greenidge and Mudassar Nazar. It is perhaps no coincidence that since he retired in 1982 England's batting has been in a state of near-permanent crisis.

When Boycott returned from Australia in the spring of 1979, his future as a Test player looked bleak. Few who watched his leaden-footed batting in Australia would have believed that here was a man who, over the next two years, would emerge triumphant against the world's most formidable bowlers. But that is exactly what Boycott was soon to achieve against full-strength Australian and West

Indian attacks, destroying for ever the myth that he was reluctant to face quick bowling.

After his drastic loss of form on tour, Boycott took the only step he could to iron out the problems in his technique: repeated net practice. At the MCC indoor school at Lord's, he worked for session after session on returning to a more classical, side-on stance, playing with the full face of the bat rather than closing it. The fluency began to return and by the start of the 1979 season, Boycott was refreshed and eager for battle. He felt he had a point to prove for both Yorkshire and England after the disasters of the previous 12 months, and he did so in the most emphatic style. During the summer, he became the first cricketer in the history of the game to average over 100 for the second time in a domestic season, hitting 1538 runs at 102.53. At one stage for Yorkshire, he scored centuries in three successive matches, his third hundred being a massive 175 made in just four and three-quarter hours against Nottinghamshire, carrying his bat through the Yorkshire innings of 360. Against Somerset at Harrogate, he and Richard Lumb put on 288 for the first wicket, the highest opening stand for Yorkshire since Sutcliffe and Hutton had compiled 315 against Hampshire at Sheffield in 1939.

Boycott's renewed confidence was also reflected in the international arena. He performed usefully, if not dramatically, in the World Cup, as England progressed to the final. In England's response to the vast West Indies total of 286 in 60 overs, Boycott and Brearley made a reasonable start, scoring 79 in 25 overs up to the tea interval, but thereafter they needed an acceleration that never materialized, partly because of Boycott's reluctance, in Brearley's words, 'to throw caution to the winds'. In his book, *Man in the Middle*, Gordon Greenidge, the West Indies opener, revealed: 'If Brearley and Boycott had been more ambitious and adventurous, the outcome of the whole match might have been different. They failed to realize that we were rattled and disheartened by our inability to part them. Eventually we came to the conclusion that although Boycott and Brearley were firmly in control, they were not making their runs quickly enough and we resolved to keep them in.' Though the pair put on 129, they took 38 overs to do so. The middle order was left with an unattainable rate and England were bowled out for 192.

Boycott fared better in the four Tests against India, scoring 378 runs at 75.60 with two hundreds at Edgbaston and the Oval. The latter match was the most exciting played on English soil since the Lord's Test of 1963. Set 438 to win, the Indians fell just nine runs short, with Gavaskar's monumental 221 carrying them to the brink of victory. For Alan Butcher, who opened with Boycott, this match was to be his sole Test appearance. He says, 'I actually found him quite helpful. At breakfast on the first day, he sat next to me and shared his muesli and fruit salad – what he always had. We talked a little bit about the Indian attack and I of course knew the wicket at the Oval. However, when we went out to bat, there were two things that struck me. First, on a really flat wicket with the ball not doing much, he did contrive to make it look exceedingly difficult; he was very suspicious of any movement. He came down the wicket on one occasion to tell me that Kapil Dev had just bowled a "right firecracker". I thought all it did was move a little off the wicket so I just said, "Yeah, right, Boycs." Second, there was his running between the wickets. After a while it was obvious that I was going to have to be pretty sharp about running his runs but some of my calls were turned down. He said, "Sorry, I have not got used to your running and calling." The implication was that I was expected to trust him. He found it difficult to trust his partners.'

When Butcher was preparing to bat on the first morning, chairman of selectors Alec Bedser took him to one side and said, 'Don't do anything stupid, will you?' a remark that only increased his anxiety. This is contrary to what Brearley had written in his book *The Art of Captaincy* where he claimed that it was Boycott who had increased Butcher's 'nervous, new-boy feeling' by giving him a lecture on the toughness of Test cricket. Butcher recalls, 'If anything was detrimental to my play it was what Bedser said rather than Boycott.' In the summer of 1997, at Edgbaston – where his son Mark was making his England début – Butcher by chance met Boycott and told him of the misattribution in Brearley's book. Butcher continues: 'Bear in mind this was eighteen years later. And Boycott replied, "I'm glad you told me that. I read what Brearley wrote and it has always worried me. With all his psychology degrees he does not always get it right."' At the next Test match at Lord's, Butcher then ran into Brearley, who said: 'I have an apology to make to you, Alan.'

'What do you mean?'

'Boycott has written to me.'

'You what?'

'Yes, he has written to me to tell me that I made a mistake in my book about your Test match. It's typical of him. However long it takes, he will always want to be proved right.'

That winter Boycott went to Australia under Brearley for the second winter in succession. The tour had been quickly arranged following the agreement that ended the division in world cricket between the Packer organization and the official Test authorities. Only three Tests were played between England and Australia. Because of the unique circumstances, the Ashes were not at stake, while greater priority was given to a triangular one-day World Series competition, which included the West Indies.

After his nightmare on the previous winter's trip, Boycott was a revelation on this tour, especially in the one-day games. Not since the Gillette Cup final in 1965 had he been so explosive on the cricket field, regularly punishing top-quality bowling with an array of dashing strokes. Several times, Dennis Lillee and Michael Holding found themselves staring down the pitch in disbelief as Boycott crashed their deliveries through the covers or back over their heads. What made his one-day form all the more astonishing was that he was initially left out of the side on the grounds that he was too slow a scorer – Brearley no doubt remembering his stodgy innings in the World Cup final. Recalled to the one-day side in the first match against Australia, his 68 was the top score and helped bring England victory by three wickets. Even better followed three nights later at Sydney when he hit a match-winning 105 in 46 overs, reaching his century with a perfect off-drive. His powers of concentration during this innings were remarkable, for he had to deal with not only Lillee and Thomson but also the racket from a nearby speedway meeting and firework display. Afterwards his captain Mike Brearley said this of his performance: 'It was almost unbelievable. I have never seen him bat like that before. I think we probably helped him by leaving him out of the first one-day match. When he got back in I'm sure he thought to himself, I'll bloody well show them they can't leave me out. The incredible thing is that he never had to slog once to make his runs.'

Boycott's brilliant sequence continued during the one-day series, with successive scores of 68 against the West Indies, 86 not out against Australia, and in the two finals against the West Indies (both lost) 35 and 63.

Yet, in the face of this great success, Boycott still managed to add to his already bulging catalogue of quarrels and incidents. As usual, his moody, sensitive nature was to blame for this latest string of clashes. Before a ball had been bowled in the first Test he had indulged in a petulant exchange with Mike Brearley, who asked for his advice on the state of the wicket. 'I have given my advice before and it hasn't been taken, so bugger it,' replied Boycott. Boycott felt just as aggrieved at the end of the game, which England lost by 138 runs when they should have saved it.

On the last day, he was the only batsman to show any application or technique. As the wickets fell all around him, he moved slowly towards another Test century. Then, to his horror, he was still on 97 not out when he was joined by last man Bob Willis. From the first delivery of a Lillee over, Boycott pushed the ball into the leg-side for an easy three, but Willis refused the third run on the grounds that Boycott should keep the strike in an attempt to pro-long England's innings. Unfortunately Boycott was unable to score off the next five, which left Willis to face an entire over from Geoff Dymock. One ball was enough. Willis immediately edged the left-arm seamer to slip, leaving Boycott stranded on 99 not out. Peter Willey, who was on his first tour with Boycott, says, with Geordie cynicism, 'Boycs came into the dressing room and he was in tears. And we thought, He's crying because he's missed his hundred, not because we've lost the Test. Mind you, he did deserve a ton, the way he played that day.'

More trouble followed in the second Test at Sydney. At the traditional eve-of-Test dinner, Boycott turned up with a thick scarf round his neck, complaining that he had hurt it playing a round of golf that day and was a doubtful starter for the Test. This im-mediately led to a lot of teasing from the other players, who put their napkins round their necks and pretended they, too, were suffering from the same ailment. They were sceptical about Boycott's injury, having seen the dampness of the wicket they were about to play on. Left uncovered during a torrential storm, it was almost tailor-made for Lillee, Dymock and Pascoe.

But Brearley did not see the joke. 'You're in. You're in. And that's all there is to it,' he told Boycott. He continued in the same vein the next morning, and ordered Boycott to take a fitness test. Bernard Thomas, the physiotherapist, explains what happened: 'I took him off for the test in the nets and, after watching him, I said, "Geoff, I'm sorry, but I think you should be playing. I know you're in pain but you, even injured, are worth at least 20 per cent more than anyone else in the side." I felt that even if he had a problem, it would not be further irritated by his playing. But he replied, "I'm not going to play, I'm not going to play." So we went back to the dressing room and I said to Brears, "Mike, it's up to you to sort it out. I think he should play." Now from what we had available that morning, he was the best man, even if he was not 100 per cent. So Mike and Geoff had this argument in the dressing room. Geoff made himself very unpopular, putting himself before the team.' Under duress, Boycott finally agreed to play but appeared to prove his point by making only eight and 18 as England crashed to an eight-wicket defeat.

Boycott landed in even deeper trouble after this Test with some self-pitying comments to journalist Tony Francis, then a sports reporter with ITN before his rise to TV-presenting fame. 'They'd have me out there on one leg if it suited them. I tell the selectors I'm not fit and they don't listen. They took the vice-captaincy away from me, then removed me from the selection panel. You'd think I didn't know anything about cricket, wouldn't you? I play best when I'm surrounded by people who appreciate me. I'm just fed up with the whole set-up.' Francis printed his words in a *Sunday Telegraph* article, and soon they were plastered across Australia, landing him in more difficulties with management.

'No one can deny that Geoff is a world-class opening batsman,' wrote Derek Underwood in his 1980 book about the tour, *Deadly Down Under*, 'but he is a mighty complex man. He is basically so egotistically minded about his cricket that he gives the impression that his own performance matters far more than the end result. He isn't particularly interested in watching the game once he is out and always seems geared up for only two things: his batting and his reputation.'

Yet Boycott could also show a lighter side of himself on tour. One night several of the England players, Emburey, Dilley, Bairstow and assistant manager Ken Barrington, went off to a downmarket night-club near Sydney's red-light district, where they watched the great Yorkshireman give one of the more unconventional performances of his career – as a disc jockey. Boycott had been paid £100 for the guest spot, and appeared to relish this early foray behind the micro-phone. Frank Keating gave *Guardian* readers this wonderful description of Sydney's new king of the turntable: 'Geoffrey wore tight black slacks and a frightful gaudy shirt of purply flowers. Not a hair of his hairpiece, preened and pomaded, was out of place. The lights kept changing – red, green, amber, you name it. His bright, blue-tinted contact lenses turned positively and glaringly Martian green when the lights were on amber.' As the evening wore on, wrote Keating, Boycott's famous lopsided grin 'got wider and wonkier'. One black girl with golden glitter on her eyelids asked England's number one to join her on the dance floor. With characteristic devotion to his task, Boycott resisted. 'I can't, luv. I'm putting on records, see,' he replied. But the old anxieties remained.

'I were all right, weren't I?' he asked Keating at the end of the evening.

'Yes, Geoffrey, you were absolutely terrific. They really loved you.'

'Yes, they did seem to, didn't they?'

For England, the brief series was a disaster as they lost 3–0. There was one bonus, however, in the way that Boycott and Graham Gooch cemented their opening partnership. In the third Test at Melbourne, they put on a brilliant 116, the best start England had enjoyed since Boycott and Brearley compiled 185 at Hyderabad two years earlier. With 49 stands together between 1978 and 1982, Boycott and Gooch opened more frequently for England than any other pair except Washbrook and Hutton (51 partnerships). Looking back on their time spent at the crease, Gooch is full of praise for Boycott. 'If you asked me who was the bloke I liked batting with best, it would probably be Boycott,' he told me. 'He was like a superstar, a legend in the game in both deed and as a person, someone who was utterly single-minded about his cricket. When I played with him on tour, I always got on with him pretty well. He tended to respect you if you stood up to him. He liked people who were like himself, a bit fiery. He could be a difficult guy, but out on the field, he was the ultra-professional, an excellent Test match player right to the end of his career. I learnt a lot in watching him play at the other end and in seeing how he prepared himself so well for every innings.' Gooch also believes that Boycott's running had greatly improved by the time they opened. 'He was not a bad runner at all. Short singles were a big part of his game plan, to keep the strike turning over and to accumulate. We had a good relationship there. The most important thing about running is that you shout and call early, you back up and you should be aware of the need for quick singles. It worked pretty well between us and we never had any problems.'

England needed Gooch and Boycott operating smoothly, for they were about to face twelve torrid months of international cricket against the might of the West Indies, whose terrifying battery of fast bowlers was at the peak of its potency. For the five-Test 1980 series, England had a new captain in 24-year-old Ian Botham, Brearley having announced his retirement after the winter tour. It was a poor appointment, for Botham possessed neither the tactical awareness nor the personal authority for the job. Too often he was the boisterous, practical-joking lieutenant who wanted to impress his troops rather than the hardened, scheming general who analysed how to win the war.

Boycott was disappointed to be passed over for the England job again in favour of a player sixteen years his junior, though after the New Zealand tour of 1977/78 he could hardly have expected otherwise. He did not allow his resentment to show in his form against the West Indies, scoring 368 runs in the series at a creditable average of 40.88 and hitting three half-centuries. Thanks partly to his sound batting, England managed to retain their dignity in the face of the extreme pace assault, losing the series just 1–0 – and that defeat, at Nottingham, was by the margin of just two wickets.

The respect in which Boycott was held by the West Indies is reflected in the words of the late Malcolm Marshall, who said that, when his side was preparing for the first Test, 'the conversation never strayed far from Boycott. He was the key to the match and possibly the series. As a batsman, he commanded the respect of

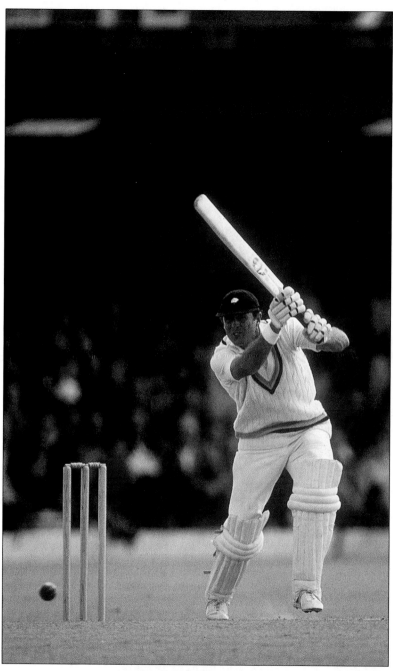

The Master Craftsman. Patrick Eagar

The century of centuries: Boycott drives Greg Chappell to reach this historic milestone, England v. Australia, Headingley, 1977. Colorsport

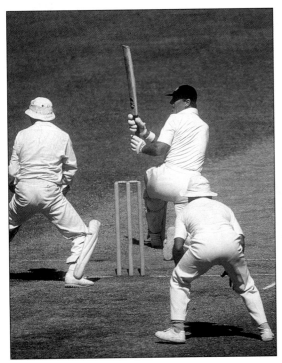

The great accumulator: Boycott batting against India, 1981/82, the series in which he became the highest run-scorer in the history of Test cricket.

Patrick Eagar

Yorkshire's pride: (*above*) Boycott on his way to a double-hundred against Essex, 1971, the year when he became the first Englishman to average over 100 in a season; (*below*) playing defensively in his last season in county cricket, Yorkshire v. Middlesex, Lord's, 1986. Patrick Eagar

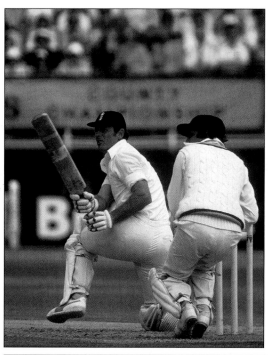

Boycott sweeps, England v. India, Edgbaston, 1979. He made 155. Patrick Eagar

Boycott bowled Holding for a duck at the end of one of the fastest overs ever bowled, England v. West Indies, Bridgetown, 1981. In the next Test in Antigua Boycott made a century against the same opposition. Patrick Eagar

In retirement: the coach (*right*) and the commentator (*below*). Patrick Eagar

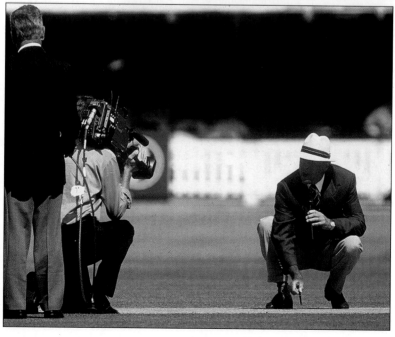

Boycott on trial: (*above*) Margaret Moore confronts Boycott; (*below*) Boycott's team arrive back from France, bloodied but unbowed. Max Clifford is at left; solicitor Richard Knaggs stands between him and Boycott. Among the women are Shirley Western (*next to Boycott*) and (*beside her*) Rachael Swinglehurst. © News of the World, PA News

Boycott, collecting his OBE in 1980, with his long-term companion
Anne Wyatt. News of the World

'Just a dad': Boycott, Rachael Swinglehurst and their daughter, Emma.

Daily Mail/Solo

Yet another comeback: behind the microphone again, after his trial in France.

Patrick Eagar

every bowler in the world and he was still very much in his prime when I faced him.' Graham Gooch recalls: 'There is no way he ducked out of fast bowling. People sometimes said that he used to try to avoid the strike but against the West Indies in those two series in 1980 and 1981, against probably the best quick attack there has been in the last twenty-five years, there was no quiet end. To score runs against that lot you had to have bravery, character and technique – Boycs had all three.'

Boycott's courage was amply demonstrated in the fourth Test at the Oval when the West Indies implemented a theory that Boycott might be vulnerable to fast, short bowling delivered round the wicket. Despite the intimidation, Boycott coped well until a bouncer from Colin Croft hit his forearm, then cannoned through the visor of his helmet so hard that it drew blood from his right eyebrow and left him with two black eyes for the rest of the match. Forced to retire hurt, Boycott returned at the fall of the next wicket and hit a stoical 53 before he was run out by Greenidge.

It is interesting to note here that Boycott was one of the last England professionals to adopt the helmet. He first wore one during the World Cup against the West Indies in 1979, then increased his protection by adding a perspex visor during the winter tour of Australia. There is a lot of nostalgic drivel talked about the 'heresy' of modern players wearing helmets, with airy claims that neither Compton nor Bradman nor Hutton would have been seen in one. How does anyone know? And what, precisely, is the moral difference between a helmet and any other form of protection, whether it be pads or gloves? Boycott took the perfectly rational line, which surely most of the other batting greats would have adopted, that something which improved safety and effectiveness at the crease should not be eschewed on the grounds of some spurious Puritan dogma.

For the first time since his return to Test cricket, Boycott looked like going through a summer without an international hundred. He rectified that with 128 not out on the last day of the Centenary Test against Australia, although, predictably, it was not an innings without controversy. The match had nothing like the excitement or romance of the 1977 Centenary Test in Australia, largely as a result of poor weather and the safety-first attitudes of the teams towards playing on a damp surface. The paying public felt almost as frustrated on the last afternoon when England, set a target of 370 runs in 350 minutes, refused to go for the runs after losing two early wickets. Instead, with Boycott at the helm, they blocked their way to a draw. Many, including ex-captain Mike Brearley, felt they were wrong not to make at least an attempt to accelerate. In fact at the tea interval, there had been a discussion in the England dressing room about going on the attack, which Boycott stifled by saying, 'This is a Test match against Australia. I'm not going out and playing it like a ruddy one-day game.' Half an hour after tea, when Mike Gatting hinted that he might be ready to hit out, Boycott told him severely, 'No, lad, get your head down.' So, amidst slow hand-claps and booing Boycott completed the nineteenth century of his Test career, passing an aggregate of 7000 Test runs on the way.

Surrey fast bowler Robin Jackman, who was England's twelfth man and was later to be a broadcasting colleague of Boycott's, also has cause to remember the Centenary Test, as he explained to me: 'I had tremendous respect for Boycs as a player, but my relationship with him in the England set-up was kind of non-existent because he was always very distant.' Jackman said that amongst his memorabilia at home, there is a Centenary Test dinner menu. The only signature missing from it is Boycott's because Jackman could not get hold of him at the official dinner. 'On the last day he told me as twelfth man that he wanted a taxi outside the door downstairs in order to get away. So I organized this for him and I also had his bag virtually packed. All he had to do was strip, shower and get out. And as he left the dressing room, I got my menu out of my cricket bag and said, "Oh, Geoff, there's just one thing before you go. Would you mind signing this card?" And he told me, "I haven't the time." I felt kind of miffed by that.'

A far more appalling Boycott incident occurred on England's tour of the West Indies that winter. Legendary in the cricket world but rarely referred to in print, it reveals the depths of that social ineptitude which left Boycott unpopular with many of his team-mates. During the Barbados Test, the England side had suffered the terrible blow of the death of Kenny Barrington. On the night of 14 March, he had a heart-attack and was dead before he arrived at the local hospital. The news shook the England side to its core. Rarely has a manager been more loved and missed by his charges. Nervous, devoted, conscientious and often tongue-tied – he went up to a bar on this trip and asked for 'one of those Peter Granadas' – he was a father-figure to most of the players. Professionals are often inclined to be contemptuous of the advice of 'old timers' but that was never the case with Barrington, who commanded their total respect. At the minute's silence on the ground the morning after his death, much of the England party was in tears.

With the shadow of his loss hanging over the team, England then flew from Barbados to Montserrat for a game against the Leeward Islands. It was at this moment that Boycott committed one of the worst social blunders of his career. The plane carrying the England team on this brief trip was very short of space, though Boycott has insisted that there was some room for wives and girlfriends. Then Boycott, with an insensitivity that only the Yorkshire committee could have equalled, asked if Ken Barrington's vacant place could be taken by his companion Anne Wyatt. At a time when arrangements were still being made to embalm Barrington's body and bring it home to England, this request could hardly have been more tactless. It was treated with the contempt it deserved.

I have had this story confirmed by two impeccable sources, one of whom received the request and the other who witnessed it being made. Neither of them have any axe to grind against Boycott; indeed, one says that the incident did not even cause that much bad feeling 'because everyone expected that sort of thing of Geoff, being at the front of the queue for what he wanted'. It is interesting that Boycott has always denied, not this specific tale, but a grossly distorted version of it. In this more lurid, and false, account, he is supposed to have gone to the tour management to request Barrington's first-class air ticket home from the Caribbean to England. That could never have been true, for the TCCB could not afford first-class air fares.

Peter Willey also witnessed the clumsy side of Boycott during the tour, albeit on a far lesser scale: 'We roomed together for about two weeks on the trip. The most amazing part of that was when we went down to the restaurant in the hotel, he'd say, "Just follow me," and then we'd go into the kitchens and he'd be telling the staff, "We want this, we want that." I was embarrassed really.' But Willey saw much to admire in Boycott. 'He made a rod for his own back with the way he kept upsetting people, but he was really good when he talked to me about cricket. He would give me some technical advice suggesting a different guard or a different grip. I think he liked being asked for a few tips; it showed he was appreciated. There was a mutual respect there. We were both down-to-earth. I could tell him to sod off, and he'd tell me the same.'

David Gower says that the tours in the 1980s to the Caribbean were 'the hardest things I ever had to do in cricket' because of the strength of the West Indies pace attack, but he found that 'Boycs was not always that helpful. At team meetings, you might find him slagging people off, "He can't play," but quite a lot of the time he just said nothing. I think that was partly because he felt he should be captaining England.' Gower recalls 'a classic example' of Boycott's tactlessness during the Barbados Test. Gower had just returned to the dressing room in a fury having been bowled by the occasional spin of Viv Richards, after seeing off Roberts and Holding. 'Just as I was taking my pads off Geoffrey came up to me and said, "I could tell you were going to get out. I saw you getting all easy, all loose. I knew you were going to get out."

'"Oh, sod off, will you, Geoffrey?"

'That was pure Boycott. He could read the game, read the batsmen but couldn't tell the appropriate time to say it.'

Given all the problems England faced on this tour over the pace attack, the death of Kenny Barrington and the Jackman affair – the Marxist regime of Guyana refused entry to Jackman because of his South African connections, thereby causing the cancellation of the second Test – the team did well to lose only 2–0, compared to the 'blackwashes' of 1984 and 1985/6. In the opening match at Trinidad they went down by an innings and 79 runs, with Boycott's 70 in the second innings England's only half-century of the Test. After the Guyana fiasco, England suffered another massive defeat, this one by 298 runs, in the third Test at Barbados. The most memorable incident of the game was Michael Holding's ferocious first over to Boycott. What made it so dramatic was that Holding took no time at all to reach his full, lethal pace. Most quick bowlers need a few deliveries to get their rhythm but here, in the words of Graham Gooch who was standing at the other end, 'It was nought to ninety in 3.4 seconds. There was no warming up with him. He was sensationally fast from the first ball.'

The Saturday afternoon crowd, packed into the stands or sitting on the corrugated iron roofs, sensed they were in for something special as Holding reached his marker, turned and began his graceful, gliding run to the wicket. The first ball, short of length, rapped Boycott on the gloves. The second, of a similar length, had him groping outside his off-stump. The third ball cut back and hit him on the inside of the left thigh. The fourth and fifth deliveries, again short of a length, were fended off by Boycott down into gully. Then came the final, quickest ball of all, a fuller one that sent the off-stump cartwheeling twenty yards before Boycott had completed his stroke. Most seasoned observers watching this electrifying passage of cricket agreed that this was the fastest over they had ever seen in their lives. Even Boycott, usually such a stern critic of his own game, felt there was nothing he could have done. 'For the first time in my life I can look at a scoreboard with a duck against my name and not feel a profound sense of failure,' he wrote, in the tour diary he recorded for his book *In the Fast Lane*. In the second innings he suffered almost as badly, caught in the gully off Holding for one.

Many lesser players would have been in a state of psychological shock for the rest of the tour after that experience. Indeed, there were increasingly loud claims that he was finished as a Test cricketer. Even before the tour had begun, Fred Trueman was demanding his exclusion from the England side: 'He's not picking up the line and length of fast bowlers as quickly as he used to. I dread to think what might happen over there.' But Boycott now delivered a magnificent response to this chorus of pessimism. Instead of crumpling, he asked for a video of Holding's over from the BBC, replayed it three times, then returned to the nets to work on his game. In the fourth Test at Antigua Boycott demonstrated his extraordinary determination with one of the bravest performances of his career. In England's first innings, he and Gooch gave England a solid start of 60, with Boycott making 38. Even better followed in the second, when England had to bat through the last day to save the game. The opening pair put on 144, and shortly before the close, Boycott reached his twentieth Test century. Peter Willey was at the other end: 'It was a great knock. He never seemed bothered about facing the West Indies attack. He had the courage and technique to handle them.' And this is what one of the world's great fast bowlers, Imran Khan, wrote in 1983: 'Geoffrey Boycott is one English batsman I have admired greatly over the years and I wish Pakistan had a few like him. I was particularly impressed by the way he battled through against the West Indies fast bowlers in 1980 to 1981. That took guts, technique and nerve.'

Boycott was now approaching 41, an age by which most batsmen had long since retired from Test cricket. He carried on, motivated not just by his remorseless professionalism but also the chance of overtaking Gary Sobers' record as the greatest run-scorer in the history of Test cricket. For that goal was now in sight. Sobers' aggregate stood at 8032, while by the end of the West Indies tour, Boycott's total was 7410 at 49.7. Two more satisfactory series and the record would be his.

The 1981 summer against Australia turned out to be something of a disappointment for Boycott. The series was dominated, of course, by the incredible performances of Ian Botham, who, freed from the England captaincy after the second Test, achieved feats with both bat and ball that instantly became part of Ashes history.

While Boycott may have fallen below his usual standard, his contribution to England's 3–1 victory in the series should not be overlooked. At Lord's in the second Test, playing in his hundredth Test match, he appeared set for another hundred when he chased a wide ball from Lillee and was caught for 60. The miracle of Headingley in the next Test was fashioned by Botham's wondrous century, Willis's awesome bowling and Brearley's cool leadership. But, in retrospect, Boycott's painstaking innings of 46 in three and a half hours was vital in wearing down the Australian bowlers before they were blown away by Botham's hurricane. 'I was full of admiration for Geoff's skill; he hardly played and missed at all,' wrote Brearley later.

Boycott achieved little in the following two Tests at Edgbaston and Old Trafford. On the eve of the fifth Test, he expressed to Brearley his worry that he might be dropped for the forthcoming tour of India and would thereby lose the opportunity of overtaking Sobers' record. He was also concerned that, like Robin Jackman, his connections with South Africa – he regularly holidayed and coached there – might discourage the selectors from picking him for fear of the political reaction from India. 'Boycott was curiously in need of reassurance. I tried to encourage him towards a less anxious, less cautious frame of mind,' said Brearley.

Brearley's efforts were to little avail. While Botham was indulging in another epic of sustained hitting, Boycott only made 10 and 37, though in the former innings he passed Colin Cowdrey's Test aggregate of 7624 to become England's greatest run-scorer. He came good in the drawn sixth Test at the Oval, scoring 137 in England's first innings and winning, in Brearley's words, 'a contest of rare vintage with Dennis Lillee'. In the second innings, Lillee had his revenge by bowling Boycott for a duck. 'It was like a random knockout punch at the end of the long and even bout,' wrote Lillee later, in his autobiography. The bout had lasted 11 years, stretching back to the 1970/71 tour. Lillee, widely regarded as the greatest of all fast bowlers, had an interesting analysis of Boycott, arguing that he would not have selected him in his side because he was not a mixer and sometimes scored so slowly that he could become a liability. On bowling to Boycott he said: 'I always fancied getting him with the short-pitched ball directed at his body or the shortish ball outside off, which he tries to parry or push away square. He gets out a lot to that shot. But keep the ball up to him on leg stump and he'll always look champion.'

19

Constructing the Image

By the early eighties, Geoff Boycott was one of the biggest sports stars of Britain. His record-breaking achievements, his talent for causing controversy, and his vivid character made him a dream subject for tabloid editors and TV producers. Almost any story, no matter how trivial, that had the name Boycott attached to it was guaranteed coverage. Far from detracting from his public standing, his endless rows with Yorkshire and England only added to his reputation as a colourful celebrity. As Mike Brearley said ruefully, during the 1979/80 tour of Australia: 'It really is extraordinary how anything to do with him is inflated out of all proportion.'

Boycott's attitude towards his celebrity status was ambiguous. For an insecure man who craved recognition of his talent, the adulation of the public was the boost that his ego constantly needed. Only through the cheers of his adoring fans could he feel truly validated as a cricketer and an individual. Yet Boycott was also a very private man: shy, awkward, and sensitive. He often grew weary of the endless media and public intrusion into his personal life. As Rachael Swinglehurst puts it, 'He's been living in a goldfish bowl for more than thirty years.' Kevin Sharp, who played with Boycott at Yorkshire, tells a story that reflects his sense of exhaustion: 'I remember once we were playing a Sunday league game at Hove, and myself and one of the other lads went for a walk along the seafront just to get some fresh air in the morning. When we got back to the hotel, Boycs was at the reception desk reading a paper.

' "Where have you been?" he asked.

'I replied: "I just went for a walk along the front."

'He looked at me and said, "I wish I could do that. I can't even go to the toilet in peace." '

Boycott's upbringing in a tightly knit working-class family from a Yorkshire mining village left him ill-equipped to cope with the intense demands of stardom. It should be remembered that other British sporting greats have found it impossible to handle such pressures. Ian Botham, the only cricketer since the seventies who achieved a similar level of fame to Boycott, was often involved in appalling publicity over drugs, drink and women. George Best, brought up in the back streets of Belfast, turned to drink at the height of his career, while Paul Gascoigne's personal life reads like *The Rake's Progress*. Boycott was too self-disciplined to sink into the quagmire of alcohol that dragged down Best and Gascoigne but his frustrations found an outlet in his legendary displays of bad temper and rudeness.

'The dressing room, the car and the field are private places. It's the bits in between – the autograph hunters and the newspapermen, the cameras and the outsiders, that are difficult to endure. Our craft is performed on a public stage,' wrote Peter Roebuck in *It Never Rains*. Now, it might seem odd that a man who valued his privacy should pursue such a very public career throughout his adult life. If he disliked media attention, why did he follow the spotlight of fame?

The answer lies in the contradiction that can often be observed in great public performers who need an audience but loathe intimacy. Many of our finest comedians, singers, actors, sportsmen and politicians feel far more at ease in front of a crowd of strangers than they do with a small gathering of friends. On the stage, at the crease or at the despatch box, they are playing out a role. They have both anonymity and attention. But in private they no longer have the shield of their public image. They are vulnerable, exposed to the gaze of those immediately around them. The comedian Barry Humphries, creator of Dame Edna Everage and Sir Les Patterson and, like Boycott, the most private of public men, spoke recently about his relationship with his work. 'After a long, stressful day, I step into my costume, my persona, walk into the light and think to myself, Alone at last.' For Geoff Boycott, one can imagine a similar sigh of relief as he walked out on to the field. All the compromises of everyday life, the demands of other people, the conflicts and the questions, suddenly fell away. He, too, was alone at last, responsible for no one and nothing but his mastery of the moment. Able to focus on his batting – just as Humphries focused on his act – he had created the one environment where he could feel entirely comfortable with himself.

The resort to a public image of irascibility was one of the mechanisms Boycott adopted to keep the public at bay. No one wanted to get too close to someone with a reputation for being wilfully difficult and dismissive. With such an attitude, which barely mellowed with the passage of time, it is no surprise to find his career littered with social disasters – and not just in the cricket world. In December 1985, for instance, he visited the Saxone shoe store at the Ridings centre in Wakefield and subjected a young salesgirl to a tirade of abuse. The assistant was so terrified by Boycott, who had gone into the shop to return a pair of shoes, that she collapsed in tears and security had to be called to escort him from the centre. 'The girl was upset and didn't know what to do. His attitude was appalling,' said one of her colleagues.

At a social evening in Dorset in September 1982, Boycott created another row: 230 guests had paid £5.50 a head to attend a cricket dinner organized by the Wimborne Community Association, at which Boycott was the main speaker, but his conduct was said to be so outrageous that the Association's social chairman Les Philips stated: 'I will lose no sleep if I never see him again. I was absolutely amazed and appalled by his behaviour.' Philips claimed that Boycott kept the guests waiting while he sat naked in his hotel room watching cricket on TV, then arrived 20 minutes late for the dinner, told Mr Philips to 'shut up' when he tried to inform him of the dinner arrangements, abused local journalists with four-letter words over their request to report his speech, demanded his £650 fee in cash and, once he had counted it out, left before the other speakers. The editor of the *Wimborne and Ferndown Journal*, John Dudley, said afterwards: 'Boycott is the rudest man I have ever met.'

But Boycott later provided a very different version of events, which, yet again, shows how he felt his actions could be misinterpreted. He insisted that he had told organizers beforehand that, because of his long journey, he would not be ready until at least seven fifteen, when the dinner was due to start. The lurid accounts of his hotel-room nudity had been grossly misrepresented. 'While I was bathing and changing I had one eye on the TV Test highlights. What's wrong with that?' He said that he had also forewarned the Association that he could not stay for all the speeches because his habit was to retire early. On the question of his fee, he denied demanding the money in cash but explained that the Association had been only too keen to pay him in this way. Boycott said it was 'totally untrue' that he had counted out the money three times before leaving the dinner. Finally he quoted a statement he had been given by the Wimborne chairman Ken Richmond: 'You went down very well and we all enjoyed the evening. We were flabbergasted when we saw the press reports.'

Sid Fielden recalls the time that, as a Yorkshire committee member, he had to deal with a bizarre three-page complaint from Warwickshire about Boycott's behaviour during a Benson and Hedges Cup tie at Edgbaston, where Boycott was said to have: (a) gone round the place settings in the dining room and removed the meat from the sandwiches; (b) answered the telephone in an abusive manner; (c) told a photographer to 'fucking get lost' when she had asked him to take part in a team photograph, because he said he was watching the television.

At the request of the committee, Fielden, a detective sergeant, questioned Boycott about the complaint. To the first charge about the sandwiches, Boycott replied: 'I went into the dining area, took what I wanted but you know I don't eat much bread, so I left most of it on the plate and had the meat.' It is true that Boycott eats in this manner. Jim White noticed it immediately when he interviewed Boycott for the *Independent* in November 1992. As he reported: 'Boycott picks up two sandwiches at once, strips the ham from one and carefully pops it into the other, discarding the excess bread.' On the second charge, Boycott said he was watching the Rugby League cup final on the TV when the phone rang with 'some bloody woman wanting so-and-so'. He claimed that he only swore after he had put down the receiver. On the third charge, Boycott said that the photographer 'shouted down the corridor and I shouted back'.

'Did you swear?' asked Fielden.

'I can't remember.'

'That means you probably did.'

Though Boycott hardly came out well from the saga, no disciplinary action was taken, because only one of the charges – swearing at the photographer – was clear-cut.

On another occasion, during a game against the Leeward Islands on the 1980/81 tour to the Caribbean, Boycott returned to the England dressing room after being given out lbw, a decision he later described as 'the worst of my life'. An attendant, standing outside, began to laugh and point at Boycott, who responded by leaning out the dressing-room window and chucking a glass of water over him. The soaked attendant then picked up a brick and strode towards Boycott. Only through the intervention of those around him was he restrained. Though some of the England squad were amused by the incident, it might not have been too funny for Boycott. The attendant wanted to press charges and Alan Smith warned Boycott that he could end up in prison if the case went wrong. In the end, the squalid business was settled by mutual apologies.

Again, Boycott's robust dealings with professionals were not confined to the cricket world. A London painter called Ivan Rose had produced a coloured illustration of Boycott for a book published in 1983 called *The 50 Greatest Cricketers*. The portrait, taken from a photograph, showed a grim and defiant Boycott in his favourite pose, about to play the forward defensive. Soon after the book was published, Rose was the surprised recipient of a call from Boycott demanding a replica of the illustration. 'I want that picture. But I want it bigger and bloody better.' Rose suggested that Boycott could come to London for a portrait sitting. 'No point in that. I just want the same one as in t' bloody book.'

One radio presenter also experienced the sharpness of Boycott's tongue. In September 1980, Boycott, visiting Bristol to play in a flood-lit international, was scheduled to appear on local radio. At the last minute, however, he decided to cancel his interview in favour of some batting practice, prompting the presenter, John Turner, to complain to listeners about Boycott's attitude. Unfortunately, Boycott, travelling to the ground, heard the jibe on his car radio. Immediately, he ordered his driver to take him to the radio station, where he burst into Turner's studio: 'John Turner, eh, I'll give you John Turner.' He was then put on air, telling the audience: 'I was listening, and I were bloody annoyed.' There followed a typically fluent twenty-minute interview.

Even children were sometimes at the receiving end of Boycott's ungraciousness. One Essex supporter, who now works for the BBC, remembers trying to get his signature when Boycott came to Chelmsford in the early seventies: 'At first he refused but then said that if some friends and I washed his car for him he would sign later. So we did as instructed, washing the car very thoroughly. We waited for him beside the car at the end of the game but he just got into it and drove off. I remember the absolute indignity of being a pre-teen kid and being snubbed and used in that way. Maybe he had a bad day but we were standing there with our little books open. He was a total bastard.'

Against such tales, however, should be set the many acts of kindness or generosity Boycott has performed, particularly for those in his trusted circle of family and friends. Such testimony shows that the picture about Boycott is far more complex than his enemies would admit. Tony Vann, for instance, recalls that Boycott was a great help in arranging for his wife to see a senior consultant when she was suffering badly from arthritis, the same complaint that afflicted Boycott's mother. 'That is the sort of man Geoffrey is but people out there don't know him.' John Callaghan, the journalist, says he has never given him any anxiety over money in all the various projects on which they have co-operated. 'He's not mean. That's just a label. In fact, he sometimes pays me more if he thinks I have had more work than expected. He is absolutely straight. If Geoff says, "I will give you a cheque for a thousand pounds in three weeks' time," the cheque will arrive on the exact date he promised. He never forgets.'

Boycott's colleague on Talk Radio, Jack Bannister, told me of an event that Boycott held at his local golf club near Barnsley, with several top cricket stars including Dennis Amiss and Tony Lewis. 'He laid on everything: sandwiches, drinks, green fees, caddies. Then in the evening he organized a dinner at Barnsley's best restaurant on a generous scale. By the end of the night, I was starting to query the cost of it all, and he nearly bit my head off. "One more word about it and you can find your own way out of Barnsley," he said.'

The writer and editor Adam Sisman says that in 1990 Boycott sent him a cheque for five hundred pounds as a sign of gratitude for his editorial assistance on the book *Boycott on Cricket*. 'I had already been fully paid by Transworld for my work so I was both surprised and touched to receive this present from Boycott out of the blue. There was no reason for him to pay me in this way and his generosity counters some of the stories about his meanness.'

Partly because of the insecurities about his background and his long struggle to attain greatness, Boycott sees himself as a figure in constant battle with the world around him. He is therefore inclined to be black-and-white about people, regarding them as either supporters or enemies, while he also sets great store by loyalty to his cause. The worst crime, in Boycott's eyes, is to break a trust. His public life is littered with accusations of betrayal and deceit against a vast gallery of institutions and individuals. For instance, in his last book, *Geoffrey Boycott on Cricket*, he bitterly attacked the commentator Henry Blofeld for going into print with complaints about Boycott's behaviour and for refusing to back his legal appeal against Margaret Moore, despite having enjoyed, claimed Boycott, a mutually supportive friendship in the past. 'He seems to have been only too eager to latch on to me in his hour of need, but when I was in trouble, instead of helping me, he appears to have relished exploiting my vulnerability.'

Alternatively, Peter Briggs, a friend of Boycott from the Yorkshire Reform Group days, told me: 'He retains the loyalty of people he considers his friends. Whatever anyone says, Geoff Boycott is as honest as the day is long. He would never let you down or lie to you. If we meet up on tour when I'm travelling overseas, he will always take me out to dinner and insist on paying.' George Hepworth, whose friendship with Boycott stretches back to his days at Ackworth, feels the same way: 'When I had an accident at work, he was the first on the phone, and he took me along to see Paddy Armour, the physiotherapist who used to deal with him. When my son Peter was trying to get into the Leicestershire side in the eighties, he was very supportive, always urging his mates in Leicester, like Jack Birkenshaw, to put him in the side. At Yorkshire when Graham Stevenson had to retire because of injury, he fought tooth and nail for him and eventually got him a settlement of £7000 when Yorkshire had only offered Graham £4000. He has done so many things that are never talked about. For instance he raised a lot of money in his benefit year for a local spina bifida charity. Again, in the seventies when I mentioned to Geoff that the Pontefract and

District Cricket League were struggling for money, he arranged a fund-raising game, got the league on a firm footing and built a healthy bank balance. In recognition of his work, the league made him a life member.'

Backing up this point about Boycott's charity work is the evidence of Brian Hazell, a councillor in Wakefield, who has run the Suzy Fund, a campaign for third-world relief, for 24 years, amassing £300,000 over that period. Councillor Hazell told me: 'I have regularly asked Geoff to help, auctioning the cricket gear, presenting the raffle prizes, signing autographs. He has always responded favourably. Over the years he has helped us raise thousands for Ethiopia and other projects. He has a genuine concern for suffering. He might not be a socialite, a beer-swiller or a raconteur but, in my experience, he is a gentleman, even if he is a little blinkered in his obsessive love for cricket.'

It has occasionally been claimed that Boycott, because of his attitude, is without friends in the cricket world. Brian Close, at the height of the Yorkshire row in 1984, told him, 'You ought to be the most popular man in cricket but you can't name me two blokes in the game who have a good word to say for you.' Well, that, as we have seen, is patently untrue. Top cricketers like Bob Barber, Tony Greig, Brian Luckhurst, Dennis Amiss, and M. J. K. Smith have all been keen to sing the praises of Boycott.

Probably his closest friend on the England circuit in the 1970s, Alan Knott, wrote in his autobiography *It's Knott Cricket*: 'I owe him a great deal for his encouragement of my batting throughout my career. He is a very sensitive person and that means that occasionally he can get hurt very easily, but that sensitivity, when channelled in another direction, makes him a very friendly, warm person with a special brand of humour.' And in the Yorkshire dressing room of 1984 there were several players, such as Paul Jarvis, Arnie Sidebottom, David Bairstow, Graham Stevenson and Kevin Sharp, who were big admirers of Boycott.

Sharp complains that the media never seem interested in the good side of Boycott: 'I think that Boycs overawed a lot of people just with his presence. Many people seemed unable to be themselves in front of him but for me personally it was never an issue. I felt some form of affinity to him because he was a guy who always said what he thought, who didn't pull his punches. Personally I enjoyed being around him. When I got married, I even bought a brand new bed off him that had never been used – very cheaply, I should add. He was good to me that way. Geoff was also instrumental in setting up some coaching courses for me in the Wakefield area that helped me make a living in the winter.'

Yet Sharp, like many others, admits that Boycott could be a 'Jekyll and Hyde character'. 'Some days he could be very mellow, pleasant, nice to people and then on other days he would be rude, short. He could be contrary in the dressing room as well. At times he would be very quiet, doing his own thing and hardly speaking to anyone. Then there were other occasions when he would join in and have a laugh.' Paul Jarvis, who says that he 'enjoyed having Boycott around and felt a real sadness when he retired', remembers this side of Boycott with affection, particularly the time in 1982 when Boycott, playing at the Oval against Surrey, received a cruel blow in the box from a Sylvester Clarke delivery. 'The box had broken and there was a lot of bruising to his manhood. Suddenly, as Boycott stripped off and lay on the table waiting for treatment from the physio, the lads gathered round and threw him in an ice-cold bath. A lot of people would have gone absolutely ballistic but he took it really well. I think he quite enjoyed the attention.'

On another level, when Boycott was at his most acerbic and dis-agreeable, he might have been motivated partly by the urge to live up to his image as the gruff, no-nonsense Yorkshireman content to be the loner. For this image was a vital part of Boycott the celebrity. Once his reputation had become lodged in the public mind by the late seventies, he may have felt he had to behave in the way his audience expected. It is fascinating to listen to a tape recording of Boycott's quiet, measured, shy monotone in 1965, when he was just beginning his Test career, and compare it with the noisy, opinion-ated, forthright voice of 1987, when he had just retired. Apart from the accent, you would hardly believe the two voices came from the same individual. Always a perceptive admirer of Boycott, Bob Barber says: 'About three years ago, a friend and I met Geoffrey in Johannesburg. He almost seemed to be playing up to the image he had established. He spoke in a louder voice than I would have expected, as though he was putting on an act.'

Boycott was certainly aware of his image as a leading Test cricketer and could be absurdly jealous of any slight on his reputation as a batsman. Rodney Cass was working at a school in South Africa in 1967 while Boycott was coaching at King David College. 'We had a match between our schools and at the end of the game, all these kids were gathered around Geoff, wanting autographs. He was signing away and talking and I said to him: "What do you think of my number three, not a bad little player, is he?" And with two hundred kids listening, he replied, "Ay, he's a good player him, all right."

'I said, "I think he plays the on-drive as well as anybody I've ever seen."

'And Geoff exploded: "He doesn't play it as good as me." And he meant it.'

Boycott the perfectionist was a vital part of his public image: the endless net practice, the Spartan routine, the concern for his equipment, the contempt for sunbathing, the rigid personal habits. There were the famous trademarks of his attention to detail, like the handkerchief removed from the pocket as he walked to the crease so he could check the direction of the wind. 'In the dressing room, if I was twelfth man and he was batting,' says Paul Jarvis, 'I would know that there were certain things that had to be there for him. At lunch he would have to have some boiling hot water in a cup for his honey and ginseng tea. He would have to have certain sandwiches, digestive biscuits with cheese, and water, not orange juice.' Boycott was famously rigid about the need to have eight hours' sleep every night, arguing that he had to be asleep by eleven thirty because, he said, the half-hour before twelve was worth an hour after it.

Perhaps the most graphic example of Boycott's perfectionism was the attention he gave to his bats. During much of the seventies he used equipment made by County Sports, a subsidiary of St Peter's Sports, where Alf Evans was in charge of fashioning Boycott's blades. 'He used to spend a lot of time getting his bats absolutely right,' Evans told me. 'His bats weighed up to two pounds five ounces but never any heavier. He knew immediately if a bat was a fraction above this weight just by its feel. The top of the handle had to be thinner than with most other bats because, he said, this helped with the grip of his left hand, which had been weakened by a wrist injury in Australia in 1971.' As with many others trusted by Boycott, Evans contradicts the idea that he was an awkward customer: 'I worked with him for ten years and I have nothing but admiration for him. I dealt with him in a business-like way and he was always friendly. Nothing was too much trouble, whether it be signing autographs or doing other favours.'

In 1977, as part of a sponsorship deal, Boycott switched over to Slazenger's. When he first moved, he ignored the increasing preference for heavy blades, like Graham Gooch's three-pound cudgel, and stuck with his lightweight models. He would often use a heavier bat in the morning, say two pounds five ounces, and then in the late afternoon would go out with one weighing two pounds three and a half ounces.

His individualism about his equipment was also expressed in other ways. At a length of 33.75 inches, his bats were a quarter of an inch shorter than the professional average. The shoulders and edges of the bat were thinner than on most others. The hump at the back of the bat ran for a shorter length, four inches rather the usual six, and was nearer the bottom of the blade. This was because Boycott preferred to drive the ball along the ground than hit over the top. Indeed, the entire construction of his bats reflected an emphasis on timing and skill rather than brute force. 'What mattered to him was the balance and the pick-up,' I was told by Eric Loxton, who made his bats for Slazenger. 'He wasn't bothered about size and power. I once gave him a bat and said, "This is a brilliant one, Geoff, the ball will fly to the boundary." He replied, "I don't want it flying to the boundary. I just want it to roll over the rope. I'll still get four for it." He always knew what he wanted. He would often drive over forty miles just to get an ounce taken off the blade.' Like Alf Evans, Loxton is fond of Boycott: 'I know he isn't very popular in the cricket world but he has always been kind to me. If he arranged for me to go to a Test, he always made sure I was well looked after, got the VIP treatment. If I ever wanted tickets for a game, I only had to ring him up and he would make sure I got them.'

Boycott was equally concerned to have all the right accoutrements, the house, the clothes and the car, to go with his status as a leading professional. Understandably, given a tough upbringing made worse by his father's disability and premature death, he was haunted throughout his career by the spectre of financial insecurity. But if he had been interested solely in money, he was definitely in the wrong game, for cricketers have always been poorly rewarded compared to their professional counterparts in football, golf, tennis and motor-racing. In Boycott's day, financial rewards were limited. When he started, his basic salary with Yorkshire was around £600 a year, plus up to twenty pounds in match fees, while even in the late seventies his pay from Yorkshire was only about £8000 a year. As Ric Sissons put it, in his revealing study *The Players: A Social History of the Professional Cricketer*, by 1977 'the earnings of English cricketers had declined to such an extent that capped players found themselves receiving less per year than the skilled worker, while a "star" player was only two times better off'. Boycott's income, of course, was supplemented by his Test fees but, again, before the advent of Packer, these amounted to only £210 per match. The position improved after the establishment of World Series Cricket, with the fee rising to £1000 per match. In addition, the minimum tour fee went up to £5000, with extra payments for long service, which meant that Boycott received over £9000 for his immediate post-Packer MCC tours. The new commercial environment brought better rewards to all professionals, from the uncapped colts to the top stars. When Boycott finally retired in 1986, his salary from Yorkshire was around £28,000 a year.

Boycott's direct income from cricket in the eighties was considerably enhanced not just by sponsorship – like his £10,000 sponsored equipment deal with Slazenger's – but also three other hefty lump sums. The first was the fee he received from the rebel tour of South Africa in March 1982, estimated to be in excess of £50,000. The second was his 1984 testimonial with Yorkshire, which raised the record sum of £147,000, though it was overtaken the following year by Graham Gooch's 1985 benefit of £153,900. The third was the tax-free bequest of £100,000 left to him by his most devoted fan, Miss Phyllis Culpan, a retired schoolmistress, who died in November 1985 at the age of seventy-five. A lifelong Yorkshire supporter from Skipton, Miss Culpan had admired Boycott from the beginning of his career and travelled the world watching him. Such sums, of course, pale beside the income of other performers, and it was not until Boycott embarked upon his second career as a media star that he began his progress towards millionaire status. As he explained in an interview with *FHM* magazine in September 1999: 'As for when I was playing, I never earned good money at Yorkshire. It's an illusion. There were not great spin-offs back then. I've earned far more since I stopped playing. These days I am a wealthy man.'

Nevertheless, his lifestyle towards the end of his career could hardly be described as deprived. In December 1979, more than a year after his mother died, he and Anne Wyatt bought a luxurious 200-year-old converted farmhouse in the upmarket village of Woolley at a cost of around £70,000. With four bedrooms, a sitting room, lounge, dining room and a large garden, it was a world away from the two-storey Coal Board house in Fitzwilliam where Boycott had spent his life.

Top of the range BMWs and Mercedes were the only cars that a great cricketer could possibly own when he reached celebrity status. As so often with Boycott, however, his attitude towards driving has been complex. In direct contrast to his cautious approach as a batsman, there was a part of him that enjoyed high speed. Once, in December 1977, he was fined by Derbyshire magistrates for driving at 91 m.p.h. on the M1 near Chesterfield. Howard Cooper, the Yorkshire medium-pacer, recalls that he was 'a very fast driver. I remember joining the M1 at Bradford, and within an hour and fifty minutes, we were in the hotel in London, exactly 200 miles away. We must have been flying down at about 120 m.p.h. almost the whole way. But he had intense concentration, just like when he was batting. I felt quite safe.' Intriguingly, for someone who was so well organized, he has a poor sense of direction. 'If Boycs didn't carry a map in his car, he wouldn't be able to find his way home,' the late David Bairstow once said.

In more recent years, Boycott drives himself much less, preferring to be chauffeured or to travel by first-class rail. Tony Vann explains: 'I love driving but he hates it now. He has a BMW 7 series but if we go anywhere I always drive. It once got to the stage that he actually put me on his insurance because I was driving him so frequently.'

David Lloyd, the broadcaster and former England coach, told me this story of giving Boycott a lift from Yorkshire to Cardiff, which shows him at his most gloriously impatient. 'I picked him up in my old BMW. He put his feet up on the dashboard, his hat pulled down over his head and he said, "Wake me up when we're in Cardiff." Unfortunately, I lost my way, and I finished up in Safeway's super-market in Derby. I was trying to drive slowly and quietly so as not to wake Boycs. But I failed. "Where the fook are we?"

'"We're in Safeway's supermarket in Derby."

'"You fookin' idiot. What are we doing here?"

'"I'm lost."

'"Well, that's with me not driving." He went bananas. Then we started off once I had looked at the map but soon we had to stop again, this time for petrol.

'"Have you not filled up?"

'"Well, I have but it's empty again."

'"Good gracious." His hat's off his head and he steams into the motorway service station. And he shouts, "I'm not paying. That idiot out there will pay, him filling up. He never were planning. He never had any plan, even when he were batting. That's why he never got any runs. Where's your toilet?" And he disappeared, muttering to himself: "Brains of a fookin' chocolate mousse."'

Boycott, as we have seen, takes great pride in his appearance. Balding since his early twenties, he famously joined Elton John in the mid-seventies in having a hair transplant. His new look was first seen in public at a function in Huddersfield in January 1975, giving delight to the headline writers of the *Sun*: 'Boycott Scores a Thatch Trick: Geoff's Hair Rising Extra Cover Has Everyone Stumped.' Apart from his coiffure, high-quality tailoring has long been an essential element of the Boycott image. He favours designer-label suits and coats, while he has made the Panama his trademark. 'I might not spend twenty pounds in a bar but I spend it on luxuries I enjoy. I've got nice jackets for TV and I wear nice shoes,' he said in his *FHM* interview. Some critics have derided his style as 'man at C&A' but more sophisticated observers think that he can be quite chic. Sarah Cook, one of Max Clifford's young consultants, says, 'He is very dapper, with that trade-mark Panama. I would say that he is a bit European in the way he dresses. He always wears stylish trenchcoats, or has a good suit. He's not over the top but is very conscious of looking nice.'

One of the tailors he used most frequently was the firm of Carl Stuart in Ossett. I spoke to Nigel Grimes, one of the managers. 'There was no compromise. He got exactly what he wanted or he didn't get anything. He was very meticulous but his attitude would depend on what mood he was in. If he was in a pleasant mood there would be no problem with him whatsoever. But if he was in a demanding mood we would have to set a member of staff to be with him for he would be thumping around the place a bit. I have the endearing memory of him trying on trousers and standing in just his boxer shorts in the shop, much to the consternation of the female staff.' Lack of embarrassment in front of women over such eccentric behaviour has been a trait of Boycott's. One of his peculiar habits on tour was to wear pyjama tops but no bottoms. Once, when England were touring abroad, a member of the management team gently complained to him about this, saying it could give offence to the young maids doing room service. But he took no notice.

As well as being well groomed, Boycott has always rigorously maintained his 11-stone-7-pound figure. Even now, long after his retirement, he carries no excess weight. Strong and well-built, he has kept in shape both through years of training as a professional and through meticulous attention to his diet. Like Alan Knott, he is careful about his food. Lord MacLaurin, chairman of the England Cricket Board, first met Boycott in 1977 when he asked him to coach the Hertfordshire colts, his son's cricket team. He recalls: 'He came to stay, and at the evening meal, he was very pernickety about what he ate, keen on all the healthy things, vegetables, meat with no fat. He went to bed, got up the next morning, came down to breakfast and he brought with him his own honey and some ginseng. We then went off to coach the boys and I thought to myself, This is a complex character.' However, Boycott and Lord MacLaurin became firm friends over subsequent years: 'I like Geoffrey Boycott. I read all these stories about him but I have always had a good association with him and I have never had any reason to doubt him. He has caused social blunders but that is the guy's nature, he can upset people. Partly it is because he feels so passionately about cricket that he ends up clashing with someone at a function.'

Though not a teetotaller, Boycott rarely indulges in alcohol apart from a few glasses of champagne, wine or Cinzano. Just occasionally, he has loosened himself from the strait-jacket of his enormous self-discipline. Kevin Sharp recalls one such time when the Yorkshire squad went on a brief tour to Gibraltar. 'One of our fixtures was against an army team and the night after the game Yorkshire were invited to the army barracks. Boycs had a few drinks in there and started playing darts with the local guys. He was shouting, and laughing. He couldn't even hit the dartboard, he was fooling around that much. I remember saying to the other lads, "Look at Boycs over there, having a great time." It was fantastic to see but it was sad he could not do it more often.'

Boycott is often dismissed as a monomaniac, and certainly this might have been true of his early days when he lived only for cricket. But as he has matured, he has developed a wider range of interests beyond his own profession. He enjoys music, not only middle-of-the-road material like the Stylistics, Frank Sinatra, the Carpenters, Fleetwood Mac and Neil Diamond, but also light opera. Surprisingly, for a blunt Yorkshire sportsman, he also likes the ballet and regularly took his mother while she was alive. As a technical perfectionist, though, he only follows the classical kind. 'I don't understand modern ballet,' he once said. He is fond of his cats, the only type of pet whose sense of independence matches his own. Again, contrary to his mean image, he has been a substantial donor to the local RSPCA. He once gave half of his fee for a Shredded Wheat commercial to this cause. Reading is another form of relaxation, especially books about major celebrities with whom he could feel some empathy. 'I've read biographies of Joan Collins, Richard Burton, Maria Callas and Frank Sinatra in the past year. What wonderful characters they were! What pros!' he told the *Yorkshire Post*, in September 1990. Boycott has always been drawn to professional success, and it is no wonder that some of his closest friends have been high achievers in their own fields, like Brian Clough, Ian MacLaurin and Michael Parkinson. In an interview with the BBC in 1977 Parkinson spoke about Boycott's wider interests: 'He is a very intelligent man. He is inquisitive and would make a very good interviewer. He asks you about books, about television, about politics, anything that he doesn't know about. He has a memory like a steel trap, and once it is in there, he'll bring back a point of conversation five years later and contradict you.'

Other sports interest him. He plays tennis, is an avid fan of Manchester United and is an eight-handicapper at golf. Given his powers of concentration and his fascination with technique, it is not surprising that he should be a sound golfer. Mark Nicholas, who has played a lot of golf with him, says: 'The whole thing is exactly the same as his cricket, deeply professional. Everything is calculated, worked out, practised, absolute knowledge of strengths and weaknesses. "Poor driver but I can do the irons, beautiful putter," he'll tell you.' Jack Bannister has also been a golfing partner: 'He is just about the most introspective sporting bloke I have ever come across. Out on the course, just as with his batting, he can be utterly oblivious to the people around him, then, at the end of the round, he'll be talking away.' There are, of course, the usual stories about his poor behaviour, like the time he offended one professional golfer on the tee. The PA system announced that this player was sixty-seventh on the European Tour Order of Merit, which is not a bad ranking, pulling in about £140,000 a year. But Boycott was unimpressed. 'If I were sixty-seventh in anything, I wouldn't go around bloody boasting about it.'

Like most top sportsmen, who live by competition and individualism, Boycott's political views are firmly on the right. Indeed, he could almost be described as the identikit Thatcherite, the miner's son who built his own fortune through diligence and hard-nosed professionalism. However, though he might be inclined towards Conservatism, he has never been involved in Tory politics. In fact, his only foray into political activism was when he lent his support to Sir James Goldsmith's Referendum Party in the run-up to the 1997 general election, explaining that his Euro-scepticism was motivated by his patriotism. But Boycott was quick to turn down any idea that he wanted formally to enter politics: 'I am not a political animal and as someone who prefers to speak his mind I might find it impossible to follow a specific line of policy in Parliament.'

Boycott's spiritual outlook is as unconventional and contradictory as the rest of his life. He has an ostentatious dislike of superstition on the cricket field. Brian Luckhurst recalls opening with Boycott in a Test against Australia in 1972 when one of their colleagues cheerily wished them good luck. 'You don't need luck, you need ability,' barked Boycott in reply. Yet despite this blunt rationalism and his upbringing as an Anglican, he has long been fascinated with alternative faiths. A firm believer in astrology, he once said that he could deal with the endless crises of his life because 'I'm a Libran and they cope.' In the early eighties, at the depth of the crisis in Yorkshire, Boycott visited a medium, as he explained to Anthony Clare during his interview *In the Psychiatrist's Chair*: 'She told me things about myself that no one could have known, detailed, personal things. I sat up very quickly then.' It was also at this time that Boycott first began to study Chinese horoscopes. He eventually became such an expert that he was able to use his knowledge on others, like PR executive Kathy McLeman, who discussed the subject with him when they met in a Bradford optician's shop in November 1994. As Ms McLeman explained to the *Yorkshire Post*: 'I know about Chinese horoscopes and what he told me was spot on. He asked me what year I was born and when I told him he said I was a Goat, which is correct.' Not exactly the usual Boycott chat-up line but Ms McLeman seemed impressed. 'You wouldn't expect such a through and through Yorkshireman to be into anything like that but he was really keen.'

But, then, Boycott has never been one to swim with the tide.

20
'Look, Ma, Top of the World'

Geoffrey Boycott once told Mike Brearley that his relationship with Yorkshire was like a marriage. If that is the case, it was a pretty stormy union, racked by bitter jealousy, frequent talk of separation and regular accusations of betrayal. Years before the final divorce, Yorkshire tried to send Boycott packing, while he showed his wounded pride by flirting with other partners.

The cracks in the alliance had been widening throughout the seventies, under the continuing failure of Boycott's team to bring the success that the Yorkshire public craved. His sacking as captain in 1978 had almost led to his departure. Though he decided, at the eleventh hour, to remain, the committee's decision left a festering dispute that was never resolved in the rest of Boycott's time at the club. His relationship with Illingworth as manager was fractious from the start. Boycott's critics would claim that he was largely to blame for the breakdown in trust between manager and senior professional during this turbulent period. Hadn't Illingworth been a brilliant captain of Leicestershire, they ask, and a highly successful captain of England?

Yet following his reign as England supremo between 1994 and 1997, real doubt must be cast on Illingworth's abilities as a cricket manager. His record over these years was disappointing. By the end of his spell he had lost the respect of the players under his control. He had a disastrous fall-out in South Africa with Devon Malcolm and, more tellingly, his relationship with that most phlegmatic and modest of individuals, England's captain Mike Atherton, had badly deterioriated by the end of his term in office. As David Norrie put it in his 1997 authorized biography of Atherton: 'Illingworth has often acted in ways that seem almost designed to make Atherton's life a misery over the last three years.'

The Illingworth–Hampshire partnership limped through the 1980 season without any revival in fortunes. A dispirited Hampshire resigned and was replaced by Chris Old as captain. Despite some rhetoric from Old about being an 'attacking captain', Yorkshire plunged to new depths of farce in 1981, which saw the Reform Group mount an increasingly vociferous campaign against Ray Illingworth as manager. Illingworth had never been popular with the Reformers because of the role he was perceived to have played behind the scenes in the sacking of Boycott as captain in 1978, and now his reign was in danger of slipping into chaos. Yorkshire had no fewer than four captains that summer. When Old was away on Test duty or out with his usual niggles, the job was taken by John Hampshire or the wicket-keeper David Bairstow or, more bizarrely, Neil Hartley who, as an uncapped player, was struggling for his place in the side.

Boycott himself was involved in another of his predictable, petty controversies early in the season, invoking a complaint from Derbyshire after he had given the V-sign in public when told over the public-address system to stop practising on the playing area before the start of a cup tie at Derby. In addition, he could be as uncooperative with his new captain, Chris Old, as he had been with Old's predecessor, John Hampshire. Having discussed the future of Yorkshire with Boycott during the England tour of the West Indies in 1981, Old thought he had established some sort of rapport. He was soon disabused of the idea. At a match against Kent at Dartford in May, he consulted Boycott over tactics once Yorkshire took the field. 'It's nothing to do with me. You're the captain. Get on with it,' came Boycott's reply.

Far more serious, however, was the clash at Scarborough on 9 September just as Yorkshire were about to play Northamptonshire in the last home county championship match of the season. By this stage of the season Boycott was fuming with Illingworth, who had left him out of the Yorkshire side for several games in the Scarborough Festival. Boycott's seething discontent exploded during a TV interview in a York bookshop, where he said he would be seeking a 'showdown' with the manager. Understandably outraged at this inflammatory remark, Illingworth discussed the matter with Chris Old and they both agreed to suspend Boycott. When Illingworth arrived at the ground in Scarborough, he immediately told Boycott to pack his bags and leave.

What followed was one of the most extraordinary scenes ever witnessed in a county championship game in England. As news of Boycott's suspension filtered around the North Marine Road ground, there was whistling and booing from large sections of the crowd, some of whom spilled on to the field in protest at Illingworth's action. So prolonged was the uproar that the umpires could not even start the match on time, while the hostile mood of the Yorkshire supporters made Illingworth concerned for the safety of his wife and daughter. Meanwhile, Sid Fielden was busy organizing a petition of no confidence in Illingworth as manager, quickly gathering over 350 signatures. About 75 minutes after the game started, Boycott left the ground. According to *The Times*, 'most of the 5000 spectators rose to their feet and applauded him as he passed out of the gates in full view of the players'.

Illingworth, in trying to lance the boil of Yorkshire's feuding, had ended up causing more trouble. His main reason for suspending Boycott was for alleged breach of his contract which, Illingworth believed, contained a clause prohibiting unauthorized statements to the media. The problem was that Boycott, ever the individualist, had a different contract from the rest of the Yorkshire team. He had no such gagging clause in his. Therefore, on strictly legal grounds, Boycott's suspension had been dubious. Further disciplinary action was impossible and future moves against Boycott became all the more difficult.

Just as this storm was subsiding, another swept through the club. This arose from the notorious poll conducted in the Yorkshire dressing room by captain Chris Old, which revealed that the majority of players no longer wanted Boycott in the side. Old later justified his action by saying he had been 'incensed by the local newspaper claim that Geoff had the players' support'. In an unprecedented move, the committee decided to make the results public on 23 September, less than a fortnight after the Scarborough fiasco. The findings were as follows:

Question 1: Do you want Geoff Boycott as captain?
15 against. 3 abstentions.
Question 2: Do you wish to have him in the side next season?
10 no; 2 yes; 4 abstentions.
Question 3: Do you want Raymond Illingworth to continue as manager?
13 yes; 3 abstentions.

The decision to hold the poll was bad enough, providing official sanction and a spurious democratic legitimacy for what was little more than a vendetta against one individual. Far worse was the committee's grossly irresponsible decision to make the findings public. In doing so, the club's administrators gave the impression that they had all but given up control to an insidious form of player power. Indeed, one committee man virtually admitted that they had surrendered: 'A majority think that these sorts of things are best kept within the dressing room. But there has been such an agitation in the last fortnight that we felt it our duty to inform the members.'

If the committee felt that decisive action was needed, why not take it themselves instead of trying to hide behind the views of players? Far from strengthening their position, their shabby behaviour only weakened their authority and built up support for the Reformers. Eric Baines, a committee member from Doncaster, resigned in disgust and Sid Fielden was elected in his place. The press and cricket worlds were united in their condemnation of the committee and *Wisden* spoke for many in its editorial: 'It seemed an absurdity when young members of the Yorkshire team, unfit in terms of cricketing ability and commitment so much as to tie up Boycott's bootlaces, were asked to vote on whether or not they wanted to play with him any more, let alone when their feelings were made public.' Even Chris Old, who had been in charge of the poll, began to have his doubts. The next spring he confessed that it had been a mistake: 'It was my first year as captain and I was very naïve in such matters. I was never anti-Boycott but I was pushed into a corner. Certainly, I would not do the same thing again, knowing what the consequences have been.'

Anxious to dig itself out of the mess it had helped to create, Yorkshire then resorted to that device traditionally favoured by bureaucracies under attack. It set up a sub-committee to carry out an 'in-depth' inquiry into all aspects of the club's management. Headed by retired accountant Peter Dobson, the sub-committee went about its work busily, holding 15 meetings and conducting 32 interviews over the next two months.

They were not, initially, able to interview Boycott, who was abroad on what turned out to be his last, and perhaps most controversial, England tour, the 1981/82 trip to India under Keith Fletcher. For once, Boycott had been keen to make the visit to the Asian sub-continent because his Test aggregate now stood at 7802, only 230 runs behind Gary Sobers' total of 8032. Yet, after all the debate about his self-imposed exclusion from the 1972/73 and 1976/77 sides, it was now his inclusion in the England party that was to be a source of trouble. In March 1981, Boycott had been placed on United Nations blacklist because he had played and coached in South Africa. Though the Indian Cricket Board raised no objection to Boycott and the other UN blacklisted England player, the Northamptonshire batsman Geoff Cook, the Indian government made noises about refusing entry to both of them. For several months the tour was thrown into doubt, until the Indian government relented, apparently satisfied by a statement that Boycott had made in his book *In the Fast Lane* in which he expressed his loathing of apartheid. Later, during the tour, Boycott committed one of his inevitable social gaffes by offering a copy of this book to Mrs Gandhi when the teams were presented to her during the Test match at Delhi. The Indian Prime Minister seemed somewhat bemused at Boycott's unorthodox approach to international diplomacy. 'I will accept your book because you caused me so much trouble before this tour,' she said, with a smile.

Worried about his immediate health and his future at Yorkshire, Boycott was more withdrawn and unsociable than ever on this trip, grumbling about the hotels, the food, the management and the transport, while his insecurities and idiosyncrasies became all too apparent. The tour captain, Keith Fletcher, told me, 'I don't dislike Boycs but he was always difficult. You had to be so careful what you said since he could easily take things the wrong way. On that tour, he was still a bloody good player but he would never help at all. If I asked him for advice, he'd just say, "Well, you're the captain." Or if we went out to look at the wicket, I'd say, "Boycs, what do you reckon?" And he'd reply, "You're in charge." He had a lot of things he could have given but he never did. He was certainly very aware of the Test record. As far as I was concerned, he came to India simply to overtake Gary Sobers. Once he had got that, his interest in the tour waned completely.'

Boycott had a row with Fletcher over his scoring rate in the Bangalore Test, which again highlighted his excessive touchiness. Never a man for extravagant language, Fletcher had casually remarked to the press that Boycott and Chris Tavare had been told to hurry the score along during their stand. When he read the reports of Fletcher's comments about the need for acceleration, Boycott exploded, denying he had received any such instruction, and demanded an apology. So obsessed did he become about the issue that he acquired a tape-recording of Fletcher's press interview, replaying it a dozen times to the captain and manager Raman Subba Row as well as bombarding them with heavily underlined newspaper cuttings which Anne Wyatt had brought over from England when she came out to see Boycott. Fletcher was 'baffled' by the level of Boycott's outrage but he eventually gave the sought-after apology, explaining that 'it seemed the simplest way out'. Understandably, relations between Boycott and Fletcher were not easy after that.

One of Fletcher's other complaints against Boycott was of his 'uncooperative, sometimes embarrassing behaviour' at functions, when he would sit in a corner and refuse to socialize. But Derek Underwood, who was also making his final England trip, says that he sympathized with Boycott: 'The last thing you want in the middle of a Test match is to go to a cocktail party at the British High Commission, having been playing all day in a cauldron.' Of course, the rest of the team rightly pointed out that they had to endure exactly the same as Boycott.

The 1981/82 Indian tour could be described as a microcosm of Boycott's entire Test career: glorious achievement marred by crass and self-indulgent actions. It took him only three matches to pass Gary Sobers' record. He hit 60 in the first Test at Bombay, where England were beaten by 138 runs in the only result of this flaccid series; then he scored 36 and 50 in the second Test at Bangalore, which left him just 81 runs short. The climax came at Delhi in the third Test on 23 December, when he and Gooch put on 132 for the first wicket after Fletcher had won the toss. Shortly before the close Boycott clipped left-arm spinner Dilip Dohsi into the leg-side and took the single that made him the heaviest run-scorer in the history of Test cricket.

It was a glorious moment for the balding 41-year-old with poor eyesight and a bent wrist. There could be no greater vindication of all the years of loneliness and dedication, of unforgiving practice and analysis, of criticism and rejection. Vic Wilson had said exactly 20 years ago that he was not worth persevering with. Well, he had shown him; he had shown them all. It had taken almost 452 hours of batting at the Test match crease but now he could say, like James Cagney's character in *White Heat*: 'Look, Ma, Top of the World!' But Boycott was never a man to throw a celebratory party; after all, he was 86 not out overnight and there was still a century to be had the next morning. With an air of inevitability, he thus completed his twenty-second and last century for England, putting him on the same number of tons as Wally Hammond and Colin Cowdrey.

Health problems have long been an inevitable part of touring India and most England players have succumbed at some stage during a visit. Once during a 1937/38 tour to India the Surrey fast bowler Alf Gover charged in to bowl and then, after completing his delivery, carried on running straight into the pavilion. A dodgy lunch was blamed for this rapid 100-yard dash. Despite his fastidious attentions to his diet and hygiene, Boycott gradually became more unwell as the tour progressed. He felt ill at the end of his triumphant Delhi Test and in the fourth Test, in Calcutta, after he was lbw to Madan Lal in England's second innings for just six, he retired to his bed suffering from diarrhoea and a temperature. Bernard Thomas, the England physiotherapist, recalls, 'I visited him twice a day and he was certainly very poorly. By the last day of the Test, however, he was getting better. I said to him, "Look, Geoff, you've got to get down to the ground again. For one thing, you have to pack your bag and, in any case, the air will do you good."' Thomas had always been sympathetic to Boycott. 'I never found him difficult, though he was a perfectionist, which isolated him from the rest of the team. He was quite vulnerable, always insecure. You were conscious that he was in constant need of reassurance.'

Unfortunately Boycott misinterpreted Thomas's instructions. Yes, he went down to the ground at Eden Gardens but instead of staying there he asked two of the players, Paul Allott and Geoff Cook, if they fancied joining him at the golf course at Tollygunge in the suburbs of Calcutta. To Boycott, this seemed perfectly reasonable. He had been told by Bernie Thomas to get some air. That was impossible in the smog-ridden streets of Calcutta so what better alternative was there than the greenery of the fairways? The England players hardly saw it that way. Here was the senior professional, ostensibly still a member of the Test XI, saying he preferred a round of golf to watching his colleagues battle it out against India. And if he was well enough to swing a driver, was he not well enough to take the field?

Oblivious to such considerations, Boycott went off to Tollygunge where he enjoyed a stroll and gently played 14 holes. When he returned from what he felt was a recuperative afternoon, he had to face the wrath of both management and team, who all believed he had behaved disgracefully. Boycott was hauled into a meeting at room 201 of the Grand Hotel with Subba Row the manager, Bernie Thomas, Fletcher and Bob Willis the vice-captain.

'Is it true you played golf without permission from either captain or manager?' he was asked.

'Yes, but Bernie told me to get some fresh air and the golf club seemed the best place, because downtown here you can't walk a step without having to plough through or step over a body,' replied Boycott.

'Well, why didn't you ask permission?'

'Because I thought I had it from Bernie.'

Thomas is surprised at the suggestion he had done this. 'I never said anything like that at all. That was totally untrue. I only encouraged him to get some fresh air,' he says.

Boycott was then informed that the team were extremely angry and were demanding an apology. Before he acceded to this, Boycott said that he wanted to fly to Delhi to consult the British Consulate doctor. The request was refused, at which Boycott said angrily that he would resign from the tour. He wrote an apology to his England colleagues, which he tried to stick to the fridge in the team room but it kept falling off, so he pinned it to the table with a bottle-opener. It had been agreed at the meeting that Boycott and the management would think again in the morning about his wish to return to England.

Overnight Boycott changed his mind. He told Subba Row and Fletcher at another meeting in his own room the next morning that he was prepared to stay. 'All I ever wanted was to play for England,' said Boycott. It was too late. The decision to allow him to return to England was confirmed. Fletcher and Subba Row thought that his change of mind was just another sign of his inner depression and turmoil. While most of the England team and the press pack travelled to a regional game at Jamshedpur, Subba Row accompanied Boycott to the airport. After Boycott was on his way home, Subba Row issued this statement: 'It was felt that two weeks of physical health problems had affected his perspective. His mental approach manifested itself by his spending a large amount of time in his own room, not going out with other people or colleagues, making him more introverted.'

It is important to note that Boycott was not sent home in disgrace, merely that the tour management agreed to his resignation. It was, however, an ignominious end to an 18-year Test career. Keith Fletcher later expressed the view that 'Boycott's apparent reluctance to contribute anything made it very clear to me that he should never tour with England again.' What surprised Fletcher was the relief with which the rest of the England team greeted Boycott's departure. Derek Underwood was the only one who had anything good to say about him, and even that was conditional. 'I had the highest regard for him as a cricketer, and I had a great admiration for his guts and determination. And over all our years together in the Test team, I had grown very tolerant, very patient with him. But I must admit that what he did in Calcutta did not show much respect for the team.'

David Gower recalls: 'Keith Fletcher was livid. He'd got to the stage where he saw that he couldn't have someone like that in the team much longer. Looking back, it was a desperately sad way to leave Test cricket.' Gower also has one fascinating memory of that tour, which shows the vulnerable side of Boycott. 'We went to a reception at the Maharajah's palace at Buruda and it was a lavish occasion. Boycs and I were wandering through the garden when he turned to me and asked, "Why do people not like me, David? I'm just an ordinary bloke trying to do a job." It was a little awkward to be shown that side of him then, for I was only a young player. But I have subsequently seen it a few times over the years. As a commentator, he can be punchy, forthright, not holding anything back. Then afterwards will come all his insecurities, "Did I get it right there?" type of stuff.'

Public relations had never been one of Boycott's gifts. Now he was at it again, digging a hole for himself during an interview with David Coleman on the BBC's *Sportsnight* just after his return to England. In explaining his visit to the golf course, he displayed a surprising interest in ornithology: 'I was stopping every couple of holes and standing around enjoying a different setting, a bit of piece and quiet. I watched the birds on one or two of the fairways. You have got a couple of dozen great big black and white vultures, then lovely green parrots that fly past and birds with red bushy tails. [There is laughter in the BBC studio at this point.] While I am talking to you here I can see you on television laughing but it's true.' After further elaboration on the nature of his golfing trip, he concluded by saying he still hoped to play for England: 'To suggest that I have played my last Test because I have come home seems grossly unfair.'

In fact, far from pressing his case for a return to the England side, Boycott almost immediately confirmed his ostracism by taking part in the rebel tour to South Africa the following month. The suspicion soon arose that, as the most senior of the rebels, he had come back to England early from India to oversee the final preparations for this venture. But the idea of Boycott as some sort of James Bond villain, jetting in from the East to mastermind a smooth and sinister operation, obscures the reality, that the build-up to the trip could hardly have been more chaotic and rushed, with Boycott playing only a minor role at the end.

It was in December 1980 that the idea of a visit by a quasi-England party had first been discussed by Boycott, out on his usual winter holiday in the Republic, and his friend Peter Cooke, a cricket enthusiast and executive in the music business. Two months later, during the England trip to the West Indies, Boycott, following more discussions with Cooke, put the proposal to five other England players, David Gower, John Emburey, Graham Gooch, Ian Botham and Graham Dilley, in a meeting at the Pegasus hotel in Guyana. The meeting took place at the very moment at which politicians and administrators were deciding the future of an England tour thrown into jeopardy by the row over Robin Jackman's links with South Africa. As Graham Dilley later said: 'Heaven knows what the Guyanese would have done had they found out that the six of us were sitting in a hotel room under the noses of their security men giving birth to a project that was to cause an even greater furore in the cricket world just over a year later.' The plans at this stage were vague. There were hints that Holiday Inns might act as a sponsor, but the shape of the tour and its timetable were unclear.

After the end of the 1981 season and then on the England tour of India, more discussions were held between the would-be rebels and their South African organizers, with Boycott acting as a go-between. Then the whole venture began to fall apart. Two of the biggest stars, Ian Botham and David Gower, decided to pull out, fearing that a ban from Test cricket would reduce their earning power. Botham was also concerned, understandably, about the reaction of his closest friend in cricket, Viv Richards. At the news of Gower and Botham's withdrawal, Holiday Inns withdrew their sponsorship.

As Boycott flew home to England from India, it looked as if the South African trip was definitely off. But Peter Cooke had a sense of determination to rival Boycott's. He soon found another sponsor, the South African Breweries company. He then managed, through a remarkable telephonic endurance test, to contact potential tourists all over the world and, within a few weeks, had assembled the core of another team, ready to fly to South Africa at the end of February. That the tour began at all was a tribute to Peter Cooke's high energy and England cricketers' low earnings.

But the disarray of the rebel party continued on their arrival in South Africa on 28 February. Bob Willis had been the first-choice captain. With his late withdrawal, the rebels tried to entice Keith Fletcher to join them but he refused, hoping to remain as England captain. Boycott would have been an obvious replacement but he declined the job, to the relief of some of the other players, including Gooch. 'We all had too much on our plate to say anything more to the man about his exit from India, but words were not necessary. Feelings still ran deep, the incident had not been entirely forgotten or forgiven, and to accept Boycott as leader would have been illogical,' wrote Gooch in his book *Out of the Wilderness*. Alan Knott's name was briefly touted, but he had never seen himself as a captain, so the burden fell on Graham Gooch.

He could hardly have had a more difficult task, given the uproar surrounding the tour, the makeshift nature of his side, the lack of match practice and the quality of the South African opposition. His XI failed to win any of the four so-called 'Test' matches and, apart from himself, few of the other players showed any sort of form at all. Boycott was a disappointment against the excellent Springbok attack of Garth le Roux, Steve Jeffries, and that bald giant of a fast bowler, Vincent van der Bijl. Once more, as in Australia three years earlier, there were mutterings that the great man's reflexes were finally slowing down. Off the field, although he had one row with South African cricket chiefs Ali Bacher and Joe Pamensky over the selection of the rebel side and its playing schedule, Boycott was far more at ease on this expedition than on any of his other recent England tours. Since his first visit to the country in 1964/65, he had grown to love it, and by 1982 he had a large number of friends and business contacts there. Indeed, it was rumoured in March 1982 that, because of the dark cloud over his Yorkshire career, Boycott might soon settle there. 'If Geoff wants to come here permanently he could do a wonderful job for our cricket on and off the field,' said the South African Cricket Union.

It certainly might have seemed an attractive option as Boycott came home to face the twin crises of the fall-out from South Africa and the continuing storm at Yorkshire. On his arrival at Heathrow at the end of March, he farcically undermined the image that the rebels were trying to present of solid professionals who had nothing to be ashamed of by trying to sneak through customs dressed in an absurd outfit of thick-collared sheepskin coat and baseball-cap pulled far down over his forehead, looking like 'a third baseman for the Milwaukee Braves' in the memorable words of the *Daily Mail*'s Ian Wooldridge. Peter Willey was one of many angered by Boycott's behaviour. 'I said to him, "We've done nothing wrong. Let's walk through with our heads high. We haven't broken any laws." But he went through with that hat down and collar up. I told him, "What's the point? They know who you are." I think he made it worse.'

While the rebels were in South Africa, the TCCB had imposed a three-year ban on their playing Test cricket. Once back in the country, Boycott, Emburey and Gooch consulted the lawyers Linklaters and Paines, who had handled the Packer case, but it emerged that the TCCB could not be easily challenged in the courts. The rebels also turned to the Professional Cricketers Association for support, but made a bad error in appointing Boycott as one of their chief spokesmen. Jack Bannister, the commentator who was also secretary of the PCA, recalls, 'For the first three or four minutes when Geoffrey got up to speak he was getting quite a sympathetic hearing. Then suddenly, as he became more aggressive, you could feel the room freezing. When he sat down, I knew what was going to happen. Whatever chances they had had of getting support had been damaged. As a result the ban went unchallenged.' The final vote was 190 to 35. The position of the PCA was understandable. If the TCCB had not imposed such a harsh sentence, then the West Indies, Pakistan and India would probably have cancelled their forthcoming visits to England, and the Test match revenues, on which the salaries of the county professionals depended, would have been severely reduced.

The whole sad saga of South African sporting links was riddled with hypocrisies and double standards on all sides. It was legitimate of the rebels' supporters to ask why they had been banned yet white South Africans like Allan Lamb and Chris Smith could play for England without any objections. Why were Boycott and company allowed to play against the South Africans on the county scene but not in the Republic? In a wider context, why were sportsmen singled out for punishment over their South African connections when other professionals, especially in business, could carry on working and trading there? Indeed, why was South Africa the subject of this unique boycott when there were many other tyrannical regimes across the world with whom sporting links were maintained? Yet the rebels weakened their case by entering into political arguments about the nature of apartheid. This was especially true when, instead of admitting that they were free agents selling their wares, some feebly tried to claim there was some moral purpose about their trip, even arguing that they had gone to South Africa because they wanted to further the cause of multi-racial cricket. Ultimately all those who railed against South African sporting isolation were proved wrong, for the boycott was undoubtedly an important weapon in the destruction of apartheid.

As well as being banned from Test cricket, Boycott also felt the consequences of the move in his pocket, as the Labour-controlled West Yorkshire County Council terminated his £5000-a-year contract promoting the county. Councillor John Gunnell, now a Labour MP, explained that Boycott had failed the test for political correctness: 'When talking of industrial promotion you have to be careful of the image you want to project. It is not clear where Geoffrey Boycott stands on certain fundamental issues.' The BBC also dropped him from the list of cricketers to be invited occasionally into the commentary box. Yet Boycott never actually said in his book *In the Fast Lane* that he would not play cricket in South Africa. And there is another crucial point about Boycott that is rarely mentioned: he is utterly without any personal feelings of racial prejudice. Unlike many other northerners born in the 1940s, he is broad-minded on questions of race. A television producer who worked with him says: 'He may be rude, bitter, mean and many other things, but he is totally colour-blind. For all his foibles, I have never, ever heard him utter anything that is remotely racist. He just judges players on their ability.' Bill Sinrich, the vice-president of TransWorld TV, who, as an American, is keenly aware of the sensitivities on issues of race, says: 'He is hugely popular in India, Pakistan and the West Indies. One of the reasons is that he has none of the cultural baggage that others carry. Geoffrey is the most purely colour-blind person that I am aware of in cricket.' It is perhaps telling that one of Boycott's noisiest fans during his playing career was Ron Griffiths, a Barbados-born British Rail electrician from Wembley who, in 1973, was the first cricket follower to christen him 'Sir Geoffrey'. Sadly for Griffiths, Boycott had to make do with an OBE, awarded in 1980.

Boycott had perfectly good personal and financial reasons for joining the rebel tour, with his Test career apparently over and his future at Yorkshire in doubt. His concerns about Yorkshire were greatly increased by the report, dated 19 February, produced by Peter Dobson's 'in-depth investigation' into the running of Yorkshire. The report made some criticisms of Illingworth as manager, suggesting that unless there was an improvement in results, it was unlikely that his contract would be renewed at the end of the 1982 season. But its real firepower was reserved for Boycott. 'In the continuing absence of a strong enough captain, morale can only be rebuilt and true unity of purpose re-established within the team when Mr Boycott is no longer in the team. It is therefore the reluctant recommendation of the majority of the sub-committee that Mr Boycott's services be dispensed with as soon as possible.' The 'in-depth' report was circulated to Yorkshire's general committee and, inevitably, its explosive conclusions soon leaked out.

But the commotion over the report, led by the Reform Group, ensured that there was no possibility that Yorkshire would dare implement its recommendations immediately, especially since the Reform Group was now more powerful than ever. Boycott was therefore allowed to stay. Rather than taking any steps towards sacking him, the club, in yet another piece of bureaucratic tinkering, decided to set up a three-man 'peace-keeping' sub-committee, consisting of Ronnie Burnett, Billy Sutcliffe and Fred Trueman, all committee men and distinguished ex-Yorkshire cricketers. It was hardly a move likely to inspire confidence in Yorkshire's sense of direction and firmness.

The atmosphere of crisis worsened in the middle of the 1982 season, when Chris Old was replaced as skipper with fifty-year-old Ray Illingworth. This dramatic move was prompted by a woeful team performance at Middlesbrough against Northamptonshire, where Old had virtually lost control of proceedings. It may have reeked of nostalgia and romance to have as captain a quinquagenarian who had first played for Yorkshire when Clement Attlee was still prime minister but it did little for results. Yorkshire staggered through another season, sinking to tenth place in the championship and sixteenth place in the John Player. Through the gloom, the form of Boycott shone like a beacon. Relieved to be allowed to continue his career with his beloved club and freed from the pressures of Test cricket, he enjoyed his best summer since 1979, scoring 1941 runs for Yorkshire at 61.70 and hitting no fewer than six centuries. In doing so he went past Sir Len Hutton's total of 129 first-class hundreds.

Looking back, this fine season only represented the calm before the storm.

21

Boycottshire

Margaret Thatcher thrived on conflict. It was the dominant theme of her first years in office. Hostilities raged abroad in the Falklands and at home in the inner cities of Birmingham and Brixton. Ulster was torn apart by the IRA hunger strike led by Bobby Sands. There were the struggles against Lambeth and Livingstone, against Arthur Scargill's miners and Derek Hatton's Militants. The Soviet Union, Brussels, Tory wets, CND and Labour were all enemies that had to be faced down and beaten.

In its own way, Yorkshire County Cricket Club seems to have been caught up in this mood of strife. Starting with its Winter of Discontent in 1978/79 over the Boycott captaincy row, by the early eighties a once-great club had descended into near anarchy and civil war. And throughout, the one central factor in this slide towards destruction was the personality of Geoffrey Boycott. Around this volatile, magnetic, flawed and potent figure was fought Yorkshire's bitter dispute. To his devoted supporters, he was the greatest cricketer in England, the sole source of pride in a club of growing mediocrity. To his implacable opponents, he was the cause of all Yorkshire's problems, the man who had brought the county to the brink of ruin through his wilful selfishness.

Until Saturday 13 August 1983 at Cheltenham, Boycott's season had been one of steady run-accumulation. There were no rows, no show-downs with Illingworth, no front-page incidents. But that all changed when the Yorkshire team arrived at the Cheltenham College ground, one of the most attractive settings for cricket in England with the glorious college chapel and elegant marquees acting as a backdrop for the play. There was very little attractive about Boycott's behaviour when he turned up. Just as the Yorkshire team were going out on to the field for a photo-call before the start, a small boy came up to Boycott and asked for his autograph. 'Fuck off,' was the reply. Once the photograph had been taken, the players were walking back to the dressing room when Boycott was approached by a gaggle of young autograph hunters, only to greet them with the same two-syllable response. Unfortunately, several Gloucestershire members had overheard him and Illingworth felt compelled to apologize to them. 'I am very sorry. I can't defend him. He was wrong and has been told about it.'

Yorkshire won the toss and batted. What followed was to become the cause of the most belligerent debate. In bright sunshine, on a good wicket and a fast outfield, Boycott stayed at the crease all day, taking 347 balls to score 140 runs. He took 262 balls to reach his century but, even after that, failed to accelerate, collecting another 20 singles, four twos and just three boundaries. Incredibly in the last half-hour, when Yorkshire were chasing a fourth bonus batting point, he scored just eight runs. The torpor of his approach looked all the more dismal when contrasted with a dashing century made by Kevin Sharp, who passed Boycott on 110 despite having come in 22 overs later.

Illingworth was aggrieved by the way Boycott ran Sharp out when the left-hander was dominating the bowling. Attempting his old trick of retaining the strike off the last ball of one over, Boycott pushed his shot straight to mid-wicket and called Sharp through for a suicidal single. But what really angered Illingworth was his belief that Boycott had deliberately ignored his instructions. When Jim Love was batting with Boycott towards the end of the day, Illingworth sent out twelfth man Nick Taylor with an urgent message to get a move on.

According to the account Illingworth gave later to the Yorkshire committee – backed up by the testimony of Nick Taylor and Jim Love – Boycott told Taylor, 'Go and talk to the other man. I'll continue batting in my own way.' Illingworth's anger forced the committee to take action. The so-called peace-keeping group of Burnett, Sutcliffe and Trueman received a report from him, summoned Boycott to a meeting and then, six days later, issued this statement to the media: 'We are satisfied in this instance his batting was not in the best interests of the side and he has been told again that he must at all times play the sort of innings the side needs, irrespective of his own personal ambitions.'

Boycott and his supporters were furious. While Boycott took to the airwaves to deny that he had been officially reprimanded, Brian Clough passionately defended Boycott's batting in the *Mirror*. The Reformers, led by Sid Fielden, demanded a special meeting of Yorkshire's general committee to discuss the Cheltenham affair.

Under pressure from the Reformers, Illingworth was now threatening to resign but his mood was lightened somewhat by Yorkshire's success in winning the John Player League, their first major trophy for 14 years, and Illingworth began to talk once more of remaining at the club in some sort of managerial capacity or even, perhaps, as a skipper. Yet that still would not have resolved the problem of the rancour between himself and Boycott.

The cricket committee decided to resolve it for him. At their meeting on 3 October, members voted unanimously not to offer Boycott a contract for the next season. In an attempt to assuage the inevitable reaction from the Boycott supporters, they also decided that Illingworth would be replaced as captain by David Bairstow, one of Boycott's strongest supporters in the Yorkshire dressing room. When they went before the general committee in the afternoon of 3 October, these two decisions were approved by 19 votes to 7.

Sid Fielden recalls Boycott's mood the evening of the sacking. 'I rang him up from Headingley, spoke to him about the decision, and he said, "Come here. But don't come to the house. Park further down the lane and cut across the fields because you can't get into the village with all the press." So I did that and I ripped my suit actually getting through a wire fence. I got there in the late evening and we talked way into the night. In the early hours of the morning we went for a walk around the village. I kept promising that we would fight for him. He was very upset, of course, more distressed than I have ever seen him. But that night was the beginning of the campaign to reinstate him.'

On 9 October, the Boycott supporters gathered in the Post House hotel in Ossett to demand that he be reinstated. The strength of feeling surprised even the keenest loyalists, as Tony Vann, soon to be a key figure in the pro-Boycott movement, remembers: 'Inspired by the injustice of the sacking, I went to this meeting which was fixed for 7.30 p.m. I got there at 7.10 and could not park the car it was so full. I went in and there were over 400 people in a single room – we were like sardines. The debate went on for a couple of hours and was 90 per cent in favour of Boycott.' Even with this campaign under way, the committee merely reaffirmed at its next meeting the earlier decision to sack Boycott by 18 votes to 8. In a lengthy statement, chairman Michael Crawford set out the reasons for his dismissal: the need to encourage younger players without the current atmosphere of 'dissension and discord which creates a lack of confidence'; the public bickering after the Cheltenham affair; the need to put the interests of Yorkshire before one individual; and the threat of established players leaving the club, especially Bill Athey. The sacking of Boycott, though, came too late to persuade Athey to stay.

Boycott has always refused to acknowledge that he played any part in Athey's departure from Yorkshire in 1983. In his *Autobiography* he wrote: 'To the best of my knowledge, Athey has never gone on record as saying he left Yorkshire because of me, though I know the committee would have liked him to.' Well, he has now. In his interview with me, Athey said: 'Boycott's attitude and the atmosphere he created had everything to do with my decision to leave Yorkshire. In the dressing room with Boycott around, there was always a tense, highly charged atmosphere. Spirit was always poor because it was never relaxed in there. Even after he lost the captaincy and Hamps took over, the very fact that Boycs was still there was a problem. Half of Yorkshire were vehemently on his side and the other half were vehemently against him. It wasn't good for people to play cricket in that atmosphere. It was such a relief to go to Gloucestershire. My career was much more fruitful there. I averaged around forty-three compared to twenty-eight at Yorkshire. That's a huge difference.'

Another incident in the season may have had an influence on the committee's decision. Richard Lumb had been Boycott's regular opening partner since the mid-seventies but by 1983 he had grown heartily sick of Boycott's running between the wickets. In the match against Gloucestershire at Bradford Lumb was run out twice. On the second occasion he was so indignant that he sat in the dressing room with his pads on waiting for Boycott's return at the close of play. Normally a quiet man, he could hide his frustration no longer. Lumb recalls: 'Most of the other players had scattered to the bar while I let him have it. "What do you think you're doing? Twice in the match. That's eleven–nil on run-outs now."

'"Sorry," replied Boycs. "I must be bad at it. What should I do?"

'"You should fuck off like you should have done ten years ago."

'It did affect me that time. I was so fed up that I told the chairman that I did not want to bat with him any more.' 1983 was Lumb's penultimate season with Yorkshire. He left in 1984 and emigrated to South Africa.

Encouraged by the turn-out at the first Ossett meeting on 9 October, Boycott's supporters fought on to overthrow his sacking. A new campaign group, known as Members 84 Group, was formed with Tony Vann as secretary and Peter Charles as chairman. The necessary signatures to force the club to hold a special meeting were quickly gathered. The committee now had no option but to put their decision to the test of the popular will. The meeting was fixed for 3 December at Harrogate, where three resolutions were to be debated: (a) that Boycott's contract should be renewed; (b) no confidence in the cricket committee; (c) no confidence in the general committee.

It has been fashionable in certain circles to dismiss the Members 84 Group as little more than a hysterical personality cult. In the *Sun* in January 1984 Brian Close called them 'all the nobodies of the Geoff Boycott fan club'. Yet such abuse – even if it might be understandable in the feverish climate of the 1984 revolution – hardly provides an answer as to why so many devoted Yorkshire cricket followers felt so passionately about the sacking of Boycott. The senior figures of the Members 84 Group were all intelligent, responsible men in serious occupations, not a bunch of wild student radicals or starry-eyed celebrity groupies. In any other context they would have been regarded as moderate, even conservative individuals. Not one of the leading six was under 40. Peter Briggs was in that most sober of professions, accountancy, as was Peter Charles. Reg Kirk was a 62-year-old chartered secretary. Sid Fielden was a detective sergeant in the South Yorkshire police. Tony Vann was a successful businessman, owning a garage in Bradford, while Bob Slicer was also in the motor trade at the top of National Breakdown.

The overwhelming feeling of the Members 84 Group – and, as was soon to be demonstrated, the Yorkshire cricketing public – was that Boycott was being made the scapegoat for the wider failings of Yorkshire. Here was a man who, through sheer force of will and dedication, had made himself into one of the world's greatest batsmen, yet he was now to be sacked because the rest of the team came nowhere near his standard. That view was summed up by Bob Slicer at the first Ossett meeting: 'What sort of theatre is it that sacks the top of the bill because the rest of the supporting acts are rubbish?' And, they could also ask, what other Yorkshire player had brought anything like the same moments of recent glory, such as the hundredth hundred in 1977 at Headingley? Yes, he had faults, they said, but they were the faults of someone who had made Yorkshire cricket his life. Which other player had demonstrated the same loyalty? The committee said he had been a poor captain, so they had thrown him out of that job. Yet look at the results since: in the last five years of Boycott's reign (1974–78), Yorkshire had finished eleventh, second, eighth, twelfth and fourth in the county championship. During Illingworth's five years in charge (1979–83), they had finished seventh, sixth, tenth, tenth and seventeenth, the first time in history that Yorkshire had been bottom of the table. As Anthony Woodhouse wrote of the 1983 season in his *History of Yorkshire County Cricket Club*: 'To finish bottom of the championship was a disgrace never envisaged either in their 75 years of almost complete domination or even in the 1970s, when the side had at least had periods of success which gave great hope for the future.' Through some logical inconsistency, Boycott was blamed for disappointing results as captain in the seventies, yet on his return to the ranks he carried the can for even worse performances in the eighties, while the skipper/manager of the side, Ray Illingworth, appeared to be absolved of all responsibility.

Furthermore, apart from debate about Boycott's personality, the decision of the committee just seemed the latest misjudgment in a sorry recent history of bungling, autocracy and prevarication. There was the Wardle sacking in 1958, the departure of Illingworth in 1968, the dismissal of Close in 1970, which led to the creation of the Yorkshire Action Group, the removal of the captaincy from Boycott in 1978, which fired the establishment of the Reform Group, and now this. The management of Yorkshire CCC had been failing in almost every area for decades – youth policy, maintenance of grounds and facilities, commercial sponsorship, involvement of members, coaching, even basic administration. Ray Illingworth complained that he once tried to give a game to a young pace bowler, Steve Stuchbury, only to discover that the club had forgotten to register him. To the Members 84 Group, it again appeared that Boycott's presence was being blamed for problems that had nothing to do with him.

One particular committee decision over Boycott crystallized the seething mood of injustice. This was the agreement, made during the summer, to grant him a testimonial in the 1984 season as recognition of 20 years' service for the club. Even to the most disinterested observer, such a move seemed bizarre. On one hand, the committee was saying he was such a malign influence that his immediate departure was vital. On the other, they were admitting he was such a wonderful servant of the club that he deserved this rare and special reward. Such a two-faced attitude made no sense to either his campaigners or the Yorkshire public.

The question of his testimonial was a key issue for Boycott. After the first committee vote to sack him on 3 October, he indicated to the club that he would be willing to retire as a Yorkshire player in 1984 if he was allowed to play out his testimonial season. The Yorkshire committee rejected this compromise, partly because they felt they had to bite the bullet and partly because Boycott had previously told the club that he wanted to carry on playing for several more years – indeed, he had expressed the hope that he might regain his England place once the TCCB ban had expired in 1985. If he had a great season in 1984, could they have prevented another renewal of his contract for the following year?

Two more acts of disastrous ineptitude by Yorkshire, on top of the testimonial fiasco, helped the Boycott campaign. The first error occurred over subscriptions. With the crucial meeting at Harrogate due on 3 December, the committee decided to send out ballot papers only to members who had paid their subscriptions by that date. This was a piece of nonsense, for a year's subscription lasted through 12 months, not just up to some arbitrary date fixed by the club. It was estimated that almost 700 legitimate members had been disenfranchised by this move. Thanks to the powerful case set out by one of its legal advisers, Matthew Caswell, the Members 84 Group took the Yorkshire committee to court and won. The special meeting had to be postponed until 21 January so that new voting papers could be sent out.

The second important mistake by the committee was a reflection of the pressure they were now feeling. On 19 December, the leading officers of the Members 84 Group, Tony Vann, Bob Slicer and Peter Briggs, were called to a meeting at Headingley. There, the chairman and secretary of Yorkshire made an outlandish offer. They said that because Boycott's testimonial might suffer if he was not playing he could take part in six championship games and one John Player League fixture. It was, as Peter Briggs said later, a ludicrous idea. If Boycott was good enough for six first-class games, why not the whole programme? How was Boycott expected to maintain any form if he was in and out of the team? And, just as importantly, how would the Yorkshire batsmen feel about having to chop and change all season to make room for his sporadic appearances? 'Frankly, if we had known that this is what they had in mind, we would not have bothered to turn up to the meeting,' said Briggs.

Tony Vann recalls that the Yorkshire committee were looking increasingly shambolic after this latest mess. 'Initially, the meeting about Geoff's future was fixed for 3 December. I don't think we would have won then. But in the following weeks there was the problem over the subscriptions, which meant that the December meeting had to be postponed. The club lost a lot of face over that. Matthew Caswell's legal brain shone through there. Then there was the botched proposal over his testimonial. It was a crazy proposal. It just showed how bankrupt the committee had become in their thinking. Those two issues were symbolic of the mismanagement of the club. After that, we had a lot of credibility.'

The committee were now sinking faster than the *Titanic*. They finally went under water at Harrogate on 21 January. Amid scenes in the Royal Hall of almost evangelical fervour, all three pro-Boycott resolutions were carried, as follows: (a) that Boycott be offered a contract for 1984: for 4115; against 3109; majority of 1006; (b) no confidence in the cricket committee: for 3609; against 3578; majority of 31; (c) no confidence in the general committee:

for 3997; against 3209; majority of 78.

It was a sweeping victory for the Members 84 Group. Only four months ago, Boycott's career had looked finished. Now the horizons were stretching further into the distance. 'If Boycott is fit enough and still making runs, his contract should be renewed, whether it be at the end of the 1984, 1985 or 1986 seasons or whenever it may be. Age doesn't matter. It is ability that counts,' announced Sid Fielden.

Tony Vann recalls that there was no air of triumphalism that night from Boycott: 'When he turned up, he was actually very modest, explaining at his press conference how grateful he was for the support and how glad he was to carry on playing for Yorkshire. He pitched it just right. There were about thirty of us there that night and he went round, shaking each of us by the hand and thanking us. Though he disguised it quite well, he was on a high because he knew he could continue playing cricket.'

Though the votes were not technically binding on the committee, Ronnie Burnett, Billy Sutcliffe, Fred Trueman and their colleagues felt they had no alternative but to resign. In every seat throughout the county, there were now to be elections for a new committee. Here again, Tony Vann's organizational skills came into their own in turning the Members 84 Group into a formidable election machine. 'Tony did an absolutely marvellous job,' says Peter Briggs. 'He pulled the whole thing together and worked so hard. No one could have done it better.'

Vann does not deny the effort he put in: 'In the five months after Geoff's sacking, I was working about thirty hours a week, lobbying, canvassing, knocking on doors, telephoning, corresponding. I did put myself out for Geoff but, then, organization has always been my strength. I must say that Geoff has never forgotten that. He has always been very loyal to me.'

A mixture of contempt for the old committee, support for Boycott, and the organization's own diligence, ensured a landslide for the Members 84 Group. Of their 21 candidates, 17 stormed to victory. Ex-players like Sutcliffe, Burnett and Bob Platt all lost. So did Fred Trueman, the biggest name in Yorkshire cricket aside from Boycott. In his Craven district, Trueman polled just 65 votes to the 128 of the Members 84 Group's candidate, the unknown Peter Fretwell. Among the victors was Geoffrey Boycott, standing in his own district of Wakefield, where he beat the incumbent, Dr John Turner, by 203 votes to 147. It was a unique occurrence for a current professional to be elected on to the general committee. Boycott, however, had submitted his nomination papers in December when his playing future was unclear. Given that nothing in the rules prohibited a professional from serving, he decided to take up his seat.

Because of these all-conquering elections, Boycott was seen by his enemies in Yorkshire as a sinister Machiavellian figure, plotting and pulling the strings of the Members 84 Group in his bid for absolute power. But this implies far too much political subtlety and cunning in Boycott. He was, in fact, just the opposite: forthright, open and rude. The backroom deals and clever arguments so beloved of politicians were not his style. In many ways, he was a curiously naïve figure. He could never be described as streetwise or sophisticated. Cocooned in his cricket and reluctant to socialize, he had never managed to understand the easy compromises and deceptions that run through most human interactions. The victims of the 1984 revolution might guffaw when he said all he wanted was to do his best for Yorkshire, but in his own eccentric, blinkered, childlike way, it was probably true.

Yet even with the most straightforward of intentions, in standing for the new committee, Boycott had planted the seeds of his own destruction.

22
The End of an Era

After the triumph at Harrogate and the subsequent electoral land-slide, the new committee took two immediate decisions. One was to confirm the award of a new contract to Geoffrey Boycott; the other was to sack Ray Illingworth as cricket manager. Illingworth was glad to go, bruised by the years of strife. Understandably, he never had anything to do with the management of the club again.

When Illingworth was sacked, he received a letter from Molly Staines, a former committee member who had lost her seat in the committee revolution. She wrote: 'I've always felt that you were to be the scapegoat, especially when you dared to criticize G. Boycott, surely the saddest person who ever walked on a sports field.' And, in truth, Boycott's last three seasons were probably the saddest and most negative of his career, when his presence in committee was divisive and his performance on the field increasingly self-serving. By the time of his final departure, he had alienated many of those who had fervently supported him through the winter of 1983/84.

It had always been said in the past that no man is bigger than Yorkshire cricket, but during the eighties, that was no longer the case. In the corridors of Headingley, backed by his mandate from the people, Boycott now seemed unchallengeable. And to what use would he put this dominance? Quite simply, the freedom to bat in his own way. He could wallow in the luxury of his own personal crusade to break every possible record without being distracted by the needs of the team. Such an egocentric outlook, as I have said, was hardly unique to Boycott. In a typically thoughtful article in October 1983, just after Boycott had been sacked by Yorkshire, *The Times* cricket correspondent John Woodcock wrote: 'Talk of selfishness is valid. Yet batting is a selfish business. I have watched, written about and known all the great batsmen of the past 40 years and very few of them have taken guard with only the interests of their own side in mind.' What was unique about Boycott's position after 1983 was that he had created the circumstances where he could put his own interests first.

In his final years, his strokeplay became more restricted than ever before. His defence was still sure – at the age of 45 he was still the best batsman in the country on an awkward track – but his finest attacking shots were rarely displayed. In place of the classical attacking style which, 15 years earlier in Australia, had led to comparisons with Sir Jack Hobbs, he now relied largely on pushes and nudges for his runs. Tony Lewis, who had played against Boycott at his peak then watched him as a commentator, says: 'I had thought that as he matured he would have become more expansive but just the opposite happened; he became more defensive, more limited. Eventually, I think in some ways he was a bit like Nick Faldo, so technical that he almost lost sight of the game he once played so well with all those drives straight and through the off-side.'

Examining the 1984 season, some of his scoring reached new heights of immobility: 60 in 52 overs against Somerset; 53 in 51 overs against Derbyshire; 17 in 26 overs against Leicestershire; 77 in 67 overs against Sussex; 33 in 32 overs against Nottinghamshire. His supporters could point to an average at the end of the season of 62, but it had taken him almost 1200 overs to compile his 1567 runs.

And despite being in his element at the crease, the ingrained Boycott moodiness still shone through. In his book about the 1984 season, *A Yorkshire Diary: Year of Crisis*, the late David Bairstow – in general a strong supporter of Boycott – wrote about his behaviour in a game at Headingley against Leicestershire: 'He annoyed me by his attitude. He was out cheaply, came back to the dressing room, kicked Stuart Fletcher's bag, blamed the pitch, swore at "having to play on a pitch like that" and then, when we'd won, left without saying a word. He grumbled, "I'm under so much pressure." I replied, "If people weren't behind you, you would not be out on this field today."' In another match, against Somerset, when asked his opinion, he came out with his old line, 'It's nowt to do with me. I'm not the captain.'

Whatever such problems, Boycott continued to be adored by the Yorkshire public. And they reflected their devotion in giving him a massively successful testimonial in 1984. The sum of £147,954 was a record for a cricketer, though it was beaten the following year by Graham Gooch. But not all of the Yorkshire team were so impressed with some of Boycott's fund-raising techniques. During a NatWest game against Shropshire in July, Yorkshire were chasing a target of 230 and were badly off course after Boycott took 25 overs to score 27. Then an announcement was made over the public-address system informing the 4000-strong crowd that a collection was being taken for Boycott's testimonial. Players muttered to each other that none of them could remember a similar situation with a Yorkshire player taking money on an away ground. Even worse followed. As Yorkshire's lower order were struggling desperately to win the game, another announcement explained that Boycott would be 'signing autographs in the tent on the side of the field near the church'. At very best, this showed a certain insouciance towards the outcome of a vital cup tie – which Yorkshire went on to lose badly.

That defeat was emblematic of yet another disappointing season for Yorkshire, who finished fourteenth in the county championship and bottom of the John Player League. The rumbles of discontent now started again, and this time Brian Close, Boycott's old captain, was to be at the forefront of yet another winter of crisis. During the election early in 1984, the Members 84 Group had welcomed the candidature of Close in Bradford because, though by no means part of the pro-Boycott faction, he was seen as unsympathetic to the old administration after his sacking in 1970. Following the landslide victory, Close was elected chairman of the cricket committee. But he soon became disillusioned with his position. Unimpressed with either Bairstow's leadership or Boycott's batting, he also felt he had no freedom to act because of the way the cricket and general committees were now packed with Boycott loyalists. 'In committee, Boycott just controlled his supporters. You couldn't put anything up against him. He would sit at the back, his feet up, reading the paper, then put up his arm and sixteen hands would follow,' says Close – a picture which Boycott describes as 'nonsense'. In a move of characteristic originality, Close suggested a way out of the spiral of decline: Boycott should once more become captain of Yorkshire. On the face of it, this seemed an absurd suggestion. Hadn't Boycott been branded a failure after eight years in the job in the seventies? But Close felt there was some logic behind the proposal. He told me: 'I felt that Geoff wanted power without responsibility. So I thought if Yorkshire were to recover he had to take on the responsibility for the side. I said to him, "You might actually go down as someone who has contributed something to Yorkshire cricket rather than someone who just used his final years for batting practice while the rest of the team went to pot."' But Close gave him two conditions. First, he should bat no higher than number five in the side, so he could watch the game and pass on instructions. Second, he had to resign his membership of the committee.

Boycott refused this offer. He saw the captaincy as a poisoned chalice. With Yorkshire's resources so weak, failure was certain, and that would become another means of trying to force his removal. A disillusioned Brian Close resigned from the cricket committee, precipitating another winter of warfare in Yorkshire. This time, however, the pro-Boycott Members 84 Group were the establishment rather than the outsiders, while the opposition came from a newly formed alliance of businessmen headed by David Hall, managing director of the tailoring firm John Collier. Hall's new pressure group, the 'Yorkshire Cricket Devotees', thought that the revolution had gone too far. Following the precedent set by the Reformers six years before, they drew up a motion of no confidence in the committee. After the inevitable legal wrangles and noisy exchanges of propaganda and abuse, this resolution was finally debated at the Queen's Hotel, Leeds. It was only narrowly defeated, by 1735 votes to 1483, an indicator that the anti-Boycott forces were gaining ground amongst the membership, who were increasingly tired of the way Boycott continued to be such a source of controversy in the club.

One issue lay at the heart of the growing reaction against him. This was his insistence in remaining on the general committee while still being a salaried player – the so-called 'dual role'. For many this was highly unsatisfactory. It meant that there could be no confidentiality or trust. Cricketers felt that what they said in the privacy of the dressing room might end up on the floor of the committee. Conversely, elected members feared that their words might later be bandied amongst the players. Moreover, as a committee member, Boycott could have had access to personal information about players' contracts, wages or disciplinary records. Boycott argued that five men before him had served on the committee as players, including Lord Hawke, Stanley Jackson and Brian Sellers. But the huge difference was that they had all been amateurs and not, therefore, employees of the club.

It was this question of his dual role that lay at the heart of one of the most bitter and unfortunate episodes of Boycott's last three years: the quarrel with Sid Fielden. Silver-haired, striking and eloquent, Fielden was an impassioned Boycott supporter and had become secretary of the Reform Group in 1978, lending his powerful oratory to the cause. He and Boycott had become the closest of friends. In Boycott's own words, 'For many years, I trusted him like a brother.' Fielden admits, 'Ronnie Burnett used to claim that my only fault was that I loved Geoff Boycott. And I suppose I did, in the best sense. Even my wife sometimes used to say that I thought more of Geoff Boycott than I did of her.'

The pair could hardly have been closer during the revolution of 1983/84. Yet after the Boycott victory they fell out badly. Boycott believes the enmity was caused by Fielden's resentment at not being made chairman of the club as a reward for his dedicated service. Fielden says that this is untrue. 'I disagreed with him serving on the committee – and I still think I was right about that. Sadly my stance turned people in his camp against me.' The chasm between the two widened rapidly. By late 1984, Fielden was the subject of increasingly nasty attacks. The smears and rumours deepened until, in January 1985, after a meeting of the general committee, Fielden announced, 'Geoff Boycott is a very great cricketer. I have known him for many years, through sadness and elation. But now I wish I had never met him.' He moved over to the 'Yorkshire Devotees' opposition, and by March he could be found on platforms supporting Brian Close against his former allies. Boycott, who always prized loyalty more highly than most other virtues, was incensed at what he saw as a cruel betrayal. Subsequently, the most scathing words in his autobiography were to be reserved for Fielden, where he described him as 'Judas'. Yet despite the acrimony of this period, Fielden today will say only good about Boycott. He still thinks the world of him, and becomes emotional when he looks back on the feud.

The issue that caused their split, Boycott's dual role, dragged on interminably for another year, with all the incestuous, pointless wrangling at which Yorkshire had become so expert. There were references to sub-committees, threats of legal action, special general meetings, recourse to expensive London QCs, and talk of resignations. Eventually, after a referendum of the membership had voted by 80 per cent to oppose dual role, the annual general meeting in February 1986 voted by 3370 to just 310 to introduce changes in the rules to prevent a current player serving on the committee. At the end of the 1986 season, Boycott would be faced with a stark choice about his future – unless, of course, the club decided to make it for him.

Boycott's playing career was littered with misjudgements but few decisions have been more bloody-minded than his rigid adherence to his dual role for almost three years. Technically there may have been nothing wrong with it but strategically it was disastrous, alienating many of his supporters. When the rule-change resolution was put to the AGM in February 1986, Tony Vann formally seconded it. He told me: 'He was very offended that I, his loyal friend, could not just vote in favour but would actually second the resolution. But I had seen how the issue was tearing the club apart and I thought, on balance, that it just was not right that a player could be in both the dressing room and the committee room.' Boycott might have felt aggrieved but the crucial point about this row, compared to his 1983 sacking and the 1978 captaincy removal, was that there could be no sense of justice on his side. While previously he could go before the Yorkshire public as a martyr, this time he looked like nothing more than an egocentric power-seeker.

Out on the field, where most of his followers thought he belonged, his appetite for runs showed no signs of diminishing during his last two years. In 1985, he hit 1657 runs at 75.31 and finished second in the national averages with only the great Viv Richards ahead of him, a remarkable performance for a cricketer aged nearly 45. His six centuries included 184 at Worcester, where he put on 351 for the first wicket with Martyn Moxon, the highest opening stand for Yorkshire since Holmes and Sutcliffe's famous partnership of 555 against Essex at Leyton in 1932. Boycott was out, hooking to the last ball of the day, having hit 21 boundaries, showing that his shot-making had not entirely disappeared. Even now, in the twilight of his career, he still showed the same hatred at his dismissal. Martyn Moxon recalls that, on this occasion, 'He came in and basically sat in a corner with a towel on his head for forty-five minutes and never said a word to anybody. He was absolutely distraught that he had got out playing the hook shot at that time of day, so I think that sums up his mentality on batting.' He also played two superb innings against high-quality West Indian pace bowling. When Surrey played at Sheffield in July, Tony Gray shot Yorkshire out for 133, taking 8 for 40 in 17.4 overs, yet Boycott carried his bat for 55 not out. Against Hampshire at Middlesbrough, Boycott made 115 out of a Yorkshire total of 283, with Malcolm Marshall taking 5 for 48.

Boycott was probably happier in the Yorkshire dressing room in 1985 and 1986 than at any time since the mid seventies, as he was surrounded by players with whom he felt at ease, like Arnie Sidebottom, David Bairstow, Paul Jarvis, Kevin Sharp and Phil Carrick. Paul Jarvis has happy memories of Boycott at this time, recalling the time when he was only 17 and he was in the shower room with Boycott: 'We were the only two in there. Boycott stood up, soaping himself, and said, "Look, Paul, you've got a helluva lot of ability. With your ability and my brains, you'll go a long way. If you listen to me, I can help you a lot. People write in, ask for my advice and pay for it. I'll give you it for free. Would you rather be like me or them lot in there?" – obviously meaning the rest of the team. "If you want to go on and achieve things, you've got to be more like me than them."'

Jarvis says that after this conversation Boycott was extremely helpful, sorting out his run-up and coaching him in the right line and length to trouble batsmen. Often, on the field, Boycott would stand at mid-on or mid-off, and give continual advice to Jarvis on where he should be bowling. Jarvis also cherished their net practices because he learnt so much from watching Boycott in action. 'Technically he was the finest batsman I have bowled at. He was phenomenal, really. For someone like me to have been associated with him for more than four years was a great experience. I have just got so much respect and affection for the bloke, it is almost like a love relationship.' It is interesting that both Paul Jarvis and Sid Fielden say quite openly that they loved Boycott, a tribute to the real devotion he could inspire in those around him, despite his faults.

A more mellow, helpful Boycott is also recalled by Philip Ackroyd, a Yorkshire committee member who had first come across him as an intense, withdrawn teenager. Visiting Hull for a Second XI game in the mid-eighties, Ackroyd had seen Boycott, on his first outing after a bad injury, score a superb 130. Later, in the bar, Ackroyd was talking to the young Yorkshire player Richard Blakey, who explained he was nervous about approaching Boycott for advice on his leg-side batting. 'You see, many of these young boys were terrified of Geoffrey because of his reputation for being un-cooperative,' says Ackroyd. Later, Boycott came into the bar and Ackroyd told him about Blakey's problem. Boycott went straight over to the colt: 'Ay, I noticed that, Richard, you were playing a lot of good shots but the ball was going straight to fielders. You're play-ing too early, lad, too early. Let the ball come on to you. Easiest shot in the world. I've scored most of my runs round that corner. We'll have a go in the nets tomorrow.' Ackroyd concludes: 'He's a wonder-ful coach but we have never used him properly. People don't ask and he does want asking. He always has done throughout his life.'

This is a point reinforced by Martyn Moxon, who made his Yorkshire début in 1981 and says that he learnt about batting just by standing at the other end when they opened together. Never-theless, as he told the author Richard Sydenham, 'I was in awe of him so much that I was frightened to talk to him. He wasn't the sort of bloke who would offer young players advice. It was only in later years that I found out that his theory was players should go to him if they wanted help.'

Boycott remained so fit and prolific that there was some specu-lation that he might return to the England side that summer in the Ashes series against Australia, now that his three-year ban had been served. Though he made no public statement to this effect, privately he did not disguise his ambitions to resume his Test career. But David Gower, the Test captain who had just led a highly successful tour of India, quashed such talk. 'Geoffrey's been a marvellous servant for England but we have to look to the future and, in view of his age, it wouldn't make an awful lot of sense to pick him again,' said Gower in April. Any lingering hopes that there might be a vacancy for an opener were crushed once the series began with the return of Graham Gooch and the tremendous form of Tim Robinson. When Robinson scored a brilliant 175 in the first Test at Headingley, Ian Botham led a chorus of 'Bye-bye, Boycott' from the England balcony.

With no hope of an England recall, Boycott had only Yorkshire to play for. But here, too, his days were numbered. Since the high point of the 1984 revolution, the pro-Boycott forces had been in decline, losing through both elections and defections, of which Sid Fielden was the most high profile. Brian Close had returned in 1986 as cricket chairman, with more powerful backing than he had enjoyed before, particularly from the club's president, Viscount Mountgarret, while the influential cricket committee now had an anti-Boycott majority. On top of the traditional gripes that Boycott was selfish, divided the club, batted too slowly and held back younger players, a new claim was added to this arsenal of criticism. This was the argument that, in middle age, he had become injury-prone. During the 1986 season, Boycott suffered a badly pulled hamstring, then broke his hand playing against Leicestershire – though with his usual fortitude he went on to make a century. Such injuries could have happened at any time in his career but, with the tide now turning against him, Boycott rightly sensed that they would be used against him when his contract came up for renewal.

Despite his injuries, Boycott topped the Yorkshire averages yet again in 1986, with 890 runs at 52.35. That brave century in July against Leicestershire, whose attack included Phil de Freitas and Winston Benjamin of the West Indies, was the hundred and fiftieth of his career. It was a performance typical of Boycott's late career. His defence was solid but runs only came in a trickle. Critics who said he played only for his records rather than the team could point to how this milestone took five and a half hours and some 267 balls to achieve. Perhaps even more damning was an earlier innings in June against Middlesex at Lord's. There he had scored just 69 in four hours forty minutes – with only one run coming in the last half-hour of his innings, although, as Boycott pointed out, he was the top-scorer in both Yorkshire innings and they won the game by exactly 69 runs.

The greatest disappointment of this farewell summer was that he failed to reach 1000 in a season for the first time since 1962. By the time of the last game, against Northamptonshire at Scarborough in September, he knew that the end was inevitable but he still needed 69 runs to reach those four figures. Unfortunately, in Yorkshire's first innings he was run out by Jim Love for 61, leaving him eight short. As it turned out, this was his final first-class innings. Some might say it was appropriate that it should end with dismissal of that sort. Then in response to Yorkshire's 352 for 7 declared, Northamptonshire collapsed to 197 all out. Bairstow had the chance to impose the follow-on, and he asked Boycott's advice. Given the claims about Boycott's self-centredness, it reflects well on him that he told the captain, 'Go for the win; enforce the follow-on.' Northants batted again and went right through until after 5 p.m. on the third day, denying Boycott the chance to make his final eight runs. The Yorkshire crowd were well aware of this statistic, and as the hands on the clock ticked by, they bayed more and more loudly for a Northants declaration, which would have allowed Boycott one last visit to the crease. Northants did declare, but only at 5.21 p.m., which meant that they would not have to take the field again before the close at 5.30 p.m.

Boycott knew his time was up and, savouring his final moments as a Yorkshire player, he lingered at the ground long after most others had left. Thirteen years later, in an interview with the *Sunday Telegraph*, he gave a moving description of that scene in Scarborough on 12 September: 'Something had come to an end, something wonderful. I just thought, This is it, then. I waited for the ground to clear. Then I wandered around on my own among all the newspapers and food wrappers and tin cans. It didn't feel like death exactly but I did think a part of my life was finished.'

On 23 September, the cricket committee confirmed that he would not be offered a new contract for the following season. Close announced afterwards: 'It wasn't easy. In some respects I would have loved Geoffrey to have gone on breaking records but in reality I had to say that his retention would not have helped us. We just couldn't carry on with a cult figure grinding out his personal glory while the rest of the players simply made up the numbers.' Despite the insult implied by the use of the term 'cult', this time there were no protests, no revolutions, no action groups. After almost a decade of turmoil, the Yorkshire cricketing public were sick at the thought of more conflict. Even Boycott's most enthusiastic followers had no stomach for another battle.

There was briefly some flicker of hope among his supporters that his first-class career might not be over. Soon after his sacking, Boycott received an expression of interest from Glamorgan and a verbal offer of a two-year contract from Derbyshire. Boycott loyalist Peter Briggs says: 'I wrote to Derbyshire saying he would be a great boost to their club and they were enthusiastic about the idea. In fact, their chairman, Guy Willatt, virtually went on his hands and knees begging Boycott to play for them.' Derbyshire's captain Kim Barnett expressed only minor concerns about having such a controversial figure in their midst. 'There might be some opposition in view of what has happened at Yorkshire but I would like us to take him on. We need to find an extra two thousand runs from somewhere and I believe that Geoff is the man for the job.'

Glamorgan dropped out of the race to sign Boycott, recruiting Surrey's Alan Butcher instead. The Derbyshire offer certainly attracted him and he pondered it through the autumn. Lord MacLaurin, by now a good friend of Boycott's, recalls: 'When he was thinking of playing for Derbyshire in 1986, I said to him, "Geoffrey, you are a Yorkshireman through and through. I think it would be the worst thing in the world." This was the line that Boycott eventually took. As in the Packer crisis nine years earlier, his loyalty to his native county was too great. On 12 December, Boycott issued this statement: 'My first love is Yorkshire cricket and always has been. As any Yorkshireman will understand, it was an emotional decision to consider whether to play for another county after twenty-five years.'

Even if angered by his enforced retirement from Yorkshire, Boycott could look back with pride on a wonderful set of statistics built up over a quarter of a century's batting: 48,426 runs made at an astonishing average of 56.83; only seven other men, Hobbs, Woolley, Hendren, Mead, Grace, Hammond and Sutcliffe had scored more and every single one with a lower average; 151 centuries, a total exceeded only by Hobbs, Hendren, Hammond and Mead; 1000 runs in a season 26 times; only Englishman ever to average over 100 in a season, a feat he performed twice; third highest aggregate of runs for Yorkshire, after Sutcliffe and Denton; 13 hundreds in the 1971 season, a figure exceeded only by Compton in 1947 (18), Hobbs in 1925 (16), Hammond in 1938 (15) and Sutcliffe in 1932 (14).

What is so amazing about all these figures is that Boycott played two-thirds of his career after 1969, in a greatly reduced championship programme, so his opportunities for scoring were far fewer. Moreover, in his era, compared to that of Hobbs and Sutcliffe, fielding had greatly improved; bowling attacks were much stronger because of overseas imports and more intense professionalism; and there were the additional pressures of one-day cricket, Tests and overseas tours. In a lyrical appreciation of his career in *Wisden*, Derek Hodgson wrote: 'When his career is fully assessed and settled into the record, early next century, will all his foibles and prejudices matter that much? A batting record that stretches, vast and almost unsurpassable, like a distant view of the Himalayas, must put much pettiness into perspective, leaving all the discord in his wake no more than an odd trickle down a great stone face.'

23

A New Beginning

In his 1999 book *Geoffrey Boycott on Cricket*, Boycott wrote, 'Even now, years on from my retirement, I miss playing to such an extent that I can honestly say I would exchange the rest of my life for five more years of playing for England at the height of my form.' Boycott has frequently repeated this morbid statement in print and to friends, which shows the depths of his heartbreak at the end of his career. 'I didn't enjoy playing cricket. I loved it. Every day of my life I got up wanting to play, longing to bat. Cricket's not a pastime. It's a passion. I'd have liked to have played until the day I died,' he said, in an interview in the *Sun* in December 1989.

The wrench of giving up competitive cricket was almost like a bereavement for Boycott. The fear of reawakening his anguish over loss has prevented Boycott ever returning to the crease, not in a charity game, a benefit match, a celebrity knock-out or anything. To pull on his pads, don his gloves and take guard again would have been too emotional, too distressing. It would have served only as a reminder of the world he had adored and lost, like someone who is sunk into grief by the fleeting memory of a departed lover. This might sound melodramatic, but Boycott has always been a man of intense feelings. He admitted in that *Sun* interview, conducted by John Sadler, that he tried not to touch the bat he kept at his Woolley home: 'I daren't relive the moments. When I pick up the bat, it stirs the memories. So I have to put it down.'

John Callaghan told me: 'There was a time when we were doing the latest book and we had been talking about Yorkshire. We had to break off what we were doing because he was very emotional. He said to me, "I'd give everything away if I could be twenty-five again and playing for Yorkshire."' In 1998 Rachael Swinglehurst gave an even more graphic description: 'He doesn't openly weep but he does what we call clouding up. He's done that ever since he finished playing cricket. When he's talking about something very special in his career, he wells up because he misses it so badly.'

Even when he received lucrative offers from the Lancashire League or festival organizers, he still refused them, again contradicting the reputation he has for meanness. One league team promised him twice the salary he received at Yorkshire but could not persuade him. 'There's not a price that could swing it. Geoffrey Boycott going to the wicket with a bat in his hand – that's history. It's not buyable.'

In addition to the danger of painful reminders, Boycott has had other reasons for his position. He said, for instance, that he could not play in a match without sufficient net practice. Kevin Sharp recalls: 'He was asked to play in a game, Yorkshire v. Yorkshire Exiles, at Scarborough in 1987, and he said that he would need three months to prepare for the game and he couldn't spare the time.' He also argued rightly that he had too much respect for cricket to take part in contrived matches or to play just for money. Cricket followers, he believed, would be insulted. To one of Tony Vann's friends, who had asked him to participate in a charity event, he wrote, 'I have played with the best, for the best, against the best. Only the best will do. Thank you but no thank you.' Then there was also the old terror of failure. The expectations of a festival or charity crowd would be as high as ever, and any bowler who dismissed Boycott cheaply would be able to dine out on that story for the rest of his life. Once again, he would sense the eyes of his critics watching for any error, all the more ready to mock and jeer if the bowling was of poor quality.

Like someone starting a new life after a tragedy, Boycott decided he had to make a clean break with professional cricket. Not only did he refuse to play any more, but he even put all his trophies in a bank vault rather than have them on display. 'They're locked away. I never look at them. I'm not flippant about it. I'm not going to sell them or anything. But I don't believe in living in the past. Life's very short, really, if you've got things to do,' he said recently.

The question was: what was Boycott going to do with the rest of his life? He was hardly likely to return to work in the civil service, the only occupation he had ever held outside cricket. Too mundane, too badly paid, too accountable. With his self-discipline, tough negotiating skills and attention to detail, he might have made an excellent businessman – throughout his playing career he had proved superb at making deals for himself – but it was almost inevitable that he would stay in cricket. He might not want to pick up a bat again, but he still relished watching, analysing, reading about and discussing the game. In the *Yorkshire Evening Post* in 1977, on the eve of his hundred hundreds, he looked to the future after his retirement: 'I love the game and I shall go on loving it and being fascinated by it. I'll make my living doing something tied up with cricket. Perhaps televised cricket. Even when I'm not playing I'll be there watching the beauty of it. I love the magic of it. I believe in it. Sometimes cricket writers moan and say it's been a boring day. I say, "Don't you know how lucky you are to spend all your time watching and writing about such a beautiful game?"'

Boycott was far better qualified than most ex-cricketers for a role in the media. Intelligent and articulate, he had strong opinions on the game and, just as importantly, he was never afraid to express them. Given that the professional cricket world is small, many former players have often been reluctant to criticize their 'mates' – Ian Botham's noisy advocacy of his old Worcestershire colleague Graeme Hick in the face of all the evidence is a good example. But Boycott, as a loner, never had that difficulty. He had not flinched from brutal judgements in the dressing room; he would not do so now across the airwaves. Furthermore, by the mid-eighties his public speaking had gained in confidence and fluency compared to his painful shyness of the early sixties. Philip Ackroyd, a member of the Yorkshire committee from 1984, recalls a talk that Boycott gave at a fund-raising evening for his local club: 'It was the most brilliant talk I have ever listened to. You could have heard a pin drop throughout it. He spoke about his tour of India, not just on cricket but also on the conditions of the people. There were about 120 people there and he had them all spellbound.'

Ackroyd was present at another talk, this one at a club's junior prize-giving, when Boycott demonstrated his gift for the telling phrase and the memorable image. 'One little boy asked what it was like facing the West Indian attack. He replied, "Well, the best way to describe it is like this: you go on to a motorway, stop in the fast lane and there's a car coming towards you at about a hundred miles per hour. It gets within twenty-two yards of you. You're looking straight at it. You've got to make a decision, which way are you going to go? When you face the West Indians, you have three decisions, defend it, leave it or attack it."'

Even before his retirement, Boycott had started work in the media and cricket writing. Since the late seventies he had made regular guest appearances in the BBC commentary box where, with characteristic diligence, he studied the techniques of Richie Benaud and the late Jim Laker. He was employed by the *Mail on Sunday* to comment on the disastrous England tour of the Caribbean in 1985/86, while a series of well-received books – several instruction manuals and the three tour diaries – had proved both his coherence and his appeal as a pundit.

Despite his experience and obvious talent, Boycott was somewhat disappointed that, on his retirement, he did not immediately receive a definite offer from the BBC, which then had a monopoly on domestic cricket broadcasts. 'For whatever reason, after my playing career finished, it proved difficult to catch the eye of those in charge at the BBC,' he wrote in *Geoffrey Boycott on Cricket*. Boycott believes that it may have been his blunt Yorkshire accent that did not impress the southern, public-school types who ran the BBC – exactly the same kind of establishment that he believed had thwarted his ambition to be England captain in the seventies. But Peter Baxter, producer of BBC *Test Match Special*, told me that in this period Boycott's famous brusqueness could also work against him: 'He used to come to me about it to complain, though he would never ask me directly to employ him because he thought I had no influence. He could be quite offhand. I would get disparaging remarks from him like, "It's all right for you. You get all the matches but have none of the responsibility." I just used to say, "Yes, Geoffrey." But that is hardly the way to go about getting the job you want.'

Tom Graveney, then a commentator himself, gives a further explanation for the BBC's dilatoriness in taking on Boycott: 'In the eighties, the BBC Head of Sport was pushing to get Boycott into the commentary box, but it would be fair to say that we didn't really want him once he had retired. Eventually they decided that they were going to have him irrespective of our feelings so he and I used to alternate.'

Still waiting for a BBC contract, Boycott described himself as 'cheerfully unemployed' when he launched a junior cricket competition at Headingley in December 1987. This was more than a little exaggerated. Not only was he doing freelance work but, far more importantly, he had been busy promoting the book whose huge success was already transforming his prospects and his personal wealth. Published by Macmillan on 16 June 1987 – the twenty-fifth anniversary of his début for Yorkshire – *Boycott: The Autobiography* was an instant bestseller. Within four months of its publication, it had sold 50,000 copies, an astounding total at a time when the sports-book market was much more limited than it is today. Financially, Boycott did far better out of the book than out of his batting. His £180,000 advance from Macmillan was double that paid for any other sporting memoirs, with the next best the £90,000 Greg Norman collected for his autobiography. In addition, Boycott negotiated a £200,000 newspaper deal with the *Daily Mail* for serial rights.

These phenomenal sums reflected the publishers' confidence that the book would cause a sensation. They were proved absolutely right. The British public had long been fascinated with the Boycott saga and were eager to read his account of his life. In many respects, the book reflected the strengths and flaws of the man. Analytical, compelling and honest, it was also too eager to highlight imagined wrongs and too obsessed with the internal machinations of Yorkshire County Cricket Club. Generally the reviews were enthusiastic. Christopher Martin-Jenkins wrote in the *Cricketer*: 'Boycott has told his side with conviction. It makes absorbing reading, although the life he unfolds is too strewn with physical pain and mental anguish to be described as a happy one.'

Such was its success that Boycott's book set the modern trend for the revelatory blockbuster from retired England cricketers – and umpires. Since it was published, we have had massive bestsellers from Graham Gooch, Allan Lamb, Ian Botham and, way at the top of the list, Dickie Bird. Boycott himself did much to promote his memoirs, travelling round the country with Jeffrey Archeresque energy and autographing no fewer than 14,000 copies.

Boycott may have worked hard, but he did not endear himself to the man who took him round the country, a driver called Graham hired by Macmillan for the six-week tour. These are some of Graham's other memories of that assignment: 'I found him incredibly rude, the rudest, crudest man on two legs. I was not given a chance. I was a "complete fookin' wanker" from the beginning. I found him a very strange man. He was the most miserable tightarse you could ever come across in your life. Absolutely everything had to be paid for by the publisher. He could also be quite unpredictable. One minute he could be as nice as anything, the next he could be ranting.' Graham says that one of Boycott's odd habits was to sit in the back seat, staring at the rear-view mirror and trying to glare him out. He also says that Boycott would frequently poke him in the back. 'At the end of the stint, down in Southampton, I had had enough and I told him what a shit he was and gave him a piece of my mind. We had a bust-up and he did not want to have anything to do with me on the journey back. Yet despite their differences, Boycott remained an admirer of Graham's professionalism and demanded his services for another book-signing tour in 1990. When Graham arrived at its start, Boycott said, 'Great to have you again. I told those publishers that you're a fookin' professional.' Graham recalls, 'So off we went and the whole trip went peacefully this time.'

Another group who were not happy about Boycott's attitude during the writing and promotion of his book were the Yorkshire committee. Having been re-elected for the Wakefield District, he failed to attend any meetings for a year from November 1986, claiming that he was too busy with his book. One of the most regrettable features of this long absence was his delay in autographing a set of souvenir £100 certificates bought by Yorkshire members as part of a fund-raising drive for an indoor school. The comparison of his feverish book-signing was not lost on a few Yorkshire stalwarts. Boycott did eventually sign the certificates, but his behaviour annoyed even loyalists. John Callaghan, usually one of his most eloquent defenders, wrote in the *Yorkshire Evening Post*: 'Why does he stay on the committee if he has no discernible interest in other aspects of the operation? By pursuing his lonely course,

Geoff Boycott has seriously damaged his image yet again.' Tony Vann was equally embarrassed. 'That year out is an example of Geoffrey's character, the way he lets himself down. Not only did he not attend, he did not even send apologies to most meetings. I think it was partly due to his anger at the way he had been sacked. But it was a misjudgement. I think he let himself down then and also the few friends that he still had at the time.'

Apart from the book and his possible resentment at the sacking, there was a geographical reason why Boycott was not involved with the committee in 1987. During this period he was spending much of his time abroad, in Jersey or in America, a tax exile now his book had made him a wealthy man. In August 1987, it was reported that Boycott had expressed an interest in buying a property on the island and had approached the advertising department of the local paper for advice on such a purchase. Boycott, however, denied that he was thinking of moving to Jersey. Indeed, contrary to all rumours of emigration to the Channel Islands, South Africa or Dorset, Boycott has remained at Pear Tree Farm, Woolley, since he moved there in 1979.

In his attack on Boycott in the *Yorkshire Evening Post* over his neglect of his committee duties, John Callaghan had written: 'The outstanding personality of the last two decades is already to some extent yesterday's man.' The worst mistake to make with Boycott is to write him off. Within two years, he was on the way to becoming a bigger personality in cricket than ever before, his post-playing career dramatically taking off in three directions: as columnist, coach and commentator.

It was in 1989 that Boycott was first recruited to write for the *Sun*. The relationship would last harmoniously for nine years until the paper's high-minded and hypocritical sacking of him after the Margaret Moore case. With his punchy language, talent for controversy, and strident opinions, Boycott was exactly right for Britain's flashiest, loudest tabloid. Kelvin MacKenzie, the former editor of the *Sun*, later Boycott's boss at Talk Radio, says: 'The great thing about him was that he just didn't give a stuff in his column. He would say what he thought, regardless of whether it was going to damage friendships or, much more likely, sever relationships. It was an extraordinary performance.'

John Etheridge, the *Sun*'s cricket correspondent who ghosted

Boycott's column, told me: 'He was very bright and extremely assiduous about his notes, taking the same meticulous approach to his journalism as he used to bring to his batting. The secret of the column was to make it sound just like him but that was not too difficult as he spoke in such a colourful, expressive way, full of sharp phrases. Often it was little more than a case of just transcribing our interview.' Etheridge remembers that Boycott was meticulous about checking his copy, even down to the grammar. A legacy of his rigorous English teaching from Hemsworth was his dislike of beginning any sentence with 'and' or 'but' which, of course, is universal in tabloid journalism. Etheridge continues, 'He was incredibly outspoken, never afraid to offend or take a different line from the rest of the media. For instance, when everyone else was banging on about the Pakistanis' ball-tampering, he just said that Wasim and Waqar "could have bowled England out with an orange". Unquestionably, during his time with us, he was the best sports pundit on any newspaper, the man that had everyone in the business talking. There just was no one near him for content and detail.' Perhaps most interesting of all is Etheridge's memory of his professional relationship with Boycott. 'I have nothing but praise for him. He was a dream to work with, very thorough and reliable. He always delivered. If he said he would be at a certain place at a certain time, he was there. I have worked with a number of people over the years on various columns, and he was easily the best.'

Another breakthrough of 1989 was Boycott's recruitment as one of England's coaches. Since his retirement, he had been giving private coaching and some clinics for youngsters, but nothing at official international level. There was still concern in some TCCB quarters that Boycott was too awkward a character to be involved with the Test squad. That all changed when Ted Dexter became chairman of selectors at the start of the year as successor to Peter May. Dexter was disturbed by the pitiful nature of England's batting against Australia that summer, when the series was lost 4–0, and felt that techniques had to be improved. But what really strengthened his determination that Boycott had to become part of the set-up were the reports that Boycott's private coaching had resurrected the form of Australian star Dean Jones. Having scored two important innings in Australia's victory at Headingley, Jones announced that he owed it all to Boycott's advice. 'Nothing was going my way but I had a heart-to-heart with Geoff and the result has been fantastic.' Jones had this warning for England: 'Geoff is there to be used. If England don't use him, it's their own fault.'

This is exactly what Dexter thought. Before the England tour that winter to the Caribbean, Boycott was asked to give specialist coaching to the batsmen. It took place at both the indoor school at Headingley and the training centre at Lilleshall, and Boycott helped players on both the full West Indies tour and the A trip to Zimbabwe. Mark Nicholas, who was captain of the A tour, recalls, 'He was a brilliant coach. What he gave everybody was an insight into the mental requirements of batting as much as the techniques. England were going to the Caribbean, we were going to Zimbabwe. And he was superb on what was required to be successful in those countries. He took a video of every net session, then sat and talked you through it. Hussain, Atherton and Stewart were all full of praise for him then. I was not quite a good enough player but I suspect, had Geoffrey Boycott been my coach for a long time, I might have been rather better.'

The two biggest guns of the England batting line-up, Robin Smith and Graham Gooch, were perhaps the most lavish in their praise. Smith so admired Boycott's coaching during his Test career that he regularly spent eleven hours on the return train journey from Southampton to Leeds just so he could have a 75-minute session with Boycott. Robin Smith explains, 'He had great experience of West Indian conditions and everything he said was meaningful. I always admired his total obsession and professionalism about cricket. He had this incredible knowledge of the game, which was invaluable in the nets. I only wish that, during my England days, we had made more use of him as a batting consultant. When he talked, you listened.'

Probably the most significant beneficiary of Boycott's influence as the new England batting coach was Graham Gooch. In the summer of 1989 Gooch's form had declined so badly that he asked to be dropped from the Test side. Continually falling to Terry Alderman's swing bowling, he began to wonder if his Test career was over. Several masterclasses with Boycott changed all that. Gooch told me, 'He explained that because I was shuffling across the crease, my body and head were falling away, especially when I tried to play to leg. So that was a start and I worked on what he said. Then we did some nets at Lilleshall before going to the West Indies in 1990. He was always a great player of fast bowling so his advice on how to deal with their quicks was vital. I found him excellent and I carried on working with him because he talks a lot of sense about cricket.'

Instead of disappearing from the England scene, Gooch entered on the most prolific period of his Test career. In the calendar year of 1990, only months after he had been in despair at the state of his batting, he scored 1264 runs at an average of 79, including his famous 333 at Lords against India. This transformation cannot all be attributed to Boycott, of course. Gooch says, 'He would tell you that he had a big influence on my career, though I would not give it quite the importance he does.' The responsibility of the England captaincy, growing experience, and a renewed sense of determination were also vital factors. Nevertheless Gooch, like Dean Jones, has always given large amount of credit to the technical support of Boycott. When he was made Player of the Year in 1991, Gooch said: 'I am always striving to improve my technique and that is where Geoff Boycott comes in. He's a good coach and a good friend, the first man I always turn to. I am not too proud to admit that I owe him a hell of a lot, particularly after the problems I had against the Aussies in 1989.'

After coaching the England party, Boycott went on the 1990 tour of the Caribbean in his new capacity as a Sky TV commentator. Not only was it his first major job in broadcasting – he had done only brief stints previously for the BBC and Australia's Channel Nine – but it was also the first time an England tour overseas had been televised live. Boycott was taken on by TransWorld, the TV company (no relation to the publisher) that had the contract to produce the coverage for Sky. The aim was to get away from the detached approach of the BBC by adopting a more exciting style. This involved both technical innovations and a new brand of high-octane, high-decibel commentary, for which the heavily accented and hard-hitting Boycott was perfect. Bill Sinrich, the senior vice-president of TransWorld, recruited him for his new role. An American who has developed a passionate love of cricket, Sinrich is full of praise for Boycott. 'When he and I met in October 1989, there was an immediate meeting of minds on the approach we wanted. Since then, I have never had cause to be anything other than satisfied with the work he has done for us. He is very disciplined, organized and methodical – and a very talented commentator.' Contradicting Boycott's reputation for being difficult over money, he says that 'our negotiations have always been very straightforward'. Sinrich adds that during the West Indies tour 'he fulfilled all our hopes. He was animated, intelligent, informed, with opinions that got the attentions of most people.'

As a player, Boycott had been utterly professional about the technical side of his game, and he was the same as a commentator, soon proving himself at ease with the revolutionary new techniques like super-slow-motion and the telestrator, an idea TransWorld borrowed from American football. Of this tool, Sinrich says: 'Again, this is where Geoffrey is great because he embraced it immediately whereas some others just viewed it as a gimmick they could not be bothered with. More than anyone else, Geoffrey picked it up and made it his own.' Sinrich gave me this fascinating view on what makes Boycott so special as an analyst: 'If you blindfolded Geoffrey after something happened at real speed, and then you asked him to narrate the replay in slow motion, without seeing the screen, he could do it. The incident will have formed an image in his mind so precise and immediate, he does not need to look at the replay. That is a unique skill.'

Boycott was teamed up in the Caribbean with his old friend Tony Greig to unleash the explosive new approach on Sky viewers. Boycott and Greig had previously worked together on Channel Nine in Australia, and Greig admits that 'quite a few in our commentary box in Australia had played with him and were not too excited about it. But I would always have him. If you asked me to choose one England commentator, I don't know anyone better. He's straight; he says what he thinks; he provides stuff you can work with; he's got a view; he's entertaining; you can take the mickey out of him; and people relate to him and all those lovely Yorkshire phrases.'

Jack Bannister, also working in the media, remembers Boycott's banter on that 1990 trip to the Caribbean, when he was staying at the Hilton in Trinidad. One day he had a lift from the taxi driver who ferried Boycott every day to and from Port of Spain during the Trinidad Test on Denness's 1973/74 tour. This driver told Bannister that Boycott had kept saying that he was lacking in confidence, that he was out of form. The driver had replied, 'Mr Boycott, you are the best opening batsman in the world. You will get a hundred.' But after England's victory, Boycott had disappeared so the driver had never been paid. Bannister continues, 'We turned into the Hilton and there was Geoffrey standing at the hotel entrance, holding court as usual. So I said jokingly to the driver, "Now, there's your man. You can get your money after all these years." The driver waited very politely until there was a break in the conversation and then said, "Excuse me."

'Geoffrey turned round and said, "I remember you. You once did taxi for me."

'"Yes, I did. I was just telling Mr Bannister how you weren't confident, how you were out of form. And I tried to raise your spirits."

'"That's right, you did. I remember."

'Then I intervened and said, "And you didn't see him on the last day so you have never paid him."

'And the driver said, "But I didn't mind, not after that 90 and 105."

'Geoffrey replied, "It were 99 and 112. Now you're definitely not going to get paid." With that, he walked off laughing.'

From 1990, following his success in the Caribbean, Boycott's work with the BBC became much more regular. Tony Lewis worked with him at both Sky and the BBC at the beginning of his broadcasting career: 'When he started, his weaknesses were a bullying style and a tendency towards repetition, but he just got better and better. He is very professional, absolutely top-class. And he would be thoroughly prepared, just like he was with his cricket. Off the air he would always be working at the job, writing lists of points, making notes. Indeed, he treats his broadcasting like his batting. He believes that anything is possible with practice and attention to detail.'

Despite such accolades, Boycott still betrayed the insecurity that had shone through his playing career. Steve Pierson, who was his floor manager at the BBC and now works for Channel Four, says: 'He is the most insecure man I have ever met. When we started together, he would go on the air and always come out at the end of it and say, "Was that all right? Was that OK? What did I do right? Did I do anything wrong?" He just had to be reassured all the way. There was an arrogance – or confidence – in what he was actually saying but he was very unsure when he came off the air.' Pierson says Boycott was quickly taught that he had to fit in with the rest of the BBC team and could not act like a superstar. 'For instance, when he started, Geoffrey demanded that his tea be served in a china cup. I made absolutely sure that everyone else had tea in a china cup but he got it in a polystyrene one. He soon realized that we were going to be mates. After that we got on well, and I actually like him. You can put him in his place and he is all right, he's good fun. I once said to him, "Geoffrey, I do like your pullover." It was one of those sponsored things. At the end of the season, in comes a parcel at home from Geoffrey with the pullover: "There you are, no need to say thanks."'

Not everyone was pleased with Boycott's new incarnation as a commentator. In June 1991 the chairman of the Professional Cricketers Association, Tim Curtis, launched an attack on Boycott's tough style. 'Boycott is apt to be very acerbic and can have a demoralizing effect on players. Why doesn't he adopt a more generous attitude?'

Boycott had absolutely no time for this kind of bleating. 'My job is to use the experience and expertise I have acquired at the highest level to make informed comment. And as for Tim Curtis criticizing me, I could point out that if he had listened to my advice he would have been a better player than he is.'

Another, even more powerful indictment of Boycott came from within the media. On 20 June 1991 in the *Daily Mail*, Ian Wooldridge, one of the most respected names in sports journalism and a friend of Boycott since his first playing days, penned a savage rebuke of Boycott's style: 'Geoffrey Boycott is the meanest-spirited commentator in the history of British televised sport. He has a limited vocabulary and no wit. His assessments of cricket matters outside the boundary ropes are frequently absurd. He is incapable of voicing criticism with either sympathy or sensitivity. I reckon Geoffrey Boycott is a rotten commentator.'

24

'Just a Dad'

In October 1996, readers of the *News of the World* were treated to a graphic analysis of Boycott's bedroom technique by one of his former lovers, Sylvia Reid. 'He always took the lead in sex. He was very experienced. His love-making was like his batting. We had a slow build-up and then it was explosive.' Ms Reid had obviously never watched Boycott play on a dodgy wicket at Middlesbrough against Derbyshire on a damp Monday afternoon. But her comment shows that Boycott remained as exuberant as ever in his personal life long after his retirement from the game. The freedom to enjoy liaisons had always been an integral part of Boycott's life as a professional cricketer. It remained so once his media career began. As he enjoyed increasing wealth and celebrity status, he showed no indication that he wanted to settle down or start a family.

'His appetite for sex and money is enormous,' one former colleague told the *Yorkshire Evening Post* in January 1998. 'He is a fine-looking man, although he was never one of the blokes. The players would be standing in a hotel bar after a match and making the usual sexual comments about some attractive young woman they all fancied. Geoffrey would appear, go straight over and pick her up. He has a very particular charisma that is very attractive to women.'

Judging by Ms Reid's tale in the *News of the World* in 1996, Boycott had lost none of his charm. A 49-year-old sales manager for a housing development company, she met Boycott in October 1991 when he came to open a new project in which she was involved. There was an immediate attraction between the two, Boycott using his knowledge of Chinese horoscopes as a vehicle for flirtation. 'He said, "I'm a Dragon and you're a Horse. We could have a passionate affair together." We all posed for group photographs and I couldn't stop laughing because he kept grabbing and teasing me,' she explained. But Boycott went no further, showing the same restraint he had as a batsman. After almost a year without a word, it was Sylvia Reid who decided to try to renew contact, which makes her complaint to the press that 'Boycott used me as his sex toy' seem a bit rich. She sent him not only a collection of Shakespeare's sonnets, but also a jokey Christmas card.

Having spelt out her message all too clearly, the affair began a few months later. It was conducted in secret in hotels and car parks near Boycott's home. Reid said he 'made me feel like a love-struck sixteen-year-old. I've got two grown-up children but I felt very young and silly.' She admitted that she was very impressed by his figure, revealing that he had 'a fantastic, suntanned body. His thighs and calves were very muscular.' She further explained that they practised safe sex, for which Boycott always carried a condom in his wallet. What impressed her less was that ingrained Boycott trait of rudeness. At one of their dinners together in a hotel, she said, Boycott upset the young waitress by moaning about the batter on his fish and then refused to sign the visitors' book because his dinner had been cooked incorrectly. She also claimed that Boycott was so reluctant to part with his cash that he only booked their hotel rooms by the hour.

Kim Freeman, described by the *News of the World* as a 'stunning brunette', was another who enjoyed a passing flicker of the media spotlight over an affair with Boycott. She told the paper how she had met him while she was on holiday in Barbados with her boyfriend Roy in 1991. Again, she said that she was besotted with his fame and, once again, Boycott's opening gambit involved Chinese horoscopes. They were both staying at the Sandy Lane Hotel and when he asked her up to his room, she responded immediately.

She turned up, she recalled, wearing just her swimming costume, only to be greeted by the ex-Test star in an even more advanced state of undress. What struck her, though, was not his fine body but the calluses on his hands from holding a bat for so long. She also claimed to be disappointed by his lovemaking, 'a big baby with the stamina of a 95-year-old', though that begs the question as to why she continued to see him sporadically in hotels across England for the next three and a half years. Freeman did admit to the *News of the World* that 'he was a very good kisser and she found his crooked-mouth smile very attractive', but she added that his habit of sleeping naked apart from a T-shirt 'made him look ridiculous'. Yet perhaps the biggest problem for Freeman was the continuing obsession of Boycott's life: 'I couldn't have a conversation with him because he was only interested in cricket,' she said.

For all their lurid and often amusing detail, these stories reflected at least as badly on the two women as they did on Boycott. After all, they were the ones who shared the secrets of their affairs with the press, using the excuse of some spurious outrage over his 'selfishness' or 'not being there when I needed him' – to quote one of Reid's phrases. Besides, Boycott was still a single man when he met both of them. The wish not to be constrained was one of the reasons he had always refused marriage. In fact, he seems almost to have a phobia about it. Talking of his relationship with Margaret Moore, Boycott once explained: 'When she first mentioned marriage I went hot and cold. It's a word Anne and Rachael have never mentioned. They know me too well.' Yet Boycott's terror of settling down is quite rare in a middle-aged man. Even in these days of rocketing divorce, co-habitation and single-parenthood, over 80 per cent of adults still get married at some stage in their lives. It is not as if Boycott had a similar outlook to W. C. Fields about children. Indeed, though he could fire off the occasional volley of expletives at a young autograph hunter, he was often very good about coaching and encouraging youngsters. And the days of all-consuming dedication to his craft were now past. He had plenty of time to share with a partner, and the excuse that marriage or children would be a distraction to his cricket no longer existed.

The reasons for his fear of family life can be found in his upbringing. Though his Fitzwilliam home meant security, it could also be a suffocating environment – hence his restless urge to travel. On a deeper level, his relationship with his mother was so definitive, so intense that it established in him a permanent sense of himself as the son, the child. It was therefore almost impossible for him to imagine being a parent. The concomitant aspect of his mother's continual validation was that it gave him such a strong sense of identity that he never needed to seek it elsewhere in a married relationship or family. He knew exactly who he was: Geoffrey Boycott, the great cricketer. His self-worth came through his achievements rather than the love of a spouse and offspring. His name would be carried on not through subsequent generations of Boycotts but through having been written into the record books.

The problem for Boycott was that despite his animosity towards the idea of parenthood, he had actually become a father soon after his retirement. Some might say that, given his colourful private life, such an event could hardly have come as a surprise. But, as we have seen, Boycott was as keen on having the right protective equipment in the bedroom as he was at the batting crease. Unfortunately on one occasion the precautionary measures taken by him and his lover were ineffective. In the spring of 1988 Boycott was informed that he was shortly to become a father.

The woman who gave him the news that she was pregnant was Rachael Swinglehurst. Described by the *Daily Mail* as a woman with the 'leggy curvaceous body of a beauty queen', Rachael first met Boycott in 1974 when she was 22. She had just left her brief marriage to her childhood sweetheart and was living with her parents in their farmhouse in the village of Thurk, near Rainton in North Yorkshire. Her father, Jack, was a successful agricultural auctioneer, well known locally. It was Boycott's benefit year and one night the local pub was holding a function to raise funds. Rachael was asked to help and went along to the do with no expectations – she did not even know what Boycott looked like. But she was smitten almost as soon as she saw him. 'Suddenly this man with the most incredible blue eyes and wearing a beautiful dark grey jacket walked in. I immediately thought, Hmm, he's nice. It was pure sexual attraction,' she explained in 1998. 'The landlord introduced us. At the end of the evening, Geoff invited himself back to my home for coffee. We chatted for hours, mainly him asking about me,' she said. Such a conversational line might have seemed unusual to more than a few of Boycott's colleagues. 'There was a lot of sexual undercurrent, but nothing happened that night.' Boycott then returned to the pub where he was meant to be staying, only to find that it was locked up so he had to drive another 50 miles home. A few days later, Boycott rang her up. 'He invited me out for dinner and that was it. He was, and still is, the perfect gentleman,' Rachael explained, in an interview for *Woman's Own*.

The affair continued through the seventies. There were strict ground rules agreed by Rachael and the resolute bachelor: no living together, no demands and no exclusive rights. But Rachael began to grow disillusioned by the end of the decade, feeling that the relationship was going nowhere. In 1980 they split up, and Rachael went to America for a short period. When she returned, she and her mother bought a pub near Whitby, which she ran for six years. During this time, she saw other men but never fell in love. Then, in the mid-eighties, one of Boycott's friends telephoned her. 'Apparently he had been wittering on about whether to phone me or not. I told his friend to put him on the line and he invited me out for dinner. A few months later we were back together. The spark was still there,' she says.

This was an idyllic time in their relationship, as Boycott would fly her out to meet him while he was abroad on cricketing assignments or on holiday. 'Geoffrey would just ring up and say, "There's an airline ticket, do you want to come?" I'd pack the bags and be off. It's marvellous going out to lovely hotels and lying in the sun.' In November 1987, Boycott and she stayed together in India during the World Cup, where she was introduced to hotel staff as Mrs Boycott. It was during this trip that the long affair was first revealed in public, by the *News of the World* which quoted Boycott telling England players and officials, 'There's no local crumpet so I've had to import it.' The paper also tracked down a chambermaid at the New Kenilworth Hotel in Calcutta who said, 'Mrs Boycott is very nice. They make a lovely couple and seem very much in love.'

Only a few months later Rachael discovered she would soon be a mother. 'I'd been on the pill and I hadn't a clue I was pregnant. Then, when I was twenty-four weeks gone, I felt a flutter in my tummy. It hit me like a brick. Geoffrey was in New Zealand at the time so I had to tell him over the phone. The first thing he said was, "I knew you were," but he was as gob-smacked as I was. He never asked me if it was his, he never has. But, then, Emma is so like him,' Rachael told *Woman's Own*. The last thing Boycott wanted was a baby but then Rachael felt the same way. Neither maternal nor broody, she relished her independence, which would be shattered by the birth of their child. The impending arrival of Emma led to serious arguments between Rachael and Boycott, each of them feeling let down by the other. Yet, despite the clashes, Boycott never once became aggressive – one reason why Rachael is so certain that he did not hit Margaret Moore. Baby Emma was born on 5 September 1988. On the birth certificate, Rachael left the space for the father's name blank to protect Boycott.

Boycott provided a lump sum for his daughter's education and maintenance but there was still no question of a traditional family. Rachael knew her relationship with him was changed for ever. 'I knew I would lose him. I could hardly ask him to settle down and start changing nappies. Nor could I carry on flitting around the world with him whenever he asked me.' With her life in a state of upheaval, Rachael moved with 18-month-old Emma to Tenerife, where she remained for four years. During her stay out there, she did not allow Boycott to see his daughter, which led to more confrontations. Rachael wanted to be sure that Boycott was committed to Emma and until she was certain he had agreed to that, she would not allow a visit.

In 1994, she returned to England and bought another pub, this time near Skipton. Through sheer hard work – often putting in more than 14 hours a day – she made a success of this venture. By now she and Boycott had rebuilt the trust between them, and Boycott was easing himself into the least likely role of his life: that of the doting father. 'Emma can twist him round her little finger. He calls her Half-pint and I think he is gob-smacked by his reaction to her.' Rachael says that she is iron-willed and strong, just like her father. Emma is immensely proud of him and has taken to calling herself Emma Swinglehurst Boycott. 'He might be this big, extrovert personality to the public, but to Emma he's just a dad,' Rachael said to me. Though Boycott has expressed his concern about her growing up with such a famous and controversial father, he also appears to harbour some ambitions for her, recently complaining to his old friend Shirley Western that Emma was not learning enough competitive sports at her junior school.

Boycott and Swinglehurst became romantically involved again in the wake of Margaret Moore's allegations about his violence.

Appalled by what she felt were utterly baseless claims, Rachael leapt to Boycott's defence and they were drawn together once more. She admits that she would marry him tomorrow if he asked her, but she still appears to be comfortable in their unconventional relationship. They have never lived together, and Rachael has her own cottage near York. As a successful businesswoman, she cannot see herself as the homely wife, doing his laundry and ironing. In fact, she says that she is much better than he is at the traditionally masculine jobs around the house. 'I'm far more practical than him. I change the fuses, decorate and do the tiling. Geoffrey's totally hopeless.' Equally hopeless, it seems, when it comes to the shopping. 'About ten years ago he came to the supermarket with me. It was the first time he had ever done proper shopping.'

Shopping? Parenthood? Rachael Swinglehurst has certainly managed to see a different side of Boycott. And she also contradicts the image of Boycott as boorish, loud and self-centred. 'He is tremendously loyal and caring. He has known Anne for around forty years and me for twenty-five, and he has always been very protective towards both of us. Whatever other things people say about him, that must be a big plus in his favour,' Rachael told me. 'Yes, he can be difficult and impatient sometimes, even putting my back up occasionally. But I think that's because he's not streetwise. All he ever did was play cricket so he can be very naïve, taking what people say at face value. He doesn't always understand the way other people operate. He was criticized for being mean and selfish but that's because he didn't like to spend all his time going into bars. He's not mean at all, certainly not with me. I have seen him do tremendous things for other people, acts of kindness that are never talked about. I have seen him standing for over an hour at the cricket ground, signing autographs for a long queue of kids. Basically, he's fair and honest. And never, ever violent. If anything, he would always walk away from confrontations. That is why it's appalling what Margaret Moore has done to such a proud, decent man.'

Throughout most of Boycott's involvement with Rachael, as she says, he was still living with Anne Wyatt, his companion since 1960. But as she moved into her seventies and with the passion gone from their relationship, Anne hankered for a move from Yorkshire to warmer climes on the south coast where she had a brother. In 1997, she and Boycott paid £475,000 for a four-bedroom home in the village of Sandbanks, five miles from Bournemouth, in Dorset. The property, substantially refurbished before she moved in, was in an exclusive area. At the same time, Boycott put his farmhouse in Woolley on the market for £600,000, apparently providing confirmation of his planned move to the deepest south of England.

By this stage of his life, Boycott certainly had few worries about money, having become a millionaire several times over. The huge success of his book had launched him into a new wealth bracket, but his subsequent earnings from the media consolidated his position. As well as having an offshore account in Jersey and two properties worth over £1 million, Boycott jointly owns with Anne Wyatt a sports company called Partcount. According to the records at Companies House, Partcount's assets in 1998 were worth £1.14 million. When Boycott started his *Sun* column, it was estimated to earn him around £50,000 a year. By 1998, his new three-year contract with the paper was worth £350,000. At the same time, his other income from broadcasting was estimated at over £100,000 while on the after-dinner circuit he could command at least £5000 a night. 'He's done well for himself, but he's earned every penny,' says his old Ackworth friend George Hepworth. Again, countering his image of parsimony, Boycott enjoys spending his wealth on luxuries like top hotels and first-class air travel. When commentating in the West Indies, for example, he usually stays at the Sandy Lane in Barbados, the island's most exclusive establishment, while also enjoying the use of the hotel's white Rolls Royce limousine. In contrast, most of the other commentators are content to cram themselves into a minibus. 'He does like his personal comforts. He wants the trappings of his wealth and status. And he certainly doesn't mind spending a bit on getting the best rooms,' says David Gower.

Interestingly, the property next door to Boycott's old home in Milton Terrace, Fitzwilliam, was up for sale at the same time. At an auction, it attracted a single bid of just £5600, less than 1 per cent of the value of Pear Tree Farm – another graphic indicator of the journey Boycott had travelled from his humble birth to his present fame and wealth. Estate agent Tony Webber said: 'I wish more people knew that Geoff Boycott used to live in this street because it might improve demand.'

Reports that Boycott was leaving the White Rose county led to a tidal wave of astonishment and regret across the press, with Yorkshire's other great cricketing son, Dickie Bird, leading the way: 'He's Yorkshire born and bred and I thought he would never leave. I would never move from Yorkshire and I could have sworn Geoffrey would be the same. To me, it's the finest place in the world. I have known for some time that he was going to be leaving but it is still a big surprise.' Jack Sokell, of the Wombwell Cricket Lovers Society, put a brave face on the news: 'Geoffrey will be no less of a Yorkshireman because he lives in the south. Every Yorkshireman is proud of his heritage no matter where he lives and I am sure he will keep his links with the club.'

But as Boycott often says to his friends, 'You shouldn't believe everything you read in the papers.' For the move to Poole Harbour was purely for Anne Wyatt's benefit. Boycott was never planning to move down there with her and, indeed, he has only visited the property once since she took up occupation. The truth is that Boycott had placed Pear Tree Farm on the market because he was planning to base himself abroad, given that he was commentating overseas for most of the year outside the English cricket season. Even when he was in the UK during the summer, he spent much of his time in hotels because of his media work.

But, after the catastrophe of the Margaret Moore trial, this plan fell through. As his TV and newspaper contracts were torn up one by one, Pear Tree Farm was quietly taken off the market.

25

Before the Fall

At first glance, it might seem to be yet another paradox of Boycott's career that the most dour of Test batsmen should become the most sparkling of Test broadcasters. His detractors might say that his commentaries have all the ingredients that his batting so conspicuously lacked: fire, excitement, animation and energy. As Fred Trueman once put it: 'If Geoffrey had played cricket the way he talked, he would have had people queuing up to get into the ground instead of queuing up to leave.'

But on another level there is no contradiction at all. For Boycott the commentator is merely a reflection of Boycott the man, the passionate, enthusiastic, intense soul who has lived his life for cricket. In all Boycott's media work, two of his most intrinsic qualities have shone through. The first is his total absorption in the game. Dennis Lillee joked in 1987 that 'Geoff Boycott is the only fellow I've met who fell in love with himself at a young age and has remained faithful ever since.' It's a nice line but it's untrue. Boycott's fidelity since his youth has been to cricket, not to himself. He is gripped by every minute of the play and conveys that enthusiasm to the viewers. The second quality is his knowledge. Precisely because he did not have a vast natural talent, he has studied every aspect of the game in greater detail than almost any other top professional. With this unparalleled technical and psychological grasp, Boycott is a phenomenal reader of the game. His colleague at Talk Sport, Jack Bannister, who also commentated with him for many years at the BBC, says: 'I would put Boycott top for content. If you take the people I have worked with, Illingworth, Graveney, Graeme Pollock, Barry Richards, Hadlee, Gavaskar,

Boycott is a mile ahead of them, he really is. His great strength is that he can see batting problems and faults more quickly, more incisively and to a greater depth than anyone else.' It is a judgement shared by Mark Nicholas: 'Along with Ian Chappell, he gives you the best insights into what may happen next in the game.'

Moreover, because Boycott played for England in the seventies and early eighties, when Test cricket had become a more intense sport – reflected in the depth of pace bowling, the quality of the fielding, and the far greater strength of the sides like India, Pakistan and New Zealand – he has a much deeper understanding of the pressures faced by the modern cricketer. That is why he never indulges in the moaning nostalgia so beloved of former players like Trueman, who retired in 1965 and subsequently turned his exasperated ignorance of the current game – 'I don't understand what's going off out there' – into the central feature of his work.

Because of these virtues, in the nineties Boycott the pundit has been an even bigger – and certainly much wealthier – star in the media than he was in his playing days. Before the French trial, he was in demand throughout the world. His trademark hat, lopsided grin and Yorkshire vowels were a gift to TV companies and impressionists alike. The coverage of the game moved up a gear when Boycott was involved, whether it be through his famous pitch inspections with his car keys or his loud jousting with his colleagues in the commentary box. His phrases like 'corridor of uncertainty', 'roon, you lazy booger', 'my moom could have hit that with a toothbroosh', 'add two wickets, then see how comfortable you feel', 'daft creekit' and, of course, 'that's roobish, that is' have entered the lexicon of the game. Hugely popular in Asia, South Africa and the West Indies, and used by a host of companies like Sky, the BBC, TransWorld and Star TV of India, he had almost become a modern cricketing icon.

The Sky TV presenter Charles Colvile has worked closely with Boycott, and his analysis of a generally enjoyable working relationship provides several fascinating insights into the man. Colvile first met Boycott when he was working for the BBC Radio Four *Today* programme in 1984 and had to arrange an interview with him about the Yorkshire crisis. 'It was like dealing with royalty or the Prime Minister. It took me about four weeks of phone calls and phone calls before he agreed to do it.'

Six years later, they were working together at Sky TV: 'My first canter with Boycs was for a Sunday League game and I must admit I was terrified. He fixes you with this stare from his very pale blue eyes, probing. There are only two other people I have met with eyes like that which look right through you: Enoch Powell and Mrs Thatcher.' After this initial anxiety, however, Colvile says that he and Boycott became 'the firmest of friends'. The only time they clashed was during a dinner on the 1993/94 tour of the West Indies, when Boycott was being 'wound up unmercifully' by other guests, and Colvile made the mistake of venturing an opinion. 'What would you know about it, ya tuppenny-ha'penny club cricketer?' snapped Boycott, though he had the grace to apologize the next day. 'He is a volatile character but whenever I have worked with him he has usually been as good as gold.' Colvile recalls only one occasion on air when Boycott completely misread the situation. This occurred when they were at the St Johns ground, Antigua, in 1994, just after Brian Lara had scored his world record 375, and he and Boycott were getting reaction from all sorts of different people around the ground.

'With me is a man whose highest score in Test cricket was nowhere near 375. Terrific knock, Geoffrey?' asked Colvile.

'My highest Test score were 246 not out against India in 1967 and I were dropped for it.'

'Well, I don't imagine Brian Lara's going to be dropped for this.'

'And I should never have been dropped either.'

Colvile sees Boycott as 'an intensely private person who keeps himself to himself, almost fanatically so. The secretive veneer, the exclusiveness is part of his image. He is also a great wheeler-dealer. If he had not been a cricketer he would have still made a million somewhere.' As an example of this streak, Colvile explains that Boycott acquired a little franchise to sell Sky TV sports team ties at £20 each. Some time later, when Colvile had to get another, he rang up the supplier and was told there were several still available. 'I asked "How much?"'

'"Twelve pounds."' Colvile found it amusing that a wealthy and famous ex-sportsman should descend to such a small-scale money-making enterprise.

Mark Nicholas also worked with Boycott at Sky before his

high-profile move to Channel Four. He told me: 'I don't mind admitting that I like him. We are all riddled with faults and he is one whose faults have become public property. He is a very organized, fastidious person and therefore is frustrated by people around him who aren't.' However, Nicholas argues that Boycott is responsible for a lot of his own troubles through his lack of diplomacy and impolite behaviour, which in hotels 'can be extra-ordinary.' Nicholas believes that Boycott is 'deeply insecure. Like everybody, he wants to be told that he's done well, and he is very cross with himself when he gets it wrong. He is not a natural at doing pieces solo to camera, so he prepares fastidiously for them.' Nicholas has also witnessed his moodiness. 'There are mornings in the commentary box when he is a lot quieter than others. Or he goes into his dark side, hibernates in his room or disappears.' But when he is feeling more jovial, according to Nicholas, 'he can belie his public face with a real sense of humour. I have been on the air a fair bit with him on overseas tours and he is a great deal better at having the mickey taken out of him than he is often given credit. That comes out on the air abroad because he does not feel that everyone is prying and waiting to knock him. And he's a damn sight better with words than he would have you believe. He tells it as it is.'

Boycott's work with the BBC also increased in the early nineties, because, according to the director of BBC cricket in the 1990s, Alan Griffiths, 'He gave us a bit of grit, ensuring that our commentaries weren't so bland as they had been in the past.' Professionally, Griffiths found Boycott 'excellent. When you told him, for example, at a pitch report, "Geoffrey, I want thirty seconds," he would always deliver exactly. He wouldn't go on for fifty seconds." Nor did Griffiths find him difficult to work with, despite his reputation: 'In my job, I dealt with many people with their large egos, and he was by no means the worst.'

Yet, as with Shakespeare's love, the course of Boycott's career 'never did run smooth'. In the early nineties there were growing complaints about a conflict of interest between his media commitments and his work as England's batting coach. It was the old question of 'dual role' again, this time in a different guise. One day Boycott would be seen coaching the England players; the next he would be heard criticizing them on TV. In a reflection of his innocence or, to be more harsh, his lack of sensitivity, Boycott saw no problem with this. 'I coach them. They play badly. I say so. Doesn't mean I don't want to coach them,' he told Mark Nicholas. But in his autobiography Allan Lamb summed up the views of the England team: 'It couldn't have been right for him to coach the players and then have a go at them behind the microphone. One instance that upset us was when he had been coaching the players and then outlined on television the best way for the Aussies to get Jack Russell out.'

The issue came to a head during England's tour of New Zealand in 1991/92, just before the World Cup, when Boycott's criticisms of the Test side led to fierce resentment. In particular, Ian Botham was angered by Boycott's *Sun* column, which described his attitude towards training as 'totally unprofessional and unacceptable'. Though Boycott carried on advising for the rest of the tour, at the insistence of Mickey Stewart, who said 'it would be a crying shame if his expertise were lost,' his days at the England nets were numbered. his days When Keith Fletcher succeeded Mickey Stewart as manager in 1992, he stated categorically that he did not want Boycott at any training sessions. His place as batting coach was taken by Clive Radley, the former Middlesex batsman.

There have been occasional attempts since to involve Boycott with the England set-up. In 1993, when Ted Dexter stood down as chairman of selectors, Boycott's name was on a shortlist of 20 as a possible successor but in the end the choice was between Ray Illingworth and M.J.K. Smith. Then, in 1995, Illingworth tried to persuade him once more to become one of England's part-time batting coaches. But all such negotiations have always run up against the stumbling block of Boycott's media earnings.

Understandably, Boycott has felt that if he was forced to give up writing and broadcasting, he should be properly compensated. The England authorities say they simply cannot meet his asking price. Lord MacLaurin, chairman of the England Cricket Board, told me, 'With a lot of these ex-players we would dearly like to have them involved in English cricket but quite frankly we can't afford them. Boycott, Botham, Gower are all earning a huge amount of money in the media and we just could not employ them.'

This is, of course, a vicious circle. Without the input from top ex-players, England can never expect to improve their standards and thereby become a more popular and richer sport. Boycott thinks the solution is for the ECB and Test players to stop being so sensitive about employing broadcasters and to follow the more robust Australian example, where, for instance, Allan Border is both a selector and a commentator. But given Boycott's unique gifts for causing controversy and arousing resentment, it would probably have never worked.

Boycott's media career, especially his heavy commitments abroad, also left many Yorkshire members dissatisfied. In the 1993 elections for the committee – whose membership had been trimmed from 23 to 12 – Boycott was defeated in the newly created West district behind another ex-player Bob Platt. Far from recognizing that Boycott's popularity had been in decline, his supporters had been talking before the poll about his taking over from Brian Close as cricket chairman. Now he was without any formal influence in the club at all. Yet Tony Vann, though he was disappointed at the time, thinks the result was probably good for Boycott because it freed him to concentrate on his burgeoning media work.

That career soon had its own change of fortune, when, in October 1994, Boycott left Sky's commentary team and Ian Botham was signed up as his long-term replacement. Negotiations with Boycott were said to have broken down not just over his pay demands but also over the feeling in Sky that the channel needed a brighter image. 'We think we have come up with the youngest, freshest and most committed cricket team we have ever selected' with commentators who had a 'positive and constructive' approach, announced the Sky publicity department on the ditching of Boycott in favour of Botham. But Boycott was hardly out of TV work. Shortly afterwards he signed a four-year deal with the BBC worth £100,000. Indeed, Richard Knaggs, Boycott's solicitor, says that Boycott was keen to move from Sky, despite a lucrative offer, to the BBC so he could be broadcasting live on TV during the domestic season.

His work at the BBC brought him into the same commentary team as Simon Hughes. Again, like many others, Hughes says that he and Boycott had a good relationship, though he was fascinated by many of Boycott's habits: 'He is meticulous about the way he approaches his gear. His hat is hung up. He always wears a sleeveless pullover. He will carefully take it off and fold it up, inside out. He tends to bring his own food, which he is very fussy about. He has his own little shield for the microphone. We have our water cups labelled and he makes sure he keeps hold of his own, doesn't allow anyone else to drink out of it. When he was not on air, you heard him in the next box, discussing contracts and signing fees. He had a special arrangement for expenses, and he claimed everything from taxis to porters' fees in hotels. It was a bit like his batting, always trying to squeeze every last ounce.' Hughes says that, as a broadcaster, Boycott was 'absolutely first-class but always in his own world, just like when he was a player'. According to Hughes, the BBC commentary team were always amazed at the range of his expletives off the air and were certain that, one day, he would slip up and swear while broadcasting. 'But he had the uncanny knack of always reverting to expletive-free speech once behind the microphone.' Hughes also says that he enjoyed Boycott's 'dry wit, though he was a bit of a piss-taker. He always thought that David Gower was a fence-sitter and sometimes, off mike, he would say, "Come on, David, get off that fookin' fence."' Gower himself says he enjoyed working with Boycott, precisely because 'there was a chance to have a real debate on the air. With Geoffrey, it is always easy to get an argument going.'

Peter Baxter, the producer of *Test Match Special*, told me that he has enjoyed a good working relationship with Boycott and admires his brilliance at reading the game, a view that was shared by *TMS*'s most famous commentator, the late Brian Johnston. 'Brian would sometimes say to me of Boycs: "You know, he's really very good." Even Boycott's most trenchant critic, Ian Wooldridge, has changed his opinion: "When he started he was embarrassingly awful: biased, dogmatic but, above all, scathingly dismissive of the younger generation of batsmen new to the trenches. But Boycott's whole style has changed. The strident dogma has been jettisoned, the abrasive criticism modulated. There is now a generosity of spirit,"' he wrote in the *Daily Mail* in September 1995.

A far more damning view of Boycott at the BBC comes from a senior producer whom I spoke to during the World Cup. Some of his opinions have appeared elsewhere in the text. 'There is a bullying aspect to him. When we started Gower's cricket monthly in 1995, we deliberately did not have Boycott in it. The production team did not want him because we were trying to do something more youthful. He got terribly upset and he collared us at the Oval, when we were conducting some interviews. "It's crap, it's absolute fookin' bollocks, worst bloody television show," he told us. He is an odd man. There is no consistency with him. He can go so quickly from being intensely rude, condescending, shouting and swearing, and then, the next time you see him, it is as if you are his best buddy. The saddest thing is that he is actually great at his job. He provides an edge that other commentators lack.'

Even with his growing success as a commentator during the nineties, Boycott remained a source of perpetual conflict and controversy. He was in the vanguard of demands for Mike Atherton's resignation as England captain in 1994 over the soil-in-the-pocket affair, when the cricketing media and establishment showed itself at its most ludicrously pompous. Given some of the rows that Boycott had been involved in during his career, his stance looked particularly hollow. The next summer he managed to offend England's new star, Dominic Cork, with some derogatory remarks. Boycott was inspecting the pitch before the start of the fifth Test at Trent Bridge, and Brian Lara, the scourge of England during that series, was in the vicinity. Boycott told Lara, 'Don't let that little twat Cork get you out. With his pace, he'll never get you going back. Get a hundred against him.' Cork, as he wrote in his 1996 book *Uncorked*, was understandably upset. The feud between Cork and Boycott was fuelled further when, in June 1997, Boycott called Cork 'a show pony'. Cork was so furious that he demanded a television debate with Boycott to air his grievances. Yet even if Boycott was tactless and offensive, his assessment was given substance by the decline in Cork's Test career in the late nineties.

In the summer of 1998 at the Oval, soon after his return to the commentary box following his French trial, Boycott was involved in another clash, this time with David Lloyd at the Sri Lankan Test, which resulted from Boycott claiming that Lloyd was 'out of order' for complaining about Muralitharan's action. Simon Hughes recalls, 'Lloyd came in, as soon as the broadcast ended, stormed across, wagged his finger and said, "You haven't spoken to me for two years and then you criticize me on air. Why couldn't you say it to my face?" I think, though Boycott defended his ground, he was a bit hurt by that. He came to me later in the day and said, "I haven't said anything unfair, have I? Lloyd was out of line, wasn't he?" So underneath this brusque façade there is a sensitive soul, a soul that wants to be loved but does not really know how to get it.'

A much more humorous clash arose in the summer of 1996, when Boycott was a witness for Imran Khan in his libel case against Ian Botham and Allan Lamb, who unsuccessfully sued Khan over remarks he had made about their alleged racism in relation to the international ball-tampering saga. Called as a witness for Imran while he was commentating at Lord's, Boycott appeared before the judge without his jacket but with a Reebok cricket boot, with which he hoped to demonstrate some ball-scratching techniques. He never got the chance after an entertaining performance in the box. After apologizing for appearing in his shirtsleeves because of his rush in leaving Lord's, he then gave his full postal address in Yorkshire, adding, 'That's in England.' George Carman, QC, Imran's lawyer, enquired, 'It hasn't declared independence yet?' Boycott replied, 'We like to think we are a bit different.' There followed some questions about ball-tampering, in which Boycott said that it was 'done privately and surreptitiously all the time'. But his real problems started when he tried to make an impromptu speech in response to the appearance earlier in the proceedings by Brian Close, who had refused to comment when asked whether Boycott was an honest man. 'Can I say one thing? It will only take three minutes,' asked Boycott, wanting to air his grievances against Close. The judge tried to explain the rules of English jurisprudence to Boycott, but he batted on regardless, to the increasing annoyance of Botham and Lamb's counsel George Gray, QC, who protested that Close was not present to hear Boycott's testimony. Eventually the judge said, 'It appears this witness's evidence is in danger of getting completely out of control. I think he should now leave the witness stand. You are released.'

Boycott (bounding out of the box): 'That's a pity.'

Botham's relations with Boycott, never easy from the start, became even worse after his high-profile appearance for Imran. They were, however, soon forced to work together again when Boycott was recruited by TransWorld (TWI) to be part of the commentary team for the England trip to the West Indies in 1997/98. Boycott had left Sky's commentary team to work for the BBC in 1994, but since TransWorld were responsible for the production of the tour's coverage, the company had the right to choose three of its own commentators to work alongside those chosen by Sky. Given Bill Sinrich's admiration for Boycott, there was little surprise about his choice. Besides, as Mark Nicholas points out, Boycott is extremely popular in the Caribbean because of his frankness and his refusal to act as a 'homer' or cheerleader for the England side.

Boycott has perhaps an even greater following in southern Asia, where his unique delivery, trenchant observations and infectious enthusiasm have brought him a cult following on Indian TV, where broadcasters are usually much more restrained. In an article in *The Times* on 24 December 1997, the Indian writer Tunku Varadarajan expanded on the reasons for Boycott's appeal in the sub-continent: 'The key to his popularity lies in his pithy approach. Indian viewers, accustomed to stilted commentators whose language veers between the ornate and the long-winded, enjoy his devil-may-care independence. He used words such as mad, crazy, silly, stupid and pathetic. A roar of laughter could be heard across India when he criticized an umpire's decision with the words, "If that's out, then I'm a Pakistani." Not since Rex Harrison took India by storm in *My Fair Lady* has an Englishman's accent been as widely imitated.' Indeed, so imitated was he that one Indian prep-school headmaster decided to give a group of pupils six of the best for speaking at all times in their version of Boycott's accent. Their favourite word, inevitably, was 'roobish'. It is ironic that Boycott should now probably be more popular in India than anywhere else in the world, apart from Yorkshire, in view of his reluctance as a player to travel in the country and his early departure from the 1981/82 tour. Yet Boycott, in another contradiction of his dour Yorkshire image, now embraces parts of Indian culture. He enjoys watching Indian satellite TV and is a fan of the Sikh pop star Daler Mehndi.

'It is the nicest thing that the Indian people have taken to me and I have taken to them,' says Boycott, whose celebrity status in the sub-continent has also brought him a series of lucrative sponsorship deals. From Honda motorbikes to Whyte and Mackay whisky,

Boycott now advertises them. As Gulu Ezekiel wrote in the January 2000 edition of *Wisden Cricket Monthly*, 'Thanks to the reach of TV in India today he is one of the most recognized faces and voices and he is mobbed at every ground. No party or promotional campaign is complete without his presence. Even his well-known roving eye is deemed acceptable in the high-society circles in which he mixes.'

Despite such warm feelings, Boycott can still behave just as badly in south Asia as anywhere else. His fellow commentator Henry Blofeld described in his 1998 book, *Cakes and Bails*, a series of embarrassing incidents arising from Boycott's attitude during a visit to Pakistan. These included Boycott's continual complaints about his 'shit hotel' and his rudeness to taxi drivers, waiters, even his hosts at dinner. On one occasion, when Boycott was asked to dinner with Imran Khan's cousin, Javed Zaman, the driver was late in picking him up, said Blofeld, which led to a 'torrent of abuse' at the hotel and in the car. Then, when he arrived, he was infuriated to discover that the meal would not be served until 10.30 p.m., even though that is the normal time for eating in Lahore. Having soon become involved in a heated argument with a member of the Pakistan Cricket Board, he stormed out of the party, saying, 'I'm not going to waste my time talking to you.' In a later interview, Blofeld added: 'I had dinner with him quite by chance about six times in a row in Lahore and he didn't cover himself with glory. He calls all Pakistani waiters George and says, "George, you've got the brains of a bloody chocolate mousse." And it's not said in a friendly manner.'

Boycott's relationship with one of Blofeld's colleagues, the BBC cricket correspondent Jonathan Agnew, is a 'love-hate' one, to use Agnew's phrase. There is mutual respect for the other's ability as a commentator, but their exchanges are spiced by a regular stream of belittling comments from Boycott about Agnew's ability as a fast bowler. Agnew has written: 'I know listeners cannot always be aware of it but I promise you that Geoffrey is smiling whenever he has a go at me. He has the kind of voice that does not always reveal that he is being humorous but, believe me, he is trying to be.'

Out in South Africa, Boycott has worked regularly with Robin Jackman, another former England fast bowler whose Test record with both bat and ball was the subject of Boycott teasing. Fed up with continual Boycott sarcasm, Jackman plucked up the courage to confront him. 'Look, Geoff, I'm not enjoying what's going on. Can you stick to the cricket, give your expert opinions, which are brilliant, and leave me out of this?' said Jackman.

'I were only jokin'.'

'But I don't find it funny. So if I don't find it funny, do you mind not joking? Half the time I think you're taking the piss and that offends me.'

'OK.'

Since this incident, Jackman says their working relationship has been much better, with Boycott only occasionally slipping back into his jibes. 'I have got great respect for his work and for the authority with which he speaks. As a batsman, nobody ever practised harder than him and, as a commentator, he is meticulous in everything he does.' In their joint broadcasts, Jackman is the anchor and Boycott provides the expert opinion. 'I enjoy asking him to talk the viewer through the slow motion of a particular shot or a certain delivery. Because he's so sharp on any flaw in technique, he is excellent at that kind of analysis.' Jackman says, however, that if he were to sum up Boycott in one word, sadly it would be selfish. 'He often played that way and appears to have carried that trait into other areas. Perhaps it is because he has worked really hard to achieve his ambitions – but then again, many of us have had to work equally hard.'

26

En Grasse

In January 1998, Geoff Boycott was convicted in a French court of assaulting his lover, Margaret Moore, a verdict that was upheld both at a retrial ten months later and at an appeal in May 2000. Branded a criminal, Boycott's public career collapsed as dramatically as Jeffrey Archer's.

Superficially, the conviction looked safe. Didn't Margaret Moore have photographs of her bruised and battered face? How else could those injuries have come about? She was hardly likely to hit herself. Didn't the concierge of the hotel where they were staying hear her screams of pain and fear? And, in any case, why would she make up such a story? Surely not for money. Wasn't she a rich woman with her own successful computer business?

Deeper probing, however, reveals a rather different picture.

Boycott first met Margaret Moore at the Sandy Lane Hotel in Barbados in 1992. Never someone to dissemble, he admits that it was her looks that attracted him when they first met. 'If you've got a good figure and you're in a bikini, you look good on the beach, don't you? Yes, I was taken with her. We got talking, we had dinner and when we were back in England I rang her up,' he recalled after the first trial. This was the beginning of an on-off affair that was to last until the disastrous events of 2 October 1996. It was precisely because the relationship was, from Boycott's perspective, largely sexual, apparently without any strings, that he liked it. In a revealing interview on Nicky Campbell's show on BBC Radio Five Live: 'I was travelling all over the world with my work. There was nothing for us to pay. She would just fly in to join me. It did not alter my work or lifestyle. It wasn't like going home to a wife or living together. If that makes me look bad, well, I'm not trying to make myself look good. I'm not saying it's right or wrong but it seemed to suit both of us. I would have breakfast with her and then go to the cricket all day to do my job. She said she was going to meet clients for her software firm. I would then see her in the evening, we'd have dinner and go to bed. So it was a pleasant, convenient relationship. It suited both of us. We were both independent.'

Boycott touched there on another of Margaret Moore's attractions, her supposed wealth, which meant that he never had to go too deep into his pocket. She told Boycott that her computer company was worth over £20 million. Her love of first-class air flights, expensive clothes, top restaurants and luxury hotels all helped to build the image of the fashionable millionairess.

But the reality was different. By the time of the alleged incident with Boycott, her business was in dire trouble, while her personal finances had spiralled out of control. In July 1997 – more than six months before the first French trial – she was declared bankrupt, with liabilities of £713,375, while in the same year the company that she and her husband had created, Rapid Gen Systems, went into liquidation. The failure of that company exposes the preposterous claim from Margaret Moore that one of the reasons Boycott became aggressive was because he resented her career: 'He was jealous of me. I am a successful businesswoman and travel all over the world. In his eyes I was successful and I think he found that difficult.' Not only were the riches a sham, but also, if she had really understood the man she claims to have loved, she would have recognized that Boycott much prefers his women to be strong-minded and success-ful. That way there is less danger of their being dependent on him.

'Margaret Moore is the sort of person who will do anything to achieve what she wants', her ex-husband Ritchie McGladdery once said. Born in Hull, the daughter of a salesman who worked for Hoover, Moore moved to Ulster as a young child when her father took up a job selling fire equipment. She and McGladdery met in Belfast in 1969 when she was just seventeen, married four years later and had two children. The son of a leading Unionist politician who was a senator in the Stormont Parliament, Ritchie McGladdery was a computer expert and graduate of Queen's University, Belfast. In 1976 he and Margaret founded Rapid Gen Systems, a computer software company. Thanks to his technological skills and her talent for marketing, Rapid Gen took off and by 1990 the McGladdery family were living in some style in Belgravia. They threw lavish parties and were active in the Westminster Conservative Association. Another Westminster Tory recalls Margaret's love of socializing: 'She was marvellous. She would open champagne at the slightest excuse. You'd have thought champagne was made just for her.'

But the good times did not last much longer for the ambitious couple as their marriage collapsed in acrimony. In 1991 Margaret and her husband had arranged to go on holiday together to the Caribbean. Claiming to be delayed by work, Moore told McGladdery to fly on to Jamaica where she would join him later. While he was out there he received a call from Moore saying that the marriage was over. She then voted her brother on to the board, took control of Rapid Gen and sacked McGladdery from his own company. In March 1992 they were formally divorced.

Moore was later to claim that she was traumatized by this split and that Boycott exploited her when she was at her most vulnerable. In an interview with the *Daily Express* in November 1998 she said: 'I had just come out of an eighteen-year marriage which I began when I was seventeen years old. It was very much on the rebound. I was in a very vulnerable stage of my life and I didn't realize that men could be nicer.' But Boycott was not the only man she took up with after she was single again. She also had an affair with businessman Ken McLachan, who was even briefly engaged to her. Like Boycott, McLachan admitted that he was attracted to her instantly. 'Margaret was strikingly beautiful, glamorous and good fun,' he told the *Daily Mail* in November 1996. The relationship ended, however, when McLachan began to have doubts as to whether their marriage could work. 'I got cold feet and told her I couldn't go through with it. I saw her flitting off round the world on business. She had the highest taste in food and clothes. The normal man could have never kept her.'

Madeline Woodward, a previous fiancée of McLachan's, is far more scathing about Margaret Moore. She lived with McLachan for four years and has said that Moore 'stole him' from her. 'She knew how much I was in love with Ken but I believe she didn't care. She just took him.' On one occasion, after the break-up, she ran into Margaret and Ken in a London hotel. 'We all sat down together but she did not show the slightest embarrassment or discomfort. I sensed that she was very competitive – someone who always wants to be a winner and hates to lose.'

Meanwhile, the bitter divorce from Ritchie McGladdery continued to cast a shadow over Moore's life and her business. Since the verdict in the second French trial in 1998, Margaret Moore has been described as 'fraudulent and dishonourable' by three appeal court judges in a long-running legal battle with her ex-husband. In a case heard at the Court of Appeal in July 1999, McGladdery attempted to recover money representing both assets she had stripped from the company and maintenance due to him. The court was told that in 1993 and 1996 Ms Moore was ordered to pay her former husband maintenance of £25,000 a year, a lump sum of £120,000 and to repay £110,000 to members of his family, which she failed to do. Though the judges decided it was too late to reopen this case, they said that Ms Moore had used 'dishonourable tactics' in failing to comply with legal demands, had 'embarked on a strategy to frustrate the orders', 'had not paid debts due and had fraudulently removed assets'.

Without McGladdery, difficulties soon mounted for the business. While Moore put on an expensive front, in private she was increasingly concerned at the crisis into which the company was sliding. When in 1997 she was declared bankrupt, she was found to have built up trade debts of some £404,875, as well as owing the Inland Revenue £250,000 and various credit card companies £13,000. One of her attempts to deal with her money problems, setting up another firm into which Rapid Gen's assets and service agreements could be transferred, elicited a warning of the risks involved from her legal advisers, Memery Crystal. In a letter to Margaret Moore of 22 November 1966 – later placed in the High Court after the bankruptcy hearing – they advised that 'since the company [Rapid Gen] is to be put into liquidation, there is a possibility that a liquidator would seek to challenge the agreement, for example on the basis that it is a transfer at an undervalue or an attempt to defraud creditors.' According to Sue Sims-Steward, Moore's former solicitor: 'She saw Boycott as a way to settle her financial problems. She said, "Of course, if Geoff and I ever fall out, I could go to the press and get a lot of money for my story." ' Ms Sims-Steward is a vital witness in this tale for, having worked as Moore's legal adviser, she was so outraged by the claims of assault against Boycott that, after the first trial, she switched sides and gave him her support, after confirming with the Law Society that this was acceptable. In a statement setting out her reasons for backing Boycott, she painted a disturbing portrait of Moore as a devious, difficult woman, a portrait made all the more damning because it comes from a former associate and friend who knew her intimately. In the statement she explained that she first met Margaret Moore in 1995 and became her solicitor, representing her company Rapid Gen Systems. Soon after the commencement of the retainer, Sims-Steward records: 'I witnessed Margaret Moore's ability to turn on the tears at will when not getting her own way. It looked to me like an orchestrated scene. I was totally fooled.' Sims-Steward was also made quickly aware of her involvement with Boycott, which led to the most wild mood swings: 'A call from Geoff Boycott on her mobile or private line would either result in a foul mood, tears, depression or elation. Margaret Moore's family did not share her love for Geoff Boycott and urged her to end the relationship, saying it was bound to end in tears.' Sims-Steward was disturbed by Moore's spending: 'Champagne flowed. Hundreds of pounds was spent on entertaining, foreign travel and clothes. She had to be suitably attired to accompany Geoff Boycott at any cost. The image to the outside was one of wealth. The reality was a picture of increasing debt and despair. Margaret Moore could not tell Geoff the truth for fear that she would lose him.'

In 1996 Sims-Steward set up a firm to meet Margaret Moore's needs, but she was worried about the mounting money and emotional pressures. On one occasion in January, Moore became depressed over a decision by Boycott to take Anne Wyatt, not her, to Barbados. That night, after an embarrassing scene in Langan's restaurant in London's West End, she threatened to kill herself. Sims-Steward sat up until five in the morning with her talking her out of it.

Despite all the support from Sims-Steward, Moore now turned on her. In May 1996, Sims-Steward's retainer was ended because of

Moore's refusal to pay fees of £35,000. 'My firm ceased trading and I registered unemployed. Margaret Moore was angry that I was not intimidated by her and had stood up to her threats. She made endless calls to my home by day and late into the night. The illusion of a charming woman had long since gone.'

Sims-Steward then took Moore to court to recover the money owed and on 15 October her application for a summary judgement against Moore was granted. This was just a fortnight after the alleged Boycott assault and, behind Moore's sunglasses, the remnants of two black eyes could be seen. Intriguingly, in view of later events, Moore made no reference to any health problems and did not ask the court for an adjournment, explaining that her injury was the result of an accident. This is what she also told members of her staff, making no mention of the assault. This is confirmed by an affidavit sworn by her former personal assistant, Ms Valerie Thompson, during bankruptcy proceedings against Moore in 1997. In this document, placed in the High Court, Thompson says: 'When I first saw Ms Moore during this period I noted that her face was badly swollen and bruised. She stated by way of explanation that she had had a terrible accident.'

It was after this first court appearance over her financial troubles that press coverage about the alleged assault began. On 27 October 1996, the *News of the World* had the headline: 'Give Me £2 Million And I'll Tell You Who Did It: Boycott's Battered Mistress Wants Cash To Say Who Beat Her.' In one bizarre move, she even claimed that the summary judgement against her of 15 October was invalid because she had not been in court as a result of her injuries. As Sue Sims-Steward put it, 'She pursued these arguments in the face of confirmation of her attendance by third parties, including a note from the judge, that she was present. It seemed that no matter what was said, she simply would not accept that she could be wrong.' At last, after 10 months of legal wrangling, the final bankruptcy hearing took place on 18 July. In court, the judge, unimpressed by Moore's tears, made a bankruptcy order. One witness of this hearing, a retired magistrate, later recalled that Ms Moore's evidence was 'characterized by inconsistency which was of such a degree as to suggest a deliberate lack of truthfulness.'

Sue Sims-Steward says that she was finally driven to act against

Moore by the reports of the hearing in January in France, which she had read with incredulity, especially because she had clearly heard Moore say in October that she had suffered 'an accident'. She spoke to Boycott's solicitor, Richard Knaggs, who explained that Boycott was unaware of either the bankruptcy or Margaret Moore's cash-flow problems. Looking further into the case, Sims-Steward saw a close parallel between Boycott's story and her own experience. Sims-Steward concluded her statement: 'I am not prepared to see a famous man destroyed at the whim of a woman who has no regard for others, and, in my experience, no perception of the truth. This is not, in view of my dealings with her, an innocent woman telling of an assault. I believe that Geoffrey Boycott is telling the truth and I am content to support him in any way I can, even though I do not know him personally. As I am by nature a very private person, the steps which I am taking are a measure of the strength of my feeling for Geoff Boycott's innocence and my desire that justice should be done.'

Boycott was not aware of any of this background, but by 1996 he was tiring of Moore. What particularly annoyed him was the way she kept bringing up the question of marriage. 'She wanted to marry me and said so constantly during the summer of 1996. It was getting me down. It was just so claustrophobic and oppressive. She wanted me to move to Monaco where she could run her company. I told her that I wanted to live in England, that I didn't want to leave Anne Wyatt.' So why didn't Boycott just leave her? 'I don't know why I didn't. I was still physically attracted to her and kept thinking she would drop the subject and the relationship would go back to how it was. I was naïve.' So when Margaret Moore fixed up a stay at the beginning of October in the Hôtel du Cap, Antibes, he agreed to come over, on the condition that 'she cut out all the Monaco talk, because I was sick of it'.

She did not stick to this agreement. On the third day of their holiday, when they were having lunch, Moore once more started to ask for an engagement. That was it for Boycott. He decided he had to return to England. He went up to their room, put his suitcase on the bed and started to pack. At this moment Margaret Moore entered in a rage. Then, according to Boycott, she climbed out on to the window-ledge, threatening to kill herself and screaming,

'After all I've done for you.' Boycott did not respond but instead sat on the bed with his head in his hands. This drove Moore to only greater fury, and she began to throw Boycott's things out of the window: his underpants, socks, papers, and toiletries.

It is perhaps a reflection of how much Boycott cherishes his clothes that only when she grabbed one of his best suits from the wardrobe did he finally react. 'You're never having that,' he said. In his account, they were both struggling so hard over the suit that they fell together, both crashing into the tiled white marble floor. Boycott badly bruised his left elbow, while Moore sustained a bump on her head. 'You hit me,' she said, as she lay on the ground. 'I haven't hit you. It was an accident,' replied Boycott. He put some ice on the swelling and a doctor was called, who logged the injury. In Boycott's account, they slept in the same bed together for two more nights – 'and we had sex, if you want to be blunt'. Despite her black eyes, Moore went sunbathing the day after her fall, and on their return journey to England she bought a silk tie for Boycott at Nice airport. Moore's critics point out that, by her own admission, she took several days to log a complaint with the police, a delay which she explains thus: 'You don't just stop having feelings like that after four years. I was confused and didn't know what to do.'

In her version, Moore said that after she had thrown his belongings out the window, 'he just totally flipped. All I remember is him pinning me down and punching me in the face. I thought it would never stop. He was smiling as he hit me and was like a wild man.' She said that he only ceased his attack when the telephone rang. It was the concierge who, allegedly, had been so disturbed by her screams that he had rung to see what was the matter. This was strongly disputed by Boycott's defence team, who say that it was actually Moore who telephoned the concierge to complain that Boycott was hitting her. She then claimed that, still in a state of shock, she slept on the bathroom floor for the next two nights behind a locked door before joining Boycott on the return flight.

Moore told the *Daily Express* that Boycott beat her 'at least twenty times' while she was on the floor. It is the numerical detail of this statement that is so questionable, for such a brutal and sustained assault is hardly consistent with her injuries. If Boycott, a professional sportsman for more than twenty-five years, had really mounted this kind of attack, she would have probably suffered major fractures and permanent damage. As it was, there was no swelling at all around the eyes, nose or mouth, just a single egg-shaped lump on her forehead. Moreover, the discoloration on her upper face could have been the well-documented effect from a bump on the head known as a tracking injury where, through the force of gravity, internal bleeding seeps into the pouches beneath each eye. In fact, exactly this type of injury had happened to Boycott against the West Indies in 1980, when a ball from Colin Croft hit him on the head, giving him two black eyes for the rest of the match.

Several senior medical experts, who supported Boycott at his second trial, have cast doubt on Margaret Moore's evidence. Dr D. C. Fieldhouse, a former senior police surgeon, said in his written statement: 'It is clear that the only injury is the swelling on the right side of the forehead. There is no evidence that she has been hit by Geoff Boycott or anyone else. I have read Mrs Moore's account of her being beaten twenty times about the face and body and I can confirm from vast professional experience that anyone receiving such a beating would have displayed severe physical injuries requiring immediate hospital investigation and treatment. I can also confirm that the large lump on Margaret Moore's forehead is consistent with an impact injury such as contact with a hard tiled floor and not a blow with a fist, which would have produced an entirely different appearance.'

One of Britain's leading experts in facial injuries, Professor Jonathan Shepherd of Cardiff University, agrees with this analysis. In his written statement to the French court in support of Boycott, Professor Shepherd asserted: 'The doctor who first examined Mrs Moore on 2 October did not find any evidence of left-sided bruising, neither did he find any evidence of bleeding from the nose. The alleged assailant in this case, Geoff Boycott, is well known to be right-handed and this makes it even more unlikely that this particular injury was caused by a fist. In my opinion the evidence in this case points towards a single injury of the right forehead, sustained in a fall and not an assault.'

Then there is testimony from Philip Chisholm, a highly experienced specialist in the photography of criminal and accidental injuries. Chisholm is sceptical about the pictures of a battered

Moore, which were widely circulated in the press in the run-up to the first trial and were used by the French prosecution. In fact, Chisholm argues that the pictures support Boycott's case. 'The bruising under the eyes and on Ms Moore's right temple correlate to that of an injury which I am regularly called upon to photograph, where a client has fallen and hit their head on a hard surface.' Chisholm said that injuries from a clenched fist 'would cause massive swelling around the eyes, cheek bones, mouth and nose. None can be seen in the photographic evidence provided.'

On top of these expert statements, there is also, crucially, the question of Boycott's character. His enemies might say that his history of moodiness and social gaffes demonstrates that he would be easily capable of descending to such violence. But any serious study of Boycott must lead to the conclusion that he is not a violent man. He may be loud, self-centred, arrogant, impatient and awkward, but he has never demonstrated any instinct for physical aggression during his life. In all the many interviews I have conducted for this book, I have not come across one person, even among his fiercest critics, who thinks that he is guilty as charged. Despite many rows, there is no instance of him getting into a serious brawl with any of his colleagues, unlike Ian Botham who admits that he 'has a reputation for talking with his fists' and famously threw a punch at Ian Chappell in a bar in Australia in 1977. And in all his other affairs, there has never once been a claim of violence. Two of the most important women in his life, Rachael Swinglehurst and Shirley Western, both travelled to court to testify on his behalf. Rachael, who gave tremendous assistance and support to Boycott in the run-up to his trial, has described him as the 'most gentle man I have ever met'. Shirley told me: 'Having known him at close contact for years, I never once saw a streak of violence. And I know violent men – one of my relationships was with a man who could turn nasty. But Geoff would never lay a hand on anybody. He would be more likely just to walk away.'

There is one other point about Boycott's character: his obsession with being straight. He is the blunt Yorkshireman who delights in speaking what he sees as the truth, no matter what the offence given or the cost to himself. 'I have never known Geoffrey to lie to me on any issue. He has always been absolutely honest,' says his friend

Tony Vann. Throughout the grim saga of Yorkshire's turmoil, he was accused of many crimes but lying was never one of them. Even his critics says that he is so perversely honest that if he had hit Margaret Moore he would admit it. 'He is a thoroughly unpleasant bully, but I do not believe for one nanosecond that he attacked her, I really don't. He protests his innocence so much and there's no way he would do that if he was guilty,' says one television producer who has worked with him. It is telling that Boycott has stuck rigidly to his version of events through his many interviews and his media appearances. No one has been able to point to a single inconsistency in any of his testimony.

Moore does not deny that, despite this alleged frenzied beating, she tried to stay in touch with Boycott. He says that when he was working in India soon after the Hôtel du Cap incident, she 'was ringing me up four or five times a day, wanting to come to India. This is a woman who says she's in fear of her life. She said she loved me and wanted to carry on with the relationship. She kept on and on. But I'd had enough. It were just driving me crackers.' In a letter to Boycott dated 13 October, she wrote, 'You know I am in love with you and have been for almost five years. You are the only man in my life and the only one I want.' Boycott wanted nothing more to do with Moore and her protestations of love. 'I've absolutely got sick of hearing that word now. I don't want to hear it again.'

By 18 October, Boycott's failure to respond to her calls, faxes and letters made it obvious that he was not interested in her any more. On that day she met the PR Max Clifford at Claridges Hotel, in London, where she made her notorious demand of £1 million for her story. As soon as he met her, he felt she had no credibility. It should be stressed at this point that Clifford had never met Boycott – and was not to do so for another 18 months. Clifford told me what happened: 'I'd had a few phone calls from Margaret Moore over a period of weeks. Her line was, "I have got a story about the biggest star in the world and how much can I get?" I told her that until I knew who it is and what it is about I had no idea. So we met up at Claridges. She had been knocking back the champagne and seemed to be very – shall we say "happy"? – and she proceeded to tell me that her story concerned the "biggest star in the world, Geoffrey Boycott". And I laughed, thinking it was a wind-up. She insisted that he was a worldwide superstar, so I said, "Geoffrey Boycott is very well known in cricketing circles and used to be one of our greatest players but he is a million miles from being the world's biggest star." Nevertheless, she proceeded to tell me the story of how he had beaten her up, what he had done to her. She showed me the bruising on her face – this was not that long afterwards – and gave me photographs. Then she proceeded to tell me that he punched her numerous times, literally sitting across her and punching her in the face over twenty times.

'I looked at the pictures and I looked at her and I knew that there was no way that any man could have punched a woman's head against a marble floor – which is what she told me – twenty odd times and have had that effect. My instinct was that she had bumped her head; it was consistent with a bang where the injury spreads out and down. It was certainly not consistent with her having been punched twenty odd times by a batsman. I then said to her that her bruising did not look convincing to me and she said, "Well, it's his word against mine anyway." And I said, "No one is going to print any story unless they can prove it." She replied, "I have got the bruising and it's what I say that counts." I said, "Yeah, but you could be making the whole thing up." She laughed hysterically. She told me that the French believed her and that she was going to make him pay. I left it by saying, "No, it's not for me." I was dealing with someone who did not seem to me to have a grasp of reality. It does not take ten minutes in Margaret Moore's company to realize that. She was telling me that she had been through the most horrendous experience of her life while she was giggling, laughing and sipping champagne – a bizarre contradiction. As the conversation progressed, she made it very clear to me that, even if her story was not true, no one else could prove it so therefore she was going to take him to the cleaners and get £1 million. She emphasized this figure and said that if I was not able to get it, she could get it on her own. I told her, "I'm afraid that is what you are going to have to do, then."'

That day, 18 October, on Claridges headed notepaper, she wrote yet another letter to Boycott, which concluded, 'You persuaded me to take you to the best hotel in Europe, the Hôtel du Cap and you ended beating me up.'

The claim that Moore was seeking money for her version of the Hôtel du Cap incident is backed up by the testimony of Boycott's close friend and barrister Matthew Caswell. 'I was contacted by a person claiming to represent Ms Moore with a view to making a deal whereby, upon payment of £1 million, civil proceedings for injury would not commence. I am satisfied that had Mr Boycott been induced to part with £1 million that would have been the end of any action by Ms Moore,' Caswell said in February 1998. He has since confirmed to me the accuracy of this statement. Just as disturbing is the evidence of Boycott's own lawyer, Richard Knaggs, who also received an approach from a representative of Margaret Moore. In a written statement for the second trial, Knaggs explained that on Monday 28 October, almost four weeks after the alleged assault, he received a telephone call from a lawyer acting for Moore. 'He told me that Margaret Moore was under tremendous pressures from the newspapers for the sale of her story to them and had been offered in excess of £150,000 for her story. He went on to say that if Geoff was prepared to match or increase this figure, though she still wished to sell her story to the papers, she would publish it with a favourable light on her life with Geoff. I took that to mean not making any allegations regarding assault.' As Knaggs explained, Boycott's response was that 'he was not prepared to be involved in what he considered to be blackmail'.

Moore finally sold her story to the *News of the World*, though it seems she received much less than her original asking price. She now pursued Boycott through the courts. On 20 January the first hearing was held in Grasse, southern France, at which Boycott was found guilty of hitting Moore, given a three-month suspended jail sentence and fined 50,000 francs (£5,100). Boycott failed to turn up to this hearing. This was not, as some of his detractors have alleged, because he did not take Moore's charges seriously, but because he had been informed that the case had been adjourned. To this day, neither Boycott nor his solicitor Richard Knaggs knows why they were given this misleading information. In any case, it would have been entirely out of character for Boycott to act in so careless a fashion, for as both a cricketer and a commentator he has always been utterly meticulous in planning and preparation. Similarly, he was heavily criticized for a breezy press conference he gave after the verdict, spelling out his position with his usual assertiveness and dealing undiplomatically with some of the journalists. 'Shut up, this is my conference, not yours,' one reporter was told. A man from the *Mirror* was chastised thus: 'You and the *Sun* are like kids at each other.' But it should be noted that just as he went into this conference he was confronted by Margaret Moore, brandishing the pictures of her battered visage. This incident, set up as a publicity stunt, was bound to make him tetchy.

If Boycott had any doubts about the seriousness of the decision, they were soon dispelled by the news that both TransWorld TV and the BBC, his two most important broadcasting employers, had dropped him from their commentary teams for the immediate series against the West Indies. Boycott knew that he had a real fight on his hands. He had already applied for a retrial and he now embarked on a high-profile legal and PR campaign to restore his damaged reputation – and win round two in France.

It was now that his solicitor, Richard Knaggs, set about constructing a formidable defence. In effect, he was battling on two fronts. His twin aims were to contend the case as hard as he could – though he always knew that, given the vagaries of the French legal system, it would be difficult to triumph – and to reveal to the wider public the strength of the evidence in Boycott's favour. To achieve this, he devoted all his working hours to compiling witness statements, gathering medical evidence, and challenging Moore's claims. If Boycott was to go down, he would go down fighting.

Over the last decade, Richard Knaggs has become far more than just a solicitor for Boycott. He is also a business adviser, negotiating contracts, as well as a close friend and confidant. In many respects he is similar to Boycott: tough, competitive, frank, diligent, and fiercely loyal. He has the same attention to detail in his legal work as Boycott used to have in his batting. He is rightly proud of his achievements, having built up an impressive practice in the northern town of Redcar, where his large offices dominate the High Street. Like many of those closest to Boycott, Knaggs speaks of him as a warm, generous man who would never let him down. Knaggs was impressed by Boycott's refusal to accept defeat after the first French trial. Despite all the upheaval surrounding the case, Boycott was still considerate enough to arrange a VIP trip for

Knaggs to Old Trafford to watch his beloved Middlesbrough beat Manchester United away, 'at a time when I would have imagined that he least felt like making a public appearance'. *En route* to the ground Boycott teased Knaggs about the size of his two-seater 230 SLK Mercedes – derided by Boycott as nothing more than 'a mini-moke' only to be used by 'a middle-aged man trying to recapture his youth'. Knaggs took all this as friendly banter.

While Knaggs worked on the legal side, Max Clifford was recruited for the PR side. It was a job he was keen to take on because of his previous experience with Moore. Clifford says: 'I supported Geoffrey because what was happening was a terrible injustice. I knew better than anyone that he was innocent. I felt incredibly sorry for him. His whole life is cricket and suddenly it was being taken away from him because of Margaret Moore. It was outrageous, really. I would not have done what I did if I had not liked him and taken to him. In some ways, his lack of diplomacy attracted me to him. I know a lot of smooth-talking bastards who are the nastiest people in the world.'

During the summer, in part thanks to Clifford's and Knaggs's efforts, there was some sense of the tide turning in Boycott's favour. Press coverage became increasingly positive, especially as Clifford revealed more details about Margaret Moore's chequered life and business history. Then, in July, after three meetings with Knaggs, the BBC took the decision to allow Boycott to retake his position in the commentary box. David Gower says, 'There was a certain feeling, because of his lack of team spirit in the commentary box, that we had done all right without him, so why did we need him in again? But as soon as he returned, we saw that he does give the commentary a sharpness which it can easily lack if everyone is being nice all the time. In a way things picked up again. It didn't do us any harm at all.'

As so often before, though, Boycott proved to be his own worst enemy through a foolish incident during a Sunday League game when he was sent to interview Yorkshire's Darren Gough about the forthcoming crucial Headingley Test against South Africa. Immediately Boycott launched into a diatribe about the selection of Ian Salisbury, telling Gough, 'He couldn't bowl out my grand-mother with a rolling pin.' Gough was placed in an awkward position by this outburst against a colleague, and a letter of complaint was sent by the England Cricket Board to the BBC. However, Boycott was told not to worry by senior BBC producer Philip Bernie. After England's historic victory, some in the media felt that Boycott's churlish, negative tone was inappropriate. 'We had just won a five-test campaign for the first time in a decade and there he was, slagging off England and saying three of the players had not performed,' says a television producer.

The second trial went ahead on 20 October 1998. Having failed to appear for the first hearing, Boycott went to the other extreme by turning up with a vast supporting cast of thirteen, who included the six women quickly dubbed by the media 'Geoff's Girls'. The six were: Rachael Swinglehurst, Shirley Western, Sue Sims-Steward, and three other witnesses, Karen Berry, Sylvia Milner and Anne Bickerstaffe, who all testified to having suffered similar facial injuries to Margaret Moore's through falls. Also in the team were Philip Chisholm, the photography expert; Professor Jonathan Shepherd of Cardiff University; and Peter Wood, a consultant psychiatrist, who said he believed Moore had a 'personality disorder' with 'hysterical and psychopathic features'. In addition, Boycott had collected written character references from 58 witnesses, whose number included Jonathan Agnew, Colin Cowdrey, Pat Pocock, John Emburey, Alan Knott, Tony Lewis, Jack Russell, Alec Stewart, Sir Tim Rice and Michael Parkinson.

It may be, as some have argued, that this strategy of having a big group of defence witnesses was counter-productive in that it dragged out the hearing for more than 12 hours and thus provoked just as much resentment from the French judiciary as Boycott's non-appearance at the first trial. In other respects, though, the sheer scale of the operation showed the strength of Boycott's determination to prove his innocence. And, with a bill for his defence of around £500,000, Boycott had certainly contradicted his image as a parsimonious Yorkshireman.

Like Bill Clinton, Boycott is often at his most impressive in the depths of a crisis. Considering his career in cricket could be in the balance, Boycott appeared astonishingly calm the night before his trial. When his defence team went out to dinner, one of them asked him how he could be so self-assured. 'Whatever happens tomorrow, I will always be able to look in the mirror and not be afraid of my reflection. Because I know I didn't do it. I know the truth.' One of his witnesses later said, 'He was so dignified and so impressive with the way he handled himself. He was remarkable, really.'

It was impossible for Boycott, however, to maintain his calm through the chaotic, often bizarre proceedings in Grasse. The defence team arrived at one o'clock, having been assured that theirs would be the sole case of the day, only to find that another twenty-three cases were waiting to be heard. That meant that the hearing did not even start until after half-past four, while all Boycott's witnesses were locked up in the court library, without access to refreshments or the toilet until protests were made about their intolerable conditions. Because of all the difficulties, the final Boycott witness did not leave until after one o'clock in the morning. 'They call it Napoleonic, I call it shambolic,' says Richard Knaggs. 'It was like an abattoir, with all the screaming and rushing around. People in England, used to our system, just have no idea how difficult it was. On top of all the language problems, there was no cross-examination allowed; we were misled about the timing; and Margaret Moore was allowed to introduce extra witnesses without notification.' But, in truth, whatever strategy Boycott and his lawyer Richard Knaggs had used was unlikely to have succeeded. The trial was presided over by judge Dominique Haumant-Daumas, whose glamorous looks hardly compensated for her lack of authority in her courtroom. Several times she had to shout to make herself heard above the simultaneous conversations, while the language difficulties often turned the trial into a farce. At one stage she asked, 'Who is Shredded Wheat?' and, at another, demanded to know the size of a cricket ball. Boycott's strong accent did not assist the translation. When complaining to the judge that he'd got 'fed oop' with Moore's demands for marriage, Haumant-Daumas asked, 'What eez thees "fed oop"?'

Nor did Boycott's own belligerent manner help his cause. He became so frustrated that he lost his temper as a four-way argument raged between lawyers, prosecutors and the judge. 'Shut up. Everybody's talking in French all the time and I can't understand.'

His own lawyer replied, 'That's because we're in France.'

Boycott continued, 'They're all talking, talking, talking all at once.'

His interpreter, a middle-aged woman, interjected, 'I'm doing my best to translate for you.'

'Not very well,' said Boycott.

Many of Boycott's witnesses, kept waiting for hours in a cramped room, felt unable to make any of their points in this atmosphere. Max Clifford says: 'If the trial had not been so serious it would have been incredibly funny. It was a pantomime, really. You would be asked a question in French, you start to give your answer, whereupon someone would interject in French, you looked to the interpreter for a translation, you didn't get one, the defence would start arguing, all this was going around your head and suddenly it would be "next question" and you would think "but I have not even answered the last one." That seemed to typify what went on all bloody day. Margaret Moore was sitting there looking like the vestal virgin or Snow White. You could see the way it was going. And Geoffrey is not exactly the most diplomatic of people. He did lose his temper, totally understandably, but unfortunately that is not consistent with someone who is calm and rational. So the thinking then went, Well, he's a bad-tempered bugger so he must have hit her. I was obviously disappointed at the verdict but I cannot say that I was surprised. People who had very important evidence were not given a chance to explain. We had been there since about twelve o'clock and some people were going into the witness box at eleven o'clock at night. Everybody was sick and tired of the whole thing and you could sense the resentment. If that case had happened in England, there is no way that Margaret Moore would have won. She would have been lucky to come third.'

Sadly for Boycott, Judge Dominique Haumant-Daumas did not see it that way. On 10 November she confirmed the first trial's verdict, fined Boycott £5300 and gave him a three-month suspended sentence. In her seven-page judgement she said, 'In the court the accused didn't hesitate rudely to interrupt Ms Moore's barrister, thereby tarnishing the image of the perfect gentleman which he brought his old friends and witnesses to testify to. His arguments did not support the theory of an accidental fall that the accused man said happened and the court decided that Ms Moore was a victim on 2 October 1996 of purposeful blows.'

At this announcement the roof fell in on Boycott's world. The BBC, Sky and Channel Four all said they would not be using Boycott as a commentator again in the foreseeable future. Having promised just before the trial that 'we are agreeing to stick by

Geoffrey whatever happens in France', the *Sun* ditched him, making sure its readers got the message with the front-page headline: 'The Sun Sacks Boycott The Brute.' In pontificating tones, the paper said, 'Our readers would find repugnant the idea of us employing someone with a conviction for violence against a woman.' Boycott subsequently sued the paper for breach of contract and, in January 2000, won his case.

Yet instead of sinking along with the wreckage of his reputation and broadcasting career, Boycott once more demonstrated his astonishing tenacity and resolve, the qualities that had made him such a great batsman. Even in the immediate aftermath of the verdict, he did not allow himself to be browbeaten. Sarah Cook, from Max Clifford's office, had to liaise with him in Pakistan, where he was working as the news arrived: 'I had to type up his statement and he was obviously mortified. I said I was so sorry and he replied, "Well, love, you've just got to battle on." I then had to give him a huge list of media requests. Now, a lot of people would have said, "Hang on, give me an hour or two, let me just sort myself out," but not Geoff. He was, "Yeah, fine." I thought he was so courageous the way he was immediately willing to face the world. You just had to admire his spirit.'

That spirit also shone through as Boycott soon won a new job in broadcasting, as the cricket expert on Talk Radio. Once more the cynics mocked, thinking that Boycott was finished. What's Talk Radio got to do with cricket? they sneered. Then suddenly Talk Radio acquired the exclusive Test rights for the England tour of South Africa, for £150,000, and Boycott was back as England's leading radio commentator for the winter.

According to Kelvin MacKenzie, the chief executive of Talk Radio, there is no truth in the rumour that Boycott played some clandestine part in the negotiations for these radio rights. But MacKenzie is full of praise for him: 'I am very grateful to the other broadcasting organizations for dropping him. He's done a marvellous job for us. The bottom line is that he is a great ambassador for us, especially in India and Pakistan. Any country in the world that loves its cricket welcomes him. He says what he thinks, he's got a good clear voice, he's not a fool, I think he's great.' MacKenzie's views of Boycott's strengths as a commentator on Talk Radio – now Talk Sport – have been reinforced by his impressive performances during the winter tour to South Africa in 1999/2000. As an article in the *Guardian* put it: 'Talk's undoubted star is Geoff Boycott and his celebrated calling-a-spade-a-bloody-shovel act . . . he's the man you want in the commentary box.' The February 2000 edition of *Wisden Cricket Monthly* was full of praise for Boycott's work at Talk: 'Despite his lack of social skills, he remains a wonderfully enthusiastic and perceptive analyst.' Boycott's presence has undoubtedly increased the credibility of Talk Radio, helping the station become a serious player in cricket broadcasting.

In May 2000, Boycott travelled to Aix-en-Provence once more, aiming to persuade the French Court of Appeal to overturn his conviction for assaulting Margaret Moore. After his previous experiences of the French judicial system, he had little hope of success, but he felt he had a duty to continue the fight to clear his name. Shortly before he left for France, he telephoned me to ask for a suitable quotation, apparently thinking that, since I had written about his life, I was some sort of literary expert. I warned him that I was no such thing, but I did give him these lines from Shakespeare's Richard II: 'Mine honour is my life; both grow in one. Take honour from me, and my life is done.'

With a dramatic flourish, Boycott used these words in the French court, as well as rehearsing his previous arguments about Moore's demands of marriage and the way her injuries had been caused by an accidental fall. But even with his Shakespearean oratory, Boycott failed to convince the court. After one hour's deliberation, the Appeal Judge, Jean-Claude Vuillemin, upheld the conviction.

Outside the courtroom, Boycott was defiant. 'I never hit her. I will say that till the day I die.' Talk Sport said that the verdict would not affect his employment, explaining that 'Boycott will continue to play an important role in our cricket coverage.' And it is doubtful if Talk Sport will be Boycott's last job in English cricket. Whatever his faults, whatever the setbacks of his career, Boycott has always relished the biggest possible stage. Now aged 60, he will not be going quietly into the twilight.

Statistical Appendix

Compiled by Paul E. Dyson

Introduction
This appendix does not, in much of its content, take the form of the traditional post-biography statistics. Instead, an attempt is made to use some figures in relation to certain aspects of Boycott's career and employ them, in particular, to show how the player compared with others of his generation and possibly set the record straight on certain issues.

Brief Chronology
Born: Fitzwilliam, Wakefield, 21 October 1940
First day in first-class cricket: Yorkshire v. Pakistanis, Bradford, 16 June 1962
First first-class century: 145, Yorkshire v. Lancashire, Bramall Lane, Sheffield, 3 June 1963
Awarded County Cap: 2 October 1963
First day in Test cricket: England v. Australia, Trent Bridge, 4 June 1964
First Test century: 113, England v. Australia, The Oval, 17 August 1964
Appointed Yorkshire captain for 1971 season
Benefit season: 1974; £20,639
Scored hundredth first-class century: England v. Australia, Headingley, 11 August 1977
Captained England for first time: v. Pakistan, Karachi, 18 January 1978
Sacked as Yorkshire captain: 29 September 1978
Awarded OBE in Queen's Birthday Honours List, June 1980
Final day of last Test match: England v. India, Calcutta, 6 January 1982
Testimonial season: 1984; £147,954
Final day in first-class cricket: Yorkshire v. Northamptonshire, Scarborough, 12 September 1986

Highest Test Run-scorer

The peak of Boycott's career probably came in Delhi, India, on 23 December 1981, when he became the highest run-scorer in the history of Test cricket. At 4.23 p.m. he overtook the 8032 runs scored by West Indian Gary Sobers, and completed his Test career in the following match with a new record of 8114 runs. The leading Test run-scorers at that time are shown below:

Highest Run Aggregates in Test Cricket
(as on 6 January 1982)

		Tests	Inns	NO	HS	Runs	Avge	100s	50s
G. Boycott (England)	1964-81/82	108	193	23	246*	8114	47.73	22	42
G. St. A. Sobers (West Indies)	1953/54-73/74	93	160	21	365*	8032	57.78	26	30
M. C. Cowdrey (England)	1954/55-74/75	114	188	15	182	7624	44.06	22	38
W. R. Hammond (England)	1927/28-46/47	85	140	16	336*	7249	58.45	22	24
D. G. Bradman (Australia)	1928/29-48	52	80	10	334	6996	99.94	29	13
L. Hutton (England)	1937-54/55	79	138	15	364	6971	56.67	19	33

Boycott remained at the top of this particular table until overtaken by Sunil Gavaskar of India on 13 November 1983. A further six batsmen have since passed Boycott's total. This includes two Englishmen: David Gower (who passed Boycott's record on 6 July 1992) and Graham Gooch.

Comparing Test Careers

Direct comparisons with other batsmen are difficult: different eras have different lbw laws, different regulations concerning the covering of the pitch and, most importantly, different oppositions with different strengths and weaknesses. The only other English batsmen with Test careers of any significance who came close to being Boycott's contemporaries are Dennis Amiss and John Edrich. Edrich made his début one year before Boycott but played his final Test five and a half years earlier whereas Amiss played his first Test in 1966 and his last in 1977. A summary of their parallel careers, with the figures presented cumulatively, follows:

| | AMISS | | | | BOYCOTT | | | | EDRICH | | | |
Year	Tests	Runs	Avge	100s	Tests	Runs	Avge	100s	Tests	Runs	Avge	100s
1963	–				–				3	103	17.16	–
1964	–				4	291	48.50	1	8	340	28.33	1
1965	–				13	821	43.21	2	10	657	50.54	2
1966	1	17	17.00	–	24	1320	36.66	2	19	1107	44.28	4
1967	4	125	25.00	–	27	1613	41.36	3	21	1142	40.79	4
1968	5	125	17.88	–	35	2238	43.88	4	31	2036	45.24	6
1969	5	125	17.88	–	41	2609	42.77	6	40	2711	45.95	8
1970	5	125	17.88	–	41	2609	42.77	6	40	2711	45.95	8
1971	9	258	19.85	–	49	3548	49.28	10	54	3665	44.15	10
1972	9	258	19.85	–	51	3620	47.63	10	59	3883	41.75	10
1973	21	1235	37.42	3	57	4142	48.73	11	59	3883	41.75	10
1974	32	2488	50.78	8	63	4579	47.70	12	65	4230	42.73	11
1975	41	2865	45.48	9	63	4579	47.70	12	75	4993	43.42	12
1976	42	3084	47.45	10	63	4579	47.70	12	77	5138	43.54	12
1977	50	3612	46.30	11	66	5021	50.72	14	77	5138	43.54	12
1978	50	3612	46.30	11	74	5675	51.13	16	77	5138	43.54	12
1979	50	3612	46.30	11	84	6316	49.34	18	77	5138	43.54	12
1980	50	3612	46.30	11	94	7115	49.41	19	77	5138	43.54	12
1981	50	3612	46.30	11	104	7802	47.87	21	77	5138	43.54	12
1982	50	3612	46.30	11	108	8114	47.73	22	77	5138	43.54	12

The figures are given as on 30 September for each year in question.

They show the comparative longevity of Boycott's Test career and also his consistency. His period of self-imposed exile from the Test scene can be seen as well as the relatively slow start experienced by the other two players.

The next part of the comparative study includes a wider range of English batsmen, as the next table shows; the figures of Boycott and Cowdrey are repeated for convenience.

English Batsmen with 5000 Test Runs Who Played with Boycott
(in chronological order)

		Tests	Inns	NO	HS	Runs	Avge	100s	50s
M. C. Cowdrey	1954/55-74/75	114	188	15	182	7624	44.06	22	38
K. F. Barrington	1955-68	82	131	15	256	6806	58.67	20	35
J. H. Edrich	1963-76	77	127	9	310*	5138	43.54	12	24
G. Boycott	1964-81/82	108	193	23	246*	8114	47.73	22	42
G. A. Gooch	1975-94/95	118	215	6	333	8900	42.58	20	46
I. T. Botham	1977-92	102	161	6	208	5200	33.54	14	22
D. I. Gower	1978-92	117	204	18	215	8231	44.25	18	39

It is noticeable that only Barrington, who played several Tests when certain countries had weaker teams, has an average superior to that of Boycott. The four English batsmen who scored 5000 Test runs before Boycott's career started (D. C. S. Compton, W. R. Hammond, J. B. Hobbs, and L. Hutton) also all had better averages but, as if to emphasize the point, the two to complete the feat since (M. A. Atherton and A. J. Stewart) have much lower averages.

Now to compare the seven relevant batsmen under different criteria. Again, the consistency of Boycott is very apparent.

Comparing Batting in Tests Under Three Different Criteria
(Venue, Age and Position in Match)

	Home		Abroad		Diff in Avges	Under 30		Over 30		Diff in Avges	1st Inns		2nd Inns		Diff in Avges	Sum of Diffs
	Runs	Avge	Runs	Avge		Runs	Avge	Runs	Avge		Runs	Avge	Runs	Avge		
Edrich	3155	43.81	1983	43.10	0.71	1130	41.85	4008	44.04	2.19	3383	45.72	1755	39.89	5.83	8.73
Boycott	4356	48.40	3758	46.97	1.43	2609	42.77	5505	50.50	7.73	4795	45.67	3319	51.06	5.39	14.55
Gower	4454	42.82	3777	46.06	3.24	6553	45.50	1678	39.95	5.55	5317	46.64	2914	40.47	6.17	14.96
Cowdrey	3537	43.13	4087	44.91	1.78	3850	42.31	3774	46.02	3.71	5250	47.30	2374	38.29	14.50	19.99
Gooch	5917	46.23	2983	36.83	9.40	2540	35.77	6360	46.09	10.32	5002	42.39	3898	42.84	0.45	20.17
Botham	2969	34.93	2231	31.87	3.06	4409	36.14	791	23.97	12.17	2671	36.71	1529	27.80	8.91	24.14
Barrington	3347	50.71	3459	69.18	18.47	1056	44.00	5750	62.50	18.50	5069	65.83	1737	44.54	21.29	58.26

A complex table but one that proves that Boycott was one of the most consistent English batsmen of his era, taking into account the three criteria used.

Ways of Getting Out

Boycott prided himself on his batting being based on a firm foundation of a solid technique. The proportion of his dismissals being bowled and lbw do not seem entirely to bear this out, however, when compared with his English contemporaries. The figures are presented in order of lowest total percentage of dismissals being bowled and lbw.

	Totals					Totals as percentages				
	Inns	C	B	Lbw	Other	Inns	C	B	Lbw	Other
Edrich	118	85	16	12	5	100	72	14	10	4
Botham	155	107	23	19	6	100	69	15	12	4
Cowdrey	173	116	31	19	7	100	67	18	11	4
Boycott	170	104	30	27	9	100	61	18	16	5
Gower	186	118	28	36	4	100	63	15	19	2
Barrington	116	67	21	24	4	100	58	18	21	3
Gooch	209	114	37	49	8	100	55	18	23	4

An interesting result: who would have expected Botham to be so high?

Lots of Not Outs

Another result of Boycott's relatively good technique was that he was able to survive the onslaught from his bowling aggressors rather better than most. This meant that, for an opening batsman, he had a very high proportion of incomplete innings. The next table compares batsmen from all countries and eras who scored 5000 Test runs and who began the innings for the greater part of their career.

			Inns	NO	NO as % of inns
D. L. Haynes	West Indies	1977/78-93/94	202	25	12.38
G. Boycott	England	1964-81/82	193	23	11.92
L. Hutton	England	1937-54/55	138	15	10.87
W. M. Lawry	Australia	1961-70/71	123	12	9.76
C. G. Greenidge	West Indies	1974/75-90/91	185	16	8.65
S. M. Gavaskar	India	1970/71-86/87	214	16	7.48
J. H. Edrich	England	1963-76	127	9	7.09
J. B. Hobbs	England	1907/08-30	102	7	6.86
G. A. Gooch	England	1975-94/95	215	6	2.79

Anybody's Bunny?

It has often been stated that Boycott, like most batsmen, was particularly susceptible to one particular bowler, or type of bowling. In this case the finger often pointed in the direction of left-arm bowlers and Gary Sobers in particular. Sobers actually dismissed Boycott on seven occasions in his Test career and although no other bowler exceeded this, it was equalled by Michael Holding (also West Indies) and Dennis Lillee (Australia). However, Boycott batted in 35 innings when Sobers was in the opposition's bowling attack, 26 times against Lillee but only 18 against Holding, so it is the last-named who has the greatest success rate against Boycott. Even so, seven is a very low 'best' especially when compared with the record batsman–bowler combination, which is held by Arthur Morris (Australia), who was dismissed 18 times by Alec Bedser (England); this figure is followed by 16 dismissals each against Gooch and Atherton by the West Indians Malcolm Marshall and Curtly Ambrose respectively.

Opening Partners

Boycott opened the innings for England with 16 different partners; his stands for the first wicket with five of these feature very highly in a table of England's best Test opening pairs.

Best Average by First-Wicket Pairs for England
(minimum 15 innings)

	P	UP	HP	Runs	Avge	100s	50s
J. B. Hobbs & H. Sutcliffe	38	1	283	3249	87.81	15	10
J. B. Hobbs & W. Rhodes	36	1	323	2156	61.60	8	5
L. Hutton & C. Washbrook	51	3	359	2882	60.04	8	13
G. A. Gooch & M. A. Atherton	43	0	225	2501	58.16	7	12
G. Boycott & D. L. Amiss	19	1	209	990	55.00	3	4
G. Boycott & J. H. Edrich	35	2	172	1709	51.78	6	9
G. Boycott & R. W. Barber	26	1	234	1171	46.84	2	7
G. Boycott & J. M. Brearley	21	0	185	874	41.61	2	4
G. Boycott & G. A. Gooch	49	2	155	1900	40.42	5	10

Again, the standards of the oppositions contribute: Boycott and Gooch, for instance, opened the batting on 18 occasions against the West Indies when their feared fast-bowling resources were at their peak.

The Yorkshire Captaincy

The study now turns to a completely different aspect of Boycott's career and his unsuccessful captaincy of Yorkshire CCC. The tenure of his reign lasted from 1971 to 1978 and during this period the county won no trophies whatsoever, part of the first such decade since the Championship was officially constituted in 1890. Yorkshire had lost a number of experienced players at the end of the successful 1960s and Boycott was at the helm of a relatively young and inexperienced side. The climax came in 1975 when the county finished second in the Championship and there appeared to be two main factors: the World Cup was being played and many counties were deprived of their overseas players; Boycott had begun his period of exile from the England team and was able to devote all of his energies to leading his county.

While Boycott was unavailable to captain Yorkshire, several other players acted as his deputy. The results under their leadership are now compared.

Yorkshire's Championship Results 1971–78 by Captain

| | TOTALS | | | | TOTALS AS PERCENTAGES | | | |
	P	W	D	L	P	W	D	L
G. Boycott	106	35	51	20	100	33	48	19
J. H. Hampshire	25	8	11	6	100	32	44	24
P. J. Sharpe	19	3	11	5	100	16	58	26
D. Wilson	12	1	4	7	100	8	33	58
Others	4	0	2	2	100	0	50	50
TOTALS	166	47	79	40	100	28	48	24

The figures for Sharpe include one tied match, which is given as a draw.

In other words, Boycott's captaincy resulted in a higher proportion of victories and a lower proportion of defeats than when any of his deputies was in charge. The differences in the main three limited-overs competitions (supposedly not Boycott's forte) are even more marked:

Yorkshire's Limited-overs Results 1971–78 by Captain
(Gillette Cup, Sunday League and Benson & Hedges Cup)

| | TOTALS | | | TOTALS AS PERCENTAGES | | |
	P	W	L	P	W	L
G. Boycott	117	64	53	100	55	45
J. H. Hampshire	27	11	16	100	41	59
Others	16	7	9	100	44	56
TOTALS	160	82	78	100	51	49

Another aspect of Boycott rising to the challenge of leadership is his improved batting performance in matches when he was leader. Although Boycott's tenure as captain coincided with some of the peak years of his batting prowess, there is no doubt that he appeared to bat better when invested with the captaincy of his county.

Boycott's Batting for Yorkshire

| | First-class matches | | | | | | Limited-overs matches | | | | | |
	I	NO	HS	Runs	Avge	100s	I	NO	HS	Runs	Avge	100s
As Captain	193	34	233	11162	70.20	45	119	22	108*	4552	46.93	3
As Team Member	481	77	260*	21408	52.99	58	132	15	146	3929	33.58	3
TOTALS	674	111	260*	32570	57.85	103	251	37	146	8481	39.63	6

Speed of Scoring

However, despite these feats of run accumulation the criticism was often levelled at Boycott that he did not always bat in the best interests of the side and scored too slowly. This is difficult to prove as each innings should be taken in its own individual context, i.e. taking account of the pitch and weather conditions as well as the strength of the bowling attack. However, in Championship matches during his captaincy (when he should have been taking the lead) it is apparent in his longer innings that he outscored his partners 75 per cent of the time.

Boycott scored 40 Championship centuries as captain of Yorkshire; in 30 of these innings he scored more than 50 per cent of the runs which accrued while he was at the wicket. His best innings in this context were:

Boycott's Score	Opponents	Venue	Year	Runs Scored While Boycott at Wicket	Percentage of Runs Scored by Boycott
110	Warwickshire	Middlesbrough	1971	161	68.3
111	Hampshire	Bournemouth	1971	165	67.3
105	Lancashire	Headingley	1972	156	67.3
204*	Leicestershire	Leicester	1972	310	65.8
100	Nottinghamshire	Worksop	1972	153	65.4

On the other side of the coin, his worst innings were:

142*	Surrey	Bradford	1974	343	41.4
113	Northamptonshire	Northampton	1978	267	42.3
104	Warwickshire	Edgbaston	1977	237	43.9
124*	Northamptonshire	Harrogate	1971	266	46.6

It is worth noting that Yorkshire won the games at Bradford and Harrogate by an innings. The other two were drawn.

Incidentally, the reverse is the case in his Test centuries; in only 10 of his 22 such innings did he outscore his partners.

Some Records and Achievements

Most Test centuries for England (22), equal with Cowdrey and Hammond.

Most century partnerships (48) by an England player.

First England player to bat on all five days of a Test match – v. Australia, Trent Bridge, 1977.

First player from any country to score his hundredth first-class century in a Test match.

First player from any country to score 99 and a century in a Test match – v. West Indies, Port of Spain, 1973/74.

First player from any country to score 99 not out in a Test match – v. Australia, Perth, 1979/80.

Topped the national batting averages on six occasions – the most for one player since 1945 – including three consecutive seasons (1971–73).

Has the highest career average (56.83) of all 61 batsmen to have scored over 30,000 runs.

The only player to average over 100 in an English season twice – 1971 and 1979.

Boycott: Slow Scoring in Tests

One of the features of the 1960s was an attempt to instill 'brighter cricket' into the players. This policy affected two players in particular, from a negative point of view. Ken Barrington made 137 in 437 minutes (18.81 runs per hour) against New Zealand at Edgbaston in 1965, and Boycott scored 246 not out in 573 minutes (25.76 runs per hour) against India at Headingley in 1967. Both were dropped from the next respective Test team as a disciplinary measure. The selectors conveniently seemed to forget that they had chosen Boycott when he had been out of form. He played himself into form on the first day meticulously scoring at a rate of 17.7 runs per hour and reaching his century at a rate of 31.6 runs per 100 balls but thereafter scored the remaining 146 runs at a rate of 61.1.

It is interesting to note that Boycott's first-day score on this occasion was 106 not out. Ten years later, in scoring his hundredth hundred, he was 110 not out at close of play on the first day but such had attitudes changed that this was regarded as perfectly acceptable.

The other most notable slow innings of Boycott's occurred at Perth against Australia in 1978–79. His innings of 77 was made at a rate of 22.8 runs per 100 balls and he was only 63 not out at the close of the first day. This was at the time of his most personally difficult period and his 'managers' appeared to be happy to excuse him on this occasion. This was probably helped by the fact that, as in each of the above examples, Boycott played no small part in laying the foundations of victory.

Comparing speed of scoring is not always a valid exercise as each innings should be taken in the context of the game; Michael Atherton's marathon 185 not out (37.6 runs per 100 balls) at Johannesburg against South Africa in 1995/96, for instance, was a match-saving effort played in the fourth innings of the match – an entirely different context from the other examples mentioned above. Therefore the following table concentrates only on some innings which were made by English batsmen on home soil from the start of a Test match.

Examples of slow scoring by English batsmen at home from the start of a Test match since 1967

				Inns	Mins	Balls	Runs per hour	Runs per 100 balls	Day 1 Score
G. Boycott	Ind	Headingley	1967	246*	573	555	25.8	44.3	106*
G. Boycott	Aust	Headingley	1977	191	629	471	18.2	40.6	110*
G. A. Gooch	Ind	Lord's	1986	114	355	280	19.3	40.7	114
R. T. Robinson	Pak	Old Trafford	1987	166	528	366	18.9	27.2	62*
M. A. Atherton	SA	Headingley	1994	99	321	224	18.5	44.2	99
M. A. Atherton	WI	Trent Bridge	1995	113	336	247	20.2	45.7	113
M. A. Atherton	SA	Edgbaston	1998	103	365	279	16.9	36.9	103*

NOTE: In the case of Robinson's innings the first day did not consist of a full day's play.

So perhaps Boycott was not so slow after all.

Bibliography

The following books were consulted during the researching for this biography.

Works of Reference

Frindall, Bill, *The Wisden Book of Test Cricket 1877–1984* (Guild, 1985)

Frith, David, *England versus Australia* (Lutterworth, 1977)

Martin-Jenkins, Christopher, *The Complete Who's Who of Test Cricketers* (Orbis, 1980)

Sproat, Iain, *The Cricketers' Who's Who* (The Cricketer's Who's Who, 1983)

Sydenham, Richard, *In the Line of Fire: the Great Opening Batsmen of Test Cricket* (Country Books, 1999)

Wisden Cricketers' Almanack

Woodhouse, Anthony, *The History of Yorkshire County Cricket Club* (Christopher Helm, 1989)

Books by Geoff Boycott

Put to the Test (Arthur Barker, 1979)

Opening Up (Arthur Barker, 1980)

In the Fast Lane (Arthur Barker, 1981)

Boycott: The Autobiography (Macmillan, 1987)

Boycott on Cricket (Transworld, 1990)

Geoffrey Boycott on Cricket (Ebury Press, 1999)

Books about Geoff Boycott

Callaghan, John, *Boycott: A Cricketing Legend* (Pelham Books, 1982)

Clark, Chris, *The Test Match Career of Geoffrey Boycott* (Spellmount, 1986)

Mosey, Don, *Boycott* (Guild Publishing, 1985)

Autobiographies and Memoirs

Amiss, Dennis, with Michael Carey, *In Search of Runs* (Stanley Paul, 1976)

Bairstow, David, with Derek Hodgson, *A Yorkshire Diary* (Sidgwick & Jackson, 1984)

Bedser, Alec, *Twin Ambitions* (Stanley Paul, 1986)

Bird, Dickie, *My Autobiography* (Hodder & Stoughton, 1997)

Botham, Ian, *My Autobiography* (Collins Willow 1994)

Close, Brian, *Close to Cricket* (Stanley Paul, 1968)

Close, Brian, *I Don't Bruise Easily* (Macdonald & Jane's, 1978)

Cowdrey, Colin, *MCC: The Autobiography of a Cricketer* (Hodder & Stoughton, 1976)

Denness, Mike, *I Declare* (Arthur Barker, 1977)

Dilley, Graham, *Swings and Roundabouts* (Pelham Books, 1987)

D'Oliveira, Basil, *Time to Declare* (J. M. Dent & Sons, 1980)

Emburey, John, *Autobiography* (Partridge Press, 1987)

Gatting, Mike, *Leading from the Front* (Queen Anne Press, 1988)

Gooch, Graham, *Out of the Wilderness* (Guild Publishing, 1985)

Gooch, Graham, and Frank Keating, *My Autobiography* (Collins Willow, 1995)

Gower, David, *The Autobiography* (Collins Willow, 1992)

Greenidge, Gordon, *The Man in the Middle* (David & Charles, 1980)

Greig, Tony, *Cricket: The Men and the Game* (Hamlyn, 1976)

Greig, Tony, *My Story* (Stanley Paul, 1980)

Hadlee, Richard, *Rhythm and Swing* (Souvenir Press, 1989)

Hampshire, John, *Family Argument* (George Allen & Unwin, 1983)

Khan, Imran, *The Autobiography* (Pelham Books, 1983)

Illingworth, Ray, *Yorkshire and Back* (Queen Anne Press, 1980)

Illingworth, Ray, *The Tempestuous Years, 1979–1983* (Sidgwick & Jackson, 1987)

Illingworth, Ray, and Jack Bannister, *One Man Committee* (Headline, 1996)

Knott, Alan, *It's Knott Cricket* (Macmillan, 1985)

Lamb, Allan, *My Autobiography* (Collins Willow, 1996)

Lewis, Tony, *Playing Days* (Stanley Paul, 1985)

Lillee, Dennis, *My Life in Cricket* (Methuen, 1982)

Marshall, Malcolm, *Marshall Arts* (Queen Anne Press, 1984)

Pocock, Pat, with Patrick Collins: *Percy: the Perspicacious Memoirs of a Cricketing Man* (Clifford Frost, 1987)

Randall, Derek, *Rags* (Sport in Print, 1992)

Russell, Jack, *Unleashed* (Collins Willow, 1997)

Simmons, Jack, *Flat Jack* (Queen Anne Press, 1986)

Snow, John, *Cricket Rebel* (Hamlyn, 1976)

Taylor, Bob, *Standing Up, Standing Back* (Collins Willow, 1985)

Trueman, Fred, *Ball of Fire* (J. M. Dent & Sons, 1976)

Underwood, Derek, *Beating the Bat* (Stanley Paul, 1975)

Willis, Bob, *Lasting the Pace* (Collins Willow, 1985)

Wilson, Don, with Stephen Thorpe, *Mad Jack: An Autobiography* (Kingswood, 1992)

Woolmer, Bob, *Pirate or Rebel? An Autobiography* (Arthur Barker, 1984)

Biographies

Arlott, John, *Jack Hobbs: Profile of the Master* (John Murray, 1981)

Barnes, Simon, *Phil Edmonds: A Singular Man* (Guild Publishing, 1986)

Foot, David, *Wally Hammond: The Reasons Why* (Robson Books, 1996)

Howat, Gerald, *Len Hutton* (Heinemann Kingswood, 1988)

Low, Robert, *W. G.* (Richard Cohen, 1997)

Mosey, Don, *Botham* (Guild Publishing, 1986)

Norrie, David, *Athers* (Headline, 1997)

Steen, Rob, *David Gower: A Man Out of Time* (Victor Gollancz, 1995)

Tennant, Ivo, *Graham Gooch: The Biography* (H. F. & G. Witherby, 1992)

Williams, Charles, *Bradman* (Little, Brown, 1996)

Accounts of Test Series

Brearley, Mike, *The Return of the Ashes* (Pelham Books, 1978)

Brearley, Mike, and Dudley Doust, *The Ashes Retained* (Hodder & Stoughton, 1979)

Brearley, Mike, *Phoenix From the Ashes* (Hodder & Stoughton, 1982)

Chappell, Greg, *The Ashes '77* (Angus & Robertson, 1977)

Cork, Dominic, *Uncorked: Diary of a Cricket Year* (Richard Cohen Books, 1996)

Gooch, Graham, with Alan Lee, *My Cricket Diary '81* (Stanley Paul, 1982)

Swanton, E. W., *Swanton in Australia with MCC, 1946–1975* (Collins, 1975)

Taylor, Bob, and David Gower, *Anyone For Cricket?* (Pelham Books, 1979)

Underwood, Derek, *Deadly Down Under* (Arthur Barker, 1980)

Whitington, R. S., *Captains Outrageous?* (Hutchinson, 1972)

Willis, Bob, *Diary of a Season* (Pelham Books, 1979)

Yallop, Graham, *Lambs to the Slaughter* (Outback Press, 1979)

Other Books

Agnew, Jonathan, *Over to You, Aggers* (Victor Gollancz, 1997)

Berkmann, Marcus, *Rain Men* (Little, Brown, 1995)

Blofeld, Henry, *The Packer Affair* (Collins, 1978)

Blofeld, Henry, *Cakes and Bails* (Simon & Schuster, 1998)

Brearley, Mike, *The Art of Captaincy* (Hodder & Stoughton, 1985)

Cook, Geoff, and Neville Scott, *The Narrow Line: An Anatomy of Professional Cricket* (Kingswood Press, 1991)

Emburey, John, *Spinning in a Fast World* (Robson Books, 1989)

Laker, Jim, *Cricket Contrasts* (Stanley Paul, 1985)

Roebuck, Peter, *It Never Rains* (Allen & Unwin, 1984)

Roebuck, Peter, *Tangled Up in White* (Hodder & Stoughton, 1990)

Sissons, Ric, *The Players* (Kingswood, 1988)

Synge, Allen, *Sins of Omission: The Story of the Test Selectors, 1899–1990* (Pelham Books, 1990)

Walker, Peter, *Cricket Conversations* (Pelham Books, 1978)

Willis, Bob, *Six of the Best* (Hodder & Stoughton, 1978)

Index

A SELECTED LIST OF RELATED TITLES
AVAILABLE FROM CORGI AND PARTRIDGE PRESS

THE PRICES SHOWN BELOW WERE CORRECT AT THE TIME OF GOING TO PRESS. HOWEVER TRANSWORLD PUBLISHERS RESERVE THE RIGHT TO SHOW NEW RETAIL PRICES ON COVERS WHICH MAY DIFFER FROM THOSE PREVIOUSLY ADVERTISED IN THE TEXT OR ELSEWHERE.

25267 7	CHRIS BOARDMAN'S COMPLETE BOOK OF CYCLING (Hardback)	Chris Boardman	£17.99
14519 X	JACK CHARLTON: THE AUTOBIOGRAPHY	Jack Charlton	£5.99
14003 1	CLOUGH THE AUTOBIOGRAPHY	Brian Clough	£5.99
25262 6	HANDS AND HEELS (Hardback)	Richard Dunwoody	£20.00
13937 8	THE FIRST FIFTY – MUNRO–BAGGING WITHOUT A BEARD	Muriel Gray	£9.99
13754 5	AYRTON SENNA: THE HARD EDGE OF GENIUS	Christopher Hilton	£7.99
14494 0	AN EVENING WITH JOHNNERS	ed. Brian Johnston	£6.99
14688 9	THE GREAT NUMBER TENS	Frank Keating	£7.99
25263 4	COMING TO THE LAST: A TRIBUTE TO PETER O'SULLEVAN (Hardback)	Sean Magee	£12.99
99631 9	SUMMERS WILL NEVER BE THE SAME	Christopher Martin-Jenkins & Pat Gibson	£6.99
25268 5	THRUST: THE REMARKABLE STORY OF ONE MAN'S QUEST FOR SPEED (Hardback)	Richard Noble	£20.00
25230 8	STEVEN REDGRAVE'S COMPLETE BOOK OF ROWING (Hardback)	Steven Redgrave	£20.00
99787 0	GREG NORMAN: THE BIOGRAPHY	Lauren St John	£6.99
14552 1	DICKIE: A TRIBUTE TO UMPIRE HAROLD BIRD	ed. Brian Scovell	£6.99

All Transworld titles are available by post from:
Bookpost, PO Box 29, Douglas, Isle of Man, IM99 1BQ
Credit cards accepted. Please telephone 01624 836000,
fax 01624 837033, Internet http://www.bookpost.co.uk
or e-mail: bookshop@enterprise.net for details.
Free postage and packing in the UK. Overseas customers: allow
£1 per book (paperbacks) and £3 per book (hardbacks).